1988

A PANORAMA OF Florida

By
David A. Bice

Rodney F. Allen
Ronald F. Cold
Betty J. Davison
Debora A. Graves
Cynthia S. Hays
Barbara C. Thornton
M. K. Montpelier

Jalamap Publications, Inc.

Charleston, West Virginia
1982

i

PREFACE

Many people aided in the preparation of this book for publication. All of the authors toiled under pressure to meet deadlines. They provided that intangible ingredient showing the diversity of people and cohesiveness of pride that exists in Florida. My family provided support and understanding during the project. In addition to this they supplied countless aids. Patty, my wife, decided that the book was a good idea while our children, Penny, Cheryl, Danny, Jeffrey and Ricky gave their views of the writing. Jeffrey did all of the metric conversions.

Alfredlene Armstrong edited and read the manuscript for objectivity. Darrell Jessee designed the cover and was helpful in preparing the book for market. Larry Pauley provided graphics.

Public servants in the Florida State Government assisted greatly in providing needed documents, photographs and suggestions. I feel that no accurate book about Florida could be written without the aid of Dr. Allen Morris, Clerk of the House, and his wife Joan, the archivist of the Florida State Photographic Archives. Dr. Morris' *Florida Handbook* has been indispensable in checking facts and figures about the state. Joan Morris was extremely helpful in supplying photographs to enhance the value of the text. Dyan Lingle and Sharon McDonald of the Department of Commerce went out of their way to help obtain up to date information and photographs. Other public officials assisting included: Robert Carr, Gil Clark, George Detrio, Roger Doucha, Nancy Elliott, Dick Farwell, and Tom Henderson. Courtland Richards and Jan Hartle provided special pictures.

Federal officials and departments provided a wide variety of material. The United States Department of Labor provided information which increased the value of the unit on Careers. NASA, EROS, The Kennedy Space Center and The U.S. Immigration and Naturalization Service all aided by giving facts and photographs.

David A. Bice

Foreword

Sun Coast...Gold Coast...Big Bend...Miracle Strip...Florida Crown...all of these are terms to describe parts of Florida. Urban...Rapidly Growing...Wild and Beautiful...Rural and Picturesque...the Sunshine State...all of these are Florida. They are words to describe this unique part of the United States.

It is also possible to describe the state by listing facts:

Land Area: 140,516.5 square kilometers/ 54,262 square miles

Water Area: 11,130.1 square kilometers/ 4,298 square miles

Total Area: 151,646.6 square kilometers/ 58,560 square miles

Highest Point: 105.2 meters/ 345 feet near Lakewood in Walton County

Lowest Point: Sea level Atlantic Ocean

Length north and south: 719.2 kilometers/ 447 miles (St. Marys River to Key West)

Width east and west: 580.8 kilometers/ 361 miles (Atlantic Ocean to Perdido River)

Size: 22nd among the states

Largest Lake: Okeechobee

Borders: Georgia-Florida - From the mouth of the St. Marys River to Ellicott's Mound, then in a line to the junction of the Flint and Chattahoochee Rivers at the head of the Apalachicola River. It continues up the Chattahoochee to 31° North latitude. Alabama-Florida - From the Chattahoochee River westward along 31st parallel to the Perdido River, then south along the Perdido River to the Gulf of Mexico.
The remaining borders are the coastline of the Gulf of Mexico from the Perdido River to the coastline of the Atlantic Ocean to the St. Marys River.

Bordering States: Georgia, Alabama

Bordering Bodies of Water: The Atlantic Ocean, The Gulf of Mexico

Region: Entirely within the Southern Coastal Plain

Population: 1980 Census -- 9,739,992

First European Visit: Ponce de Leon, April 2, 1513

Oldest permanent settlement: St. Augustine, 1565

Became a Territory of the United States: Agreement with Spain, 1821

Statehood: March 3, 1845

Divisions: 67 counties

Capital: Tallahassee

State Day: April 2

State Week: March 27-April 2, Pascua Florida Week

State Emblems:

> Bird: Mockingbird
> Flower: Orange Blossom
> Tree: Sabal Palm
> Nickname: The Sunshine State
> Motto: In God We Trust

Song: S'wannee River (Old Folks at Home) by Stephen Foster
Play: Cross and Sword
Theatre: The Asolo Theatre, Sarasota
Beverage: Orange Juice
Shell: Horse Conch
Stone: Agatized Coral
Gem: Moonstone
Freshwater Fish: Largemouth Bass
Saltwater Fish: Sailfish
Mammals: Manatee (Sea Cow)
Porpoise (Dolphin)

However, these facts do not tell the complete story about the state. Florida is not just a place of facts. It is the home of people, actual people, who have shaped a state. From the earliest civilizations through today's citizens, the residents have made their mark upon Florida.

A PANORAMA OF FLORIDA tells the story of these people. It is the developing story of their lives. The story is not one of abstract facts, but of human beings who engage in work, enjoy recreation, serve in government, aid neighbors, attend churches and synagogues, and do the thousands of things required of good citizens. This is our story -- as proud Floridians and Americans!

TABLE OF CONTENTS

96A

Explanation of Map Symbols

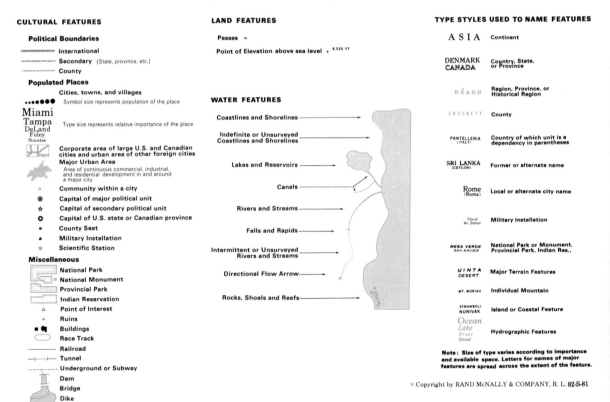

CULTURAL FEATURES

Political Boundaries
International
Secondary (State, province, etc.)
County

Populated Places
Cities, towns, and villages
Symbol size represents population of the place
Miami
Tampa
DeLand
Foley
Nocatee
Type size represents relative importance of the place

Corporate area of large U.S. and Canadian cities and urban area of other foreign cities
Major Urban Area
Area of continuous commercial, industrial, and residential development in and around a major city
○ Community within a city
⊛ Capital of major political unit
☆ Capital of secondary political unit
◉ Capital of U.S. state or Canadian province
• County Seat
▲ Military Installation
⊙ Scientific Station

Miscellaneous
National Park
National Monument
Provincial Park
Indian Reservation
△ Point of Interest
⸪ Ruins
Buildings
Race Track
Railroad
Tunnel
Underground or Subway
Dam
Bridge
Dike

LAND FEATURES

Passes ≍
Point of Elevation above sea level + 8,520 FT.

WATER FEATURES

Coastlines and Shorelines
Indefinite or Unsurveyed Coastlines and Shorelines
Lakes and Reservoirs
Canals
Rivers and Streams
Falls and Rapids
Intermittent or Unsurveyed Rivers and Streams
Directional Flow Arrow
Rocks, Shoals and Reefs

TYPE STYLES USED TO NAME FEATURES

ASIA	Continent
DENMARK CANADA	Country, State, or Province
BÉARN	Region, Province, or Historical Region
CROCKETT	County
PANTELLERIA (ITALY)	Country of which unit is a dependency in parentheses
SRI LANKA (CEYLON)	Former or alternate name
Rome (Roma)	Local or alternate city name
Naval Air Station	Military Installation
MESA VERDE SAN XAVIER	National Park or Monument, Provincial Park, Indian Res.,
UINTA DESERT	Major Terrain Features
MT. MORIAH	Individual Mountain
STROMBOLI NUNIVAK	Island or Coastal Feature
Ocean Lake River Canal	Hydrographic Features

Note: Size of type varies according to importance and available space. Letters for names of major features are spread across the extent of the feature.

Cover Photographs
Courtesy of Florida Department of Commerce

Unit 1   **Shape of the State**

Courtland Richards

Manatee

Florida Department of Commerce

Mockingbird

SHAPE OF THE STATE

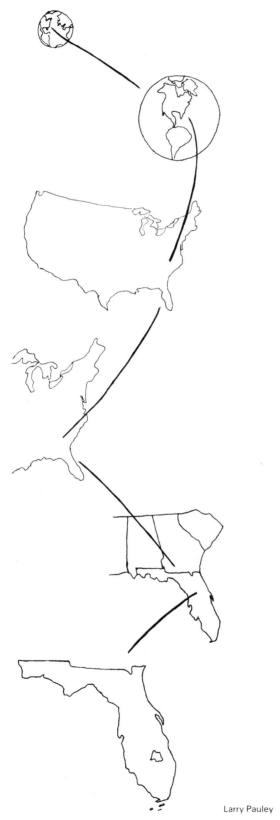

Larry Pauley

Introduction

We can look around Florida and see the results of human planning within the state. There are cities like Tallahassee, Jacksonville, Miami, Tampa, St. Petersburg, Orlando, Panama City, Pensacola, Bradenton, Daytona Beach, Fort Lauderdale, West Palm Beach, Boca Raton, and Key West. Roads and railroads crisscross the terrain. Farms and groves supply food to the state, nation and world. Recreational areas abound with people and things to do. Factories produce goods for sale everywhere.

As humans have populated the state, changes have been made. Trees were cut, land plowed, and structures built. People decided on names and part of the border, but everything done was based on what was here since the earth's creation.

Floridian Plateau

Florida completes the southeastern United States with a familiar shape that points like a huge finger toward the Caribbean Sea. Florida divides the deep waters of the Atlantic Ocean from those of the Gulf of Mexico. Florida's geography plays a large role in the geographic picture of the United States.

Most of Florida is a peninsula, a body of land which is almost surrounded by water. Extending south from the peninsula and along the coastline of Florida are numerous islands. Many of these islands have been important in the history and development of the state.

The Florida peninsula that we see on the map is just part of a much larger piece of the earth's crust called the Floridian plateau. The submerged part of this plateau is a gigantic underwater platform on which

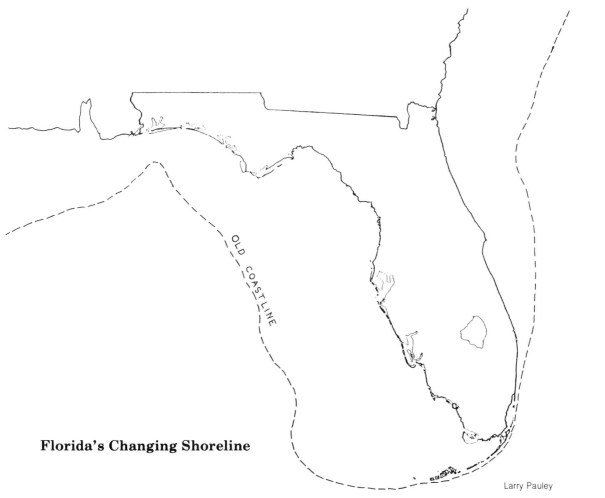

Florida's Changing Shoreline

OLD COASTLINE

Larry Pauley

3

ANCIENT SHORE LINE
PRESENT SHORE LINE

After Hoffmeister, 1974

Larry Pauley

Florida rests. It is part of the North American continental shelf. The underwater part of the Floridian Plateau slopes very gradually from the western shores of Florida. As a result, the coastal waters of the Gulf of Mexico are very shallow. If the water level of the Gulf of Mexico was lowered by just 105.2 meters/345 feet, Florida would have almost twice as much area! If the water level were raised by the same amount, Florida would be underwater. Because the continental shelf is wider beneath Florida's Gulf coast, the water is shallow. The waves, therefore, are smaller and not so rough as on the Atlantic side. This is one reason why surfing is usually better on Atlantic coast beaches than on the Gulf coast beaches.

The Floridian Plateau connects Florida to the rest of North America. It is made of rocks similar to those in Georgia and Alabama. The rock formations in the Floridian Plateau are very firm and steady. For this reason, earthquakes in Florida are uncommon, and are seldom very serious. Most of the Floridian Plateau is not a very old part of the earth's crust, according to the way geologists measure age.

The peninsular part of Florida has been either larger or smaller than it is today. These changes in size and shape have been caused by the raising or lowering of sea level.

Regions

To many people, Florida appears to be a level area that is the same across the state. However, there are different areas or regions within the state. A region is a section of the earth marked by certain common characteristics which set it apart from surrounding areas. These common characteristics may be based on any one of several factors. For example, in the United States we have regions based on agriculture, such as the Corn Belt; manufacturing, such as the industrial region of the Midwest; geographic features, such as the Rocky Mountain region; or climate, such as the Sunbelt region.

Just as our country has many regions, so does Florida. This statement would surprise many people whose mental image of Florida includes only one picture. That picture is usually of a place they have visited or seen on television or in the movies, such as: Miami Beach, Disney World, or the Everglades. While impressions of such places are important to an understanding of Florida, they are only part of a much larger picture.

One of the simplest ways to divide Florida is according to directional locations. These are north, central and south. This method is often used by television weatherpersons when they use maps in describing the weather for the state. Such directional regions can be further divided into: northeast, northwest, north central, southeast, southwest, and so on.

Such divisions can help us in terms of location, but they don't give us much descriptive information about a region. To be more specific in describing a region, geographers often base their divisions on landforms. Landforms are geographical features on the earth's surface, such as: mountains, hills, valleys or plains.

If you look at a map of the United States that shows landforms according to elevation, Florida is usually shown in one color, usually green. That color represents lower elevations. Specifically, Florida is part of the Gulf and Atlantic Coastal Plain. This is a lower elevation area touching the Atlantic Ocean and Gulf of Mexico.

Compared to places with much higher elevations like the Rocky Mountain region, Florida would indeed be thought of as a plain. The state is basically very flat. Florida has the lowest average elevation of any state, with an average elevation of 106.9 meters/ 100 feet.

However, some scientists who have carefully studied Florida have divided the state into as many as 40 landform regions. More commonly, geographers and geologists will use three to eight divisions in describing the landform regions of Florida. Florida can simply be divided into three main physical landform regions: the Atlantic Coastal Plain, the East Gulf Coastal Plain, and the Florida Uplands.

The largest of the regions is the Atlantic Coastal Plain. It is part of an important land

Red Mangrove　　　　　Ronald Cold

Florida from Landsat Photograph

region that extends along the entire eastern coast of Florida. This region extends from New Jersey through the Florida Keys. It is a low, level plain from 48.3 kilometers/ 30 miles to 160.9 kilometers/ 100 miles wide. There are sand bars, coral reefs, and islands just off the coast. The major cities of eastern Florida are in the Atlantic Coastal Plain.

There are two special subdivisions of the Atlantic Coastal Plain. The first is the Florida Keys. While not usually considered a separate region, the Florida Keys make up an interesting part of Florida's geography. The word "key" as used here comes from the Spanish word *cayo*, meaning small island. The Keys, then, are a chain of small islands that curve into the Gulf of Mexico from a point just south of Miami. The Keys are joined to the mainland by the Overseas Highway.

Like peninsular Florida, most of the Keys rest on a limestone foundation. However, those known as the "Upper Keys" are made of coral reef limestone rock. This rock is the remains of a coral reef which was once alive. This is the only part of the United States where such rock exists. At the end of the Florida Keys is Key West, the southernmost city in the continental United States.

The second subdivision of the Atlantic Coastal Plain is actually shared with part of the East Gulf Coastal Plain. This is the Everglades area. The Everglades is actually a part of a larger area called the Lake Okeechobee Everglades Basin. At one time, this whole area was part of an ancient sea. When the sea receded and the land emerged, the area that is now Lake Okeechobee was lower than the surrounding area. The word Okeechobee is from the Seminole meaning "plenty big water." This area eventually filled with fresh water. Lake Okeechobee is very shallow. It has an average depth of 2.1 meters/ 7 feet. It contains a huge amount of water because it is so large, 1,812.7 square kilometers/ 700 square miles. Lake Okeechobee is the second largest fresh water lake entirely within the United States outside of Alaska.

Between Lake Okeechobee and Florida Bay, a distance of about 160.9 kilometers/ 100 miles, lies the Everglades. The Everglades is a broad, flat plain made up mostly of grasses, but it also includes forested areas and swamps. The Everglades has always depended on Lake Okeechobee for life. Before the settlement of South Florida in the early part of this century, the overflow of water from Lake Okeechobee traveled slowly to the south. Water from the lake nourished the sawgrass marsh that is the heart of the Everglades. This gradual flow of water has been compared to that of a very wide but very shallow river. A nickname for the Everglades is the "River of Grass."

Because the Everglades contains many kinds of plants and animals in a unique habitat, large portions of the region have been made into parks and sanctuaries. Everglades National Park created in 1947, is the third largest national park outside of Alaska, covering an area of 5,660 square kilometers/ 2,188 square miles. Even so, the National Park makes up only part of the total area of the Everglades which is 10,358.4 square kilometers/ 4,000 square miles.

Today, the natural flow of water into the Everglades has been changed by man. As more and more people settled in south Florida, the coastal cities expanded inland. Parts of the Everglades were drained to make land for crops and homes. A 12.2 meter/ 40 foot dike was built around Lake Okeechobee to prevent flooding. Now, the flow of water from the lake into the Everglades is controlled by a series of pumps, gates and canals. There are disagreements among conservationists, farmers, park officials and water control officials as to how much water should be released into the Everglades.

The East Gulf Coastal Plain is also part of a larger land region. It starts at the southern tip of mainland Florida and stretches as far west as western Mississippi and north to Illinois. This region is divided into two parts in Florida. The southern part covers the southwestern part of the state. It joins the Atlantic Coastal Plain in the middle of the

Big Cypress Swamp and the Everglades. It curves upward to a point just north of Tampa Bay. The second section starts at the mouth of the Withlacoochee River and curves around to the Perdido River.

The third major region is the Florida Uplands. This region extends along the northern border of Florida to just east of the Suwannee River and south through Highlands County. It also separates the two parts of East Coast Coastal Plains. This region is sometimes referred to as "ridge country" or the "hill and lake" section.

This is rolling hill country, although in some places the land is quite flat. Lakes, springs and sinkholes are abundant in this region. Sinkholes occur when limestone rock beneath the surface dissolves and causes the ground above to collapse into the cavity that is formed. Sometimes, dry sinkholes can swallow houses!

The northern highlands part of the Florida Uplands is hilly in the eastern part of this region. In fact, it is often described as the "Tallahassee Hills." Florida's capital is located in this gently rolling and beautiful hill country. Tallahassee's elevation is 16.7 meters/55 feet above sea level.

The western part is not as hilly, but has higher elevations. It is part of an ancient plateau that has been worn down by erosion. It includes the highest point of land in Florida, a hill that rises 105.2 meters/345 feet above sea level. This hill is near the town of Lakewood in Walton County.

There are still other ways which Florida can be divided into regions. Regional divisions could be based on climate, vegetation, soil or some other geographic feature. Sometimes, a nickname based on some feature or activity becomes the basis for a regional name. Perhaps the most famous regional name is the Panhandle. The Panhandle refers to the northwestern part of Florida located between the Perdido and Chattahoochee Rivers. Other regional nicknames that are sometimes used for various parts of Florida include "Sun Coast"

Limestone wall built on outcrop　　　Ronald Cold

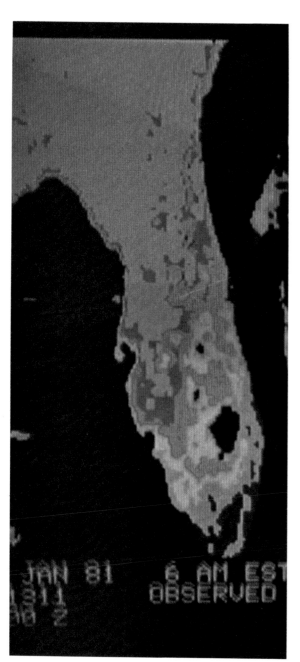

for the Tampa Bay area; the Miami and Southeast Coast or "Gold Coast"; the Daytona Beach and mideast coast or "Surf Coast"; and the "Miracle Strip" which includes Panama City and the northwestern coast.

Climate and Weather

Climate is often called Florida's most valuable resource. Florida's outstanding climate has been an important reason for attracting residents and tourists from other areas. It is certainly one of the main reasons for the population growth that has placed Florida among the seven most populous states in the union. The climate has influenced agriculture and industry in the state.

Climate is not the same as the weather. The weather of a place refers to such conditions as: temperature, rainfall, air pressure and winds from day to day. Climate is the average of these conditions for a long period of time, usually many years.

Florida's mild winters have been especially important to the development of the state. People in the northeast and midwest must bundle up and take other precautions to protect against cold weather. Floridians, however, can work, play and conduct other activities without having to worry about blizzards or shoveling snow. It is during such periods that many visitors from the colder part of our country escape to Florida for a winter vacation. These tourists contribute greatly to Florida's economy.

While northern croplands lie dormant during the winter, Florida farmers are growing a major portion of the nation's citrus fruits and winter vegetables. Florida's generally moderate climate is due to several important factors. The way these factors operate in relation to one another determines, to a large extent, the climate of the state. One of the factors is location. Florida's location is considered "subtropical" because of its nearness to the equator, lying between

This satellite photo was recorded on January 13, 1981 during a severe freeze. The light blue areas represent -11.6° C/ 11° F or colder; dark blue -11.6° C/ 11° F to -10° C/ 14° F; purple -10° C/ 14° F to -7.8° C/ 18° F; medium blue 7.6° C/18° F to -6.1° C/21° F; yellow -6.1° C/21° F to 3.9° C/25° F; green -3.9° C/25° F to -2.2° C/28° F; and black warmer than 0° C/32 ° F.

latitudes 24° North latitude and 31° North latitude. In general, places in low latitudes, those nearer the equator, are warmer than those places in high latitudes, those nearer the poles. In Florida's case, this is true. There are exceptions we should be aware of to this general rule. Exceptions can occur due to the influence of one or more of the other factors that affect climate.

One such factor is elevation or altitude. The higher a place is above sea level, the colder the climate. Another factor is distance from large bodies of water. Places located near large bodies of water have more moderate climates than inland areas.

A good example of how several climatic factors operate together can be seen in the city of Quito, Ecuador, in South America. Quito is located almost on the equator. We might suspect that Quito would have a hot climate. Quito, though, is located about 2,700 meters/ 9,000 feet above sea level. As a result, Quito has a much cooler climate than many cities in Florida. The temperatures in Quito average 14° Celsius/ 57° Fahrenheit during the year. In the evenings, temperatures of near freezing are not uncommon.

Florida, however combines several factors that contribute to a warm climate: nearness to the equator, low elevation, and nearness to large bodies of water. While coastal areas benefit most from this last factor, no place in Florida has an extreme inland location. No place in Florida is farther than 112.6 kilometers/ 70 miles from the Atlantic Ocean or the Gulf of Mexico.

In addition, Florida's climate is moderated by yet another factor, a warm ocean current. This ocean current is the Gulf Stream, a mighty ocean river which flows northeastward in the Atlantic off Florida's east coast. The Gulf Stream helps keep the southeastern part of the state warmer in winter and cooler in summer.

Still another related factor that influences Florida's climate is the direction of prevailing winds. Prevailing winds are those which blow over an area much of the time. When winds blow over the state from the waters of the Gulf of Mexico or the Atlantic Ocean, the warmth or coolness of those waters can be felt on land. Soft sea breezes in July and August can bring welcome relief from the heat of summertime!

These factors all provide the basic framework for Florida's climate. Now, we need to look at specific conditions that make up our weather and climate.

Perhaps the first condition we would think of is temperature. While we have noted that Florida has a "warm" climate, there are great variations in temperature throughout the state, especially in winter. Here we can see how averages can sometimes be misleading. The average annual temperatures for cities in North Florida and South Florida do not vary a great deal. For example, Tallahassee, in North Florida, has an average annual temperature of 20° Celsius/ 68° Fahrenheit. Key West, in South Florida, has an average annual temperature of 25° Celsius/ 77° Fahrenheit -- a difference of only 5° Celsius/ 9° Fahrenheit. The difference in coldest recorded temperatures between the two cities is much greater. Tallahassee's lowest recorded temperature is -19° Celsius/ -2° Fahrenheit, recorded in 1899. Key West's lowest recorded temperature 5° Celsius/ 41° Fahrenheit, in 1886. This is a difference of 24° Celsius or 43° Fahrenheit.

Cold spells can sometimes pull temperatures below normal for extended periods. If temperatures below freezing exist too long, crops can be damaged. During some extreme winters, 1977 and 1981 for example, agriculture and tourism suffered greatly. Fortunately, such winters are the exception. The highest and lowest temperatures in the state occurred within 48 kilometers/ 30 miles of each other. Tallahassee had the lowest on February 13, 1899 at -19° Celsius/ -2° Fahrenheit. Monticello had the highest on June 29, 1931 at 43° Celsius/ 109° Fahrenheit.

While temperatures below freezing occur occasionally in northern Florida, they are not commonplace. But, when atmospheric conditions push cold arctic air down

Tallahassee Snow of 1958

Florida's peninsula, temperatures drop and people shiver! During one such cold spell in January, 1981, the temperature in Tallahassee dropped to a low of -13° Celsius/ 8° Fahrenheit. On the same day, the low temperature in Anchorage, Alaska, was -3° Celsius/ 27° Fahrenheit! Key West's low temperature that day was 9° Celsius/ 48° Fahrenheit.

Florida's generally warm temperatures would not be half so enjoyable without the bright sunshine that usually accompanies them. While Florida does have some cloudy days, most of the time it lives up to its nickname, "The Sunshine State." Throughout the state, the sun shines about two-thirds of the time sunlight is possible. In the Keys, the percentage of possible sunshine is even higher, over 70 percent.

While there is plenty of sunshine, there is also rain, lots of it. Florida is one of the wettest states in the nation. The state has an average of 135 centimeters/ 53 inches of rain a year. Most of this, 81 centimeters/ 32 inches, falls from May to October. This rain does not fall evenly throughout the year, nor do all locations get the same amount. Rainfall throughout the state is heaviest during summer months, with winter being the dry season. This is characteristic of a subtropical climate. This uneven rainfall causes severe problems. During 1981 a severe drought or lack of rain occurred. This caused water rationing and sinkholes.

Thunderstorms are an important feature of the summer rainfall pattern. These short-lived but sometimes violent storms occur with great frequency. It may rain hard but usually the sun comes out right after the storm. Florida is known for its heavy rains, strong winds, lightning and, sometimes hail. It is the unquestioned thunderstorm capital of the nation with 80-100 days of thunderstorms observed each year. While thunderstorms can be destructive, they play an important role in helping to maintain Florida's water resources.

A location in Florida holds the record for the most rainfall in a 24 hour period. On September 5-6, 1950, Yankeetown, on the Mid-Gulf Coast, received 98.3 centimeters/ 38.70 inches of rain during a hurricane.

That's more rain than most places in the United States receive in an entire year!

More severe, but less common than thunderstorms are hurricanes. Hurricanes are intense tropical storms that can cause extensive damage with a combination of high winds and powerful storm tides. To be classified as a hurricane, a storm's winds must reach 119.0 kilometers/ 74 miles an hour. Hurricanes form near the equator in several parts of the world, including the Atlantic Ocean and the Gulf of Mexico. This means that all of Florida's coastal areas are exposed to the threat of hurricanes. Because hurricanes are such dramatic examples of nature's power, they receive much attention. Hurricanes do not strike Florida often, but when they do, they cause severe damage.

In some years, several hurricanes may strike; in others, none at all. The chances of receiving a hurricane vary according to location. In Miami, and Pensacola the chances are once every seven years. In Jacksonville, the odds are once every 85 years. Hurricanes occur mostly in August, September, and October although, the official hurricane season extends from June 1 to November 30.

While hurricanes are a greater threat to coastal areas, the more powerful ones do travel inland for considerable distances before they lose strength. One of the most destructive hurricanes in history passed across the entire peninsula in 1960. Hurricane Donna struck first in the Keys and southwest Florida. Donna finally exited near Daytona Beach, after causing $300 million worth of damage in Florida.

Thunderstorms and hurricanes both can give rise to another dangerous feature of the atmosphere, the tornado. Tornadoes can be the most destructive of storms. Although they affect a much smaller area than hurricanes, their wind speed can be higher, up to 595.3 kilometers/ 370 miles per hour. The low pressure inside a tornado funnel can cause buildings to appear to explode. Another fearsome aspect of tornadoes is the element of surprise. Whereas a hurricane may be tracked for several days or weeks before it reaches land, a tornado may appear very suddenly. It strikes quickly and can actually hop and skip over areas. One house may be destroyed while the house next door may be untouched. When a tornado funnel develops over water, it is called a waterspout.

Florida Photographic Archives

Results of 1926 Hurricane in Coral Gables

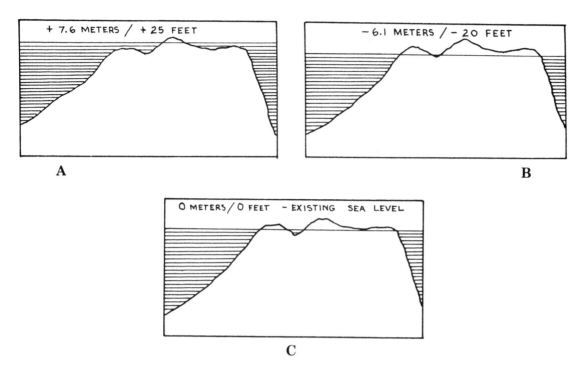

+ 7.6 METERS / + 25 FEET

A

− 6.1 METERS / − 20 FEET

B

0 METERS / 0 FEET − EXISTING SEA LEVEL

C

Cross section of Florida with different sea levels

Larry Pauley

Tornadoes are not as frequent or severe in Florida as they are in many states of the Midwest and Great Plains. On the average, Florida will experience 38 tornadoes a year. Tornadoes may occur at any time of year, but are most common in the spring.

Whatever the condition, man has made many adaptations to Florida's climate over the years. In adapting to Florida's warm, wet climate, the Seminole Indians for years have built shelters called chickees. Chickees consist of a slanted, thatched roof supported by several sturdy poles. The floor is a slightly raised platform. The tightly woven roof protects against the rain, and open sides allow cooling breezes to ventilate the chickee.

Today we adapt in a different way by air conditioning many of our homes, schools and other buildings. If energy costs continue to rise, some modern-day Floridians may consider building chickees!

Adaptations to climate are also seen in the clothes Floridians wear, and in their occupations and recreational activities. Cooler clothes made of cotton and light colors help Floridians adapt to the climate.

There is an old saying that "everybody talks about the weather but nobody does anything about it." This is no longer true. Scientists can sometimes produce rain by "seeding" clouds with chemicals. A similar technique has been used in attempts to reduce the effects of hurricanes.

Sometimes, man can cause a change in weather or climate without meaning to do so. By burning fuels such as: wood, coal, and oil in vehicles and factories, a great amount of carbon dioxide is released into the air. Some scientists feel that this is causing temperatures to rise around the world. Eventually, they believe the increase in temperatures will cause parts of the Antarctic ice sheet to melt. If this happens, sea levels around the world could be raised by 6.1 meters/ 20 feet. This would mean that all of Florida's coastal areas and the entire southern half of the peninsula would be covered by water! So far, this is just theory, but many scientists believe such events could take place within a few hundred years.

13

Borders

The natural borders of Florida have given it the nickname the "Peninsula State." Florida has more coastline than any other state except Alaska. The northern border is a combination of natural and manmade boundaries. The St. Marys River separates Georgia and Florida naturally. Then a line to the junction of the Flint and Chattahoochee Rivers is the border northward to the 31st parallel. Alabama and Florida are then separated by the 31st parallel on the north to the Perdido River, which forms Florida's western border. The remaining border is the coastline of the Gulf of Mexico and the Atlantic Ocean.

Today, the north 31st parallel comprises Florida's northernmost boundary, and its southernmost boundary is marked by the parallel 24° 30′ N. Between these two lines is a distance of 719.2 kilometers/ 447 miles. If you have every traveled by car from north Florida to south Florida, you know how long the state seems to be!

Florida also covers a great distance east to west. From the Atlantic Ocean to the Perdido River is a distance of 580.8 kilometers/ 361 miles. Florida is so wide along its northernmost border, it spans parts of two time zones. Except for part of Gulf County and nine other counties located in the Central time zone, Florida is mostly in the Eastern time zone.

Although Florida is very wide along its northern border between its eastern and western boundaries, the long, slender peninsula is fairly narrow. Its average width is less than 160.9 kilometers/ 100 miles. This means most residents of Florida are no more than 80.5 kilometers/ 50 miles away from the Gulf of Mexico or the Atlantic Ocean.

NASA

Florida, The Gulf of Mexico and the Atlantic Ocean

14

Early Divisions

When the Spanish arrived in Florida in 1513, they claimed it for the King of Spain. The land claimed was uncharted by European standards, so the extent of the claim was unknown. Phillip II of Spain, claimed almost all of southwest North America in 1564, and resisted brief French attempts to colonize Florida. A map in an atlas made in 1605 shows Florida extending westward into present day Texas and northward to the present day Carolinas. A northern border was established in 1606 when King James I of England gave a charter to the London Company to colonize as far south as 34° N. latitude. This line cuts through what is now Georgia, just north of present day Atlanta. The Spanish did not question this land claim, but it did lay the foundation for later disputes over the northern Florida border. Neither the Spanish nor the English were concerned that the natives considered the same regions to be their land.

French Lands

While the Spanish and English were settling the eastern coast, the French had moved down the Mississippi River and occupied the vast territory in central North America. By 1698, the French had settled in Biloxi and as far east as Mobile. A Spanish military post was established at Pensacola. Thus, by the 1700's, Florida was shrinking from the size of the original claim to appear, on a map, more like today's territory.

Georgia-Florida

While the Spanish were trying to expand colonization of Florida in the first half of 1700, the English were steadily moving southward. In 1721 the English established a fort on the Altamaha River, less than 1° north of the St. Marys River. In 1740, Georgians, led by James Oglethorpe, attacked St. Augustine but did not capture it. The main result of Oglethorpe's raids was to establish the St. Marys as the Florida-Georgia border. It had not been legally established until then.

North America in 1700

Spanish Florida, 1763

Larry Pauley

French and Indian War

England was successful in extending her influence in America at the expense of the French and Spanish. England and France had gone to war in 1756 over control of the Ohio Valley and worldwide trade. The Seven Year's War, 1756-1763, or the French and Indian War, gave England control of the eastern half of the continent. Spain allied herself with France, and after the war, both lost territory. France lost all of her continental possessions in America and Spain lost Florida.

England's Florida included land to the St. Marys and westward to the Mississippi River. She divided Florida into two colonies, East Florida and West Florida. They were divided by the Apalachicola River. West Florida extended to the Mississippi westward and at first to 31° N. latitude northward. Later, this area was extended to 32° 30′ N. latitude into present day Alabama and Mississippi. The capital was Pensacola. East Florida contained the peninsula with its capital at St. Augustine.

Return to Spain

England owned the two Floridas for only twenty years. In 1776, 13 of England's 17 American colonies revolted. Spain and France joined the rebellious colonies in successfully defeating England in 1783. For her part in the American Revolution, Spain received Florida back from England.

Spain, in 1783, became the largest land owner on the American continent. Her territory stretched from the Atlantic Coast of Florida to the Pacific Ocean. Florida extended to the Mississippi River. The northern borders of the new Spanish Florida were in some confusion. The St. Marys River remained the border between Georgia and Florida. A line connected the St. Marys to the head of the Apalachicola River. However, there was a disputed area between Florida and the new United States which was the Yazoo Territory. The Treaty of Paris, 1783, ending the American Revolution did not clearly define the border of West Florida. The British had placed it at 32° 30′ N. latitude, but the United States said it was part of their

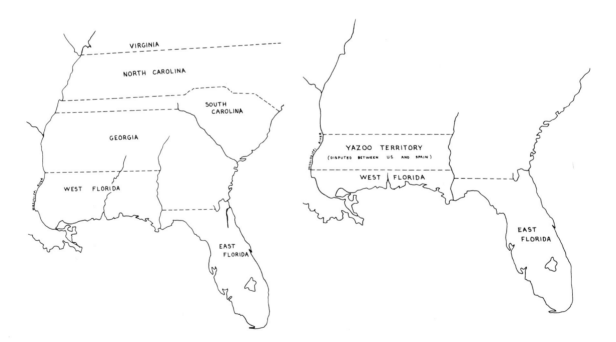

British Florida, 1763

Spanish Florida and the Yazoo Territory in 1783

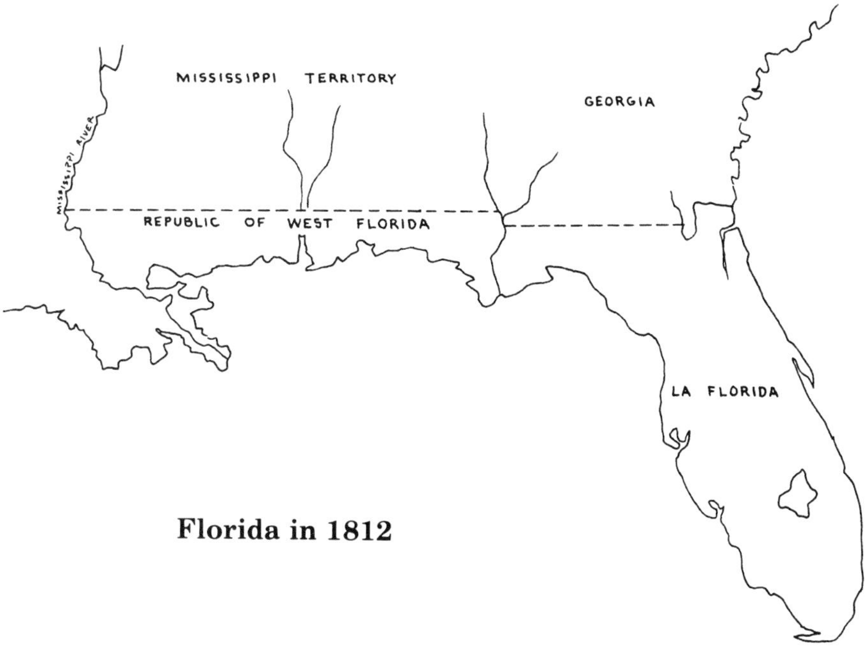

Florida in 1812

Larry Pauley

territory because of the old 31° N. latitude line which Spain had said was the border. The claims were settled in 1795 in the Treaty of San Lorenzo el Real. Spain gave up its claim to the Yazoo Territory and agreed that the Mississippi was the western boundary of America.

Surveying the Northern Border

The Americans were determined to establish the total northern border of Florida between the St. Marys and Apalachicola Rivers. Andrew Ellicott, an American surveyor, began surveying a line eastward from the Apalachicola River. He was to meet a group of surveyors coming west from the St. Marys River. They were unable to complete the survey because of Spanish opposition, Indian attacks, swamps, illness, hunger and insects. The line, completed later, is the Georgia-Florida border between Ellicott's Mound on the North Prong of the St. Marys to the head of the Apalachicola. The line runs at an angle of N. 87° 17′ 22″ W. and is the only manmade outside border of Florida besides 31° N. latitude.

Louisiana Purchase

Spain, weakened from many wars in Europe, was persuaded by France to give up a vast section of land in 1800. The Treaty of San Ildefonso, between Spain and France had been secret, and the terms would cause problems over the size of Florida. The area, called Louisiana, included a triangle of land from New Orleans up the Mississippi River and over to Oregon. In 1803, France needed money, and fearful that Spain could not keep England from getting Louisiana, sold the land to the United States for $15,000,000. This purchase helped America in taking over Florida.

Republic of West Florida

The terms and area of the Louisiana Purchase were vague. America claimed the territory including West Florida between the Pearl River and the Mississippi River. This would give the United States control of both shores of the Mississippi. Spain, on the other hand, disagreed. The issue was settled in 1810 when a group of Americans marched on Baton Rouge and forced the Spanish to

17

surrender. They asked to be annexed to the United States, but President James Madison believed the area already belonged to America, under the Louisiana Purchase. Madison sent in troops and occupied the territory. Thus, he reduced Florida to its present size.

Florida Joins the United States

Pressure from the United States on Spain during the War of 1812, including raids by General Andrew Jackson in Florida, made Spain realize she could not keep Florida. In 1821, Spain ceded Florida in its present size to the United States in the Adams - Onis Treaty.

Andrew Jackson was made the first governor of Florida. He organized it into one territory with two counties, Escambia and St. Johns, divided by the Suwannee River. One year later two new counties, Jackson and Duval, were added. Counties were added until 1925, when Gilchrist became the 67th county in Florida.

Land Surveying

Florida became a territory under some of the provisions of the Northwest Ordinance of 1787. The Northwest Ordinance was created during the first government of the 13 new states, The Articles of Confederation. One of the laws under the Northwest Ordinance provided for a system of rectangular survey. This created a system whereby all land would be laid off in sections of equal proportions and then subdivided. The result of this system can be seen by looking at a county map of Florida. Except for minor geographical divisions the counties of Florida are based on straight lines of latitude and longitude. Counties formed in territories and states created before 1787 do not have rectangular borders, but natural boundaries.

The basis for all surveying in Florida is at the Tallahassee meridian near the state capitol. This is the beginning point for almost all land descriptions in Florida, and is how surveyors identify land in Florida.

Florida joins the United States, 1821

Larry Pauley

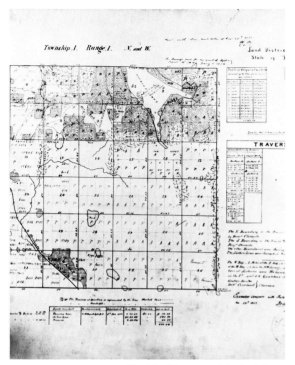

Florida Photographic Archives

Tallahassee Township
Township 1, Range 1, 1853

From Allen Morris' Florida Handbook

System of Rectangular Survey

Florida Photographic Archives

Tallahassee

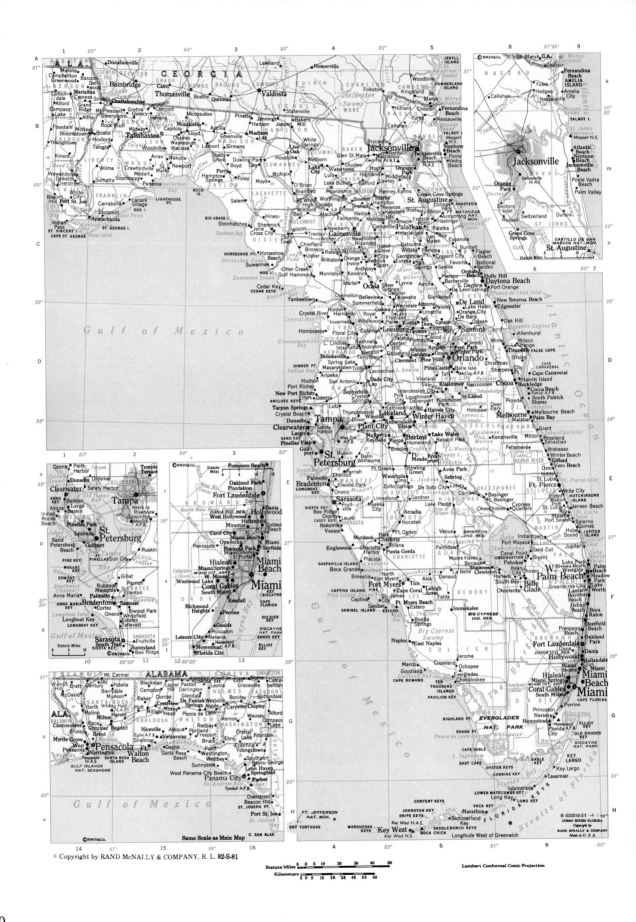

20

EROS

Orlando from Landsat

EROS

Miami from Landsat

Tampa from Landsat

St. Petersburg from Landsat

22

Exact and Relative Location

In describing Florida's boundaries, we are defining its location very specifically. Geographers speak of two kinds of locations: exact location and relative location. Exact location is determined by the latitude and longitude of a place. No other place on earth can have the same coordinates of latitude and longitude as Florida. An exact location in Florida is its geographical center, in Hernando County, 19.3 kilometers/ 12 miles NNW of Brooksville.

Relative location, on the other hand, refers to the position of a particular place in relation to the position of other places. For example, no state, except Hawaii, lies closer to the equator than Florida. Southernmost Florida at parallel 24° N is just north of the Tropic of Cancer at 23½° N latitude. Because Florida is so close to the tropics, it is often described as "subtropical" or "semitropical." This nearness to the equator and tropical regions greatly influences Florida's climate, vegetation and animal life.

Florida's subtropical location, with its mild, sunny winters, makes the state a very desirable vacation spot for visitors from colder northern places. Florida is closer to these cold-climate cities of northeastern and midwestern North America than are other subtropical places. Florida's location relative to these cities and to the tropics is very advantageous.

From a different point of view, Florida's location is very convenient for visitors from the countries of South America and the Caribbean. Florida is closer to these countries than any other state. South American tourists and businesspersons are visiting the state in increasing numbers to buy and sell goods, and to enjoy Florida's many attractions. This feature of Florida's relative location has earned it the nickname of "Gateway to Latin America." The important position of Florida in the Americas has been recognized since the early days of exploration, and is as important now, as it was then for economic and military reasons.

Land and Water Resources

The land and water within Florida's boundaries combine to make it the second largest state east of the Mississippi River. Florida's total area of 151,646.6 square kilometers/ 58,560 square miles gives it a rank of 22nd among all the fifty states. Of Florida's total area, 140,190 square kilometers/ 54,136 square miles is land and 11,456.4 square kilometers/ 4,424 square miles is water.

Soils and Vegetation

In discussing Florida's land resources, we should return for a moment to the structure of the state. The very deep, 915 meters/ 3,000 feet and more below the surface, rocks of Florida's foundation are made of hard, fire-formed, igneous rocks, such as granite. Lying above this foundation like a huge, thick cap are many layers of limestone. Limestone is a general term for a common class of sedimentary rocks. Sedimentary rocks are those formed by the banding together of sediments or particles of rock, shells and the secretions of animals, such as corals.

Limestone is found in abundance on every continent, and occurs in a variety of forms. The limestone of Florida has great variety also, but shares the same basic characteristics. Limestone can be used in many ways, as in the construction of buildings, monuments, highways and airfields. On top of the limestone are various soil layers, most of them rather thin and sandy. Soil consists of finely ground particles of rock, shell and decayed plant and animal matter. There are also various organisms living in it. In some parts of the state there are layers of sand, gravel or clay between the topsoil and the limestone.

Florida's betters soils are found in the northern part of the state, in the region we described as the northern highlands . These soils are generally thicker and richer than those in other parts of the state. They are often recognized by their reddish-yellow color, much like soils found in parts of Alabama and Georgia. Among the crops grown in these soils are corn, soybeans, oats, peanuts and tobacco.

This area is Florida's leading tree farming region. Forests here are made up mostly of pine trees. The pine is Florida's most important commercial tree. Some of the pine tree harvest is used for lumber, but most of it goes into the production of pulpwood. Pulpwood is used to make paper, cardboard and similar products. The soils of north Florida also support a number of hardwood species, including oak and hickory. These woods are used mainly for lumber and furniture.

The soils in the central Florida Uplands are sandy and well drained. In general, they are not as high in quality as those to the north. They do, however, support the majority of Florida's famous citrus groves. Many other agricultural products are grown here as well, including corn, watermelon and peanuts. There is pasture land for horses, cattle and other livestock. Pine and oak trees are grown in this region. They are not as widespread as in northern Florida.

Probably the least fertile natural soils in Florida are found in the coastal lowlands. These soils are sandy and often poorly drained, but they can still be made very productive. In many parts of the coastal lowlands, farmers have drained the land and added fertilizers and minerals to the soil to create useful croplands.

Many different kinds of vegetables are raised here, as well as potatoes, strawberries and pasture grasses. In the southern part of the coastal lowlands, tropical fruit crops such as mangoes, avocados and limes are among the leading agricultural products. In the southwestern part of this region, flowers have become a major crop. Native tree growth in the coastal lowlands consists primarily of scrub oak, pine, and especially in the south, palmetto. Along the shoreline of the southern coastal areas are forests of a very special tree, the mangrove. The mangrove does not have great commercial significance at present, but it is extremely important to the ecology of this area. One kind of mangrove, the red mangrove, grows right at the water's edge or in the shallow parts of the sea. The tangled prop roots of this tree collect leaves, sand and other material washed up by the sea. Eventually, "new land" is formed. Because of this process, the mangrove is sometimes called the "land builder tree." Mangroves help protect the shoreline from erosion, and lessen the damage from hurricane winds and tides. They provide shelter for a great number of smaller marine animals that are part of the food chain.

Another major soil type is found in low-lying, swampy areas. The largest area of these soils is found in the Everglades, but they can be found around lakes and rivers in other parts of the state. Such soils are composed largely of peat and muck, and are often covered by water. After draining, these soils can be made productive. Mucklands appear black and lush, but as soils they are actually quite fragile. If not managed with care, they can be easily lost. When exposed to the air, the mucky soils begin to disintegrate. When dried, they can catch fire and burn for long periods of time. Farmers protect and enrich these soils by keeping them moist and by adding minerals. When not in use for a cash crop, they are often planted with a "cover crop" such as clover.

As a result of careful management, farmers are able to harvest vegetable crops throughout the year, including a large portion of the state's important winter vegetable crop. In addition, many hectares/ acres are devoted to grasses for the grazing of livestock. By far, the most valuable crop in this region is sugar cane.

Perhaps the most distinctive tree of this region is the stately cypress, which gives its name to the Big Cypress Swamp. The Big Cypress Swamp is now a national preserve. Other swamp trees include the pond apple, custard apple and pop ash. In drier sections of the region, palms, pines and oaks are common. Florida's soils, with proper management and the advantages of a warm climate, have helped make Florida a very

important agricultural state. Florida's soils support a large variety of trees. Almost half of the tree species grown in the United States can be found in Florida. Florida also has many species of trees that are found in no other state.

Minerals

In considering resources of the land, it has been natural to start with soils and vegetation. In combination, they are a main source of food and other products that we use in daily living. The land areas of Florida contain many other riches, including such important minerals as phosphate and petroleum.

Beaches

Another very important land resource is contained within the narrow band of beaches that borders the state. Looking down on Florida's coastline from an airplane, you can see how narrow this strip really is. Yet this relatively small area is surely one of the state's major resources. The value of Florida's beaches can be seen in the high rating they receive from tourists. Year after year, visitors to the sunshine state rank beaches at the top of their list of reasons for coming to Florida. Beaches are, of course, very popular with residents of the state as well.

While we may not think of beaches in the same category as the inland soils of the state, they too, are subject to erosion. Protective measures must be taken if our beaches are to be enjoyed by future generations of tourists and residents. Florida is very fortunate that most of the beaches along its very long coastline are outstanding for recreational purposes. Some coastal areas of the world are rocky or swampy and have almost no beaches. Florida has excellent beaches on both coasts, but the beaches of the Atlantic are different from those of the Gulf in several ways. The beaches of the Atlantic are generally wider and experience stronger wave action than those on the Gulf side. The best surfing beaches are found around Daytona Beach. There are also differences in the composition of beaches. Atlantic beaches are usually coarser, composed of sand mixed with tiny pieces of broken shell. They are mostly tan to golden brown in color.

Gulf coast beaches are finer grained and lighter in color, ranging from tan to grey to pure white. On the northwest Gulf coast, a high percentage of white quartz sand is mixed with finely ground shells. Many people feel that the beaches in this region near Panama City are the most spectacular of Florida's many fine beaches. Here, the sand is as white as refined sugar, and when

RIVERS IN THE OCEAN

Ocean currents transport huge quantities of water from one part of an ocean to another. They are like giant rivers in the ocean. The Gulf Stream has a flow that is 1,000 times greater than that of the Mississippi River -- more than 3,628.8 metric tons/ 4,000 tons of water a minute! This great current influences climates in Europe. That is why London and Amsterdam are warmer than cities directly on the same parallel in the United States. This is why the Pilgrims were surprised their first winter in Massachusetts. They sailed south but landed in an area touched by the cold Labrador current. Many of them froze to death that first winter.

Ocean currents may be warm, like the Gulf Stream, or cold. On many world maps and globes, you can find ocean currents marked, usually by arrows. Sometimes the warm currents are shown in red, and the cold currents in blue.

130,652

Florida Department of Commerce & Tourism

Gulf of Mexico Beach at Sunset

you walk on it, it squeaks!

Beaches in every part of the state are endangered by the threat of erosion, sometimes brought on by the actions of man. Beaches are maintained naturally when new sand is deposited by the action of tides and currents. These same forces remove sand from the beach also, sometimes at a rate faster than it is deposited. When man builds structures at the water's edge or into the water, this natural process is interrupted, and serious erosion can take place. Unfortunately, this has happened all too frequently in Florida's past. Efforts to repair the damage to beaches are very costly, and their effectiveness is uncertain.

One of the best known beaches in Florida is the one at Miami Beach. Here, large hotels, condominiums and sea walls have been built right up to the edge of the ocean. As a result, large portions of the famous beach have disappeared. Concerned at the loss of this local trademark, officials decided to restore ten miles of beachfront. To do this, sand was pumped up from the ocean's bottom 1,830 to 3,660 meters/ 6,000 to 12,000 feet offshore. The new beach is 76.3 meters/ 250 ft. wide, but many experts think it will be washed away if Miami Beach is struck by a hurricane. This project is the largest beach restoration program in the world. Its estimated cost is $73 million.

Barrier Islands

Florida's land resources includes the state's numerous islands. Florida has over 4,500 islands that are 4.1 hectares/ 10 acres in size or larger. Many of these islands are classified as barrier islands. Barrier islands lie parallel to the coast, and are usually long and sandy. As barriers to the open sea, these islands produce sheltered waterways between themselves and the mainland. In Florida and several other coastal states, such sheltered waterways are connected to the Intracoastal Waterway.

Barrier islands are very popular as recreation areas, and a number of them have been developed for residential purposes as well. Miami Beach and Palm Beach are both built on barrier islands. In addition to the many natural islands in the state, developers have created a number of artificial islands. Usually, this has been done by dredging or pumping sand and rock from the bottom of a body of water, such as a shallow bay. The material collected in this way is then deposited in the desired location to form an island or to extend an existing shoreline. While this process can be useful in creating new land for homes, port facilities or recreational sites, it can cause damage to the natural surroundings.

Saltwater Resources

Water is important to the shape of Florida. Without the Atlantic Ocean and the Gulf of Mexico, there would be no beaches and no offshore islands. More importantly, there would be much less fresh water. The sea is the source, through evaporation, of much of the moisture that eventually falls on Florida as rain. The presence of the surrounding seas has been an asset for transportation throughout Florida's history. Spaced along Florida's long coastline are numerous ports, 14 of which are classified as deep water ports. These ports enable Florida to ship and receive a broad variety of products. Some of Florida's ports serve cruise ships, military vessels, and ocean research ships.

The seas around Florida provide a wealth of seafood, including shrimp, oysters, crabs, snapper, mackerel, grouper and many other species. This abundance has helped make Florida one of the leading fishing states in the nation. In addition to their importance for commercial fishing, the salt water areas around Florida are very popular with sport fisherman, who match their skills against such fighters as tarpon, bonefish and sailfish.

Various other treasures are contained in Florida's offshore waters. The most widely publicized of these is petroleum. Geologists suspect that the continental shelf surrounding Florida may contain considerable quantities of oil and natural gas. In 1981, several oil companies were conducting oil drilling operations in the Gulf of Mexico about 128.7 kilometers/80 miles off Florida's southwest coast.

Less known, but of possible future importance are minerals that may someday be mined from the sea. The oceans contain huge quantities of minerals. Some are in deposits on the ocean floor, some are in mixtures in sea water, and others in solution. There are problems in removing these minerals economically. With present methods, it often costs more to extract a mineral from the sea than it is worth. New inventions and techniques may change this situation.

In early 1981, enormous deposits of phosphate were discovered in the continental shelf off the coast of North Carolina. Perhaps similar deposits exist off of Florida's coast. Such deposits would be a welcome addition to Florida's land based phosphate, which is a non-renewable resource.

Estuaries

Not all of Florida's coastline is fringed with beaches. Some parts of the coastal landscape are made up of estuaries. Estuaries are tidal areas where the saltwater of the sea mixes with freshwater draining from the land. This brackish water is loaded with nutrients. It provides nourishment for many marine animals that spend at least part of their lives in the sheltered environment of the estuary. Shrimp, lobster and many species of fish that are caught miles offshore began their lives in the estuary. Estuaries, which are sometimes called the "nurseries of the sea," are very important areas indeed.

Fresh Water Resources

Florida's fresh water resources are controlled by the natural processes of the water cycle or hydrological cycle, and by the activities of man. Let's take a closer look at the water cycle. Florida receives large amounts of rainfall, about 134.6 centimeters/

53 inches a year on the average. Some of this rainfall drains into rivers and streams, and then into the Atlantic Ocean or the Gulf of Mexico. Some of the rain goes back into the air through evaporation and by transpiration, through plants. The rainfall that remains on or in the land, we may think of as stored water. Some of this water is stored on the surface, in lakes, rivers, swamps and reservoirs. The remainder is stored in the ground. The ground water that is not absorbed by soil filters down into huge underground reservoirs known as aquifers.

Aquifers

Aquifers in Florida are made of layers of porous limestone rock which act something like a sponge to retain water. Two aquifer formations supply most of the state's water. The largest is the Floridian Aquifer, which serves most of the state north of Lake Okeechobee. The other is the Biscayne Aquifer, which supplies southeast Florida. Water is taken from aquifers by the drilling of wells. Before it is used for human consumption, the water is processed in treatment plants where various ingredients are added. Chemical softeners are usually added, because water drawn from limestone rock is "hard," or mineralized. A disinfecting agent, usually chlorine, is added to kill harmful bacteria. In some communities, small quantities of fluoride are added to help prevent tooth decay.

Rivers

Places not served by aquifers may get their water from rivers, lakes, or springs. Despite its heavy rainfall, Florida does not have a great many large rivers. Florida's largest rivers, in terms of amount of average flow, are the Apalachicola and the Suwannee. The longest river in the state is the St. Johns, which winds its way for 439.3 kilometers/ 273 miles through the northeastern part of the state before emptying into the Atlantic Ocean.

Florida has over 1,700 rivers, streams and creeks. They help to provide drainage for the land, and refill the aquifers. They are also valuable for recreation, and some of the larger rivers are important for transportation.

Lakes

Florida has over 7,700 fresh water lakes that exceed 4.1 hectares/ 10 acres in size. Nineteen of these lakes have an area of 25.9 square kilometers/ 10 square miles or more. The largest is the giant Lake Okeechobee. Lakes are distributed throughout most of the state, but the majority of the larger ones are located in the central highlands. There are few lakes of any size south of Lake Okeechobee. Lakes are storage places for water, and like rivers, they help to refill aquifers. Florida's lakes represent a tremendous recreational resource. They provide a setting for swimming, boating, fishing, waterskiing and many other activities. Not surprisingly, homesites on lakes are very much in demand.

Springs

Springs are another significant feature of Florida's fresh water resources. We might think of springs as "leaks" or overflow from aquifers. Springs usually seep through cavities in the limestone rock near the surface of the land. The flow of springs can vary considerably, due primarily to changes in rainfall.

Florida has over 200 springs, most of them located in the north and central portions of the state. Of this number, 27 are "super springs," or first magnitude springs, as geologists call them. A first magnitude spring is one which has an average flow of more than 8.5 cubic meters/ 100 cubic feet per second. This is equal to about 245.7 million liters/ 65 million gallons a day! Florida has more first magnitude springs than any other state. Silver Springs, near Ocala, is Florida's most famous spring, although Wakulla Springs, near Tallahassee, has the greatest flow among Florida's springs.

The combined flow of all Florida's springs is about 26.46 billion liters/ 7 billion gallons a day. This quantity is several times the amount of water used by the public water systems in the state. However, springs have not been used very extensively as a water supply source. This may change in the future, but at present the main use of springs is for recreation. Florida's springs are frequently located in beautiful natural settings. Some people prefer Florida's springs to all other locations for water-based recreation. The waters of Florida's springs are refreshingly clear, clean and cool. They have temperatures averaging about 21° Celsius/ 70° Fahrenheit.

Water Problems

Despite the abundance of fresh water contained in Florida's aquifers, rivers, lakes and springs, some communities experience occasional water shortages. These shortages are expected to become more frequent and more widespread in the future. This is due to higher usage by the increasing population and industries. We should understand, however, that the problem is not with the total amount of the water supply. Less than

five percent of the fresh water available throughout the year is used by man for his purposes, including industry, agriculture and personal use.

Part of the problem is explained by the fact that this water is not always available at the right time nor the right place. We should remember, Florida's rainfall, though heavy, is not evenly distributed throughout the year. Dry spells and even droughts do occur. When they do, the water levels in Florida's surface water and ground water supplies go down even though human demand for water remains constant. In fact, it can increase during parts of the dry season when large numbers of tourists are in the state. With little or no rain, more demand is placed on stored water supplies for irrigation of crops and for the watering of lawns and plants. Some of Florida's faster growing communities are located considerable distances from water sources. Even when an adequate supply is located nearby, shortages can occur if a city does not have the equipment to treat enough water to meet the

Jan Hartle

Sinkhole at Winter Park in 1981

demands of a rapidly growing population.

Another part of the problem occurs with salt water intrusion. Many of Florida's faster growing communities are located in coastal areas. As they have drawn more and more fresh water from wells near the coast, sea water has seeped in through the porous limestone to replace it. This makes the water unfit for human consumption or for agriculture. Under natural conditions, there is usually enough pressure in the aquifer to keep the salt water out of the fresh water supply.

Man has done other things to alter the natural balance of Florida's water supply. As cities and roadways are built, the areas that are paved over reduce the amount of open land that is available to soak up rainfall. Even when attempts are made to regulate water supplies, new problems affecting water resources can emerge. The state government has established five water management districts to help manage the water supply for counties within the districts. In south Florida, the South Florida Water Mangement District has done a very effective job of flood prevention by controlling the water level in Lake Okeechobee and in a series of canals that drain excess water from the land. The district also operates large water conservation areas which store water that can be used during dry periods.

Yet, some groups are not always happy with this system. Some conservationists complain that too much fresh water is allowed to drain through the canals into the Atlantic Ocean or the Gulf of Mexico. Others, including outdoor clubs and naturalists, complain about too much water being stored in the conservation areas, which threatens the lives of raccoons, opossum, deer and other animals. If the water is released from the conservation areas into the Everglades National Park, park officials may object because the water would affect wildlife, such as nesting alligators. On the other hand, farmers will complain if they don't get the right amount of water they need for their crops. In other parts of the state, different conflicts have arisen. People in north Florida have not been pleased with proposals to deliver water from the Suwannee River to the Tampa Bay area through a long pipeline. With many competing interests, the problems of water management become very complicated.

As if all these problems were not enough Florida's fresh water resources are threatened by various sources of pollution. In some areas, sewage and a wide range of industrial and agricultural wastes enter canals, rivers and lakes either through direct dumping or runoff. These substances, often toxic or poisonous, also seep into aquifers. Water treatment removes many of these substances, but recent studies have shown that potentially dangerous quantities of some chemicals remain in the finished water produced by some water treatment systems in Florida.

So we can see, Florida's water problem is not really one of abundance. Rather, it is one of providing the water where and when it is needed. This water must be of a quality that is suitable for man and other living things. Solving this problem will be one of the biggest challenges for Floridians in the 1980's.

Special Places/Natural Wonders

Almost everyone who has lived in Florida or visited for any length of time has a special place. We might begin with a place that is truly unique in the United States, Pennekamp State Park. "Unique" is an often misused word; it means "of which there is but one." Many people use "unique" when they mean "rare" or "unusual." Pennekamp Park is unique because it contains the only living coral reef in the United States. It is also the nation's first underwater park. Pennekamp Park is located off the coast of Key Largo. It is an underwater fantasy of incredible colors and shapes. The corals that make up the reef are small, primitive animals that often live in huge colonies. Coral can survive only within limited conditions of light, temperatures and water quality. Billions and billions of corals

Everglades

make up the reef. When they die, their skeletons are cemented together with sand and debris to become part of the limestone shelf that underlies the living part of the reef. The reef provides a protected environment for a number of other marine animals, including over 200 species of fish.

Another special place is Florida Caverns State Park in Jackson County. It is not unique, but it is unusual for Florida. Despite all the limestone in the state, there are very few caves or caverns not covered by water. Florida Caverns has more than a dozen rooms, complete with stalactites and stalagmites.

In a state having mostly flat areas, parts of the land that have any elevation or relief can be of interest. On the upper portion of the Apalachicola River, bluffs rise above the river. Such bluffs are not typical of the Florida landscape, and are worth viewing and preserving.

Florida has many fine beaches. It has two that are classified as national seashores. These are Cape Canaveral National Seashore and Gulf Islands National Seashore. National seashores are coastal areas that have been reserved by the U.S. government for recreational use by the public. They are designed to provide protection for many different kinds of plants and animals, including sea oats, sand palmetto and sea turtles. Also preserved will be features of the beach landscape such as dunes, salt marshes and wooded areas. Like its wild rivers, Florida's two national seashores are special because they are natural. There are no hotels, condominiums, seawalls, or dune buggies.

Everglades

The Everglades is a unique area in Florida. Marjory Stoneman Douglas called it "The River of Grass." It is the greatest expanse of sawgrass on earth, and the "widest, shallowest, and strongest river in America." It is 80.5 kilometers/ 50 miles wide in places and averages 22.9 centimeters/ 9 inches in depth during the rainy season only to be dry in the summer.

Draining of the Everglades has disrupted the ecosystem, but man is working to balance the flow of water in order to preserve the vegetation and wildlife of the area.

White Egret in the Everglades

Wildlife

Florida is home to a wide variety of wildlife, but the numbers of many species are not as great as they once were. As man has cleared the land for his own use, the space available for wild animals has been reduced. This area continues to shrink as communities expand to meet the needs of Florida's rapidly growing human population. Fortunately, Florida has set aside a number of protected areas where wildlife can roam free, undisturbed by the threat of civilization. In addition to national and state parks and forests, the state has a number of wildlife reserves, refuges and sanctuaries, as well as several breeding grounds and fish hatcheries. In some of these areas, hunting is permitted, while in others it is strictly prohibited. Where hunting is allowed, it is regulated by the Florida Game and Fresh Water Fish Commission.

Florida has many of the same animals found in states to the north, since many species migrated to Florida during the colder periods of the Ice Age. Animals in this group include deer, bear, raccoon, opossum, fox, bobcat, rabbit, skunk and squirrel. Florida has a number of tropical species, mostly reptiles and birds. The Florida Panther is the last of the big cats to be found east of the Mississippi River. This animal is seldom seen. No one knows how many are left, but estimates range from 20 to 50. The black panther is considered to be an endangered species.

An animal species is classified as endangered if it is expected to become extinct unless given special protection. Endangered species lists have been drawn up by conservation and wildlife organizations, but the official list for the state of Florida is the one prepared by the Game and Fresh Water

Fish Commission. The federal government also has a list of endangered species. Florida is required by law to protect the animals on both the state and federal lists.

Not yet on the endangered list is Florida's largest mammal, the black bear. There are only 1,000 black bears left, therefore, this places them on the threatened list. This means they may become "endangered" soon. Some animals threatened with extinction have made remarkable comebacks. One of these is the rare key deer. This tiny deer is not much bigger than a collie, and is found only in the Florida keys. It is related to the larger white-tailed deer which is found throughout the state. The establishment of the National Key Deer Refuge helped save this animal from extinction. In 1954, when the refuge was created, there were fewer than 50 key deer. By 1981, this number had increased to around 500.

Florida's famous alligator has made an amazing comeback. Hunting and destruction of habitats led to the gator being placed on the endangered species list. With state and federal protection, the alligator population has increased remarkably. The alligator is found throughout Florida in swamps, rivers, lakes and canals. In some waterfront residential areas, the alligator can become a dangerous nuisance.

Similar to but much less abundant than the alligator is the American crocodile. This reptile is found only at the southern tip of the peninsula, usually in salt or brackish water. Other reptiles in Florida include a wide variety of lizards and snakes. Poisonous snakes found in Florida are the rattlesnake, copperhead, coral snake and the cottonmouth moccasin.

The waters in and around Florida abound with fish. This makes Florida a leading state for commercial and sport fishermen. Among the freshwater fish that are popular with fishermen are bass, bream, and catfish. In addition to the saltwater fish, the waters off Florida contain a spectacular variety of colorful fish that delight skindivers. These include the angelfish, parrotfish and tang.

Such fish are highly prized for saltwater aquariums.

Two other marine animals of special interest are the manatee and the porpoise. The manatee also known as the sea cow, has been designated as Florida's state marine mammal. This huge, gentle animal is found mainly in coastal waters and rivers, especially the St. Johns, Suwannee and Crystal Rivers. The manatee is a useful animal because it feeds on water hyacinths and other aquatic plants that clog Florida's waterways. Manatees are on the list of threatened species. Many manatees are killed or injured by the propellers of power boats. It is estimated that 1,000 manatees are left in Florida.

The porpoise, commonly known as the dolphin, has been designated as the Florida state salt water mammal. Dolphins are often spotted along Florida's coastal waters, especially in shallow bays. Dolphins are highly intelligent animals and are sometimes caught for use in marine shows. In Florida, this can only be done through special permits issued by the federal government and the Florida Department of Natural Resources. These permits set strict rules to protect the health of these animals while they are in captivity.

Florida is a bird lover's paradise. Throughout Florida's history, explorers and visitors have marveled at the quantity and variety of birdlife found here. The most famous of these visitors was John James Audubon, whose beautiful paintings of Florida birds are known around the world. In addition to many native species, Florida is host to thousands of winged tourists. Florida is a "flyway" for migrant birds. Some spend the winter here, others go on to islands in the Caribbean or to Central or South America. Among the common song birds found in Florida are the cardinal, blue jay and oriole. Florida's state bird is the mocking bird. Florida has many kinds of ducks, doves, quail and turkey. Birds of prey include hawks, falcons, osprey and the Southern Bald Eagle. The eagle is on the list of threatened species. Of great appeal to bird lovers are wading birds such as herons, storks, cranes and the colorful roseate spoonbill, found mainly in the Florida Bay area.

Many factors resulted in the shape of Florida. How will the shape of the state change in the future?

No one knows... perhaps a river changing course... maybe a drought... a surveyor remarking boundaries... new flora and fauna... or a new county.

Whatever happens in the future can not change the fact that at present Florida is in beautiful shape.

Unit 2   Exploration

NASA

The Space Shuttle Columbia lifts off a few seconds past 7 a.m. on April 12, 1981

EXPLORATION

Larry Pauley

Introduction

"Beautiful!" "Dramatic!" "Futuristic!" "Patriotic!" and "Historical!" These were the messages of congratulations sent to the United States from nations around the world. They were in response to the successful: launching, orbiting and landing of the space shuttle Columbia as it opened up a new frontier for all mankind.

The space shuttle roared skyward from its launch pad at Cape Canaveral, Florida on April 12, 1981. It went into orbit 36 times around the earth without a flaw, and glided down into a pin-point landing on the Mojave Desert in California on April 14, 1981. The world watched breathlessly! It was a sight to behold!

What is the shuttle? It is a spacefaring cargo ship that can be used over and over again. It is launched like a rocket, orbits like a spacecraft and lands like an airplane. It will take satellites, military hardware, and people into space and bring them back. It will transport telescopes, earth-scanning cameras, laboratories, and construction equipment into orbit. So then, the prospects and the promises are grand! Space colonies, orbiting factories, and flights to planets are planned for the future. Mankind is reaching out to make space work for people, and to make space travel a common reality.

Other nations will follow the United States in this opening of space exploration. They too, will be building their own hardware to send into space. Just as a new frontier brings growth and achievement, it also carries with it the struggle for survival and supremacy.

This frontier of space relates back to another time, another era in earth's history when the "ocean" was the unknown and the "continents" sat like planets, waiting to be discovered and explored. Then, as well as today, mankind was courageous, taking risks to step into the unknown. They too returned as conquerors, heroes and heroines.

Florida was like space 500 years ago as far as Europeans were concerned. In a period of time when we can cross continents and

NASA

Underside of the Space Shuttle

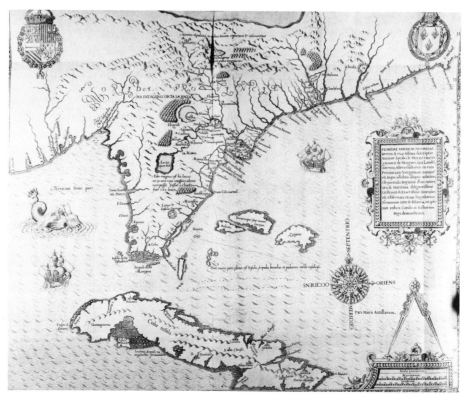

Early Explorer's Map of Florida, 1591

oceans in hours, it is difficult to imagine Florida as being remote. Europeans, in the late 15th and early 16th century, were just beginning to spread their cultures. Nations were developing as we know them today and each nation was looking for markets and riches.

Trade had opened with far off "Cathay," the Republic of China today, and fierce competition was taking place between Spain, Portugal, France, England, The Netherlands and Italy.

Europeans had been limited in their ability to sail far from shore for centuries. During the 15th century several inventions paved the way for sailing to distant lands. The astrolabe, sextant, and compass allowed adventurers to leave the sight of land and sail in uncharted waters. The invention of the movable type printing press spread knowledge and excited people about far off lands. The science of cartography or map making was developing to aid explorers.

The explorers of the 15th and 16th centuries were not totally without knowledge of the earth. Early scientists and mathematicians had proved the earth was round. Ptolemy of Egypt in about 150 A.D. had shown the earth was round and not flat. He also mapped areas with latitude and longitude. Ptolemy's work was not perfect. First, he thought the universe revolved around earth and second, he underestimated the distance from Spain to China. It was this mistake that caused Columbus to think he was in the East Indies when he touched the islands of the western hemisphere.

Columbus and other adventuresome sailors had heard or read of Ptolemy's theories and of Vikings making voyages to land across the sea. This knowledge and new inventions did not take away from the courage it took to set sail westward to arrive in the East. Columbus arrived in the New World in 1492 and started a gusher of exploration.

The voyage by Columbus gave Spain claim to the New World, but other nations were soon to follow. In 1498, John Cabot sailing for England set sail on a secret voyage to find a water passage to China. He had been to Labrador earlier, but now he sailed into Spanish territory. He sailed southward along the coast and rounded the southern tip of Florida. He sailed northward until the land turned westward. At that point he probably realized that this New World was a continent and not an island. Cabot turned back, retracing his trip around the peninsula. On the east coast he sighted a great bay, possibly Miami's Biscayne Bay. He and his sailors, weary from almost a year-long voyage, rested on the shores and then set sail for England.

Europeans had now seen the lush lands of what was soon to be called Florida. They probably had seen the bronze skinned natives of the peninsula. Even though the Europeans thought they had "discovered" a new land, it had long ago been discovered by these natives.

Early Cultures

The natives of Florida also were explorers of the peninsula. They were part of the migration of Mongoloid people across the Bering Strait, thousands of years before. The first explorers of Florida came from Asia and not from Europe. It took several thousand years for these people to cross North America and arrive in the St. Johns River area.

We know the St. Johns culture existed because of artifacts they left behind. These artifacts were left mostly in mounds and "middens" or trash heaps. Other Indian groups, as they came to be called, moved into Florida and by the time the Europeans arrived they had sparsely settled the peninsula.

Juan Ponce de Leon

It was 17 years after Cabot's sighting of Florida, before an organized exploration of the pensinsula began. Juan Ponce de Leon was the first Spaniard to set foot on Florida and he proceeded to name it.

Juan Ponce de Leon came from a family of ancient nobility. Born in 1460 in the north of Spain, he served as a page and later as a knight in the court of King Ferdinand. There he learned good manners and there he learned to be a strong soldier. In court, he listened to the reports of the great explorers.

When Columbus made his second trip to the New World in 1493, Ponce de Leon was on board one of the ships. He liked his new life on the island of Hispaniola and proved himself a capable leader and colonizer. As governor of a local province, he developed a plantation which raised food crops, cattle and horses. He sent for his Spanish wife and two daughters to join him.

In his province, Ponce de Leon allowed the native chiefs to remain in charge of their villages. They had to furnish a certain number of men for mining and agricultural work. Personal service could not be demanded from free natives, and they were allowed to raise their own food crops and attend their own needs.

Visiting natives told Ponce de Leon of gold in the rivers of the area to the north. In 1508 he was sent to colonize the island of Puerto Rico. After collecting a gratifying quantity of gold, which made him rich, he returned to Hispaniola. He later colonized Puerto Rico and became its first governor.

The next few years were disappointing to Ponce de Leon as the governorship of Puerto Rico shifted several times; and he watched its peaceful development ruin. This was one of the factors which caused him to seek new lands. Natives had been telling him of the Island of Bimini with its enchanted fountain - the magic of its water bringing youth to all who bathed or drank there.

De Leon was over fifty when he set forth on his great voyage of discovery. On March 3, 1513 his two ships moved through the familiar waters of the Bahamas and charted their course, northward. A cold, stormy wind hit; they changed their course; and angled out across the vast, rugged wind-beaten water, where they struggled for three days. On April 2, 1513, the wind abated before

Florida Photographic Archives

Juan Ponce de Leon

them; stretched across the horizon was a long smudge of land. They approached, dropped anchor and went ashore. It was probably just north of the present site of St. Augustine at 29° 32′ N. latitude that Ponce de Leon planted the flag for Spain. He called the land "La Florida" because it was the Easter season. In Spain the holiday was called, "Pasqua Florida," or "the feast of the flowers." Before returning, he sailed around the southern end and up the eastern coast. No one realized he had landed on a part of what would become the United States.

In 1521 he returned with 200 men to establish a settlement. He landed near Charlotte Harbor. While the Spaniards were putting up buildings, the fierce Calusas attacked and one of their arrows hit Ponce de Leon in the thigh. His men carried him back to the ship and set sail for Cuba, where he died within a few days.

Ponce de Leon was buried at San Juan in Puerto Rico. His tomb holds this tribute:

> *"Here rests THE LION brave,*
> *whose deeds of fame*
> *Surpassed in might and valor*
> *of his name."*

Panfilo de Narvaez

Other Spaniards were not discouraged by the fate of Ponce de Leon. Their "fire" for exploration came from a great desire to find gold, claim land and to Christianize the natives of the new world.

This fire burned in the veins of Panfilo de Narvaez who had helped conquer Cuba in 1511. He was a tall, red haired, bearded man with only one eye. His other eye, was lost in a battle, when the governor of Cuba opposed Hernando Cortes as the leader to direct the expedition to Mexico, in 1519.

King Charles of Spain authorized Panfilo de Narvaez to make the second expedition to Florida, with instructions to build three forts and start two colonies. The forts would protect the Spaniards from attacks, and the colonies would be a refuge for Spanish ships wrecked at sea.

In 1528, Narvaez sailed from Cuba up the west coast of Florida to what is now Old Tampa Bay. He arrived with six ships and six hundred people. Among them were soldiers, colonists and Franciscan priests, who hoped to convert the native Americans to Christianity. He also arrived with ample supplies of horses, cows and hogs; as well as guns, spears and crossbows for the soldiers; and hammers, hoes and seed for the settlers. Cabeza de Vaca, a devout and far-sighted nobleman, was the treasurer and historian of the expedition.

Narvaez sent his ships up the coast to await him at harbor, while he and three hundred of his men took forty horses to explore the interior. They sought food and information from the Indians, but the natives did not trust these men on horseback, with shining armor, glittering shields and noisy weapons. The Indians urged them to continue north to find their "gold." Meanwhile, the Spanish soldiers grew weary and hungry as they cut their way through thick jungles, crossed wide rivers and battled the hot sun and Indians. Disappointed by their months of fruitless wanderings, the soldiers returned to the coast, only to find no ships waiting for them. They had long since returned to Cuba having thought Narvaez and his men had perished.

Left stranded, Narvaez and his group built five crude boats with the hope of reaching Mexico in them. The strong winds, large waves, and salt water proved too much for the fragile boats. Narvaez lost his life somewhere in the Gulf. He did not accomplish what he set out to do, but he did explore the interior of Florida from Tampa Bay to what is now Tallahassee, Wakulla Springs and St. Marks.

One boatload of Narvaez's men went as far west as present day Texas before it was shipwrecked. One of the survivors was Cabeza de Vaca who managed to keep himself alive as he drifted in and out of native villages for seven years. Sometimes he was a slave; sometimes a free man. He became a "healer" to the native Americans, as well as a trader of goods. He was reunited with a band of Spaniards near Mexico City and returned to Spain. There he told his adventures to King Charles and to all who would listen.

Juan Ortiz

Another adventure story that crops up among the early explorers of Florida is that of Juan Ortiz. At the pleading of Narvaez's wife who could not believe her husband was dead Ortiz and twenty-five men set out to search for him. They found the place where he landed and were motioned ashore by native Americans. Being cautious, only Ortiz and another man rowed to shore. Ortiz was grabbed and dragged into the woods. The other man was killed and Ortiz's hands were tied. He was taken into the village where he was to be burned over a pile of wood. An Indian princess begged for his life and it was spared. Years later, this episode was to become a tale about Captain John Smith and Pocahontas in Virginia.

Ortiz was not a free man, however. He was made a slave and had to work with the women and children. One night, he was ordered to guard the dead body of a chief's son far out in the pineland. He fell asleep, but awoke to the sharp crackle of sticks that sounded like a body being dragged through the bushes. He threw his lance as hard as he could, and in the morning found that he had saved the body of the chief's son by killing a wolf. Ortiz was accepted as a tribesman.

On two other occasions, Ortiz's life was saved by native Americans. Once by the same princess, when it was thought the tribe was losing wars because of his presence, and once by a young chieftain. Around eleven years later, Ortiz heard of a Spanish expedition near Tampa Bay and went out to greet his countrymen. They were soldiers of Commander De Soto. Ortiz later became De Soto's interpreter and guide.

Hernando de Soto

One of the four most famous captains of Spain was Hernando de Soto. He had become wealthy in the Spanish conquest of Peru, and had just taken a bride, when King Charles V commissioned him to take an expedition to Florida. Because he was a nobleman and a famous soldier, hundreds of Spanish and

Hernando de Soto

Portuguese men of nobility begged him to take them with him to Florida. They believed much gold could be found there. De Soto's wife and many other noblemen's wives accompanied their husbands to Havana, Cuba, where they set up housekeeping and awaited their husbands.

In May, 1539 after a year of preparation in Cuba, De Soto anchored off Tampa Bay. His brilliant fleet of ten ships brought 600 men, among whom were monks, laborers, soldiers, carpenters, and nobles. Also, aboard were 213 horses, pigs, cattle, greyhounds and other well-stocked supplies. The natives fled as these people landed and took possession with salutes, banners, music and Masses served by priests in gold vestments.

Ortiz told De Soto that the Indians did not like the Spanish intrusion of their land. They wanted to be left alone and wished the Spaniards would leave. De Soto, determined to find gold, chose to believe the villagers when they told him wealth was just a little farther ahead

De Soto was cruel and took food that he and his men needed from the native Americans. Whenever Indians were captured, they were used as slaves or shot, and chiefs were used as captive guides to each new village.

De Soto's exploration took him through the Ocala area, across the Suwannee River north to the present site of Tallahassee. He went north through Georgia to the Savannah River, and followed it to the Blue Ridge Mountains. He and his men crossed the mountains and followed the Alabama River south to a place called Mabila. Still thinking he could find gold, he turned northwest and in May, 1541, he sighted the Father of Waters, the great Mississippi. He crossed and explored parts of Arkansas, only to return to the river. It was on the banks of the Mississippi that De Soto died and his body was buried in the river.

Tristan De Luna

It was eighteen years later, in 1559, that one more Spanish explorer made an attempt to colonize Florida. Tristan de Luna brought another well-stocked expedition and landed at Pensacola Bay. Through a series of misfortunes: a hurricane, loss of food supplies and bad calculations, the colony failed and De Luna returned to Spain, a dejected man.

After 50 years of attempting to settle Florida, the Spanish King had become discouraged and gave up on its possession. Two factors forced him to change his mind. One factor was the Spanish Plate Fleet that was bringing shiploads of gold, silver and other treasures from Mexico, Peru and Chile. They were being looted by pirates, as they rounded the end of Cuba following the Gulf Stream up the eastern coast of Florida. They also were being shipwrecked by hurricanes off Florida's coast, and they needed a safe port. The other factor was France's attempts to settle Florida, which upset the Spanish court.

Florida Photographic Archives

Jean Ribault

Jean Ribault

A new power that was rising in France was that of the Huguenots or Protestants. They followed the teachings of John Calvin and were members of the Reformed Church. The Huguenots wanted a place to worship God according to the dictates of their own conscience. So, many of them joined the sea captain Jean Ribault to establish a settlement in Florida. In May, 1562, he landed at the mouth of the St. Johns River, where he built a stone marker and claimed the land for France. Ribault returned to France for more supplies, upon finding the country at war, he turned to England for help. The English were happy for the chance to locate along the Spanish trade route. They began to mistrust Ribault and threw him in prison for two years.

Rene de Laudonniere, Ribault's lieutenant on the first voyage, led France's second expedition to Florida. He decided to stay near the mouth of the St. Johns River. There he built a small fort which was named Fort Caroline in honor of King Charles of France. The Frenchmen were not given to "work," nor learning how to raise food or to preserve the fish and game. They were busy looking for gold. Consequently, their food supply ran dangerously low. The colony was about to break up, when Jean Ribault arrived the second time bringing reinforcements.

Jacques Le Moyne, the French artist, came with Laudonniere. It is through his writings and drawings that the life and customs of the Timucuan Tribe have been preserved. He lived among them and made 42 drawings of these tall, well-built people. He also drew a map of Florida.

Pedro Menendez de Aviles

At the same time Jean Ribault and his fleet were racing to strengthen the French settlement, a great Spanish navy officer, Pedro Menendez de Aviles and his fleet were racing to establish a settlement in Florida and drive the French out. Menendez's orders read: *"If in the said coast or land there were settlers or corsairs or other nations whatsoever not subject to us, drive them out by what means you see fit."*

On August 28, 1565, Menendez entered a good harbor and called it St. Augustine, after the feast of that day. It developed into the first permanent European settlement in North America and is the nation's oldest city. Menendez left some men and supplies, then hurried north to battle the French. The French were resting and had no powder or shot in their guns. They quickly lifted anchor and sailed away. Menendez could not catch them so he returned to St. Augustine.

The Spanish under Menendez drove the French out of East Florida after several battles. Menendez now felt his colony was safe. He knew the people would have to work and not run off looking for gold. For the next two years, he built a line of small log forts for several hundred kilometers/ miles inland. The forts extended from north off the coast of South Carolina, to settlements south to Miami and west to Tampa Bay. The inland forts spread across the north to present day Pensacola.

Menendez asked the King to send over Jesuit priests to convert the native Americans to the Catholic faith. Menendez saw to it that thatched huts with crosses were built along side the forts to be used as chapels by the priests. The forts and the missions were to be a complement to each other, and for years they were.

Under Menendez, St. Augustine began to grow and develop like a Spanish village. People planted the first seedlings of orange, fig and pomegranate trees, and cleared the land to build their homes.

Menendez was energetic, resourceful and worked very hard to hold Florida together.

The King gave him greater honor and made him governor of Havana. Later in 1587, the King recalled him to Spain to assist in the building of the Spanish Armada. Florida remained the place he wanted to be.

Missions

The missionaries did more to explore interior Florida than anything else the Spanish did. They were important in Florida from 1587 to 1708.

The Franciscan friars lived among the native Americans and learned their language. They would seek out a good place for a mission, then barter with the natives for the land. They would feed and clothe the natives in exchange for their labor in building the mission and houses. Some Indians would build small huts and live near the mission. It was difficult for them to understand the white man's rules. The mission itself became a small village with huts and farmland surrounding it.

Roads were built connecting the missions, thus giving access to the interior of north Florida. Missions were not extended into central and south Florida, leaving that area unexplored by the Spanish.

Most of the early exploration of central and south Florida was by slavetraders. The search for more and more Indian slaves forced the slavers to go deeper into the interior. Captain Thomas Nairne captured Ais, Jeagas and Tequestas as far south as the Biscayne Bay. He chased the Calusas from the southwest coast northward and into the Everglades.

England

After Spain gave control of Florida to England in 1763, much of the exploration of the peninsula would be searching for interior lands for settlement. The English were restricted to sailing up or down rivers for suitable homesites.

The major exploration of Florida during this period was by William Bartram, a botanist. Bartram wrote Travels Through North and South Carolina, Georgia and

Pedro Menendez de Avilez

Florida, a description of the resources of the upper St. Johns River. His details of the springs, bird life, lakes, animal life and weather raised interest in that area.

Spain's Return

Spain regained Florida in 1783 after the American Revolution but made no efforts to explore further. Most of the exploration was under the direction of two English merchants, William Panton and John Leslie. The Panton, Leslie and Company sent agents throughout Florida to trade and barter. Friendship with the Indians gave them access to unexplored areas.

United States

Warfare caused a great surge of investigation of Florida's interior. Americans angered by Seminoles and other Indians raided Spanish Florida. General Andrew Jackson several times crossed the border to punish the Indians and to intimidate the Spanish.

Spain, after 38 years of ownership, once again gave up Florida, this time to the United States in 1821. The land hungry Americans saw central Florida as land ripe for the taking. During a series of wars with the Seminoles and Miccosukees, the Indians were driven into the Everglades, killed or sent to Oklahoma. The settlers came in right after the wars and occupied former Indian farms and ranches. They were moving southward rapidly.

Statehood and the Civil War deterred exploration for a time, but the Americans were determined to conquer "the last frontier in the East." Much of the remaining exploration of southern Florida was to be done by naturalists in search of the unknown. In 1872, Fred Beverly sailed down the Kissimmee River and entered the almost untouched Lake Okeechobee. His description of this paradise for birds and alligators was almost unbelievable to the outside world.

The Seminoles, forced into the Everglades, explored its wonders and knew it very well. They established secret paths or routes and traveled throughout the glades. Unknown numbers of outsiders entered the area in search of feathers for ladies in New York, and alligator hides for gentlemen's shoes. Many were never seen again.

Historian Frederick Jackson Turner said in 1890, that the American frontier had been settled. He overlooked a vast area in South Florida, the Everglades. In 1890, only the fringes of it and the Big Cypress Swamp had been touched. As late as 1980 a national park ranger stated that he felt "There are areas that have never been seen, even by Indians, in the glades."

Modern Exploration

The exploration of present day Florida was, for all practical purposes, ended by the early 1920's. The magnificence of this effort can be seen by the fact that it took from 1513 until 1900 and later to explore Florida, while it took from 1607 to 1890 to cover the rest of the Continental United States. It truly was and is as Marjory Stoneman Douglas subtitled her book about Florida, The Long Frontier.

Exploration of the earth's resources has taken place in Florida. This search for natural resources became a part of Florida's industrial growth.

Perhaps, it is justice that the area of the United States that took the longest to explore and conquer, is the forefront of another frontier, space. The most extensive space exploration is based at Cape Canaveral Florida, at a spot that both John Cabot and Juan Ponce de Leon sailed past in the 15th century.

Early Space Efforts

On January 31, 1958, a rocket left its pad at Cape Canaveral and thrust the United States into the Space Age. Explorer I was lifted into space and into an earth orbit. This tiny manmade satellite transmitted signals back to earth discovering the Van Allen Radiation Belt around the earth. In April 1960 the first weather satellite, Tiros I, was launched and successfully orbited.

Alan Shepard, Jr. and John Glenn

Three years after Explorer I, Commander Alan Shepard, Jr. became America's first astronaut. His suborbital flight was 187.4 kilometers/ 116.5 miles above earth and lasted 15 minutes 22 seconds, but Americans listened breathlessly to the whole event.

Less than one year after Shepard's successful flight, John Glenn soared into space and orbited the earth three times. Four years after Explorer I, the United States had successfully orbited a man in space.

Increased Activity

America's space program was rapidly progressing. During 1965, Virgil Grissom and John Young successfully changed the path of their orbiting space capsule. Three months later in June, Edward White left the confines of an orbiting capsule, connected by a tether and accomplished America's first walk in space.

NASA

Commander John Young and Pilot Robert Crippen on the flight deck of the Columbia.

It seemed the National Aeronautics and Space Administration (NASA) would do no wrong. Success had followed success! This ended on January 27, 1967, when a fire destroyed the inside of a space capsule on the launch pad. The three astronauts inside: Virgil Grissom, Edward White and Roger Chafee, died instantly. Through August 1981, no other Americans had died in the space program.

The Moon

The crowning achievement of the United State's space program occurred on July 20, 1969. The Apollo 11 mission sent the message from Tranquility Base that *"The Eagle has landed."* Inside the lunar landing module were astronauts: Neil Armstrong and Edwin Aldrin, Jr.. They were sitting on the surface of the moon, while Astronaut Michael Collins orbited the moon in the space module. Armstrong was the first out, and when he stepped on the moon, he stated, *"One small step for man, one giant leap for mankind."*

Aldrin was the second person to set foot on the moon. After which, he and Armstrong conducted scientific experiments. They gathered moon rocks and on July 24th, along with Collins, returned to earth, splashing down in the Pacific Ocean within view of their recovery ship.

America sent five more crews to the moon during the 1970's successful landings.

Other Flights

A different type of space project took place in 1975. On July 17th of that year, a United States' Apollo linked up in space with a Union of Soviet Socialist Republics' Soyuz. The astronauts and cosmonauts conducted several joint experiments.

Unmanned flights occupied the remainder of the space program until the turn of the decade. The Viking and Voyager probes have investigated Mars and Saturn.

Space Shuttle

Nineteen hundred eighty-one was the year of a dramatic change in the American space program. Until then, rockets and their payloads were lost and unusable after one launch. On April 12, 1981, the shuttle was successfully launched from the Kennedy Space Center at Cape Canaveral, with astronauts John Young and Bob Crippen aboard. The Space Shuttle Columbia returned to earth two days later ready to be launched again.

We may not achieve greatness in today's expanding frontiers, but who knows the adventures which still can be discovered in Florida. Perhaps

...distant planets... dark recesses in the Everglades... the ocean depths... an unknown plant life...

or whatever may exist that is now unknown to us.

EXPLORATION

Unit 3   **Health**

Florida Photographic Archives

Dr. John Gorrie

HEALTH

TONSORIAL
PARLOR
TEETH PULLED
BARBER   BLOODLETTING

Larry Pauley

Introduction

A doctor in an operating room in Miami slowly gives radioactive material to a cancer victim. In Orlando, an orthopedic sugeon carefully cuts into a patient's shattered elbow. After three hours of surgery, the patient is in the recovery room without having his arm amputated. Another specialist has a nurse wipe perspiration from her brow as she peers through an operating microscope to replace an eardrum in a semi-deaf boy. A six year old girl in Tallahassee is given a prescription of penicillin for a strep throat. Slowly, a paralyzed veteran of the Viet Nam conflict walks along a rail, guided by a physicial therapist.

A two month premature baby born in Tarpon Springs is rushed to the neo-natal unit at All Children's Hospital in St. Petersburg. A police officer in Ocala is burned over 90 percent of her body in an explosion. The ambulance rushes her to the hospital. The doctor decides that the patient needs more intensive care. A helicopter transports her to the burn center at Shands Teaching Hospital in Gainesville.

All of these events could happen any day in Florida. Not long ago these patients would have died, or been handicapped for life, because of the lack of proper medical attention. There have been many improvements in medical care in the last few years. Medical care, which we take for granted today, has been a fairly new addition to the social life of most Floridians. Many diseases or injuries that we now classify as minor were fatal during the early history of Florida.

Indians

Medicine in pre-European Florida was mostly based on knowledge passed down by a man or woman who knew the effect of herbs and other medicines. Indians often called upon the spirits to heel the afflicted. The Shaman, sometimes called the "medicine man," used not only spirits but such things as tobacco smoke. As the Europeans entered the peninsula, they mixed their "cures" with Indian methods.

Some of the mixtures of native American and European medicines can be seen in remedies such as the use of poultice of Indian meal on burns. Liquid from the soaked bark of trees was applied to burns, also. The Miccosukee used a variety of herbs for medicines. The most commonly used were bay leaves, cedar, sassafras and ginseng. Others included button snakeroot, lizard's tail, frost week and huckleberry. The transfer of medical knowledge can be seen with sassafras. The Miccosukee showed the Huguenots in Fort Carolina how to make tea of it. Then the French Huguenots, who survived being massacred, gave the knowledge to the Spanish.

Evidence of the use of tobacco smoke can be seen in a drawing by LeMoyne, the Huguenot artist. In the drawing the Indians can be seen inhaling tobacco smoke. Tobacco was supposed to cure headaches, lung ailments and ulcers.

In other cases cures were pure superstition. The Seminoles always had their sick lie with their heads to the east. They believed if the head was to the west, the soul would walk the Milky Way and the body would die.

The Indians had learned to deal with the maladies which existed before the arrival of the Europeans. They may not have always had cures, but we know today that some of the herbs were worthwhile. Even the Shaman's use of the spirits psychologically helped the ill. The Europeans brought new diseases to the Indians. These diseases had devasting effects on the Indians because their bodies had not built up immunity to the new diseases. Soldiers at St. Augustine in 1659 became sick with measles and many died. When the "new" disease infected the Indians, 10,000 of them died.

Early Maladies

Early diseases in Florida included consumption (tuberculosis), asthma, pleurisy, scurvy, worm fever, lockjaw, smallpox, hydrophobia (rabies), sunstroke, dysentary, cancer, typhoid, malaria, yellow fever and snakebites.

Early families were usually very large. It was not uncommon for fifteen to twenty children to be born to one family. Many of these children never reached adulthood. Childhood diseases were very common and deadly. Croup was the most common of these diseases. One cure for croup was a large dose of the juice of roasted onions or garlic to break up the congestion. To cure the accompanying fever, a concoction made of snake root would cause sweating. Worms were a common occurrence in children. Salt was given in very large doses, or sometimes, the scrapings from pewter were fed to the child to drive out the parasites.

Children and adults were always susceptible to smallpox, the most feared of the 18th century diseases. Families would burn clothing and bedding with which a victim came in contact. Until a vaccination for smallpox was developed in 1796 by Edward Jenner, an English physician, the fear of the dreaded disease led to panic and even to the abandonment of cabins. Survivors of smallpox often had terrible pox scars, especially on the face.

Measles, mumps, whooping cough, and diptheria, which today often cause slight discomfort, were serious diseases for the pioneer. Lung diseases were generally classified under the name of "consumption." Syrups and mixtures of herbs were used as a cure.

Typhoid, Yellow Fever and Malaria

These three diseases caused much suffering and death. They were very common in subtropical areas. Drainage and sanitation were often bad, so flies and mosquitos that spread these diseases multiplied. Dr. John Lorimer, the military surgeon in Pensacola from 1765 to 1781, and James Lind, a British navy doctor, both reported that the fevers were most common in July, August, and September - Florida's hottest months.

Snakebites

One of the most common maladies in early Florida was the snake bite, either from a copperhead, coral, or rattler. There were a variety of cures for this frightening experience.

Some of the most common cures for snake bites were very elaborate. One way was to take the body of the snake which had bitten the victim and cut it into pieces. The pieces were then placed on the wound in order to draw out the poison. Then the liquid of boiled leaves was poured over the wound. Another widely used cure was cutting the wound, sucking out the poison, and then filling the wound with salt and gun powder. Many times, this cure had a side effect upon the person sucking the poison from the wound. Most pioneers had bad teeth. Sometimes, the poison stayed in the cavities and was swallowed thus making the helper sick. Sometimes, ferns and roots were placed on the wound. If the flesh of an animal, such as a deer, was available, a "V" would be cut in the wound and the animal flesh would be placed over the cut.

Rabies

Much feared in early Florida was hydrophobia, which was caused by the bite of a rabid animal. There was no known cure until 1882 when Louis Pasteur of France developed a serum to be given in a series of injections. Pioneers came in contact with many animals through their lifestyle and thus, were always in danger of being bitten by a rabid animal.

There was no known cure for rabies during much of pioneer times, but medicine was given as a cure. These medicines and pills were sold by traveling peddlers and medicine men whose concoctions were supposed to cure everything. Pills for rabies were usually a mixture of herbs which had no effect. People feared some diseases so much that they would take medicine from anyone claiming to be a "doctor."

Jail Fever

Another common disease was jail or hospital fever. It was found where several persons stayed together in dirty, poorly ventilated areas. The fever was probably murine typhus, carried by the rat flea. Most supply ships were rat infested, and often brought the typhus along with the supplies.

Poor sanitation, poor drainage, hot weather, and close quarters all helped spread disease in early Florida. Another problem was with incoming ships. When they docked in Pensacola, Key West, or St. Augustine, they often left their ill crew members with the people of the town. This would cause a disease to spread further.

The common treatment for jail or hospital fever was the use of three leeches on each temple or a vein in the arm for bloodletting. The patient was removed from the area of poisoned air, if the air couldn't be cleaned. Leeches were used to treat fever headaches, also.

Fevers

One of the most common cures for fevers was bloodletting. It was thought the removal of blood would reduce the fever. Of course, that process sometimes broke the fever by killing the patient. The bloodletting was followed by causing the patient to vomit. This was done by giving them a powdered substance called "crab eye." Crab eyes came from a mass of calcium carbonate from the stomach of a European crawfish.

Other Maladies

Dentistry was very crude. Settlers teeth were usually in terrible condition. By adulthood, the few teeth a person had left were usually decayed. For toothaches, a folklore cure was to carry a hog's tooth in the pocket. When extraction could not be avoided, the offending tooth would often be pulled with tongs. This was done without the aid of an anesthetic.

Broken bones were often placed between two pieces of wood and bound with rawhide, cloth, or rope. This resulted in many disfigurements. The bones healed crooked, causing misshapen bodies.

Gunshot wounds, even the most minor ones, more often than not resulted in death. The wounds usually became infected. Because the musket balls were made of lead, the victim often died of lead poisoning. One cure for the infection, caused by a gunshot, was to "bleed" the victim. "Bloodletting" supposedly allowed "bad blood" to flow out of the body. Today, we know this practice probably hastened the death of many a patient.

Spanish Hospitals

The Spanish were concerned with health care. Governor Gonzalo Méndez de Canza, in 1598, wrote the King of Spain telling of a hospital having been formed in St. Augustine in 1597. The hospital was part of the Hermita de Nuestra Señora de La Soledad (the Church of Our Lady of Solitude). The hospital was responsible for saving the lives of many Negro royal slaves, soldiers, and Indians during an epidemic fever in 1597.

Another hospital was founded in January 1600, this one by Governor Lanzo. He paid for it himself. It was laid out with six beds arranged around an alter so the sick could observe mass without getting out of bed. The hospital was for " ...all poor and sick people..."

Fevers were still the major source of discomfort and illness in Florida. The major cure for this had become "The Bark" of quinaquina also called "Peruvian Bark." The Spanish learned of its curative powers from the Inca Indians and its use spread rapidly. The drug in the bark was quinine and for years was used to help sufferers of malaria and yellow fever.

British Health Care

The British obtained Florida at the end of the "French and Indian War" or as the Europeans called it, "The Seven Years War."

Health care during the British rule advanced somewhat, although, it was still a mixture of Indian cures, folklore, new

Kissing the middle rail of this fence was supposed to help rough lips.

Photo courtesy FSU by James Callahan

knowledge, and trial and error.

Their cures are laughed at today, but it must be remembered that the practice of medicine was just becoming a profession. For centuries the "bleeder" in most places had been the barber. This was the origin of the use of the color red on barber poles.

Medical knowledge was spiced with a bit of superstition and belief in the supernatural. Remedies were best when given during the waning moon. This was believed to cause the disease or illness to wane, also. For serious diseases it was common to call upon the seventh child of a seventh child. These people were supposed to have special healing powers.

Teas were popular in the 1800's and even into the 1900's. Sassafras tea was used as a spring tonic. It is still possible to hear the advice "drink some sassafras to help your blood." Other teas were catnip tea for colds, smartwood tea for blood poisoning, and sage tea for pneumonia.

Some people believed in hanging items around the neck. There were separate items for each health problem. If you had a fever, you put rattlesnake bones in a pouch to wear around your neck. To prevent nose bleeds, red beads were put in a bag and hung around the neck. Similar to the bags hung around the neck were copper bracelets worn for arthritis. This is a "cure" still used today.

Some folklore medicines may really have been effective even though they sound peculiar. One cure was to kiss the middle rail of a five rail fence if you had rough lips. This might have been effective if it were a pine fence because the sap would have had the same effect as today's lip balms. Another cure was washing your warts in rain water caught in an oak stump. It might have helped because the oak stump and water would have formed tannic acid. This acid slowly reduces warts. Irritated facial skin was washed in dew or in honey and buttermilk to help the rash. This probably helped because the afflicted person would stop using lye soap on his or her face.

It is hard for us to believe that some pioneer cures were effective. It is more difficult to see the effect of washing freckles in blacksmith's water to clear a complexion. Even more difficult to believe is the cure for fits—the victim's shirt was torn off and burned. Carrying a hog's tooth in the pocket was supposed to help ward off a toothache. One cure which may have been hard to endure was to pour tobacco juice into the ear for an earache.

Preventive Medicine

The British were concerned with preventing diseases. Doctors during this period believed diseases were spread by *"...particle, atoms or animalcules... from distempered, putrefying or poisoned bodies..."*

The spreading of disease was such a problem in early Florida that the British military officers set up a program for prevention. Brigadier General Frederick Haldimand arrived in Pensacola in 1767. To discourage mosquitos, he had the swamp behind the town drained. He provided a more proficient water supply. He had parts of the fort reconstructed for better air circulation. Privies (latrines or bathrooms) were built, and the men were ordered to use them.

Dr. Lorimer suggested two story barracks. He thought it was better to sleep away from the damp ground. He insisted on having the drinking water boiled in iron or tin - not copper - pots. He recommended that troop ships plan their trips to arrive in the fall when the heat was not as intense. This helped protect the supplies they carried because the mosquito population was down.

Sometimes a quarantine was used to stop the spread of disease. Santa Rosa Island was used to hold newly arrived troops with an illness before they could land in Pensacola. During a smallpox epidemic in Pensacola in 1769, Santa Rosa Island was used to treat poor civilians at government expense.

Aedes aegypti and Anopheles

Pronounciation of these words may cause you problems, but not nearly as many problems as they have caused homo sapiens for centuries.

These big words are really small insects - mosquitoes. The first one, Aedes aegypti carries the yellow fever virus from one homo sapien - human to another human. When this mosquito bites a person who is infected, the virus enters the mosquito and incubates for 9 to 12 days. From then on as long as the mosquito lives it can produce yellow fever. This disease attacks the liver of humans causing malfunctioning, which in turn creates a yellow pallor to the skin. There are headaches, fever and dizziness, also.

The second word - Anopheles is the mosquito which carries a parasite which causes malaria. It is the female Anopheles which causes problems. When the mosquito bites a person who has malaria, it sucks up red blood cells which carry the parasites. The parasites multiply in the mosquito's stomach, then move to the salivary glands. When the infected mosquito bites another person it injects saliva containing the parasites into the victim. The parasites then enter the red blood cells, causing them to burst. This causes anemia. The disease induces fever, chills, sweats and weakness.

Both these diseases are common in tropical and subtropical areas and are associated with mosquito breeding areas such as marshes and swamps. In fact, the word malaria comes from two Italian words meaning bad air.

Medications and mosquito control programs have reduced the effects and extent of these diseases.

A Man For All Seasons

Dr. John Gorrie set out to help cool sufferers of malaria and yellow fever. In doing so, he started an industry of which he never knew.

Gorrie was born in Charleston, South Carolina. He went to New York to medical school and after returning to South Carolina decided to move to Florida. He arrived in Apalachicola, Florida in 1833, where he began a successful medical practice. Dr. Gorrie also was a civic leader and politician.

In 1845, Dr. Gorrie began concentrating on how to create artificial refrigeration. Five years later, he had created ice by mechanical means. On May 6, 1851, he was granted United States Patent Number 8080. Gorrie knew he had made an important contribution to medical knowledge and society in general.

Others, however, did not immediately see the value of his invention. He could not obtain financing for a plant to prove his invention. His frustration brought on by this failure caused him to suffer a nervous collapse, and he died in 1855 at the age of 52.

Forty-five years later the Southern Ice Association recognized Gorrie's contribution and had a monument erected in his memory in Apalachicola. In 1914, the state of Florida placed a statue of Dr. Gorrie in the United States Capitol in Washington, D.C.

The next time you open your refrigerator, turn on the air conditioner, or eat a snow cone, you should thank Dr. John Gorrie - A Man For All Seasons.

Climate and Health

Letters and books written during the 18th century give differing views of the effects of Florida's climate on health. James Lind, a British Naval physician wrote of Mobile in West Florida as a place, "...where intermitting fevers prevail...." A Dutch cartographer reported in 1772 that fevers existed on the St. Johns, in East Florida and Mobile in West Florida.

The benefits of Florida were shown by another writer in 1783-84. Johann Schoept wrote in his TRAVELS IN THE CONFEDERATION:

"East Florida as regards sickliness, has often been judged with the same disfavor which experience attaches to the southern parts of North America generally; but without reason. Augustine itself is widely known to be a healthy place, so that weaklings and consumptives from the northern provinces resort hither, and always to their advantage."

Florida was to experience growth as people began to agree with Schoept. Florida's climate, despite all its problems, was an excellent place to live.

Boards of Health

Florida became a Territory of The United States in 1821. Within weeks after becoming part of America two Florida cities established boards of health. These boards were to monitor the spread of diseases and establish standards of health care. St. Augustine and Pensacola took the first steps in standardizing health care in Florida.

In St. Augustine, the mayor, an alderman, a merchant, a Catholic priest and a physician were the first members of the board of health. Governor Andrew Jackson appointed Dr. James Bronaugh, personal physician, as "resident physician and president of the board of health." Jackson instructed all medical officers at military posts to aid in public health programs.

The Legislature Council of Florida Territory met in Pensacola in the summer of 1822. Dr. Bronaugh presided. Unfortunately, a yellow fever epidemic broke out at the same time and the council fled town together. Dr. Bronaugh contracted the disease. He died on the same day Gov. DuVal signed the legislative act officially establishing a Board of Health in Pensacola and St. Augustine.

Florida Photographic Archives

**Jacksonville, 1888 with Bay Street
fires burning to
"destroy" fever germs**

Bronaugh's final words in the Pensacola "Floridian" warned about the seriousness of the fever.

Trained Physicians

Just as the rest of North America, Florida experienced problems due to the lack of trained doctors. The out and out fraud or quack found the remote areas of Florida a good place to sell their "patent" medicines. The people needed medical care and would buy any new "guaranteed to work" cure. These "medicine men" would pass through selling bottles of "miracle" cures to all who would listen. They would be gone before the buyers found out the medicine was worthless.

Others came who could not qualify under the strict rules of health or had graduated from medical schools of dubious quality. Some of these, though, did perform a service. Limited medical knowledge was better than no knowledge at all. There were, however,

well-educated doctors who came to Florida in the late 18th and early 19th century. In fact, large numbers came. There were a variety of things which drew them here. It may have been cheap land, desire to serve where needed or just plain adventurism.

The better doctors became leaders of their communities. Not only were they doctors, but leaders in religion, politics, and education. Dr. John Wells, Jr., from England, published the first Florida newspaper. The "East Florida Gazette" was first issued in 1783. The first paper published in the Florida Keys, the "Key West Gazette," was also started by a doctor. Dr. John Gorrie came to Florida from South Carolina in 1833. He settled in Apalachicola where he became the postmaster, a city councilman, city treasurer, and mayor. Dr. Gorrie maintained a successful medical practice and invented the first mechanical refrigeration.

Midwives

Doctors coming into Florida usually stayed in communities and towns. This left the remote areas without trained medical care. One medical person who worked throughout the frontier era into the mid 1900's was the midwife. These women were called upon to help when a child was to be born. As more doctors became available, the use of midwives as medical persons almost disappeared. After the Civil War, women were relegated to nurses or doctor's assistants. In the 1980's the role of the midwife has been justified. Women are being trained as professional midwives. They are now recognized as professional medical personnel.

Changing Health Care

The Civil War (1861-65) caused the nation to recognize the need for good medical care. Soldiers died from minor wounds due to filthy conditions. Operations, such as leg amputations, were done without anesthesia. The patient would often faint because of the pain. Physicians recognized the need for

Gorrie Ice Machine in Gorrie Museum

Yellow fever immunity card

Jan Hartle

Modern hospital in Orlando

better training and standards, but this required money.

Yellow Fever was one of the reasons for better health control in Florida. An epidemic in 1889 caused the state legislature to create a State Board of Health. This board began setting standards of health care and disease control.

When it was proven that yellow fever was carried by a mosquito, both the State Board of Health and the federal government worked to drain the mosquitoes' breeding place.

General Practice

During the first half of the twentieth century in Florida, doctors were mostly general practitioners. These M.D.'s dealt with every type of disease and injury. One different aspect of medical care in that period was the "house call." The doctor would go to a patient's house to attend to the illness instead of requiring the patient to come to the doctor's office for care. General practitioners were on call twenty-four hours a day. They were the chief factor in the fight against the epidemics of yellow fever and other diseases which were common in Florida.

The doctors in the state began to specialize after World War II. The trend toward specialization created a shortage of general practitioners in the 1970's. Today, doctors are returning to the general practitioner idea of medical care.

Hospitals

Florida's hospitals have improved tremendously since the first one established in 1597 in St. Augustine. Not only has the quality of medical care improved, but so has its availability.

In 1980, there were 255 hospitals in the state of Florida, 50,925 medical and surgical beds, and 17,288 physicians practicing medicine in these facilities.

The state operates seven residential mental health facilities. These are located in: Chattahoochee, Arcadia, Hollywood, MacClenny, Avon Park, Tampa, and Gainesville.

The Federal Veteran's Administration also operates five hospitals in the state of Florida. These are located in Tampa, Miami, Lake City, Gainesville, and Bay Pines. Persons living in Florida who are veterans of military service may be treated here.

Medical Schools

Three universities in Florida have medical schools. These train physicians in all specialties from anesthesiology to gynecology and pediatrics. The University of Florida, University of South Florida, and University of Miami are the locations of our three medical schools.

There are many health service personnel other than physicians, these include: nursing home administrators, optometrists, physicians, osteopaths, pharmacists, podiatrists, chiropractors, dental hygienists, dentists, physical therapists, and nurses. These health service personnel must be licensed by the state of Florida, for the protection of Florida's citizens, before they are employed.

Health and Rehabilitative Services

The Department of Health and Rehabilitative Services (HRS), located in Tallahassee, oversees the health services and programs offered to Floridians. HRS is responsible for: disease control, personal health, environmental health, radiological health, and emergency medical service programs.

The department helps handicapped children whose parents cannot afford medical care. It maintains alcohol and drug abuse programs. It provides for community mental health services. The retardation program helps mentally disabled citizens strive for as much independence as possible. The Aging and Adult Services Program provide for the special needs of Florida's senior citizens.

HRS does provide other kinds of services, but these health services are important to Floridians in need.

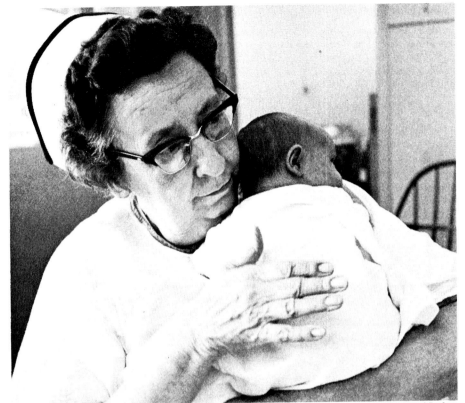

U.S. Dept. of Labor

Babies born in the 1980's will have a longer life span than their parents and grandparents.

Life Expectancy

Floridians are staying healthier and living longer. In Florida today, the life expectancy of a woman is 77.9 years. A man's life expectancy is 70.0 years. This is an increase over 1970, when a woman's life expectancy was 75.3 years and a man's was 66.9 years. But, compare that to the early 1800's, when the life expectancy of a Florida settler was about 35 years.

Vaccinations

The required vaccination of school aged children has caused many improvements. Almost every child has received the DPT shot. The combination shot has almost done away with the childhood diseases of diptheria, pertussis (whooping cough), and tetanus. Other improvements include the measles vaccine, and the Salk and Sabin polio vaccines. These vaccines have been so effective that some parents believe that the diseases are no longer dangerous. However, this is not true. It is still extremely important for all children to be vaccinated.

The value of these vaccinations can easily be seen. In 1978, the United Nations Health Organizations declared that not one case of smallpox existed on earth. An accomplishment such as this is a result of the smallpox vaccine.

Aging Population

Floridians are enjoying longer and healthier lives past the age of 65. Florida's warm climate attracts persons from colder states. Many of these persons move to Florida to retire or finish out their working years. As a result, Florida has a higher percentage of citizens over the age of 65 than other states in the United States. While California and New York have a higher number of residents over 65, Florida's percentage is greater. Attention to the needs of the elderly has been aided by Representative Claude Pepper of Florida. He has caused national attention to be focused on this age group.

In 1979, 17.7 percent of Florida's population was over the age of 65. The actual number was 1,633,873. By comparison, there are 2,350,692 Floridians from ages 0 to 17, and 5,260,666 from ages 18 to 64.

Charlotte County (31.2%), Sarasota County (35.1%), and Pasco County (34.1%) have the highest percentage of residents over age 65. Okaloosa County (4.8%), Leon County (6.1%), and Alachua County (6.9%) have the lowest percentage.

Health Problems

Senior citizens have different health problems than young people. For example, among young people from ages 5-14 in Florida, the five leading causes of death are (1) accidents, (2) malignant neoplasms (cancer), (3) congenital anomalies (birth defects), (4) influenza - pneumonia and (5) heart disease. For Floridians 65 and over, the five leading causes of death are (1) heart disease, (2) malignant neoplasms, (3) cerebrovascular diseases (stroke), (4) chronic obstructive respiratory disease (bronchitis, asthma, emphysema), and (5) influenza - pneumonia.

As a person ages, there are physical changes to deal with. Gradually, there are vision and hearing losses. Short-term memory can be affected, as well as loss of mobility. Bones become brittle, are easily broken and more difficult to mend.

Doctors are becoming more interested in the special health needs of the senior citizens. This medical specialty is known as geriatrics. In 1978, 29 physicians in the state of Florida specialized in geriatric medicine.

Another problem for senior citizens is the cost of health care. This is a time when they are most likely to suffer from a long, expensive illness. Many senior citizens live on a fixed income such as a pension, investments, or social security. For this reason, Medicare helps senior citizens' medical expenses. Medicare is a program funded through the federal government.

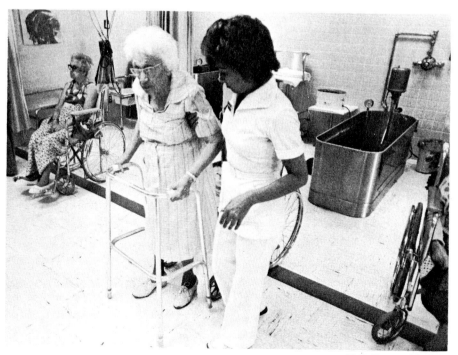

U.S. Dept. of Labor

The elderly have different health problems than the young.

Staying Active

Increasing age is no reason to become less active. In Florida, there are many ways for a senior citizen to stay active and busy. Some volunteer for SCORE, the Service Corps of Retired Executives, which offers help to younger professionals. Others work with the Foster Grandparents' program helping children whose grandparents may be far away.

Many senior citizens take classes, join clubs, play golf or tennis, travel, work part-time, or continue in the job they began as a young person.

Some spend their time writing letters to Congressmen, lobbying the State Legislature or speaking to the City Council. They hope to make conditions in Florida even better for senior citizens and other citizens.

Medicine Today

Health care in Florida continues to improve. The universities are graduating highly trained physicians. New cures are found for old diseases. Modern technology creates helpful new machines. Unfortunately, there are still problems.

Some rural counties need physicians, clinics, and hospitals. Transportation to hospitals is sometimes difficult and the cost of medical care is rising. As Florida's population grows, so does the need for trained medical personnel and health facilities.

With time and effort, the problems can be solved. So what does the future hold?

...perhaps a cure for cancer... a vaccine for the common cold... artifical limbs which work like natural ones... miniature cameras to replace blindness... artificial hearts and other organs... or whatever is needed in the continuing quest for good health?

Young people are challenged to meet the medical demands of Florida and improve the health of fellow citizens.

H
E
A
L
T
H

Unit 4   **Wars and Conflicts**

Florida Department of Commerce & Tourism

Castillo de San Marcos in St. Augustine

WARS AND CONFLICTS

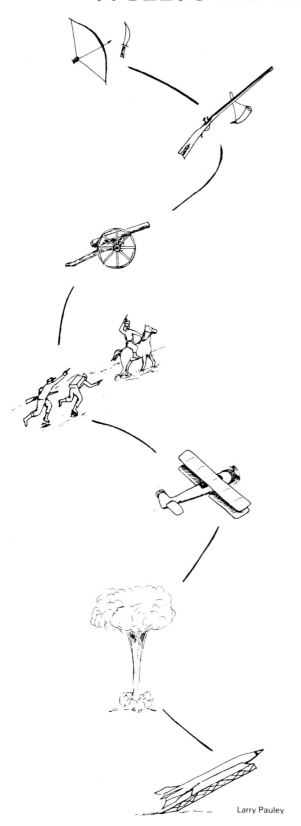

Larry Pauley

Introduction

Throughout the course of history five different countries have flown their flags over Florida's soil. Today, Florida proudly displays a state flag and the flag of the United States. Florida and the nation ended the 1970's free of armed conflict. At the beginning of the decade, citizens of Florida were part of the nation's Vietnam conflict. The history of Florida is one of many wars and conflicts. Floridians value their democracy and will take whatever steps are necessary to preserve it.

Indians

Before the Spanish explorers came to Florida in the early 1500's, it was already inhabited by many Indian groups. Some of the most important early Indian tribes were the Timucuans, Apalachee, Ais, Calusa, Jaega, and Tequesta. Fighting was common between the Indians as one tribe felt threatened by the other. Most of these conflicts were over territory.

Indians of northern Florida had a high level of social, political, and economic organization. They were farmers because of the rich soil in the north. The Indians worked together for the benefit of the whole village life. On the other hand, Indians in southern Florida were nomadic (wanderers). They hunted, fished and gathered foods. The Indians developed different cultures as was evident in their farming style, craft work, tool-making, and ways of practicing religion.

The coming of the Europeans into the Florida territory was a direct threat to the Indians. According to the Indians, this land already belonged to the Indian tribes. This territory was settled by the Indians long before the Europeans made their discovery. However, the Europeans thought of this as unclaimed land and sought this territory for imperial power. They also sought after valuable treasures of gold and silver.

The Indian's way of life was much different than that of the settlers. The Indians accepted the land as it was and adapted their way of life to the land, whereas, the settlers tried to change the land to fit their way of living. The settlers cut down the forests to clear the area for farming, while the Indians wanted to keep the forests which were their hunting grounds for food. As you can see great conflict existed between the settlers and the Indians.

The Indians realized that in order to resist the European soldiers, cooperation would be needed among the tribes. The fierce Calusas tribe forced other southern tribes into a peaceful federation to band together under one head. This was one of the first Indian organizations in North America. The Calusas were the most warlike of all the Florida Indians and fought savagely against Spanish invasion. Ponde de Leon was fatally wounded by the Calusas when he attempted to establish a colony at Charlotte Harbor.

During the European conquest for Florida, many Indians lost their lives. Early Indians either were killed in battle, died of diseases brought to the New World by the Europeans, were taken and sold as slaves, or disappeared for unknown reasons. European settlement had a tremendous effect on the Florida Indians. Today, many of the Indian customs and their ways are unknown to us and lost forever.

Spanish Claim

A Spanish explorer, Ponce de Leon, had been told by the Indians a story of an island rich in silver and gold. The Indian legend further claimed that another treasure could be found. This was the "fountain of youth" -- a priceless treasure which would make people young forever if they drank the water from this fountain.

In 1513 Ponce de Leon set sail from the island of Puerto Rico in hope of finding these riches. After about three weeks at sea, the expedition landed near present day St. Johns River. It was here that Ponce de Leon claimed the entire land for Spain. When coming ashore, he was enchanted by the sight of beautiful flowers and named this land "Pascua Florida," meaning "the Feast of Flowers at Eastertime."

WARS AND CONFLICTS

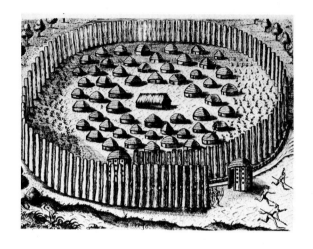

Timucuan fortified village by LeMoyne

Timucuans attack an enemy town by LeMoyne

The French choose a fort site by LeMoyne

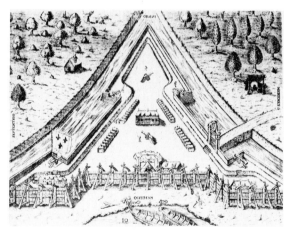

Fort Caroline by LeMoyne

Florida Photographic Archives

Rene de Laudonniere

Dios, Oro y Gloria

It has been said that Los Españoles were interested in three things as they extended their culture. These were GOD, GOLD and GLORY. They wanted to extend the Catholic faith and Christianize the Indians. Each one also hoped to find riches in the new world. The expectation of conquering new lands and returning to Spain a hero never left their minds.

The conquistadores did receive fame by conquering new lands; they sometimes did become wealthy; but their most lasting contribution to the cultures of the western hemisphere was their religion. Catholicism is spread throughout the Americas.

The Spanish used missions to spread their religion. Franciscan missionaries built a chain of missions from St. Augustine to San Luis, present day Tallahassee. Over 20 missions were established and were interconnected by roads.

Indians near each mission were encouraged to move close to the missions. Here they were regularly taught Catholicism. They were also encouraged to raise crops and cattle. The missionaries wanted them to settle in villages   to aid in defense of the missions and to make it easier to teach them.

After the discovery of Florida by the Spaniard, Ponce de Leon, Spanish conquest began in the New World. Sailing under the Spanish flag were famous "conquistadores" or conquerors such as Alonso de Pineda, Panfilo de Narvaez, Hernando de Soto, and Tristan de Luna.

Throughout a 40 year period of Spanish exploration in Florida, attempts were made to establish permanent settlements but were met with defeat each time. The Indians did not like the Spanish invading their lands. The Spanish soon became their enemies. Many times the Spanish were attacked by fierce Indians. The bow and arrows used by the Indians were a deadly threat to the newcomers.

Some of the direct conflicts to the Spanish were attributed to Indian hostility, sickness, lack of food and supplies, and poor leadership. After meeting with defeat each time, the king declared in 1561 that Spain would not try to colonize in Florida.

French Settlements

France was also interested in the New World. The French had a particular interest in Spanish Florida. The chief reasons for colonizing in Florida were to establish a base from which French ships could raid Spanish vessels; establish a colonial power in the New World, and act as a haven where French Huguenots (Protestants) could practice religious freedom.

In 1562, Jean Ribault led the first French expedition to Florida. The expedition landed near St. Johns River close to the area where Ponce de Leon had landed 50 years earlier claiming the land for Spain. The French established a settlement just north of this region. Unlike the Spanish, the French found the Indians to be friendly.

Ribault returned to France for supplies after the colony was established. This settlement only lasted a few months before it was abandoned by the colonists.

Two years later another Frenchman by the name of Rene de Laudonniere tried to establish a colony in Florida. This expedition, likewise, landed near the St. Johns River. At the mouth of the river a wooden fort was built. The settlement was named Fort Caroline. This was in honor of Charles IX, King of France.

Spain at War with France

The Spanish king became furious when he learned the French were invading their land in Florida. This land and all of Florida had already been claimed for Spain by Ponce de Leon.

The Spanish king immediately took measures to destroy the French colony at Fort Caroline. In 1565, Pedro Menendez de Aviles and his soldiers set sail for Florida to put an end to French colonization. Menendez and his men landed near the present site of St. Augustine. Here, they immediately built a wooden fort to protect themselves against the French. St. Augustine became the first permanent settlement in the New World.

Both the Spanish and French were preparing for war. Meanwhile, Ribault had returned to Florida with needed supplies and soldiers. The French, led by Ribault, made plans to attack the newly established fort at St. Augustine. However, efforts were halted by a storm that shipwrecked the French voyage.

Learning of the French misfortune, Menendez and his soldiers proceeded with their plans to attack the nearly deserted fort — Fort Caroline. After four days of marching through a storm, Menendez and his soldiers successfully captured Fort Caroline. Those Frenchmen not killed in the battle were hanged. A sign over them stated, *"I do this, not as to Frenchmen, but as to Lutherans (Huguenots)."*

Menendez, still seeking French blood, learned the whereabouts of the shipwrecked French. They had taken shelter on a nearby island. The French were ordered to surrender. But as the French surrendered, Menendez had them all executed. Ribault and 210 Frenchmen met with death at the inlet known as Matanzas -- meaning "place of slaughter." Menendez, a Catholic, killed all the Huguenots and allowed only 10 French Catholics to live.

The French had met defeat from the powerful Spanish. The remaining French soldiers and settlers were forced to evacuate Florida.

The French government did not seek revenge for the massacre at Matanzas. However, in 1568, a French Catholic, Dominique de Gourgues, privately assembled a force of three vessels with 80 sailors and 100 soldiers. He set out to attack Fort Caroline. The fort, renamed San Mateo, by the Spanish was unprepared for an attack. De Gourgues and his followers overran the fort easily. They burned the fort and hanged those not killed in the attack. As revenge against Menendez, de Gourgues placed a sign over those being executed. It read, *"Not as to Spaniards, but as to traitors, thieves, and murderers."* His revenge completed, de Gourgues set sail for France.

In 1586, an English explorer, Sir Francis Drake led an attack which sacked and burned St. Augustine. The Spaniards later reoccupied St. Augustine. However, periodic wars with the Indians and concerns over further European invasions remained a constant threat.

Spain, once again, made efforts to colonize in Florida. Menendez began to establish forts throughout the territory. Settlers were eager to move into the fertile lands of Florida. Rich soil was plentiful for the farmers. The Spanish had hoped that the Indians would be friendly. This proved difficult because the eastern coast Indians were the Calusa. The Calusa, under their chief, King Carlos, had for years been capturing shipwrecked Spaniards and enslaving or killing them. Menendez was able to gain the release of the survivors, but he was unable to stop the Calusa from taking future shipwreck survivors.

Spanish settlers attempted to live off the land but were constantly driven back inside their fortifications by the Calusas. The Spaniards had to depend on ships from Havana for food and supplies. A better relationship needed to be established between the Spanish and the Indians. To do so, Spain sent missionaries to work with the Indians. Missions were set up, mainly in northern Florida, to teach the Indians the Spanish ways and to convert them to Christianity. The missions were not always successful in stopping the hostility of the Indians.

Spain was also establishing forts and colonies in western Florida. San Marcos de Apalache, present day St. Marks, included both a settlement and a fort. A wooden fort was also built on the Pensacola Bay. It was established in 1698 with 300 settlers and soldiers.

France and England

After suffering defeat at the hands of the Spanish in Florida, the French continued their exploration in other parts of the "New World." In the 1600's, the French explored the interior of the North American continent and settled near the mouth of the Mississippi River. Over a period of years the French began drifting east of the Mississippi River into Florida territory. This land, already claimed by Spain and the French, once again, became a problem.

Spain was greatly concerned about France moving into western Florida. However, this was not her only worry. The English were also interested in Florida. Both France and England wanted the fur trade with the Creek Indians of Alabama and Georgia. Spain realized that if either of her enemies were successful in signing a trading treaty with the Creeks, Spain would be at a military disadvantage because of the alliance.

War of the Spanish Succession

Events in Europe between 1700 and 1763 would settle not only the question of the fur trade but also control of Florida. European wars spilled over into North America and began to alter the history of the new world.

The first was the War of the Spanish Succession or Queen Anne's War in America. King Charles II of Spain had no children to succeed him as ruler. He named Philip of Anjou, a French duke, as heir to the Spanish Throne. Philip was the grandson of the French King. When Charles II died in 1700, Philip became King of Spain. This, in effect, gave France control of the Spanish crown. England, The Netherlands and other European nations went to war against France and Spain to stop the alliance. The war lasted from 1701 until 1713 in Europe.

Florida was directly affected by this conflict in 1702 and 1704. The Carolina assembly authorized an expedition to seize St. Augustine before France could help reinforce the Spanish fort. Governor James Moore led a mixed force of 500 colonists and Indians in a siege against St. Augustine. Unable to capture the fort in a two month siege, the Carolinians burned and pillaged the town. They withdrew when a Spanish fleet arrived. In 1704, the now former Governor Moore organized a new force to attack the Spanish colony. This time Moore attacked the Spanish missions, destroying all but one of the 14 missions in the Apalache Country. He intended to use this opening as a route into Louisiana to attack the French, but the Choctaw Indians stopped him.

Treaty of Utrecht

The War of the Spanish succession ended with the Treaty of Utrecht on April 11, 1713. Spain did not lose her American colonies, but England did receive a concession from her. England received the *Asiento*, a contract allowing an English company to import into the Spanish Colonies 4,800 black slaves a year for 30 years. England would be allowed to send one trading ship a year to the Spanish colonies.

Conflicts Between Major Wars

Western Florida was still desired by the French. In 1719, France captured Pensacola but returned the outpost in alliance with Spain against England. France retained the land west of Pensacola.

A brief Anglo-Spanish war occurred in 1727-28. Carolinians once again marched into Florida. This time they destroyed a Yamassee village near St. Augustine and quickly withdrew.

Founding of Georgia

The English colonies were expanding closer to Florida. There had existed an area between the Carolinas and Florida that was relatively unsettled, but in 1732 a charter was given to settle this area, now known as Georgia. James Oglethorpe, the leader of the new colony founded Savannah in 1733. He began establishing military outposts north of Spanish Florida.

War of Jenkins Ear

Great Britian was upset by stories of Spain mistreating English merchant seamen. Spain had been upset by British abuses of the *Asiento* and problems along the Florida border. A Spanish *guardcoasta* had boarded the English brig, **Rebecca** searching for contraband. The Spanish commander insulted and abused the English master mariner Robert Jenkins and finally cut off his ears. This and other problems caused the outbreak of the War of Jenkins Ear from 1739 to 1743.

James Oglethorpe in Georgia saw this as an opportune time to invade Florida. His western flank was protected by the friendly Creeks, Cherokee, and Chickasaw and England's fleet controlled the Atlantic Ocean. Oglethorpe invaded Florida in January 1740, capturing Forts San Francisco de Pupo and Picolata on the San Juan River. He proceeded to St. Augustine and sieged the Castillo de San Marcos in May. The 2,500 people, including 1,500 soldiers, stayed outside until July. He broke off his siege when the hot sun, lack of provisions, insects and the arrival of a Spanish fleet forced him to flee. The Spanish counterattacked, but were crushed in the Battle of Bloody Swamp on St. Simon's Island in 1742.

Wars in Europe once again united Spain and France against England, but very little fighting took place in America until 1754.

French and Indian War

France and England declared war on each other over world trade in 1754. The war was called Seven Years' War in Europe and the French and Indian War in America. Spain allied itself with France and lost Florida because of it.

In America, England and France wanted to control the Ohio Valley and its trade. They also had disputes in India and other parts of the world. England was able to defeat the French in 1763 and impose harsh penalties on France and her ally, Spain.

The Treaty of Paris, 1763 gave to England all France's territory in continental North America, but it also gave her Florida from Spain. So after 250 years of Spanish control, Florida became an English colony.

England divided Florida into two political units becoming know as East and West Florida. The Chattahoochee and Apalachicola Rivers were the boundaries separating these colonies. East Florida included the lands to the east of these rivers with St. Augustine as the capital. The lands to the west were called West Florida with Pensacola named as its capital.

England now made efforts to attract investors and settlers to Florida. To encourage settlement they offered land to those who promised to farm it. During this time, two English settlements were established but lasted just a short time. One was called Rollestown near present day Palatka. The other was New Smyrna founded south of St. Augustine.

The American Revolution

Great Britain, in 1776, had 17 colonies on mainland North America. These were East Florida, West Florida, Upper Canada, Lower Canada, and what were known as the 13 original colonies. The 13 original colonies had been unhappy under British control and wanted more independence. These 13 colonies had a heritage of self government and resented British attempts to impose stricter rule.

This was not true of the four colonies which had been added after the Treaty of Paris, 1763. Upper and Lower Canada were inhabited by French people, who had no experience in democracy, such as in the Virginia House of Burgesses or the Massachusetts Assembly. Neither did the Spaniards, Italians, French, Greeks, Indians, and Minorcans of the Floridas have any real grievances against England. Those citizens who were truly loyal to Spain had gone to Cuba when the Spanish withdrew.

When the Continental Congress invited the four new colonies to join them in their Revolution against England, they refused. The cry of *"Taxation without representation is tyranny"* and *"...give me liberty or give me death,"* had no substantial meaning to the colonies north and south of the 13 middle ones. They were predominantly Catholic and felt no kinship to the protestant majority in the 13 other colonies.

The war in the other colonies brought prosperity to Florida. Fleeing Tories, or those loyal to England, poured into Florida. When escaping from the Patriots, they brought their money, black slaves, and skills to Florida. Houses sprang up in and around St. Augustine. Products from Florida were in demand by England, because she could no longer obtain them from her rebellious colonies.

Military Action in Florida

Minor skirmishes occurred in East Florida during the American Revolution. The people of St. Augustine feared an invasion by Patriots from Georgia. There was one serious attempt but it failed. Loyalists in East Florida under Thomas Brown and Daniel McGirtt did attack Georgia to kill and burn. Farmers along the border suffered greatly while settlements escaped capture.

France and Spain observed the fighting in America waiting for a chance to get back at England. They had never accepted the results of the Treaty of Paris, 1763. Their opportunity came after the Americans defeated the British at the Battle of Saratoga. Benjamin Franklin persuaded France to aid the American colonies and then France persuaded Spain to do the same in 1779.

Spanish forces in New Orleans and Havana immediately began preparations to attack the Floridas. In 1780, Bernardo de Galvez, the Governor of Louisiana, captured the British Florida settlements along the Mississippi River. He then proceeded to capture Mobile. Following these successes Galvez made plans to attack Pensacola. In 1781, with a force of 6,000 men, he sieged Fort George at Pensacola. The Spanish were able to gain entrance to the fort after shelling the walls. This victory gave Spain control of West Florida.

Treaty of Paris, 1783

England's forces surrendered to General George Washington and the French fleet at Yorktown, Virginia in 1783. The 13 rebellious colonies had achieved their independence. The treaty ending the war was a shock to the residents of British East and West Florida. Spain wanted compensation for her part in the war and received Florida.

Twenty years earlier England had wanted Florida in order to control the entire eastern half of North America. Now, with the loss of the 13 colonies, England realized Florida was unimportant to her.

English Departure

The Loyalists in Florida felt betrayed when they first heard the term of the Treaty of Paris, 1783. However, England did not want her subjects left at the mercy of the Spanish. She paid them for the loss of property and offered to relocate them in other British colonies. Almost 6,000 of the English settlers left Florida for the Bahamas and other colonies. Another 4,000 English settlers moved to remote areas in Florida or the American frontier. The non-English residents of Florida stayed in Florida and accepted the Spanish return.

Spain Reenters Florida

With the Treaty of Paris, 1783, Spain owned land from the Atlantic Ocean to the Pacific Ocean and almost all of Central and South America. This apparently gave Spain a powerful position in the Western hemisphere. Spain, though, had been weakened by continual warfare for almost two centuries. In effect, Spain owned the land but had difficulty controlling the huge territory.

Spanish Florida actually increased in size over the land the British owned. A disputed territory, called the Yazoo Territory, was claimed by both the new American Government and Spain. Americans moved into this territory and confronted Spanish authority. The Americans used not only the Yazoo Territory, but Florida to trade with areas that England tried to restrict. England did not allow American trade with the West Indies, but trade occurred anyway. Fernandina Harbor was busy with American ships illegally trading with the Spanish and British.

Louisiana Purchase

European events again influenced Florida's future. The people of France became restless under their king. French people had seen their country aid the English colonies, throw off their king and establish a republic. This made them realize their position in France, and in 1789 they revolted against the king of France. They established a republic, but a period of unrest allowed Napoleon Bonaparte to become dictator in 1799. Napolean obtained Louisiana, a vast region west of the Mississippi River, from Spain in 1800. He planned to build a large American Empire. Several disasters, both medical and military, caused his plans to come to an end. In 1803, when he needed money, Napolean sold the entire area to the United States. He did not want to return it to Spain, because he thought Spain was too weak to protect Louisiana from England. Napoleon also thought the United States was weak enough that he could take back Louisiana if he wanted it.

Florida and the Purchase

The United States cast an eye toward Florida and Cuba after obtaining the Louisiana Purchase. The European nations were unable to prevent the United States from making moves toward taking Florida. Napoleon was trying to extend his territory and caused Europe to be torn by what was called the Napoleonic Wars.

During the time of the Louisiana Purchase President Jefferson wanted to buy West Florida. The peninsula not only threatened shipping from New Orleans to the Atlantic ports, but all navigable rivers from present day Alabama, Mississippi, and Georgia flowed through Florida. To Jefferson, Florida looked like a gun with the West Florida barrel pointed at New Orleans. In 1805, Jefferson hinted about raising an army of 300,000 men. This was to threaten Spain into giving up West Florida. He also asked Congress for $2,000,000 to aid negotiations, but was turned down. Jefferson failed in his attempts, but upon leaving office said, *"We must have the Floridas and Cuba."*

Republic of West Florida

President Madison realized that the Americans in West Florida resented Spanish Rule. This group of settlers saw a chance to throw off this rule when revolutions broke out in South America against Spain. The Americans rose in revolt in 1810. They captured the Spanish fort at Baton Rouge, tore down the Spanish flag and dragged it through the dirt. A blue woolen flag with a single silver star was raised and the "Republic of West Florida" was declared. After proclaiming independence, they asked to become part of the United States.

President Madison moved rapidly to claim West Florida. He issued a proclamation on October 27, 1810, claiming American control to the Perdido River, but only occupied the area to the Pearl River. Madison justified his action on the ground that the area actually was meant to be part of the Louisiana Purchase. He must have been concerned though because he changed dates on documents to make his actions look better. European nations did not like what had happened, but they were too busy fighting to stop it.

East Florida

Madison thought that if direct action worked in West Florida, it would also work in East Florida. Madison and other authorities in Washington, D.C. secretly encouraged a 72 year old former governor of Georgia, George Mathews, to aid discontented Americans in East Florida. Mathews and 200 insurgents, using American gunboats, captured Fernandina on Amelia Island. Fernandina was a smuggler's paradise near Georgia and easily attacked. Mathews took over in the name of the United States and began extending his "rule." President Madison was politically embarrassed by Mathews' actions. When Mathews and his troops reached St. Augustine in June 1812, Madison declared he was operating on his own and the United States was not invovled. Mathews was angered by this, but fortunately for Madison, Mathews suddenly died.

War of 1812

Shortly after the Mathews invasion of East Florida, the United States went to war against England. France and England were still engaged in the Napoleonic Wars, and both were interfering with American trade. England's interference, however, was more open. The British ships stopped American merchant ships, searched them, and forced them to English ports to take off goods bound for France. Sometimes they would "impress" or make American sailors serve on British warships.

A group of American westerners and southerners called War Hawks wanted war with England. They saw it as a chance to take Canada and Florida while England was too busy to fight America. Spain was an ally of England against France and this created a reason to take Florida. The United States

**Two Seminole chiefs captured with British citizen at St. Marks
by General Andrew Jackson**

Marines looking for Seminoles in the second Seminole War

Congress had formally annexed all of West Florida between the Pearl and Perdido Rivers on May 14, 1812. Mobile, however, was still occupied by Spanish troops. General James Wilkinson, in April 1813, took Mobile without bloodshed. Despite all the boasting of the War Hawks, Mobile was the only permanent territory gained by the United States in the War of 1812.

In West Florida the British agents stirred up trouble with the Creek Indians. The Indians, with the aid of British weapons, attacked an American for killing over 400 people. In 1814, a British fleet entered Pensacola and British garrisons took control of the forts. Meanwhile, the Seminoles had built Fort Negro. Some Creeks and many fugitive Negro slaves moved to this fort. Many times Indians and runaway slaves would cross over the border to attack American communities. Southerners asked the U.S. government to send troops into Florida to punish the Indians and runaway slaves. American military units crossed over into Florida to capture and destroy Fort Negro in 1814. General Andrew Jackson of

the U.S. Army was called upon to put an end to the fighting. In March 1814, Jackson and his troops were victorious in the Battle of Tohopeka or Horseshoe Bend on the Tallapoosa River.

Jackson's Second Invasion

Spain was rapidly losing control of Florida. Her South American colonies were revolting, and Spain had to take troops from Florida to fight. Amelia Island, once again, became a pirate's hideout and the Spanish could do nothing about it. In 1817, the United States seized the island and drove out the pirates. The pirates were less of a problem to the settlers on the American border than were the Indians of Florida, runaway slaves, and white renegades. These loose knit bands, grouped under the name Seminoles, would cross the border to raid the American settlements. Again, Spain was powerless to stop the raids.

First Seminole War

President Monroe, in 1817, commissioned Andrew Jackson, the hero of the Battle of

---

Castillo de San Marcos

Castillo de San Marcos is an important part of Florida's unique heritage. This fortress is symbolic of the long struggle among European nations for control of Florida. Because of increasing British threats to St. Augustine, work began in 1672 to strengthen this Spanish settlement. Built of coquina, a stone formed from shells and sand, Castillo de San Marcos, replaced the wooden forts which offered greater protection to the town and harbor of St. Augustine. This fort later withstood two major English attacks. One was led by Governor James Moore of Carolina in 1702 who left the city in ashes and the other by James Oglethorpe of Georgia in 1740.

During the American Revolution Florida remained loyal to England. The Castillo de San Marcos became a British prison for American patriots and seamen. In 1783, Florida again became Spanish property. The new threat now arose from the newly formed nation, the United States of America. In 1821, the U.S. flag flew high above this great fortress.

In later years, the fort's name was changed to Fort Marion. The fortress served as a military post and stockade throughout the Spanish-American War. In 1942, by the Act of Congress, the original name of Castillo de San Marcos was restored.

New Orleans, to teach the Indians a lesson. Jackson was given authority to chase the Indians into Florida, if necessary, but not to attack the Spanish. Jackson insisted and Monroe denied that the instructions were changed to give Jackson authority to seize Spanish Towns.

General Jackson, who hated the Indians and Spanish with equal rage, burst into Florida. His hot pursuit led him to the capture of St. Marks, in April 1818. He tore down the Spanish flag and raised the stars and stripes. Jackson also captured two British subjects and charged them with inciting the Indians against the whites. They were speedily tried by a court martial and hanged. Jackson wrote the Secretary of War of the United States,

"I hope the execution of these two... villains will prove an... example to the world, and convince... Britain... that certain... retribution awaits those unchristian wretches who... excite an Indian tribe... to... war."

Jackson then turned toward Pensacola. He made a forced march westward and captured the town. Within a few weeks he had captured every important post in Florida, except St. Augustine, punished the Indians, deposed of the Spanish governor and named an American in his place, executed two British subjects, and declared *"the... laws of the United States"* in force. His only regret was that he did not hang the Spanish governor.

Adams-Onis Treaty

Jackson's invasion of Florida almost ruined negotiations between Spain and America over Florida. Secretary of State John Quincy Adams and the Spanish minister in Washington, Luis de Onis, had been discussing possible settling of the Florida problem. Talks stopped with Jackson's attack on Florida and Spanish citizens. However, because Jackson was so successful and supported by the people of the United States, Spain realized Florida would eventually fall to America.

Onis realized it was better to lose Florida gracefully than after a long, bloody, costly and humiliating war. The Adams-Onis treaty was signed in Washington on February 22, 1819. The United States received East Florida, confirmed the right to West Florida, and a definite western boundary for the Louisiana Purchase. Vague claims by America to Texas were given up in the settlement. The United States also agreed to pay claims its citizens had against Florida. The amount of claims was estimated to be $5,000,000 and in the end the United States paid its citizens about $4,100,000. Spain actually was paid no money at all for giving up the valuable possession of Florida.

The rulers in Madrid, Spain held up ratifying the treaty past the 16 month deadline stated in the treaty. President Monroe considered a military occupation of Florida, but Madrid finally yielded. The United States Senate again ratified the treaty on February 19, 1821.

Florida was transferred to General Andrew Jackson on July 17, 1821. Jackson became United States Commissioner and Governor of the Territories of East and West Florida.

The Seminole Wars

For many years the Seminole Indians have lived in Florida. The Seminoles, a large powerful Indian group, occupied the best lands in Florida. The new settlers coming into Florida wanted this land. Their greed caused several major conflicts with the Seminoles. The U.S. government made efforts to persuade the Seminoles to move to new lands in Oklahoma. Treaties were drawn up with promises to the Indians for a new and better life out west. Few Indians agreed to these terms. The powerful Seminoles insisted on staying. They were ready to fight to the end to protect their lands. The Seminoles built their strength by absorbing other Indians and fugitive slaves to their tribes. The Indians knew they had to join forces to fight to keep their lands. This fighting resulted in the "First Seminole War" of 1816-

Micanopy

Coacoochee (Wildcat)

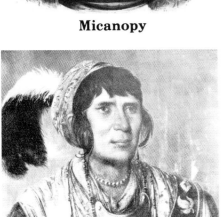

Osceola

Billy Bowlegs

Seminole Chieftains

1818 which was fought before the United States took over Florida.

After the "First Seminole War" numerous conflicts developed with the Indians. The settlers continued their movement into Florida taking lands from the Indians. Indians were being moved westward or pushed deeper into southern Florida. In 1823, several years after the "First Seminole War," the Treaty of Moultrie Creek was signed by government officials and Indian representatives. This plan called for Indians to be placed on a reservation in Central Florida. The treaty failed because of violations by both white settlers and Seminoles. The next step called for complete removal of the Seminoles from Florida to "Indian Territory" in the West (Oklahoma). Two treaties were signed by several leaders of the Seminole nation to activate the relocation of the Indians. These were the Treaty of Payne's Landing (1823) and the Treaty of Fort Gibson (1833). However, most of the Seminoles reacted violently to this removal. One of the bloodiest battles in history was about to begin. Under the leadership of such men as Osceola, Wildcat, Micanopy, Billy Bowlegs, Jumper, and Alligator, the Seminoles prepared for the battle against the U.S. armies. Osceola emerged as the leader. His devotion to the Seminole territory was expressed when he said they would fight, *"...till the last drop of Seminole blood has moistened the dust of his hunting ground."*

Dade Massacre

On December 23, 1835, Major Francis L. Dade led his troops from Fort Brooke in Tampa to reinforce the garrison at Fort King, now Ocala. The Seminoles intently watched the movement of the Federal troops. After several days of following Dade and his men, the Indians made their plans to attack. The Seminoles had taken the troops by surprise. The battle ended in bloody warfare and defeat for the Federal troops. With the exception of three men, Major Dade and this entire force were destroyed. Of the three survivors, one met death while escaping, one died from wounds received in battle after reaching Fort King and the other survived to tell the story of the "Dade Massacre." This battle marked the beginning of the "Second Seminole War," 1835-1842. This was the most costly American Indian war in American history.

The Second Seminole War

The "Second Seminole War" took place from 1835-1842. As a result of this outbreak in December, the United States began to strengthen its forces. Numerous stockades and forts were built immediately. Some of the United States forts that played a role in the Second Seminole War were Fort King Ocala, Fort Alabama-Hillsborough River, north of Tampa, Fort Foster built on the site of Fort Alabama after its destruction, Ft. Brooke-Tampa, Ft. Christmas-Christmas, Ft. Mellon-Sanford, and Ft. Meade.

In 1835, the Indians won two battles. One was near Busnell in Sumter County (Dade Massacre) and the other was near the Withlacoochee River in central Florida. By late 1837, Osceola, Wildcat and other leaders were ready to discuss ways to end the war. The Indians agreed to meet with the

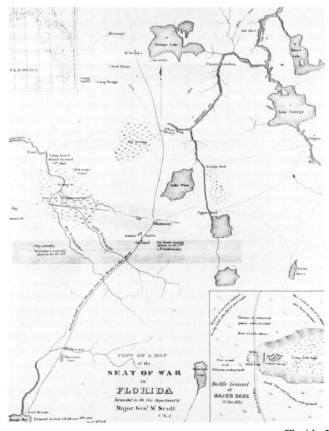

Map of Fort Dade battlefield

Asi-Yaholo

Someone said that, "Greatness is determined by one's devotion to a cause." If that is so then, Asi-Yaholo or Osceola or Powell was a great man.

Osceola, as he is best known, was three-quarters Creek Indian and one-quarter Scottish on his grandfather's side. After Osceola's father died, his Indian mother married a white man named Powell and Osceola was sometimes called by his stepfather's name.

He took the name of Asi-Yaholo from an Indian ceremony and drink. Asi was a black, caffeine drink used in tribal ceremonies. Yaholo was a long-drawn-out cry sung by the person serving the drink to the braves. The pronunciation of his chosen name caused it to be spelled Osceola.

Born in Georgia on the Tallapoosa River around 1803, Osceola became a "runaway" or Seminole. He rose to leadership of the Seminole and led them in the Second Seminole War. He led his troops in the Everglades and inflicted several defeats on American troops. Osceola was treacherously captured under a flag of truce in 1837. He was imprisoned at Fort Moultrie in South Carolina, where he died in 1838.

Osceola Knifing treaty   Florida Photographic Archives

Americans leaders. However, under the flag of truce, the Indians were captured and placed in prison at St. Augustine. Osceola and his family were among those taken. Fearing that Osceola might try to escape, he was sent to a prison in South Carolina. It was a few months later, while in prison, he died. The Seminoles had lost their powerful leader.

Another important leader of the Seminoles that had been captured was Coacoochee. He was better known as Wildcat. He had been placed in prison at St. Augustine. Wildcat made a successful escape from this prison. After his escape, Wildcat continued to lead revolts in Florida. He later led the Indians in a battle near Lake Okeechobee.

The Battle of Okeechobee was the last major battle fought in the Second Seminole War. It was one of the worst battles fought. The U.S. Army was triumphant over the Indians. Zachary Taylor, known as "Old Rough and Ready," was the U.S. commander in this battle. Many Indians and soldiers lost their lives in this battle near Okeechobee.

Only a few hundred Indians survived to escape to the southern part of Florida.

As the wars continued many of the Seminoles were rounded up and transported to Indian reservations in Oklahoma, while other Seminoles were pushed further in to the swampy lands of Florida. These are the regions of the Everglades and Big Cypress Swamp.

By 1842, most of the fighting had ended, but Seminole raiding parties continued occasional attacks on the settlers until 1858. This was a costly war for both the white settlers and Indians.

Statehood for Florida

During the period of the "Second Seminole War" Florida had become a territory of the United States (1821). Of course, the Indian wars had a direct effect upon the growth of Florida. However, Florida had already established Tallahassee as its capital. Tallahassee had been selected as the central location between Pensacola and St.

Stephen R. Mallory

Augustine. This became Florida's permanent seat of government.

By 1839, Florida had a state constitution. Florida had been a territory of the United States since 1821 and was seeking statehood. At the time, the United States was having problems over an issue of slavery. When admitting territories to statehood, the U.S. government tried to balance the number of free and slave states.

In 1845, Florida was admitted as a state to the Union. Florida was admitted as a "slave" state to keep the balance of slave and free states equal. The people of Florida could now select a governor. Before now, the national government had ruled the territory of Florida. The U.S. President had selected the governors. The first elected governor for the state of Florida was William D. Moseley. Florida's first U.S. Senators were David Levy Yulee and James D. Westcott.

Florida began to grow as a state. By 1860, the population of the state had grown to 140,424. Florida had been affected by a number of things such as: the shipping industry, railroads, cattle raising, and farming. Many changes took place as Florida grew as a state.

When Florida became a state, it was evident that major differences existed between the North and South. The difference later led to the internal struggle called the Civil War. Florida seceded from the United States only 16 years after its admission.

Civil War

There were many differences between the regions of the North and South. The economy of the North was one of industry and manufacturing. The South, on the other hand, depended upon farming as their basic economy. This, of course, led to the most important issue, slavery. Through the years, the split between the slave states and free states grew wide.

There were bitter conflicts over the role of government between the North and South. The South wanted more state control over the national government. The North disagreed because they felt the national government should have greater control. This conflict was the issue of State's Rights. The differences between the North and the South were too great and could not seem to be resolved. This led to the outbreak of the Civil War.

In 1861, Florida seceded from the Union. Florida joined the newly formed country, the Confederate States of America. Thirteen southern states had made up this country. Jefferson Davis was chosen president for the nation. The vice president was Alexander Stevens. The capital for the Confederacy was Richmond, Virginia. An important Floridian was Stephen Mallory who became the Secretary of the Navy.

The Civil War was the period of internal conflict for the United States. In 1861, the Civil War began between the United States of America and the Confederate States of

America. The war between the North and South lasted four lingering years, 1861-1865.

The Civil War was the most tragic war in American history. More Americans died in the war between the states than in all wars of the United States combined, until the Vietnam conflict. The Civil War divided families. This was especially true of border areas such as: West Virginia, Maryland, Delaware, Kentucky and Tennessee. Sometimes, one brother would join the Union Army while another would join the Confederate Army.

Fort Pickens

Florida was the third state to secede from the Union in 1861. Before the Ordinance of Secession was officially adopted, Florida had already made advances to seize the federal forts. Orders were given to seize the federal arsenal at Chattahoochee, Fort Marion at St. Augustine, and Fort Clinch at Fernandina. None of the three was garrisoned with more than a handful of soldiers which led to an easy takeover. However, federal forces were prepared to fight at Pensacola and Key West. Fort Taylor at Key West and Fort Pickens in Pensacola were the two remaining major coastal defenses. The Union commander in the battle for Pensacola Bay was Lt. Adam Slemmer stationed at Fort Barrancas. Fearful that this fort could not hold out against attack, Lt. Slemmer moved his troops to Fort Pickens on Santa Rosa Island.

Meanwhile, on January 12, Confederate troops seized the Navy yard at Pensacola and occupied Fort Barrancas and McRae. But Slemmer refused to surrender Fort Pickens. The war between the states had not officially commenced and both sides were reluctant to start fighting. A truce called the "Fort Pickens Truce" was agreed upon by Union and Confederate leaders on January 29, 1861.

On April 12, 1861, under the orders of President Lincoln, Federal troops were sent to reinforce Fort Pickens. The truce had now been broken. A few hours earlier the Confederate forces had fired upon Fort Sumter, South Carolina, which officially began the war between the North and the South.

Confederate troops made several attempts to capture Fort Pickens but efforts seemed futile. In May 1862, Confederate troops withdrew and Federal troops occupied Pensacola. Fort Pickens remained in Federal control throughout the Civil War. In later years, this fort was used as a prison for military and political prisoners. In 1888, Geronimo, the Apache chief, and his followers were held as captives at Fort Pickens.

Battle of Olustee

Florida was not to be the scene of major battles during the War between the States because of its remote location. However, the battle of Olustee was one to be remembered. In 1864, the Union troops had occupied Jacksonville. It was the intent of the Union to break up communications between the East and West Florida, thus depriving the Confederacy of badly needed food supplies. Plans also involved the capture of cotton, turpentine and timber for northern use.

Union troops led by General Truman A. Seymour left Jacksonville traveling westward with a plan to cut supply routes from Florida into Georgia. Confederates, under the leadership of General Joseph Finegan, moved to meet the enemy and the two clashed at Olustee near Lake City.

They engaged in battle over a short period of time before the Confederates won the decisive Battle at Olustee. Even though the battle only lasted about six hours the casualties were numerous. The Confederates counted 93 killed, 847 wounded, and six missing, but the Union casualties were far greater. The Federals recorded 203 killed, 1,152 wounded and 506 missing. The union army used many black soldiers in this battle.

Battle of Natural Bridge

The battle at Natural Bridge is another major event remembered in Florida history.

Saltworks on St. Joseph's Bay under attack by the crew of the U.S. Bark "Kingfisher"

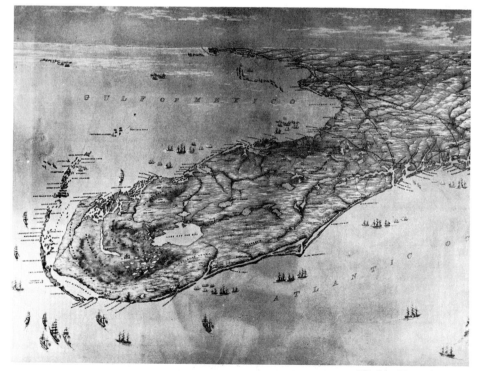

Panoramic view of Florida during the Civil War including Union ship blockade

Rebel battery at Pensacola

Ordnance Park, machine shop at Pensacola in 1865

Union signal tower at Jacksonville in 1864

W A R S   A N D   C O N F L I C T S

In March 1865, the Union planned an attack against St. Marks and Newport. These regions were important seaports and were located near Tallahassee, the state capital.

Northern leaders devised a two-fold plan. The naval operations were to capture the fort and town of St. Marks, while the military troops maneuvered into Newport. The plan from Newport was to move into Tallahassee to secure the capital. General John Newton, a Union officer, commanded the expedition. A majority of the Union troops involved in the attempt to capture Tallahassee were black.

The surprise element was destroyed when a Confederate officer learned of their plans to attack, which brought immediate response from the Confederacy. Quickly Confederate troops assembled under the leadership of General William Miller. They joined forces south of Tallahassee at Natural Bridge. Fighting was heavy, but the Confederates were victorious in the battle at Natural Bridge. Northern troops were hampered in their attempts, when their ships could not land because of the shallow waters at St. Marks. This prevented the capture of the port.

This was an important victory for Florida. The capital had been saved. By the end of the war, Tallahassee was the only Confederate capital east of the Mississippi River that had not been captured.

Florida had been successful in fighting throughout the war. However, in April 1865, the war had ended with the North being victorious. The South surrendered after four years of hardship and much human suffering, thus marking the end of another era. On May 10, 1865, Federal troops entered Tallahassee to accept the surrender of the Confederate troops. The Civil War had ended and once again the United States flag was raised over Tallahassee.

Florida's Contribution in the Civil War

Florida aided the Confederacy in many ways. Florida's seaports were of great value to help in the shipping of goods. Products such as cotton, tobacco, and turpentine were shipped out to trade with Europe for goods needed for warfare. Salt works on the coast of Florida was needed by the Army. Since there was no refrigeration at that time, salt was used to preserve meats. This enabled the armies to store meat for longer periods of time to use when needed.

Another important Florida contribution to the Confederacy was cattle. Cattle were used to provide food for the soldiers. Cowhides were used to make leather goods such as: saddles, boots, and belts. The fat from the cattle was used for candle making. Food was Florida's most effective contribution to the Southern cause.

Florida also contributed to the war in another important way. The Confederacy was aided by about 15,000 young men from Florida who joined the Southern troops. Of these men, more than 1,000 were killed in action, 5,000 were wounded, and 5,000 died of hardship and disease. One of the most famous generals of the Confederacy was General Edmund Kirby Smith, a native Floridian. There were 1,290 Floridians who joined the Union Army and Navy.

Reconstruction

The impact of the Civil War had a tremendous effect upon the South. Florida was the sight of economic, political, and social destruction. This was a time of hardships. The effects of the war upon the Floridians were numerous. People were without jobs, while many farms, homes, and stores had been destroyed by fires. Transportation systems: roads, bridges, and railroads were badly damaged. Many people were left bankrupt and destitute. Florida had many problems to overcome.

President Abraham Lincoln had proclaimed the slave's freedom in the Emancipation Proclamation. This was a period of adjustment for ex-slaves and ex-masters. President Lincoln had proposed a program for the southern states. Certain conditions had to be met by the Southern states before granting amnesty to re-join the Union. After President Lincoln's

Florida Photographic Archives

Battle of Olustee

assassination, this program continued under the leadership of President Johnson.

During the Reconstruction Period, 1865-1877, Florida was under the control of the United States Army. President Andrew Johnson appointed new leaders to control the state government in Tallahassee. In July 1865, Judge William Marvin of Key West was appointed as provisional governor. Florida's government, as in all southern states, was in a stage of reorganization.

Northerners called carpetbaggers, came to Florida for political and economic gain. They were reputed as being selfish and dishonest men. They hurried to the South bringing all their belongings in bags made of cheap carpet material. These men quickly took advantage of blacks and the southern difficulties. However, some were sincere in their efforts in helping the blacks overcome the hardships they were experiencing and to bring about reform for Florida.

Another group of influential men were the scalawags. The word derived from the terms "scamp" or "rascal." These were southern businessmen and former planters who had opposed the Confederacy. As a result, the carpetbaggers, scalawags, and even the freed men became leaders of the new state governments in the South.

These were troubled times throughout this period for Florida. White organizations, such as the Ku Klux Klan (KKK) and The Order of the White Camellia were formed. The main purpose of these groups were to keep the southern blacks from voting. These men tortured and killed many blacks. The organizations were being used to maintain white supremacy by terror and force.

It was a time of political turmoil. The Democrats and Republicans were in great conflict over many political issues. Florida's Constitution of 1865 was rejected by the Congress of the United States. This Constitution did not grant fair treatment to the blacks. Florida's efforts to re-join the Union had failed. Now a new Constitution had to be written that would be acceptable to the national government.

Jonathan Gibbs, a black leader, was elected to the Constitutional Convention of 1868. He was an important leader in writing a new constitution for the state. The Florida Constitution of 1868 reflected a tone of democracy. It provided for: equal suffrage of races, public education, a public welfare system, intermediate and circuit courts, and a state prison system. The United States Congress adopted the constitution and Florida was readmitted into the Union.

Finally, in 1877, federal troops were removed from Florida, thus putting an end to the Reconstruction Period. In spite of all the problems encountered during this period, Florida's population grew to 269,493 which was a tremendous increase for the state. Many of the political adventurers became good citizens of the state. Northern capital

Florida Photographic Archives

Teddy Roosevelt and his Rough Riders in Florida

brought to the state aided in the restoration of railroads, buildings, and roads. This money also backed the lumber industry and financed orange groves. Florida could look forward to better times ahead.

Spanish-American War

At the end of the nineteenth century, America became involved in a short war. The Spanish-American War began in 1898 and lasted only three months. Before the war began, arms and supplies had been illegally shipped from Florida to patriots who wanted to overthrow Cuba's government. Napoleon Bonaparte Broward was one of the leaders of these expeditions. He later became governor of Florida and later served as a U.S. Senator.

There were many Americans concerned with the way the Spanish were treating the people on the island of Cuba. Others were interested in Cuba because they had investments in sugar plantations. With the Cubans revolting against Spain, their investments were not safe. Later, the battleship "Maine" was mysteriously blown up.

Shortly after the sinking of the "Maine," the United States declared war on Spain. Florida immediately became the grounds of military activities. President McKinley asked Congress for millions of dollars for national defense. Florida received a large amount of money and Key West became an important naval base. Military training camps were established in Jacksonville, Tampa, Miami, Fernandina, and Lakeland. Tampa became the principal port of embarkation to Cuba. Theodore Roosevelt and his "Rough Riders" were sent to Cuba to put an end to the fighting. Florida's Militia never made it to Cuba, because the fighting had lasted only 120 days.

Florida prospered somewhat from this war. The troops that trained in Florida spent money during their stay. Many of the servicemen were attracted to the state and later returned for vacations. Others liked it so much that they decided to move to Florida.

World War I

In 1917, the United States became involved in World War I. This war started over rivalries in Europe in 1914. America remained neutral until April 6, 1917, when war was declared on Germany. The governor of Florida was Sidney Joseph Catts. Adjustments were made in the governmental economy because of the shortage of goods and increased prices. Governor Catts appointed a food conservation committee to increase food production for the war effort.

Thousands of Floridians volunteered and other thousands were drafted to serve in the armed forces. Nearly fifty thousand served from the entire state. The number of Florida men that were killed in action totaled 1,046. Three future governors of Florida served in the armed forces during W.W.I. They were David Sholtz, Spessard L. Holland, and Millard F. Caldwell. Spessard Holland was honored by receiving the Distinguished Service Cross.

Florida became the training grounds for the military. Major military and naval training centers were established throughout the state. Some of these bases were located in: Jacksonville, Pensacola, Arcadia, Miami, and Key West. Two major shipyards which attracted many new residents to Florida were located in Jacksonville and Tampa.

The Florida Keys played an important role during W.W.I. A Submarine station and a naval training station were set up in Key West. From the island bases the military could easily watch for enemy operations. Planes, patrol vessels and observation balloons were dispersed in all directions to accomplish this mission. Florida's long coastline became a matter of great concern during the war.

A tragic aftermath of the war came in the fall of 1918 with the outbreak of an influenza epidemic. The influenza hit Florida and the entire nation. The spread of the disease was attributed to the movement of military personnel. There were 30,000 cases reported in Jacksonville with 464 deaths from influenza. In 1919 the "flu" returned with 621 cases reported and 64 deaths. Once again, it hit in 1920 with 2,541 cases reported and 79 deaths.

Period of Boom and Bust

A period of prosperity came to Florida following World War I. At the close of the war, people had enough money to satisfy their basic needs as well as investments. The boom days were from 1921-1925 which was the time of economic prosperity.

Florida's population increased following the war. Many American servicemen assigned to Florida for military training returned to make their homes here. Improved rail transportation and highways made Florida's lands an attractive investment. It further enabled greater means of travel throughout the state. Florida's boom can be attributed to factors such as land development and speculation, favorable climate, greater use of automobiles, and a state-wide system of public roads. The Gandy Bridge and the Tamiami Trail were two major highways built at this time.

Florida Photographic Archives

Ft. Taylor at Key West during World War I.

During the boom days, national advertisements for Florida lands brought thousands of people to the state. Land speculators were attracted to Florida and bought land in hope of making a good profit. A piece of land would be bought and sold two or three times, increasing its value after each sale. People even bought land sight unseen.

The boom day period was the time when beach resorts were being developed along the Atlantic coast. This became known as the "Gold Coast" of Florida. Miami Beach became a major tourist resort town. A greater interest in Florida was created. Florida's population increased rapidly bringing growth to cities such as Jacksonville, Miami, Tampa, and St. Petersburg.

The decline of the boom days began in 1925 as Florida faced a number of problems. The rapid population growth led to a shortage of housing. Transportation services were disrupted and slowed down the movement of supplies for building. The boom days were coming to an end.

On September 19, 1926, a major hurricane struck Miami bringing much destruction to Florida. Total casualties from this hurricane disaster were 392 dead, 6,281 injured, and 17,784 families affected by losses. The greatest loss was at Moore Haven where some 300 people died when the Okeechobee dike crumbled sending a tidal wave on the town. Florida was unable to recover from this disaster before another hurricane struck on September 16, 1928, at Palm Beach and then moved inland. About 2,000 lives were lost during this hurricane. The severe storms of 1926 and 1928 resulted in millions of dollars worth of damage to Florida. Much of the boom-time construction was destroyed, including Florida's "Gold Coast." Unfavorable publicity was given to Florida at this time.

With the collapse of the land boom, Florida's economy was sinking into a state of depression and despair. The entire nation's economy felt the effects of a depression with the stock market crash of 1929. The failure of the banks came in the late 1920's and early

Florida Photographic Archives

Riflemen on field maneuvers at Camp Blanding, Florida in World War II.

1930's. Many businesses and individuals lost large sums of money. Businesses and factories suffered great losses which left many workers without jobs. Funds were not available to begin new businesses. Most people throughout the country suffered hardships. Florida's economy, like that of the nation's, was at its lowest level. It wasn't until the late 1930's that Florida's economy began to improve.

World War II

Twenty years after World War I, Europe again became involved in war. Hitler's Germany tried to take over the continent. At the same time, the Japanese were expanding in Asia. The United States was able to remain neutral until December 7, 1941. On that Sunday morning, the Japanese in a surprise attack, bombed Pearl Harbor, Hawaii. Because Japan was an ally of

91

Germany, the United States declared war on both nations.

During the war years Spessard L. Holland served as Florida's governor. One of the first administrative steps taken was to reactivate the State Defense Council which Governor Catts had originally established during W.W.I. The Defense Council was set up to direct the efforts of civilian volunteers. There were 137 local and county councils. Floridians were taught how to protect themselves in case of attack, how to manage in emergency situations, and to help the war effort in every possible way.

Florida, once again, became the grounds for military training. Thousands of United States servicemen came to Florida to operate new army and navy installations. A new naval air station was established at Jacksonville. An army training center was established at Camp Blanding near Starke. Naval bases were reactivated at Key West and Pensacola's naval base was the scene of increased activity. Drew and McDill airfields at Tampa and Eglin at Valparaiso were also active during the war. Many pilot training bases and flying schools developed in the state because of Florida's flat lands and favorable climatic conditions which allowed increased flying time. Florida had 40 airfields in operation by 1945.

Many Floridians were directly involved in the war effort. Over a quarter of a million were in the military service. Both men and women volunteered or were drafted for service. In 1940, 3,941 Floridians were on active duty in the National Guard. By 1947 a total of 254,358 other men and women had entered the armed forces. Many women joined the armed services in World War II. They were restricted to women's branches, but they served faithfully. Women's armed forces included the Women's Army Corps or WACS, Women in the Air Force or WAF and Women Air Service Pilots or WASP.

Many of Florida's tourist facilities were converted to wartime needs. Throughout the state every major resort city turned its

Florida Photographic Archives

Shipbuilding in Tampa, 1944

principal hotels over to some branch of armed services. Resort hotels were being used as training centers, hospitals, barracks and convalescent homes. Florida's colleges and universities were used as training sites as well as living quarters for the men.

Florida's coast defense became a matter of great concern during the war. Early in 1942, German submarines moved towards Florida's coast. On February 19, the "Pan Massachusetts" went down forty miles south of Cape Canaveral. A number of other ships along the coast were sunk. A Mexican tanker went down near Miami and another off the Florida Keys.

The Civil Air Patrol was organized in March 1942 to help guard Florida's coast from the air. The Coastal Picket Patrol was organized to protect the state against submarine threat. This patrol consisted of civilian small craft, yachts, fishing and pleasure boats to secretly survey the enemy. The "Mosquito Fleet," like the Coastal Patrol, helped to guard the coast, also. With increased protection and improved ways of detecting the enemy, Florida's coastal area was soon freed of submarine threats.

During W.W.II, shipbuilding was the chief industry in Florida. The citrus industry began to have significant development at this time. Florida not only increased the production of citrus products, but began a large-scale processing of concentrated juice. This was a great advantage in wartime. Businesses developed throughout the state. Industrial plants which made war supplies and materials offered jobs to many men and women.

Floridians at home supported the war effort by providing housing and other services throughout the war. Floridians also strongly supported the Red Cross, War Bonds and provided entertainment for the servicemen.

A new dimension to warfare was added in 1945. The first atomic bomb was tested by American scientists. President Truman had demanded that Japan surrender or it would be faced with terrible danger. Japan did not

reply. On August 6, 1945 an atomic bomb was dropped on Hiroshima. Three days later, the U.S. dropped another atomic bomb on Nagasaki. These two Japanese cities were nearly all destroyed by the bombs. The Japanese were convinced that they could not win the war and surrendered on August 14, 1945. The war formally ended on September 2, 1945 when the Japanese signed the treaty of surrender.

Korean Conflict

Since 1945, the United States has engaged in two military conflicts, both of which were in Asia. In 1950, the Communists from North Korea invaded South Korea. President Truman asked for the United Nations to protect South Korea, which it did. The United States supplied the majority of troops. The war lasted until 1953. During this conflict, 972 men of the Florida National Guard were called to active duty. In addition to these, 27,823 Floridians were drafted and 84,257 voluntarily enlisted. The Korean conflict was fought under Presidential powers and was not declared a war.

Cuban Missile Crisis

Cuba is an island located only 90 miles southeast of the Florida coast. In 1959, Fidel Castro successfully overthrew the Cuban government. The United States President John Kennedy had hoped for a democratic government. Instead, Castro became a communist dictator. Prior to this overthrow, the U.S. had carried on trade relations with Cuba. Now, all trade between Cuba and the U.S. came to a halt. Castro's government became friendly with the Soviet Union and the People's Republic of China. The Soviet Union gave much support to Cuba.

The United States continued to watch the events taking place in Cuba. Much concern was shown over the possible threats to the American people. In October, 1962, the U.S. learned that missile sites for launching nuclear weapons were being installed in Cuba. This was detected by a U-2 plane with

Americans using aerial cameras to photograph the area. During this time, the dictator of the Soviet Union was Nikita Khrushchev. The missiles being installed were a direct threat to the welfare of the United States. Launching of such a missile would be capable of destroying cities throughout the nation. Floridians, in particular, were concerned for their safety, because of the nearness of Cuba.

President John Kennedy immediately took measures to end the dangerous Soviet threat. American armed forces were activated for possible war against Cuba. President Kennedy sent a letter to Khrushchev demanding the removal of the missiles and destruction of the missile sites. He also took action by ordering a "quarantine" of Cuba. This meant that the U.S. warships would not allow Soviet merchant ships to reach Cuba. Any ship carrying missiles or military supplies would be ordered to return to the Soviet Union.

This was an extremely critical time for both nations. The United States and Soviet Union faced the danger of nuclear warfare. In order to avoid war, Khrushchev agreed to the demands of President Kennedy. The missiles would be returned to the Soviet Union and the Cuban sites would be dismantled.

The United States had successfully overcome the possibility of a Cold War crisis. The American people felt a sigh of relief. However, there is still great concern over the fact that a communist country is so near the Florida coast.

Vietnam Conflict

The second conflict was not a declared war either. This was the Vietnam conflict. Vietnam was divided into North and South sections after W.W. II. To help stop the spread of communism, President Eisenhower and Kennedy sent military advisors to aid South Vietnam. Under President Johnson, almost 500,000 Americans were sent to combat in Vietnam. President Nixon started reducing the number of soldiers, and by 1972, only air bombardment by Americans aided South Vietnam. In 1973, the U.S. withdrew from Vietnam and North Vietnam took over South Vietnam. War was still being waged in Vietnam and neighboring countries in 1979. During this conflict one Florida Army National Guard unit was called to active duty. Additionally, 40,352 men were drafted through the Selective Service System and 146,028 voluntarily enlisted. Florida's casualties were 1,897 during the Vietnam conflict.

Florida has been the scene of many wars and conflicts. Citizens of the state have served all over the world in protecting the precious freedom we have in the United States of America. We do not know what the future holds, but we are confident the Floridians value their democracy and

with education and desire can overcome the conflicts in order to make the state and nation a strong and free place to live.

Floridians will do what is necessary to develop a peaceful world.

Unit 5 Transportation

Florida Photographic Archives

Sikorsky S-40, First Four-Engine Flying Boat

TRANSPORTATION

Larry Pauley

Introduction

It was once difficult to travel around Florida. Today modern transportation facilities have eased these problems. You can cross the state by modern highways, by water, by train, or by air.

The automobile, bus, train, ship, and airplane have helped to develop Florida. Water craft from canoes to sailing vessels, to steamboats, to modern ships and busy ports have added in turn to Florida's prosperity. Today one can travel anywhere in the state in a brief time. Cars and buses ply the highways from city to city, and from city to ranches and seacoasts. Airplanes soar from city to city, taking passengers from Miami to Tampa in less than an hour, or from Pensacola to Orlando in about the same time. Tons of fresh vegetables and citrus make their way by train and truck to northern cities almost over night. Millions of tourists make their way to Florida from those cities in less time.

Florida's geography gives us 3,700.7 kilometers/ 2,300 miles of tidal shoreline, including 14 deep water ports which can handle ships drawing up to 8.2 meters/ 27 feet of water. Florida has nine shallow water ports for vessels drawing from 2.8 to 8.2 meter/ nine feet to 27 feet of water. Four rivers have ports for commercial shipping. These ports are tied together by shipping lines over water, and by modern highways and railraods.

Florida has an excellent road system of 154,367.4 kilometers/ 95,940 miles of road, including 19,328.9 kilometers/ 12,013 miles of interstates and main highways. These highways, with city streets and country roads, allow travelers to go anywhere in the state in comfort and safety. Products grown or made in Florida make their way to market over these roads.

While the railroads no longer have passenger service to all our major cities in Florida, the national railroad passenger system, Amtrak, still links major tourist cities to northern cities. Passenger service, though declining, provides transportation for those who prefer neither to drive nor fly.

But the railroad in Florida today serves mostly to carry commercial cargoes. Florida has seven freight railroads, with 10,564.7 kilometers/ with 6,566 miles of track. All of our cities and ports are tied together by these railroads. Trees go to the paper mill by trains, and then from the mill to the port of Jacksonville by train, to be shipped to newspaper plants in Germany. Coal is carried into Florida by train, and sugar leaves Florida by train.

More exciting than trains to many people, the airplane is everywhere in Florida. There are 136 public use airports, and many private ones. Almost 90 airports have paved runways and lights for night flying. Pilots are trained in Florida and many of the largest airlines schedule flights to Florida cities. These flights serve almost two and one-half million persons a year. From any Florida city today, you can fly to any of the world's major cities.

These remarkable developments in Florida's transportation are foreshadowed by the "Age of Space Travel." At Cape Canaveral, from the Kennedy Space Center, the space shuttle's engines roar, then, the shuttle soars into the heavens. It takes off not far from where Ponce de Leon's fragile vessel first dropped anchor in 1513. Transportation in Florida has come a long way from the Indians' canoes and Ponce de Leon's vessels. The Kennedy Space Center and its roaring rocket engines are constant reminders that transportation in our state is constantly changing.

Indians

Transportation in Florida has always had problems. Coastal tides and marshes, along with shiftings and bars, were dangerous and made travel difficult. While Florida is flat, its swampy lowlands and many streams combined with thick vegetation which block travelers' ways. In the northern panhandle, Florida's terrain gets hilly. While these hills were not barriers to travel, the hills and valleys, with streams and rivers, made the

French soldiers using an Indian dugout canoe.
By LeMoyne

travelers' way more rugged.

The earliest people in Florida, the Indians, did travel. Each group had its territory and moved within that territory as they needed to secure food, supplies, and land. The Indians started many transportation routes as trails across their own territories and linked these territories through trade.

The Indians used one other form of transportation, besides walking, which today has become a popular recreational form of transportation. The canoe in Florida was made from logs which were burned in the center and "dug out" to provide a place for the travelers to sit while paddling. These canoes were called "dug out canoes" because of the way in which they were made. Many of these old canoes -- some hundreds of years old -- can be seen in Florida's museums. The canoes were small and were quite adaptable for travel on rivers, streams, ponds, and wetlands.

Using trails and canoes, Indians were able to move throughout North America and the area which is now Florida. Proof of this movement and trade can been seen through artifacts which include stone implements and jewelry in Florida and seashell jewelry in the mountains of the Carolinas and further north. The artifacts prove that many tribes traded over long distances. Stories have been told about the long distances over which Indians traded. For example, in the 1700's, one young Virginian, Gabriel Arthur, was taken by the Cherokees from Tennessee to Florida and then back north to what is now West Virginia and Ohio. Stories of travel like this one do not surprise archeologists who study Florida's Indians, because they find artifacts produced with materials which are not found in Florida. These stories of trade and travel should not surprise those Floridians who pick up stone arrowheads and spear tips in freshly plowed fields and along river banks. These stone tools could only come via trade routes from places far to the north.

Early Europeans

The early Europeans in Florida came by ship and stayed close to the coastline. The first explorers, like John Cabot of England and Giovanni da Verrazzano who sailed for France, passed by Florida's coastline. In

100

1513, Ponce de Leon came ashore around what is now St. Augustine. He claimed the land for Spain, calling it *Pascua Florida*, because it was "discovered" during the time of the Feast of Flowers. Other Spaniards explored Florida's long coastline from what is now Jacksonville to Pensacola. The Spaniards attempted settlements, as did the French near what is now Jacksonville. The Spanish settlement at St. Augustine was permanent and was the point for the first transportation routes across land into Florida.

But the seas off Florida remained what they had been for the first explorers -- dangerous routes of transportation. Storms, hurricanes, and reefs took their toll in ships. Spanish ships sailing between Spain and the New World picked up treasure at ports in South and Central America. These ships gathered at Havana, Cuba, and sailed up the Florida coast before turning to Spain. This gave them favorable winds for the sail across the Atlantic, but it also gave them trouble. Treacherous Florida reefs and hurricanes got many ships and much of their treasure. Hundreds of shipwrecks occurred. In addition, pirates soon learned of this rich trade and began to lurk in the Florida Keys and harbors to prey on the Spanish vessels. Early settlers of the keys and the southern coast of Florida were called "wreckers" -- they would rush out to a ship in distress and strip it of its cargo. Many learned to use false signals to lure ships onto the coral reefs and sand bars, so they would wreck and lose their valuable cargoes.

Early Roads

Even as late as 1821, when the United States got Florida from Spain, the settlers at Pensacola, along the St. Johns and the St. Marys Rivers were isolated. The Spanish settlements were military posts, ports, and little else. Most of Florida was unexplored by Europeans. Trips along the coast were dangerous and long. While the Indians traveled overland, on foot and with canoes and horses, overland travel was difficult even along the Indian trails.

In the 1500's, Spanish missions were built across Northern Florida to serve as places for the education and conversion of the Indians to Christianity. These missions from St. Augustine to San Luis (near present day Tallahassee) were linked by a crude roadway. It is called the Old Spanish Road and was built about 1675. After the settlement of Pensacola, travel was by water to Tallahassee, not by road or trail. From Tallahassee, travelers used the mission trail to St. Augustine. This route was safer and faster for most travelers, rather than sailing from Pensacola to St. Augustine around the Florida Keys.

In 1766, the British governor, James Grant, began construction on King's Road from St. Augustine to the St. Marys River. In 1770, a road was built from Mobile Bay to Pensacola. However, with little settlement in the interior of Florida, it was difficult to keep the roads open and the vegetation cut back. Heavy rains, quick-growing vegetation, floods, marshy lowlands, and soil erosion made roads expensive to maintain.

Life would have been easier for Spanish and English settlers if Florida's rivers had run east and west. This is the direction that the Spanish and English wanted to travel in Florida. But, alas, the rivers such as the St. Marks, St. Johns, Apalachicola, and Escambia run north and south. As such, they were barriers to road travel.

In 1824, when Florida became a territory of the United States, a road was planned from St. Augustine to Pensacola. From St. Augustine to what is now Tallahasee, the road followed the Old Spanish Road, and was built with slave labor. The United States Army built a road from Pensacola to the Apalachicola River, which was gaining importance as a port and trade route into Georgia and Alabama. A road was also constructed from Tampa Bay to Jacksonville. These roads, while crude, were open not only to horses, but to carts and wagons. Some wagons were pulled by teams of six or more oxen.

TRANSPORTATION

Wreckers at work around 1850

Rivers and Canals

As a Federal territory, Florida not only received roads, but funds were available for river improvements. These funds were used to mark the channels and to clear debris and snags in some important rivers -- the St. Johns, Apalachicola, and the St. Marks. The St. Marks River served as the port for settlements in the Tallahassee region.

The Apalachicola River was an important trade route into Georgia and Alabama. The town of Apalachicola was settled in 1821, although it was not named that until 1831. By 1837, it was the third largest cotton-shipping port on the Gulf of Mexico. Cotton was floated down the river to the town where it was loaded on large ships bound for New England and British cotton mills. The frontier town and thriving port developed with trade on the river -- its namesake -- until the Civil War.

Courtesy Florida Photographic Archives

The steamer "Princess" on the Oklahawa River

Courtesy Edward Mueller and Florida Photographic Archives

Steamer "Okeehumkee" at Palatka.

The St. Johns River, with improvements and a marked channel, was to become the route for settlers along the northeast section of our state. The river's broad mouth from the Atlantic Ocean to the site of today's Jacksonville attracted shipping and settlement. Soon, vessels were carrying settlers up the St. Johns (which is really south!) where towns and farming communities emerged.

To ease land travel, many ferry boat companies were chartered by the territorial government. For a fee, travelers, their horses, and their wagons would be carried across rivers. While not all travelers were pleased by the fee, most were more than willing to have the luxury of a dry and safe crossing.

But the big transportation development was canals. As early as 1819, some Floridians were thinking about a canal connecting the St. Marys River with the Suwannee River. This would have cut the time required for shipping heavy cargoes around the Florida Keys. Ships would sail into the St. Marys from the Atlantic Ocean and have the cargoes loaded on to barges. The barges would be pulled by mules through the canal to the mouth of the Suwannee River on the Gulf of Mexico. The cargo would be loaded on larger vessels for the trip to

"General Grant on a trip on the Oklawaha on the 'Osceola'"
Harpers Weekly sketch by Frank Taylor

Pensacola, Mobile, or New Orleans.

In 1822, the United States Army Corps of Engineers explored routes for a cross-Florida barge canal. In 1826, Congress provided $20,000 to survey a canal route across the state. But while the survey began, nothing came of the canal plans at that time.

River improvements and canal building were of great interest. In 1829, the Chipola Canal Company raised funds with a lottery to build a canal from the Chipola River to the Gulf of Mexico. In 1831, the Wacissa and Aucilla Navigation Company was formed to improve the rivers for shipping.

The first steamboat company in Florida was located on the Apalachicola River in 1827. A woodburning craft carried passengers and freight up the river, and cotton and passengers down river. By 1837, it is reported that over 30 steamboats plied the Apalachicola River alone. The United States Army, fighting the Seminole War from 1835 to 1842, used over 40 steamboats on the rivers of north central Florida.

Floridians loved the steamboat for passenger travel and for cargoes. But, the steamboats in Florida were not the broad, big Delta-Queen-type of vessel which we see in films about the Mississippi River. Florida, with its narrow rivers and canals, had smaller steamboats. But these were proud achievements.

While many people worked on the development of the steamboat, final credit goes to Robert Fulton. In 1807, Fulton demonstrated the Clermont, traveling 241.4 kilometers/ 150 miles from New York to Albany at an average speed of 12.9 kilometers/ 8 miles per hour. An innovation has no value unless it has economical and practical uses. This is why Fulton is given credit over others working on the steamboat invention. One of Fulton's wealthy supporters, Nicholas Roosevelt, saw the future of the steamboat and its possible uses.

Roosevelt, Fulton, and Robert M. Livingston, the other supporter, decided to see if steamboats could be built on the Ohio River. This would open the Ohio and Mississippi Rivers to steamboat trade. Roosevelt and his wife traveled by flatboat down the Ohio and Mississippi Rivers from Pittsburgh to New Orleans. Roosevelt could see that the flatboat could only go one way -- down stream. The steamboat could travel up and down the river. With this profitable two-way traffic in mind, Roosevelt returned to Pittsburgh and helped build the first steamboat on the Ohio and Mississippi Rivers. The **New Orleans** was launched in 1811 and successfully traveled the rivers for two years. Even though the **New Orleans** hit a snag and sank, it proved the practicality of steamboat commerce. If Fulton is the "Father of the Steamboat," then Nicholas J. Roosevelt is the "Father of the Steamboat Trade."

The new steamboats were powered by boilers which stood above the water line. This allowed them to float high in the water and travel through shallow waters. After the Civil War, little steamships traveled all of Florida rivers: the Kissimmee, Indian, Withlacoochee, St. Marys, Oklawaha, Suwannee, St. Johns, Caloosohatchee, and others. There were even steamboats on Lake Okeechobee. Around 1876, there were 13 steamers on the St. Johns River, and by 1885, it was reported that 74 steamers operated on the one river. The deBarry Line, a steamship company on the St. Johns, developed a Jacksonville to New York steamship line -- with ocean-going vessels. In the 1920's, a New York to Miami steamship line was opened for tourists.

The canal boom was aided by the steamboat. In 1879, the Apopka Canal Company linked Lake Eustis and Lake Apopka. In 1881, a Philadelphia saw maker moved to Florida and purchased four million acres of state land for twenty-five cents per acre. The buyer, Hamilton Disston, owned land that stretched from the Gulf of Mexico across central Florida. Disston believed in canals. He connected the town of Kissimmee with the Gulf of Mexico by way of the Kissimmee River, Lake Okeechobee, and the Caloosahatchee River. In Kissimmee he built boatyards and factories. Kissimmee was to be the capital of his financial empire, with canals in a network covering his lands and connecting them to the Gulf of Mexico.

Unfortunately for Hamilton Disston, the railroad came and made his canal system obsolete. Railroads did to canals what the steamboat had done to flatboats and dug-out

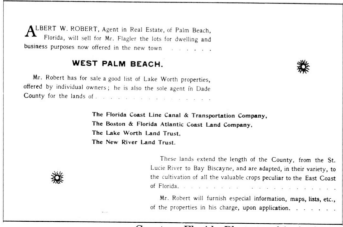

Courtesy Florida Photographic Archives

Florida: beauties of the East Coast, 1893.

St. Johns Railway 18 miles from Tacio to St. Augustine
Scribners Monthly

canoes. The steamboat on rivers was to fall in importance to the power and versatility of the new giant of transportation -- the "Iron Horse."

Today, canals are mainly for smaller pleasure crafts and water control purposes. The southern portion of the state is crossed by canals to regulate water flow, flooding, and water supplies to urban and farming areas. One canal, the St. Lucie Canal, connects Lake Okeechobee with the Atlantic Ocean. Another, the Caloosahatchee River, connects the lake with the Gulf of Mexico. The Hillsboro Canal, the North New River Canal, the West Palm Beach Canal are large ones, but the longest in Florida is the Miami Canal -- 130.3 kilometers/ 81 miles in length.

The Coming of Railroads

Railroads had many problems similar to those of the steamboat. Powered first by horses and mules, trains became important when steam was used for power. Wooden rails had been used in England for over 100 years to avoid the mud and ruts of dirt roads. Florida had its early, "plank roads," built upon wooden slabs. In England, iron strips were often nailed on the wooden rails and horses pulled the cars. At first the tracks were flanged to keep the car on the tracks, but later the wheels were flanged instead of the tracks. In 1804, an Englishman, George Stephenson, built a steam locomotive which pulled 27.2 metric tons/ 30 tons at 6.4 kilometers/ four miles per hour. This progress in England did

Courtesy Florida Photographic Archives

Florida Railway and Navigation Company 1886.

not go unnoticed in America. In 1825, John Stevens, a Revolutionary War officer, successfully ran a steam engine on a track in New Jersey. After this, the railroad began to develop as a means of transportation. Originally the boiler on trains stood erect like those on steamboats. Then with innovative thinking they were laid down allowing for larger more powerful engines.

Florida's first railroad was the St. Joseph Railroad, which was run by mule power in 1836. The railroad was eight miles long running from St. Joseph Bay on the Gulf of Mexico to Lake Wimico, on the Apalachicola River. A few months later, the railroad got a steam locomotive which covered the 12.9 kilometers/ eight miles in 25 minutes time. Actually, the Leon Railway Company had been chartered by the State Legislature in 1831, but it never got off the ground. In 1832, another railroad was chartered and died. Finally, the Tallahassee Railroad Company got its line built over the 38.6 kilometers/ twenty-four miles from Tallahassee to the port at St. Marks, and ran its locomotive over the tracks in 1837. The

Seaboard Coastline Railroad, West Palm Beach, June 24, 1924

engine was not too dependable and mules often took its place. It operated until 1855 as a mule driven system, and today is part of the Seaboard Coast Line.

David Levy Yulee, a famous character in Florida history, was a plantation owner, a businessman, a United States Senator, and a railroad builder. He wanted a railroad from Fernandina to Tampa. He planned to develop a sugar plantation on the West Coast of Florida. But, he built the railroad to Cedar Key, far north of Tampa. He received State aid and began work in 1856. He reached Cedar Key in 1860-1861, just in time for the Civil War to disrupt commerce. Neglect during the war and stripping the tracks of valuable metal for the war effort destroyed the first cross-state system. The railroad building efforts in Florida were ended until the 1880's, when the state recovered from the war, and its "reconstruction" began to think about development.

The period from 1877 to the 1920's was one of progress. The population of the state increased, and economic activity was on the upswing. The citrus industry started. Lumbering and phosphate mining began in earnest. Tourism was developing as northerners came south for their health -- and to escape the cold winters. The old railroads, financed by bonds and sales of state land, were bankrupt and in no shape to provide service. What poor management and outright cheating had not destroyed, the war had. So the railroads in 1880 were ready for new life with the right leadership.

When William D. Bloxham became governor in 1881, Florida had 885 kilometers/ 550 miles of railroad and most of that was bankrupt. The governor saw that railroads had to be revived and expanded to support progress and prosperity. Bloxham sold 1.6188 million hectares/ four million acres of land to Hamilton Disston to get the money to loan to railroad development programs. This million dollars began the railroad boom.

The first railroad "giant" was Henry Morrison Flagler, for whom Flagler County and Flagler College are named. Flagler was a partner with John D. Rockefeller I, in the development of the Standard Oil Company. At age 55, Flagler was a millionaire with an ill wife. For her health, they moved to St. Augustine. There he built the Ponce de Leon Hotel, a luxury hotel catering to wealthy northern tourists. After a time, he started to buy up older railroads and to build others. He modernized the old railroads and joined them together in the Florida East Coast Railway. Flagler proceeded down the coast of Florida, buying land, and building rail tracks. Then, he would develop resort hotels to attract tourists. Flagler's empire began with a track to bring tourists from Jacksonville to St. Augustine. By 1890, he had built railroad tracks to Daytona Beach and moved south. He bought the Ormond Hotel at Ormond Beach. In 1893, at age 63, he had reached Palm Beach. He then constructed the Royal Poinciana Hotel. This railroad reached Miami in 1896. Flagler had a railroad of 588.9 kilometers/ 366 miles from Miami to Jacksonville.

Flagler then had the most incredible idea! He wanted to link Florida and Cuba by building a railroad from Miami to Key West, overseas. He began constuction in 1904 and eight years later he had the Overseas Railroad -- an extension of his Florida East Coast Rail Way. Many died in the construction project, and it was delayed by fierce hurricanes. But Henry Morrison Flagler won! On January 22, 1912, he rode the first train from Miami to Key West. It stretched more than 160.9 kilometers/ 100 miles across water and island. The price was over twenty million dollars.

Unfortunately, a severe hurricane in 1935 destroyed the rail system and it was never operated as a railroad again. Later, the State bought the right of way and turned it into U.S. Route I. The Florida East Coast Rail Way still operates today as one of Florida's three major rail networks.

Flagler's operation down the Florida coast shows the impact of transportation upon development. St. Augustine became a boom town when the railroad reached it, and Flagler built lavish hotels. Tourists came there, for that was as far south as they could go conveniently. When Flagler extended his line further south and built new hotels, the lustre wore off the older town. Tourists went further south to the new end of the railroad. Daytona Beach surpassed St. Augustine. Ormond Beach surpassed Daytona, and so forth down the East Coast to Miami.

Another railroad "giant" was Henry B. Plant. His railroad career began in Georgia where he purchased two bankrupt railroads in 1879. In 1881, he purchased the East Florida Railroad which ran from St. Marys to Jacksonville. As he linked his companies together they were named the Savannah, Florida, and Western Railroad. With state and federal land bonuses, Plant constructed a line from Kissimmee to Tampa. He got land from the state, sold it to settlers, and used that money to pay for construction. Pleased with his railroads, Henry Plant opened a steamship line from Tampa to Key West and Cuba. All of this he kept linking to other railroads. The Plant Railroad System became part of the Atlantic Coast Line in 1902. When Henry Plant was not building a railroad, he was merging railroads. Plant's famous hotel in Tampa is now Plant Hall on the campus of the University of Tampa. Henry Plant died in 1889, one year after that lovely building had been constructed.

Plant had come to Jacksonville in 1853 to treat his ill wife. When he died in 1889, he had in such a short time, amassed an amazing railroad and steamship system. By 1902, the Plant System controlled 2,679 kilometers/ 1,665 miles of railroad track. After the merger with the Atlantic Coast Line in that same year, the total mileage was 3,620.3 kilometers/ 2,250 miles.

This railroad grew. It extended down the coast to Fort Myers, carrying citrus, phosphate rock, lumber, cows, and tourists.Henry B. Plant had made his mark. The county named Plant City, outside of Tampa, in honor of his contributions.

William D. Chipley made his railroad contribution as the manager of the Pensacola Railroad, which was bought by the Louisville and Nashville Railroad in 1887. Chipley extended the system from Pensacola to Chattahoochee. This was aided by a generous grant of 1.6188 million hectares/four million acres of land from the state. Chipley cut trees and sold them. He turned the land into farm plots and moved in settlers. The railroad business was an arm of real estate development in the Panhandle as it had been on the West and East Coasts.

Modern Railroads

Today, Florida is served by three major rail systems: The Florida East Coast, the Seaboard Line, and the Louisville and Nashville. At least eight other, short railroad lines are joined in the railroad network.

Passenger service has been turned over to AMTRAK, a federal government financed system, which provides declining service in Florida. In 1981, President Reagan proposed cutting AMTRAK's budget. The future of this rail passenger service is in doubt. Trains have lost their appeal to buses, private cars, or airplanes. Just as the railroad displaced the inland steamboats, so the car, bus, and plane have replaced the train.

In freight service, dependency upon the railroad has declined. Citrus is now rushed to market on trucks as well as trains. Trucks, running on public highways, have a competitive advantage in that they are more flexible. Roads go more places than rail tracks.

The railroad depends upon hauling heavy, bulk commodities for which there is little hurry in getting them to market. These commodities include: pine pulp logs, phosphate rock, wood chips, some citrus, lumber, some vegetables, and sugar.

The future of the railroads may be brighter with our energy problems, since they can be quite fuel efficient when compared to their competitors. The diesel engine has the handicap of using oil-based fuel. However, there is now in the developmental stage a new coal burning engine. This unit uses modern technology to burn coal in an environmentally acceptable manner. Its power unit contains a combustion and transmission system. The water is recycled and the coal fuel is in modular packs. As Florida produces more and as foreign trade increases out of Florida ports, the railroads might recapture their markets and gain a new lustre in the transportation galaxy.

Automobiles

After the 1820's, interior roads in Florida were developed to move federal troops against the Seminoles. After the Seminole Wars, these roads fell into disrepair. They were not much more than cleared paths to begin with, and erosion from heavy rains and the growth of vegetation blotted them out from the landscape. Without use and maintenance, roads do not last.

The trails of the Civil War and Reconstruction left few resources for state road networks. Roads were in the hands of city and county governments. What they did about roads depended upon the population size and tax revenues. For most counties, that meant little was accomplished because they did not have the money.

After World War I ended in 1918, the railroads were clearly the best mode of intercity transportation. But just before the war, there had appeared on the scene a noisy, sputtering machine ---- Henry Ford's automobile. Although Ford did not invent the automobile, he made it possible for almost everyone to own one. His assembly line methods, along with Eli Whitney's idea of interchangeable parts, put wheels on a nation. Florida and Floridians benefitted from the internal combustion engine and the

Flat tire and only twelve miles to Bronson.

automobile.

At first these "flivvers" were little more than a novelty and a noisy nuisance. They scared horses and sometimes were required by law to pull off the road and stop while a horse-drawn wagon passed. More than once, the owner of an automobile would hear, "Get a horse!" while trying to fix a flat tire or while pushing the car out of the mud. In spite of all the jokes and harrassments, these "horseless carriages" had advantages. They were not restricted to rails nor did they need the care horses required.

During World War I, the internal combustion engine proved useful. This was especially true when a wagon bed was added and it worked as a truck. Trucking companies and train companies fiercely competed to carry goods. The trucking industry was the winner because of its versatility. As roads and highways improved, trucks and cars could go to more places. Rural areas became accessible. Seasonal Florida foods became available in distant northern markets.

Modern Highways

Although improved, graded roads existed in Florida counties before 1900, most roads were rutted tracks out in the countryside. Each county built and maintained the roads within the county. The wealthier the county, the better the roads. Geography also played a role in road building. Counties with flat, dry land to build upon could construct better roads at a lower price, than counties with marshy areas, a lot of streams, and poor soil drainage.

In 1915, the State Legislature created the State Roads Department. For two years, it had the duty to collect maps and information on roads in Florida. The State Roads Department also gave counties advise and took a portion of the fees charged to license motor vehicles.

In 1916, the United States Congress enacted a Federal aid program for road construction, and the Legislature recreated the Roads Department with more power to build state roads. The main purpose was to link Florida's cities, towns, and villages with

TRANSPORTATION REVENUE (PRIMARY FUND)

WHERE IT COMES FROM

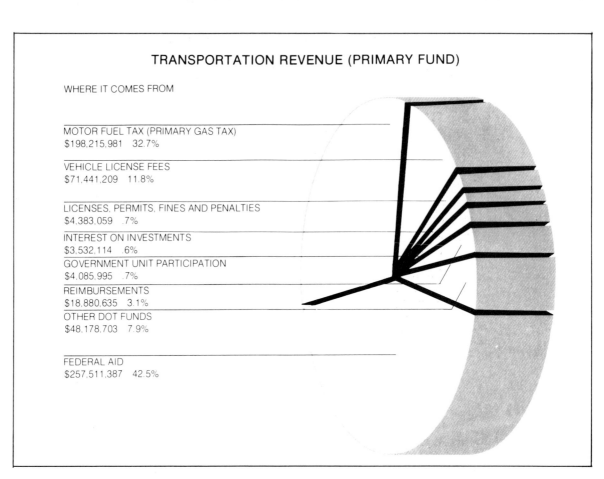

MOTOR FUEL TAX (PRIMARY GAS TAX)
$198,215,981   32.7%

VEHICLE LICENSE FEES
$71,441,209   11.8%

LICENSES, PERMITS, FINES AND PENALTIES
$4,383,059   .7%

INTEREST ON INVESTMENTS
$3,532,114   .6%

GOVERNMENT UNIT PARTICIPATION
$4,085,995   .7%

REIMBURSEMENTS
$18,880,635   3.1%

OTHER DOT FUNDS
$48,178,703   7.9%

FEDERAL AID
$257,511,387   42.5%

WHERE IT GOES

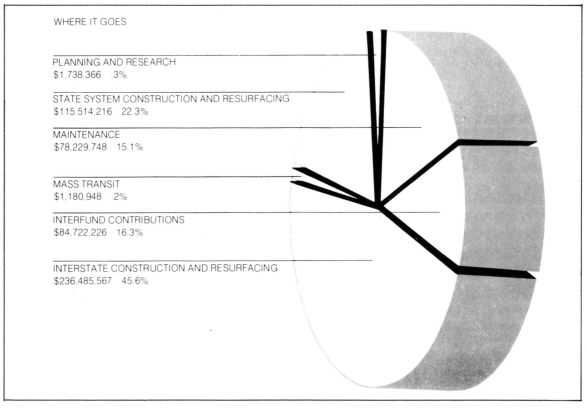

PLANNING AND RESEARCH
$1,738,366   .3%

STATE SYSTEM CONSTRUCTION AND RESURFACING
$115,514,216   22.3%

MAINTENANCE
$78,229,748   15.1%

MASS TRANSIT
$1,180,948   .2%

INTERFUND CONTRIBUTIONS
$84,722,226   16.3%

INTERSTATE CONSTRUCTION AND RESURFACING
$236,485,567   45.6%

FLORIDA INTERSTATE SYSTEM

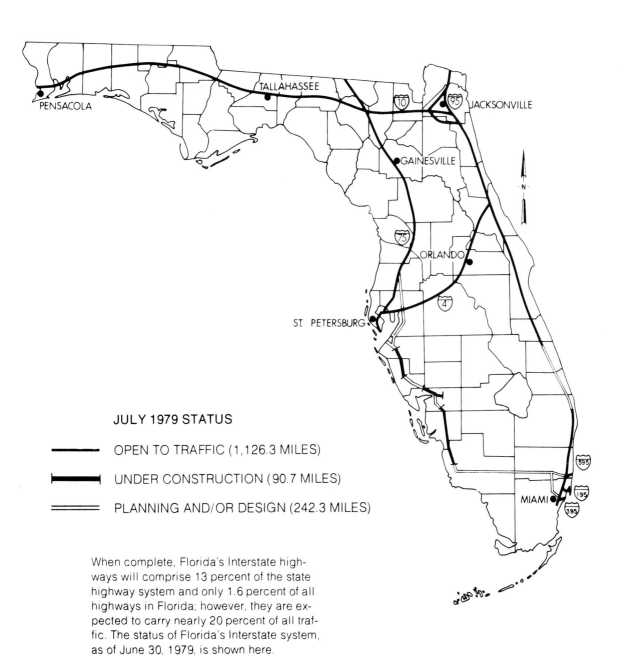

JULY 1979 STATUS

—————— OPEN TO TRAFFIC (1,126.3 MILES)

▬▬▬▬▬ UNDER CONSTRUCTION (90.7 MILES)

═════ PLANNING AND/OR DESIGN (242.3 MILES)

When complete, Florida's Interstate highways will comprise 13 percent of the state
highway system and only 1.6 percent of all
highways in Florida; however, they are expected to carry nearly 20 percent of all traffic. The status of Florida's Interstate system,
as of June 30, 1979, is shown here.

PREPARED BY FLORIDA DEPARTMENT OF TRANSPORTATION DIVISION OF TRANSPORTATION PLANNING

hard-surfaced, all-season roads. With federal and state funds, the State Roads Department grew in size and responsibility. This growth was accompanied by marked improvements in Florida's roads. By 1930, private automobiles, buses, and trucks had 5,235.7 kilometers/ 3,254 miles of state highways.

In 1928, the east and west coasts of Florida were linked with the opening of the Tamiami Trail (Tampa to Miami). In 1936, the state purchased the Overseas Railroad tracks to Key West. By 1938, in the midst of the Great Depression, the state built a 273.5 kilometers/ 170 mile road for cars and trucks. It was called U.S. Route 1 and extended from Miami to Key West. In 1938, toward the end of the Depression, the State had 14,481 kilometers/ 9,000 miles of hard-surfaced roadways.

After the delays of World War II, when new cars and trucks were almost impossible to get, the stage was set for the rapid expansion of the trucking industry and private car ownership. Cars replaced trains as common carriers for passengers, with intercity buses growing as well, while train ridership declined. Trucks displaced the central role of the railroads in hauling Florida produce and citrus to northern markets.

By 1967, the old State Road Department was renamed the Department of Transportation, with broader duties. The Transportation Department planned and set state policy. Highway sections still dealt with planning, but other divisions now dealt with: rail inspection, mass transit assistance, and aviation assistance. The gasoline tax which once only went to build and maintain highways, can now go to broader transportation purposes, such as supporting mass urban transit.

Courtesy Florida Photographic Archives

Polk County, Florida, May 5, 1917

In 1953, the State passed the Florida State Turnpike Act and the first section of the Sunshine State Parkway was built as a toll road, from Fort Pierce to Miami. In 1964, the Parkway was extended from Fort Pierce to Wildwood. It now covered 426.4 kilometers/ 265 miles. In 1980, the Parkway extends 506.8 kilometers/ 315 miles from Homestead to Wildwood.

Other toll roads were constructed following the success of the Sunshine State Parkway. The West-Dade Expressway, the Beeline from Orlando to Merritt Island, the Airport Expressway in Miami, Alligator Alley, the Sunshine Skyway connecting St. Petersburg and Bradenton, and many others were built. Some motorists, including truckers and auto clubs, complain about toll roads. They say that the gasoline tax should pay for these roads.

Florida's Interstate System will contain over 2,329.8 kilometers/ 1,448 miles of multiple-lane, well-designed limited access highways when the system is completed. The Interstate system gives even numbers to East-West routes and odd numbers to North-South routes. Supported with 90 percent paid by the federal government, the state has built I-10 from Jacksonville to Pensacola, I-4 from Tampa to Daytona Beach, I-75 from Georgia to Tampa, and I-95 from Georgia to Miami. During the 1980's, I-95 was to be completed. I-75, while complete to Tampa, should go down the West Coast of Naples, and then across Florida to Miami. The failure to complete I-75 earlier was the source of much debate and controversy, as persons in the region have felt "left out" by Department of Transportation planners and the Legislature.

A road map of Florida shows that the State's Interstate System will link the major metropolitan areas together, while providing easy road access in and out of Florida for cars, buses, and trucks. While these roads were expensive, each day they help to reduce the cost of goods brought into Florida and of goods carried out of Florida for sale to others. Roads, like canals and railroads, are investments in the future prosperity of the state's economy. The impact of the Interstate system and Turnpikes can be seen in and around Orange County. This area before 1970 was almost totally dependent on agriculture, principally oranges and related industries. Walt Disney, however, saw the future of the tourist industry based on the easy access to central Florida. Interstate 4, the Florida Turnpike, and the Beeline Expressway brought major changes to the area. It is now one of the world's most visited tourist areas. The economy has boomed with a good transportation system.

Federal Aid

The federal government in Washington, D.C. has aided transportation in ways other than the Interstate System. Under the United States Constitution, the federal government is charged with internal improvements and maintaining a postal system. These provisions have allowed federal funds to be used in improving canals, harbors, roads, railroads and airports. Road construction was aided in order for mail to travel more easily. Then, railroads received contracts to deliver the mail, but today airlines carry millions of kilograms/ pounds of mail each year.

Ports and Waterways

Roadways were not our only investments in prosperity. Over the years, vast amounts have been spent improving coastal shipping routes, ports, and waterways. From the early 1500's to the 1900's, hundreds of ship wrecks occurred off Florida's coastline. As the pirates were driven off the coast, "wreckers" appeared. These people preyed upon ships that ran aground on sand bars and reefs. Some historians have charged that the "wreckers" would use lights on stormy nights to misguide ships, so that they would run aground. Then, the wreckers would attack for fun and profit.

In 1821, when Florida became a Federal Territory, the government constructed lighthouses on the eastern seacoast. In 1825,

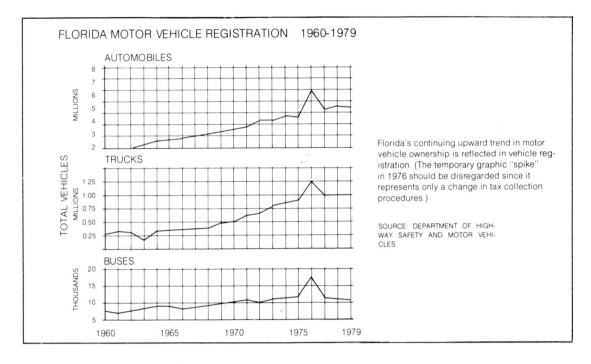

FLORIDA MOTOR VEHICLE REGISTRATION   1960-1979

AUTOMOBILES

Florida's continuing upward trend in motor vehicle ownership is reflected in vehicle registration. (The temporary graphic "spike" in 1976 should be disregarded since it represents only a change in tax collection procedures.)

SOURCE: DEPARTMENT OF HIGHWAY SAFETY AND MOTOR VEHICLES

Courtesy Florida Photographic Archives

Lighthouse at the mouth of the St. Johns River in 1874

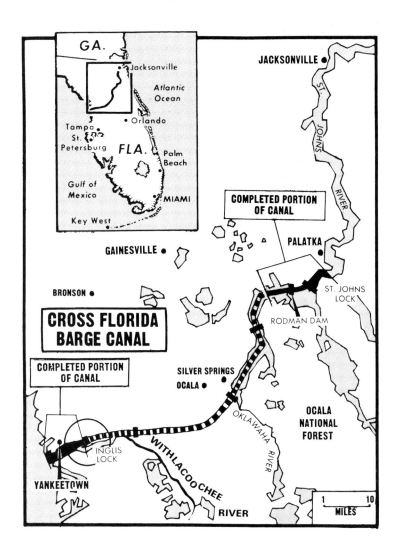

The Cross Florida Barge Canal

From the time Florida became a territory of the United States, people were interested in finding an easier way to ship goods from East to West Florida without the dangerous 965.4 kilometer/ 600-mile sailing trip around the Keys. In 1964, a 297.7 kilometer/ 185-mile route for the Cross Florida Barge Canal was selected. The port of Jacksonville was to be connected to the Gulf of Mexico near the Withlacoochee River. Traveling westward, barges would go down the St. Johns River from Jacksonville. They would go up the Oklawaha River, through locks and across Florida's Marion County, to the Gulf.

Dams had to be built to capture the water necessary to raise the barges in the locks. Locks had to be built to raise the barges and to lower them. Long and deep cuts had to be dug into the soil for the canal. In addition, the Oklawaha River, a natural, wild, free-flowing stream, would have to be channelized. That is, it would have to be straightened and deepened. It would no longer be a wilderness river.

The argument over the construction of the barge canal was long and heated. But, on January 17, 1971, President Nixon suspended work on the canal. Over $50 million had been spent on the canal by that time. It was one-third completed. Three of the five locks had been built. Three highway bridges over the canal and some 40.2 kilometers/ twenty-five miles of canal excavation were completed. One dam with a lake of 5261.1 hectares/ 13,000 acres was finished and the lake filled with water.

Yet, the Federal government withdrew from the project. President Nixon said that it was better to prevent a "past mistake" than continuing "permanent damage." Presidents Ford and Carter refused to reopen work on the canal.

MAJOR TRANSPORTATION MUSEUMS IN FLORIDA

Most of Florida's historical museums have artifacts and displays on portions of the development of transportation in our State. The following museums have displays of special transportation interest.

CAPE CANAVERAL	Kennedy Space Center: Displays of historic lauchpads and space craft used since the Center was opened in 1960.
DUNEDIN	Railroad Station Museum: Displays on the railroad and its impact on the development of Dunedin.
FLORIDA CITY/ HOMESTEAD	Florida Pioneer Museum: Displays on Henry Flagler's railroad, especially the Overseas Railroad, set in a railroad rooming house moved to Florida City from Homestead.
KEY WEST	Lighthouse Military Museum: Displays of military transportation used off Florida, such as a two-man submarine.
JUPITER	Lighthouse Museum: Displays on the perils of Florida's coastal waters, in a restored Florida Atlantic Coast Lighthouse.
PALM BEACH	Henry Morrison Flagler Museum: The private railroad car of this railroad giant is on display.
PENSACOLA	Naval Aviation Museum: Located at the Pensacola Naval Air Station, the museum has over 60 historic aircraft on display.
SARASOTA	Bellm's Cars and Music of Yesterday: Displays over 180 antique, classic, and special interest cars.
STUART	Gilbert's Bar House of Refuge -- a restored life saving station -- and Elliot Museum, which displays restored vehicles.

the Cape Florida lighthouse was built to warn ships of danger. This light is located on the southern tip of Key Biscayne, and operated until 1861. Today, it is a State Museum.

Federal aid to navigation continued. In 1871, a lifesaving agency was established in the United States Department of the Treasury. Ten "houses of refuge" were constructed along Florida's coastline from Daytona Beach to Key Biscayne. The second one built was constructed in 1875 north of Gilbert's Bar (near Jensen Beach). Gilbert's Bar was named after a pirate who used the inlet as a shelter in the 1830's. He was hanged in Boston for piracy, however, the name

remained. The House of Refuge served well until 1945 when it was decommissioned. Today, it serves as a museum for the Martin County Historical Society. It reminds us of the dangers of coastal shipping. One night in 1904, 22 seamen were sheltered there after two vessels went aground and broke up in stormy seas.

Federal aid also was directed to river and harbor improvements. Channels were marked and cleared of rocks and snags to protect ship bottoms. Money was allocated to dredge harbors to greater depths so that ships had room to navigate and the ports could load and unload larger ships.

Then the Coast Guard started participating in the inspecting of ships and ports, it also trains and licenses harbor pilots, who guide vessels safely in and out of ports.

Today, ports in Florida have a growing trade with other American ports and with foreign ports, especially those in Central and South America. Fourteen ports are classified as deep-water ports, that is, they can load and unload vessels which draw 8.3 meters/ 27 feet of water (ocean-going vessels). Huge amounts of building materials are unloaded at these ports. But, an even greater commodity is petroleum. Florida is a large importer of gasoline and fuel oil. The transportation network: airplanes, cars, trucks, and buses, are operated on this imported fuel. Petroleum is used in the generation of electricity, by almost all of the major utility companies. Asphalt and other petroleum products are imported to make road paving and other construction materials. In 1980, when the port of Tampa was closed by a serious bridge accident, supplies of petroleum were soon in short supply. Florida cannot operate for long without open, busy ports bringing in energy resources.

Small ports, with 2.8 meters/ nine feet of water or more, are important in trade along the coast. Petroleum products, such as: gasoline, fuel oil, and asphalt, are carried by barges from New Orleans and other ports.

Scrap iron, phosphates, citrus products, and other goods from Florida's fields and factories are exported. Goods from other states pass through Florida to our ports for export to Latin America.

Jacksonville, for example, is a major port for incoming Japanese cars which are sold all over the Southeastern United States. It is a major coffee port, and handles a lot of wood products from the southern forest industry.

The port of Miami serves as an excellent example of the growth of a port. In 1840, a log pier was built at the mouth of the Miami River and served as a place to dock ships and to handle cargo, especially ships serving Key West. When the Florida East Coast Railway laid tracks to Miami, trade increased. Railroads carried goods to Miami for shipment abroad. In 1915, the City of Miami developed its port with 5.5 meters/ 18 feet of water and a 30.5 meter/ 100 foot wide channel. Over the years, the facility was expanded to 10.5 hectares/ 26 acres and a wider channel.

During World War II, the profitable coastal trade at Miami was interrupted, It never returned to Miami's Biscayne port. The city turned the port over to the officials of Dade County, who developed the port in a new location. On "spoil banks" in the bay, dirt accumulated from dredging channels, the county built a 121.4 hectare/ 300 acre facility. In 1964, the new port was opened and growth has continued. Not only has the port attracted cargo vessels, but it is becoming a center for cruise ships. These cruise vessels carry tourists around the Carribbean Sea on cruises from three days to three weeks in length.

The port at Tampa is the largest Florida port in terms of tonnage handled. Vast quantities of phosphate rock and phosphate fertilizer are exported. Vast amounts of coal are handled for Tampa Electric Company, TECO, which generates electricity using coal. Petroleum products make up the other major portion of Tampa's trading activity.

Port Everglades is dominated by trade in imported petroleum products. It even has a pipeline from its docks to oil tank farms at Miami International Airport to handle vast amounts of aviation fuel.

The port at Pensacola is famous for its export of quality wood products from the forests of North Florida and Alabama. Sulfur from oil fields in Santa Rosa County is handled here. The sulfur is separated from the oil pumped out of the ground and used in many industries, including the manufacture of fertilizers.

But Florida's coastal development has involved more than lighthouses and commercial ports. Pleasure craft and smaller working boats have a much safer time now that the Intracoastal Waterway is marked out along Florida's coast. Behind barrier islands, through rivers, and hugging inlets and bays, these small vessels can travel from northern cities to Miami or from Miami to Pensacola in some shelter. The only major open portion is from the West Coast of Florida to Alligator Point in the Panhandle. Some boat-people call this the "missing link" and want the government to provide a sheltered route. But there are few coastal islands, so any shelter would be expensive to create.

This waterway and the many pleasant marinas contribute to the pleasure of living in Florida, and economically, to the pleasures of vacationing in the Sunshine State. Following the Intracoastal Waterway from Jupiter on a canal to Lake Okeechobee and then to the Gulf of Mexico is a delightful and safe experience for native Floridian and tourist alike.

Aviation

Orville and Wilbur Wright made their first heavier than air flight in 1903 at Kitty Hawk, North Carolina. Most people thought the airplane was no more than a toy. Airplanes were used by "barnstorming" pilots putting on thrill shows at fairs. Florida was no exception. Daring pilots thrilled audiences. In 1911, Lincoln Beachey made the first night flight in the skies over Tampa. Later that year, he set a new world's record for the highest flight -- 3,507.5 meters/ 11,500 feet in the air. During that same year, Glen Curtiss had a "flying school" in Miami, where he trained pilots. Later, he operated a racing team which set new records. This team was

Courtesy Florida Photographic Archives

Hialeah, Florida, Curtiss Flying School, March, 1917

120

the forerunner of the Curtiss-Wright Flying Service which carried mail and passengers in the 1930's.

Florida entered the commercial aviation age in 1914. Tony Jannus flew an "airboat" (seaplane) on the first flight of a regularly scheduled airline in America. This famous flight took place on January 1, 1914, and covered the 35.4 kilometers/ 22 miles across Tampa Bay between Tampa and St. Petersburg. The air service did not last long, but aviation schools opened to train pilots in Florida's warm skies. During World War I, many military and naval pilots were trained in Florida because the weather was excellent for year-round flying. After the war, the flying schools in Miami, Tampa,

Jacksonville, St. Augustine, and Pensacola prospered. In the 1920's, their graduates were ferrying tourists from one resort to another.

In 1926, Florida Airways Corporation had a U.S. Mail contract to carry mail from Atlanta and Miami, through Jacksonville, Tampa, and Fort Myers. This contract lasted less than a year, but in 1927, Pan American Airways carried mail to Havana, Cuba. Pan American grew to serve many cities in Latin America, just as the old 93.1 hectare/ 230 acre Pan American airport grew into the almost 1,214.1 hectare/ 3,000 acre Miami International Airport of today. National Airline, now part of Pan American, was first organized in St. Petersburg to carry mail, tourists, and businessmen. In 1930,

Courtesy Florida Photographic Archives

Aviation Airlines, St. Petersburg - Tampa Air Boat Line

Miami, Pan American Airways Airport, January 25, 1929.

Eastern Airlines was founded and connected Florida to northern cities. By 1939, Florida had 150 airports. Twenty-two had lighted fields for night time takeoffs and landings.

During World War II, many pilots were again trained in Florida. Naval air stations were located at Pensacola and Jacksonville. Army training took place across the state at many military airports. After the war, many of these training airports were given to city and county governments to run as public facilities. Orlando's McCoy Field began as an Army Air Force training center.

Aviation historically has played an important role in Florida, where the nation's first commercial flight, first night flight, first international flight, and first naval carrier landing occurred. Florida's airports are vital to the economy. Tourists by the millions come to Florida by airplane. With the energy crisis, even more tourists are leaving their cars at home and are flying here. Miami International Airport has direct flights to and from Europe, bringing tourists to the sunshine and many businesspersons to trade. Today, the Dade County metropolitan region is a center for international trade. Business people come from all over Latin America to trade, and airplanes carry tons of cargo between Miami and Latin American cities. Miami's modern airport is so busy that an aviation fuel pipeline is needed to bring fuel to the airport from Port Everglades.

Tampa's new International Airport is a link to northern cities and to Mexican and other Central American cities. This airport handles millions of passengers a year and can be expanded to handle 15 million per year. Miami, Fort Lauderdale, and West Palm Beach airports serve to link Florida with the Atlantic islands and those of the Carribbean region. Not to be outdone, Orlando is building a vast, efficient airport facility at the old McCoy Field. Orlando planners understand that air travel is a key to future tourism and business growth in Florida.

The aviation network in Florida is as large as it is important. There are 441 licensed sites in our state. There are 138 public use airports, including 87 with lighted fields, 32 with air control towers, and 24 with regular air service. The state has six international airports, with flights linking us with some of the world's great cities. These numbers include seven seaplane bases and one landing facility for dirigibles -- a blimp landing base in Dade County.

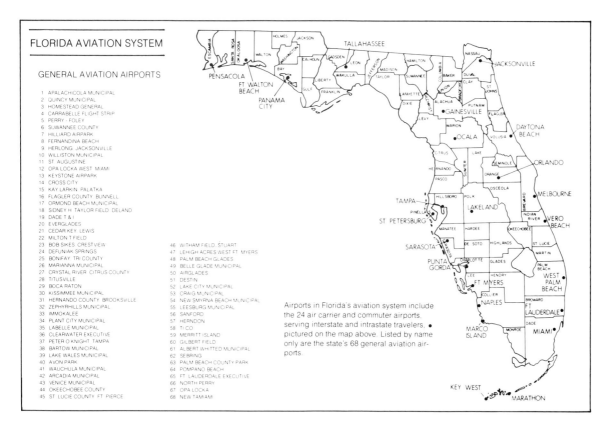

1. APALACHICOLA MUNICIPAL
2. QUINCY MUNICIPAL
3. HOMESTEAD GENERAL
4. CARRABELLE FLIGHT STRIP
5. PERRY - FOLEY
6. SUWANNEE COUNTY
7. HILLIARD AIRPARK
8. FERNANDINA BEACH
9. HERLONG JACKSONVILLE
10. WILLISTON MUNICIPAL
11. ST. AUGUSTINE
12. OPA LOCKA WEST MIAMI
13. KEYSTONE AIRPARK
14. CROSS CITY
15. KAY LARKIN PALATKA
16. FLAGLER COUNTY BUNNELL
17. ORMOND BEACH MUNICIPAL
18. SIDNEY H. TAYLOR FIELD - DELAND
19. DADE T & I
20. EVERGLADES
21. CEDAR KEY - LEWIS
22. MILTON T FIELD
23. BOB SIKES CRESTVIEW
24. DEFUNIAK SPRINGS
25. BONIFAY TRI COUNTY
26. MARIANNA MUNICIPAL
27. CRYSTAL RIVER CITRUS COUNTY
28. TITUSVILLE
29. BOCA RATON
30. KISSIMMEE MUNICIPAL
31. HERNANDO COUNTY BROOKSVILLE
32. ZEPHYRHILLS MUNICIPAL
33. IMMOKALEE
34. PLANT CITY MUNICIPAL
35. LABELLE MUNICIPAL
36. CLEARWATER EXECUTIVE
37. PETER O KNIGHT TAMPA
38. BARTOW MUNICIPAL
39. LAKE WALES MUNICIPAL
40. AVON PARK
41. WAUCHULA MUNICIPAL
42. ARCADIA MUNICIPAL
43. VENICE MUNICIPAL
44. OKEECHOBEE COUNTY
45. ST. LUCIE COUNTY FT PIERCE

46. WITHAM FIELD, STUART
47. LEHIGH ACRES WEST FT. MYERS
48. PALM BEACH GLADES
49. BELLE GLADE MUNICIPAL
50. AIRGLADES
51. DESTIN
52. LAKE CITY MUNICIPAL
53. CRAIG MUNICIPAL
54. NEW SMYRNA BEACH MUNICIPAL
55. LEESBURG MUNICIPAL
56. SANFORD
57. HERNDON
58. TI CO
59. MERRITT ISLAND
60. GILBERT FIELD
61. ALBERT WHITTED MUNICIPAL
62. SEBRING
63. PALM BEACH COUNTY PARK
64. POMPANO BEACH
65. FT. LAUDERDALE EXECUTIVE
66. NORTH PERRY
67. OPA LOCKA
68. NEW TAMIAMI

Airports in Florida's aviation system include the 24 air carrier and commuter airports, serving interstate and intrastate travelers, ● pictured on the map above. Listed by name only are the state's 68 general aviation airports.

Unusual Transportation Systems

To "transport" means to carry something from one place to another. When we talk about transportation, we usually think about airplanes, ships, trucks, and things like that. However, we do "transport" water, electricity, natural gas, and oil products. In Florida we have extensive systems to transport these commodities and we ought to understand them as well as our airports and railroads.

Pipelines

Pipelines play an important part in our Florida transportation system. They carry water, petroleum, and natural gas from producers to consumers. Let's begin with water pipelines.

Florida has an abundant supply of water. Approximately 26.49 billion liters/ seven billion gallons of fresh water are used each day in Florida. This use of fresh water is growing each year and at this time we do not have as much water as we need in some areas of the state. Every city and most towns have water systems which carry water from wells to homes and businesses. In the rural areas, people have their own household wells and pumps, but not so in cities. The larger cities in Florida now have huge pipelines carrying water from well fields to the city water system. These well fields are often kilometers/ miles from the cities which they serve, because the cities cannot get the great amounts of water they need within their own borders. Pinellas County, for example, has well fields in Hillsborough and Pasco Counties. Some Pinellas County officials would like to build a pipeline up to Hernando County and tap into new well fields and into coastal freshwater springs.

As you might guess, some Hernando County residents are not too pleased with sending water to Pinellas County. They forsee that they will need the water for Hernando County's growing number of tourists and businesses. They understand that, without safe, fresh water, an area will not grow.

This conflict will continue, since Pinellas County does not have the water available to fulfill its expanding needs. Florida has water management districts to ensure high water quality and to plan supplies for the future. But Florida's abundant water supply is far from where the shortages occur. Only conservation and very expensive pipelines seem to be the ways to handle the water issues.

Natural gas comes to Floridians through a pipeline system. There are three gas pipeline firms serving the state, but, only one is a major company -- the Florida Gas Transmission Company. It brings gas into the state from Texas and Louisiana, across the Panhandle of Florida, and then down the east coast to Miami and Tampa. Natural gas from out of state is merged with gas produced in northwest Florida, within this distribution system. Florida produces over 60 percent of its gas consumption, but this percentage is decreasing each year.

The gas pipeline system ties to city gas systems which distribute natural gas for home heating, water heating, and commercial uses. Utility companies often use natural gas, especially during the summer, for generating electricity. Factories in Florida use natural gas as a raw material in their manufacturing processes. Warm homes and schools, electricity, and jobs are as dependent upon the natural gas pipeline transportation system as they are dependent upon natural gas -- especially with the energy crisis.

There are only a few, short petroleum pipelines in Florida. One, for example, carries aviation fuel from Port Everglades to the Miami International Airport. This system is less expensive and more reliable than depending upon trucks. Another pipeline serves the Air Force base in Tampa and Tampa International Airport. Yet, another runs from the Port of Tampa to Central Florida, as an efficient way to get petroleum to Orlando distribution centers.

Electricity is produced in large generating stations (or power plants). When flying over Florida you see these huge facilities such as those at Turkey Point, Crystal River, Jacksonville, St. Marks, Tampa, and other places. The companies which produce electricity must "transport" it to their household and commercial customers. This electricity is transported through expensive systems of high voltage, overhead wires, transformers, and lower voltage wires and transformers. Unlike pipelines, most of us have seen the electric transportation system--towers, wires, and creosoted trees planted up and down streets and across the state to bring us energy.

Florida has six private (investor-owned), 35 city-owned, and 17 rural electric companies in the electricity business. These companies are linked together by the transmission lines, and to other companies throughout the Southeastern United States. If one company cannot make enough electricity, it can borrow from another through those lines. It can also help other areas when they need electricity. This is called a "power-sharing pool," and it is only possible because of the electric pipeline -- those transmission wires linking us all together, electric producers and electricity consumers.

Problems

Floridians wanting to protect the high quality of our transportation system have two pressing problems. First, is the problem of maintaining what we have in an age of rapidly rising costs. Second, is the problem of dealing with growth in an age of energy shortages and higher costs.

Costs of maintaining highways and roads are rising each day, while more fuel efficient cars and energy conservation efforts mean lower gasoline tax collections by the state. Federal cutbacks on aid to airports mean higher costs for local governments operating airport facilities, and higher costs for airlines which pass them on to consumers. Pipelines and electric transmission systems, harbor maintenance, railroad track and river dredging are increasingly expensive.

Consumers already affected by rising prices for food, health care, and similar needs are facing the inflated prices of transportation systems.

Into this spiral of prices, we have Florida's poor, its poorly paid workers, and its elderly who live on fixed incomes from social security and pensions. Can these people afford their transportation needs?

The problem of rising transportation prices is made more difficult by the growth in Florida's population. More residents and more tourists mean that each year transportation systems must be made more efficient or they must grow. Larger airports, more cars and parking lots, greater highway wear, more electric lines, larger water pipelines to cities, and so forth are natural consequences of growth. Yet, many argue that Florida must grow in order to provide jobs for our citizens.

The Promise

While the problems seem great, there is hope. Floridians are switching to more fuel efficient cars and buses. Gasoline consumption is leveling off, even in our tourist state. More tourists are flying to Florida. More Floridians are car pooling and using mass transit. Cities are developing bike paths, car pooling systems, and attractive mass transit systems. Tallahassee has a Taltran System. Pensacola has Escambia Transit. Live Oak has Suwannee Valley Transit, and Daytona Beach has VoTran.

Florida's first major rapid rail transit project is underway in Miami with Metrorail. The first stage involves 26.5 kilometers/ 16.5 miles of guideway, with a station at the University of Miami. Dade County is buying the right of way for the rails, while the state and federal

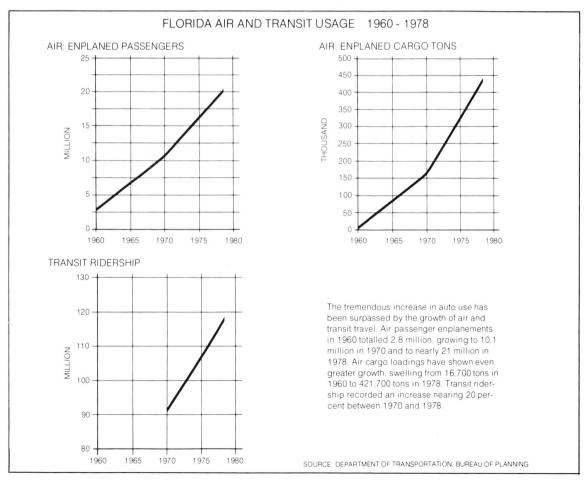

FLORIDA AIR AND TRANSIT USAGE   1960 - 1978

AIR: ENPLANED PASSENGERS

AIR: ENPLANED CARGO TONS

TRANSIT RIDERSHIP

The tremendous increase in auto use has been surpassed by the growth of air and transit travel. Air passenger enplanements in 1960 totalled 2.8 million, growing to 10.1 million in 1970 and to nearly 21 million in 1978. Air cargo loadings have shown even greater growth, swelling from 16,700 tons in 1960 to 421,700 tons in 1978. Transit ridership recorded an increase nearing 20 percent between 1970 and 1978.

SOURCE: DEPARTMENT OF TRANSPORTATION, BUREAU OF PLANNING

Miami Office of Information and Visitors.

X-Way System in the City of Miami

governments are assisting in construction. Meanwhile, both Miami and Jacksonville are exploring the possible uses of "Downtown People Movers," to get tourists and business persons out of gas consuming cars and into more conserving styles of travel. All of these systems will pay special attention to the needs of the elderly and the handicapped citizens among us.

Florida is making strides in replacing old bridges, such as the series from Miami to Key West. Funds are gathered for the completion of the Interstate System -- I-95 on the East Coast, and I-75 on the Southwest Coast of Florida. Airport facilities are being renewed such as the new Orlando International airport, or being made more efficient such as in Miami and Jacksonville.

Transportation history in Florida does not end today, but in the future is looking at the Kennedy Space Center on Cape Canaveral. It is the major American launch base for the exploration of outer space. From the shores of Florida we will reach out to new frontiers and worlds. This center was planned in 1947 and was opened in 1950. During construction, the bones of great mammoths were uncovered as were the remains of Indian villages from those first travelers in Florida. Today, as Americans are seeking new frontiers with the

Space Shuttle and other programs, the promise is bright. The leap into space will be from the site of early Indian habitation and from the place where Ponce de Leon came ashore in 1513. Transportation has changed tremendously just since the turn of the century. In 1900 very few people had ridden in an automobile and none in an airplane.

In this panorama of transportation in Florida, it can be seen that the state has a wide variety of modes of transportation. Each type of transportation has added to the economic and cultural development of the state. While different types of transportation have been preferred at one time or another, a traveler in Florida can still see all forms of transportation:

> *...hikers, strolling the many beaches . . . horseback riders trotting across the Florida Plain... a wagon pulled along a grove to gather oranges...a train ride along the eastern coast . . . boats sailing the waterways . . . an automobile or bus traveling an interstate . . . a jet liner to a far off city ... or perhaps a space shuttle to unknown worlds.*

In the future, who can imagine how transportation will change.

TRANSPORTATION

Courtland Richards

The State Seal in the Capitol

GOVERNMENT

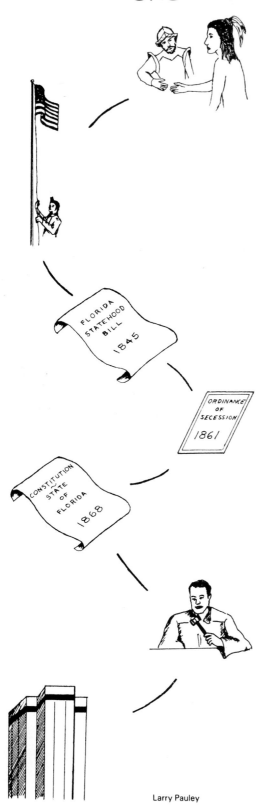

Larry Pauley

Introduction

The newspaper, radio, and television tell the same news. A new tax has just been placed on the citizens of Florida. How did it happen? Who did it? Why was it done?

Today, as a citizen of Florida, you have at least three organized governments working for you. The United States government is the government over which citizens have the least amount of direct control. This includes the executive branch, which is the President and cabinet; the legislative branch, which is the Congress; and the judicial branch which is the Supreme Court and Federal Courts. In general the federal government makes, enforces, and interprets laws and rules for the benefit of the nation as a whole. It also oversees disputes between states.

The second form of government related to the Florida citizen is the Florida state government. This government is next in power to the federal government in many areas, but it does have areas of power the federal government does not. The average Floridian has more control over the state government than over the federal government. State government also has three branches: the executive, legislative and judical. These are the governor and cabinet, the legislature and the state court system.

The third form of government affecting you as a citizen is the county system. Florida has 67 counties. Each county has its own government. This government also contains the three branches of government. The executive and legislative branches are held by the same group. This is the Board of County Trustees or Commissions. The judicial branch is the County Court.

Every citizen of Florida is related to the above governments. However, many citizens are governed by additional bodies. The fourth government affecting you if you live in a town or city is municipal government. Municipal governments in Florida only have two of the branches of government. This is due to the fact that the judicial branch is the County Court System. The executive branch is either a mayor or city manager. The legislative branch is the council.

Florida also has consolidated governments. The most successful has been the Jacksonville-Duval County consolidation. This is where the functions of the city and county have been combined to eliminate duplication of services.

A unique form of government existing in Florida is the Special District. These districts are formed, as the name implies, for special purposes. This can range from a hospital to a stadium, and even shopping centers. The special districts must be specifically authorized by law.

Perhaps, the government which affects people the most is the School Board. This form of government affects the daily life of almost every citizen in the state.

These forms of government did not happen by chance. They are the result of a long heritage of changes within the area we now call Florida. Many types of government helped shape what we call "our government" today.

Indians

We often think of the people who lived in Florida before the Spanish explorer as being "uncivilized" and without any government. This was not so. By studying artifacts, we know that the mound building cultures buried their dead. We know that some of the mounds were for chieftains. The fact that these early residents of Florida had a chieftain shows a form of government. They lived together in towns, which suggests that there had to be some form of government. We are not entirely positive as to the type they had.

We know that the Indians of the Spanish and French colonial eras had chiefs. During this period, in the 1500's, we know that some tribes dominated others. This shows they had some type of government. Any group of Indians which settled in an area and farmed had to have some type of organization. We know the Timucuans farmed and had a loose confederation of tribes.

The Calusa tribe was able to spread its dominance and influence over the Ais, Jaegas, and Tequestas. This domination required rules, which means government.

Many times all three branches of government were in one person, the chief. In other cases, a tribal council held the legislative or law making powers. One main idea of the government of the native Floridians was that the land belonged to everyone and not to individuals. This was later to be a problem between the natives and the Europeans who arrived in the sixteenth century.

Spain

It is not definite which Europeans arrived first in Florida. However, the first recorded European was Juan Ponce de Leon. He was commissioned by the King of Spain to explore for Spain. Ponce de Leon did not know that the land he set foot on in 1513 was a continent and not an island. The Europeans believed they had the right to occupy and claim any land which no other European country had already claimed. Under this idea, Ponce de Leon was appointed *"adelantado"* of the "island" of La Florida by the King. This appointment gave Florida the first of many new governments it was to have.

The Indians did not know that they had been claimed as part of the kingdom of Spain. They only knew that a different people had come to their homeland. In 1521 Ponce de Leon returned to Charlotte Harbor to begin ruling his "island." He brought soldiers, settlers, livestock, and farming equipment with him. The planned colonization was shortlived. Ponce de Leon was wounded in an encounter with Indians. He then ordered his group back to Cuba where he died. Thus, the *"adelantado"* de La Florida died without governing the land.

In 1528 another Spaniard, Panfilo de Narvaez, received a commission from the King of Spain. He was to sail to Florida and establish two colonies and build three forts. This was to be done to provide shelter for

shipwrecked sailors. Spanish ships loaded with gold and silver from Mexico often wrecked or were attacked along the Florida coast. The King wanted protection for the survivors.

Panfilo de Narvaez did not follow his orders. He probably landed at Tampa Bay, but instead of settling, he promptly took off inland looking for gold and silver. Six years later and only two survivors of the "settlers" arrived in Mexico City. The second attempt by Spain to govern Florida had failed.

Ten years after the ill-fated expedition of de Narvaez, the King of Spain appointed a governor of Florida. Hernando de Soto, the new governor, quickly fell victim to "gold fever." He arrived in Florida in 1539 and spent a year searching for gold and silver. De Soto then traveled westward, but died and was buried in the Mississippi River.

The failure of military expeditions to establish colonies in Florida was creating a change in Spain's ideas of colonization. The King had given Ponce de Leon, de Narvaez, and de Soto a royal patent or the right to found private colonies governed by them. Spain now would take control of the colonies.

The first attempt to colonize came under a priest, Father Luis Cancer de Barbasto. It may seem strange to us now that a colony was to be founded by a Catholic priest, but the King of Spain was Catholic. He wanted to spread his religion to all "uncivilized" people. During this period of time there was no separation between religion and government. Father Luis wanted to establish a colony in Florida to bring the Christian religion to the Indians. The attempt to establish a religious colony failed. Father Luis landed at Tampa Bay and was killed by Indians. The Indians believed him to be another military man who would attack them as had been done in the past.

King Charles V decided to stop colonization and attempts to govern Florida. It was not until 1560 that King Phillip II allowed another attempt. This time, the colony was to be under the control of the King as a royal colony. Tristan de Luna set sail from Vera Cruz, Mexico for Pensacola Bay to establish a town and fort. The new venture was doomed from the beginning. First, a storm destroyed much of the supplies. Then food expeditions to the interior failed even though friendly Indians helped the Spaniards. De Luna was then ordered to find a new sight. This failed because of another storm and de Luna retreated to Mexico. Another attempt by Spain to govern Florida had failed.

After years of attempts, Spain was no closer to governing Florida than when Ponce de Leon had arrived. This was soon to change because the French and English were beginning to show interest in the area.

The Spanish increased their efforts to establish control and govern Florida. The Indians had in no way come under their rule, and now their ownership was threatened by other Europeans.

France was first to challenge Spain's control of the Florida peninsula. In 1564, France sent an expedition under Jean Ribaut to settle on the St. Johns River. Although he liked the region, Ribaut decided to go further north. This attempt caused the Spanish King once more to give a new colonization contract. Pedro Menendez de Aviles would receive gifts and rights from the King on the condition he would establish three colonies and Christianize the Indians.

Menendez was able to settle at St. Augustine and stop further attempts of French colonization. Menendez, as leader of St. Augustine, felt he should establish some type of communication with the Indians in the area. He chose to meet with the Calusa chief, who the Spanish called King Carlos. This first attempt of the Spanish government to negotiate with an Indian government in Florida at first appeared successful.

King Carlos agreed with Menendez to return Spanish sailors which his tribe had captured from wrecked ships. He also agreed to protect future shipwrecked travelers. Either because of misunderstandings or deceit, the Calusas failed to uphold the agreement. This caused Menendez to begin

attacks on the Indians to protect his new settlement at St. Augustine. He also patrolled the coast in search of shipwrecked sailors.

The Spanish tried to extend their government through missionaries and military settlements, but they were never able to control the Indians. A line of missions stretched across present day northern Florida. There were about 25 missions and a road connected each. The Spanish government was trying to develop internal improvements, but this was the extent of Spanish control of interior Florida.

In the East, Spanish control was only dominant in and around St. Augustine and this was dependent on the Castillo de San Marcos. Under the Spanish, the government and military were one in the same.

English

A major change occurred in the government of Florida when the English obtained ownership of the peninsula in 1763. In the signing of a treaty, subjects of the Spanish King became subjects of the English King. Florida began a march toward self government.

An entirely different form of government was established. First, Florida was divided into two colonies, East Florida and West Florida. They were crown colonies or owned by the King. There was an appointed governor and lieutenant governor to serve as the executive branch. The chief justice was appointed and was head of the judiciary. The legislature was a Legislative Assembly with two divisions or houses. An appointed council served as the upper house. The lower house, called the House of Commons, was a first for Florida, members were elected by the citizens. A limited democracy had been established.

Governor George Johnstone of West Florida had his capital at Pensacola. In East Florida, Governor James Grant settled in the old Spanish Governor's house in St. Augustine. Both governors began an appointed lower court system under "squires" or justices of the peace. They settled problems between citizens in the new colonies.

One of Governor Grant's first actions in East Florida was to settle boundaries with the Indians. With much fanfare, the British called a meeting with all the Indian chiefs under his jurisdiction. A treaty was drawn up based on the idea that the land belonged to the Indians except for a section in the Northeast corner of the 14th colony. This area touched all or parts of the present day counties of Nassau, St. Johns, Clay, Putnam, and Flagler.

Governor Johnstone in West Florida had more difficulty in settling the 15th colony. There were problems with the Indians but more importantly there were internal problems. Several changes in the governorship caused unrest until 1770 when Governor Peter Chester was appointed. He remained governor until 1783 and helped establish a stable Indian trade. Under him, the Panton, Leslie and Company established its office in Pensacola and several trading posts.

East Florida entered into a period of unrest in 1774, two years before the other 13 colonies revolted. Governor Grant was replaced by a new governor who was the opposite of him in every way. Grant was cultured, easy going and a good administrator. His replacement, Governor Tonyn, was not pleased with his appointment to East Florida. He felt it was beneath his position and had a distrust of the democratic Legislative Assembly.

Tonyn dismissed the secretary of the upper chamber, Dr. Andrew Turnbull, and refused to call the Legislative Assembly into session. He called the members of the legislature "rebellious Americans." Tonyn finally was forced to call the Legislative Assembly into session in 1781. The legislature was loyal to the King of England and voted for 12 militia companies to be formed.

Most of the laws passed dealt with slaves. Criminal acts like arson and murder committed by slaves were to be tried by a jury and the penalty was death. Slaves could be used for public works. The governor had the right to declare martial law. Fear of what was going on in the 13 American Revolutionary Colonies, especially the Declaration of Independence, caused strict penalties for slave stealing and inciting a slave rebellion. For both crimes the penalty was death.

This brief attempt at democracy in the 14th and 15th colonies came to an abrupt end in 1783. England lost Florida to Spain in the treaty at the end of the American Revolution. England withdrew, but British ideas of government and trade remained.

SEAL OF THE PROVINCE OF WEST FLORIDA.

Florida Photographic Archives

Seal of the Province of West Florida

Spain's Lack of Control

The new governor of Florida was Don Vincente Manual de Zespedes y Velasco. He arrived in St. Augustine in 1784 to reestablish Spanish control. However, Spain would never really regain control of Florida except around St. Augustine. The Americans to the north had designs on Florida and began migrating to the Florida frontier. All people in the Spanish colony were to swear allegiance to the King, and if property was to be inherited, the heirs had to become Catholics. The Americans who had just overthrown one King and believed in freedom of religion did not willingly accept those conditions.

In the West the government was weaker than in the East. Actual influence and power was still held by the British through the Panton, Leslie and Company. Spain's wealth no longer existed, and there were not enough industries to supply the Indians with goods. William Panton saw the refusal of the Indians in St. Augustine to accept the poorly made Spanish gifts. He immediately offered Governor Zespedes British made goods on credit, and the governor accepted.

The Spanish steadily went deeper into debt to the trading company. Both Spain and the Indians began to realize who was in control. Friendship with the Indians, by the Panton, Leslie and Company was maintained through agents like Alexander McGillivray who was one-fourth Indian on his mother's side. He was so important to British control of Florida trade, that he was given military honors by England.

Spain, in her weakened condition, gave a large part of her American territory, Louisiana, to France. Louisiana then was sold to the United States, leaving Florida isolated and surrounded by Americans.

Republics of East and West Florida

Americans in West Florida saw the terms of the Louisiana Purchase as a chance to take more Spanish territory. In 1810, American citizens announced the land belonged to the United States, marched on and occupied Baton Rouge. They established a new government, the Republic of West Florida. President Madison sent in United States troops and claimed the area as American territory. Spain saw Florida reduced to its present size but could do nothing. An attempt in East Florida to imitate the success in the West was unsuccessful because St. Augustine still had some semblance of government and control.

Further expeditions were organized by Americans to go into Florida. General Andrew Jackson led several punishing campaigns into the area, because the Spanish could not control Indians who were attacking American settlers north of Florida.

Florida Becomes an American Territory

Spain realized that she was losing Florida, and in 1819 the Adam-Onis Treaty turned the area over to the United States. On July 15, 1821 in Pensacola, Andrew Jackson stood as Spanish Governor Callava of West Florida had the Spanish flag taken down. Jackson then became provisional Governor of Florida. Jackson's official title was United States Commissioner and Governor of the Territories of East and West Florida. One of his first actions was to make one Territory of Florida and divide it into two counties. St. Augustine was to be the county seat of St. Johns County and Pensacola was to serve as Escambia's County seat.

Governor Jackson was not happy to be head of government in the area and over people he disliked. His disappointment grew when President Monroe filled territorial positions with men other than Jackson's choices. Because of these factors and his wife Rachel's desire to return to Tennessee, Jackson resigned his post and left Florida in October, 1821. The government was operated until the following March by two territorial secretaries.

The Territory of Florida

Florida received its full territorial status and civil government on March 30, 1822. The first official territorial governor was William

P. DuVal of Kentucky. The rest of the exceedutive branch included one federal marshall, three tax collectors and a territorial secretary. The judicial included superior court judges and two district attorneys. The legislature was a thirteen member Legislative Council elected by the people.

Reorganizing the Territory

The first Legislative Council meeting was on July 19, 1822, with only nine members present. The remaining members were sailing from St. Augustine which took two months. The council in the first two years created four new counties. Jackson and Gadsden were carved out of Escambia while DuVal and Monroe were created out of St. Johns. These counties were named for people who had helped make Florida a United States Territory.

Ownership of land was an important issue. England had owned Florida for 20 years, Spain had owned it for 300 years and the Indians had claimed it for thousands of years. Now the Legislative Council had to settle the claims. Land boards were set up in St. Augustine and Pensacola. Americans who had squatted or been allowed to settle on Spanish land before 1821 had their claims confirmed. Spanish land titles which were granted by the King of Spain before 1819 were allowed to be kept. No Spanish grants between 1819 and 1821 were recognized. The Americans believed the Spanish king had granted land titles during that period to make sure that Spanish citizens would still have some control over Florida. New land titles were sold at $3.09 a hectare/ $1.25 and acre for territorial land.

The Spanish, American and English claimant were satisfied, but the Indians were not to fare so well. In the Treaty of Camp Moultrie, the Indians lost control of their land and were driven southward.

Tallahassee in 1842 by Francis de Castelnau

Florida Photographic Archives

Two early state seals. Notice the mountains. Compare this with Florida's terrain.

Tallahassee

Governor DuVal in 1823 commissioned John Lee Williams of Pensacola and Dr. William Simmons of St. Augustine to select a permanent seat of government. The difficulty and inconvenience of traveling from St. Augustine to Pensacola was the main consideration in locating a new capital for the territory. The site was to be between the Ochlockonee and Suwannee Rivers. This would provide a capital which was centrally located to the population.

Simmons and Williams met at the St. Marks River and proceeded to the village of the Talasi Indians. Both agreed that it was an excellent location for a town and capitol to be built. The Indians were not pleased at the selection but did not resist. The town was to be named Tallahassee from the Creek word meaning "old field." Governor DuVal accepted the recommendation and the first settlers arrived on April 9, 1824.

The Congress of the United States granted a quarter section of land to be sold to pay for a new capitol. Two planters brought their slaves to build three log cabins for the Legislative Council. When the Council met in the fall, they confirmed the name of the city as Tallahassee and named it as the county seat of the newly created Leon County.

County Government in the Territory

Florida's early counties were governed by "County Courts" which were made up of five justices of the peace. These justices were usually prominent citizens who settled disputes in their county. The County Court held all three powers of government. They made laws, administered the laws and interpreted the laws. Though the County Court's name changed over the years, the justice of the peace system was to last until 1972.

From Territory to Statehood

Floridians wanted to change their status from a Territory to a state. They did not like the idea that the governor was appointed by federal officials in Washington, D.C. Many of Florida's citizens had come from other southern states where the idea of "state's rights" was strong. This idea was founded on interpretation of the United States Constitution. The "state's rights" interpretation insisted that the states had retained most of their powers when the United States was formed. Opposing that idea, were those who felt that the federal government was the stronger and held most of the powers of government.

Many Floridians believed that with statehood they would control their own destiny. Another factor in the clamor for statehood was because of a movement by northern congressmen and senators to attempt the elimination of slavery in Washington, D.C. and the federal territories. Planters did not want to give up the lifestyle which slave labor provided them, so they wanted statehood. As a state, the planters, being the ruling class, would easily control the state and protect the "peculiar institution" of slavery.

The Legislative Assembly passed an act in 1837 providing for a vote on application for statehood. The reference passed and in December 1838, a constitutional convention was held at St. Joseph. Forty-six of the 56 delegates met at the opening meeting and the rest arrived later.

The major argument was that of being admitted as a slave state to balance the admission of Kansas as a free state. Some of the delegates considered splitting the territory and letting the planters of West Florida vote for slavery. This idea was dropped when the only slaveholder in Dade County argued that East Florida would enter the Union as a free state.

When the Constitution was finished in January, there were three clauses dealing with slavery contained in it. The General Assembly, or legislature, was prohibited from freeing the slaves, and it could not stop slave owners who moved to Florida, from bringing their slaves with them. However, the assembly could stop free blacks from entering the state.

The Constitution prohibited bank officers, clergymen and duelists from being elected to state or federal offices. The vote for the Constitution was 2,070 for it and 1,953 against it.

Florida's one representative in the U.S. Congress as a territory, David Levy (later David Yulee) proceeded to argue in the Congress for Florida's admission as a slave state. He was finally able to get the statehood bill passed by Congress as a balance, not to Kansas, but to Iowa. On March 3, 1845, President John Tyler signed into law the statehood bill, and Florida entered the Union 24 years after leaving the ownership of Spain.

Political Parties

While a territory, politics did not play an extensive role in Florida. Most offices were appointed by the federal government, thus, not leaving much room for political divisions. Those who had successfully pushed through the Statehood Constitution at the St. Joseph Convention formed the "Jefferson Republic Democratic" party. The other party was the "Whig" party, whose growth was aided by the election of a Whig President of the United States in 1840.

When Florida entered the Union in 1845, the political factions were well established. The Democrats favored strong state's rights and the Whigs were for close federal ties. The Democrats handily won the seat for Congress, electing David Yulee as Florida's first congressman. They also won the governorship with William D. Mosely. Election of a Democrat for Senator was assured by their control of the state legislature. Yulee had agreed to run for Congress on the condition that if the Democrats won the legislature, he would be appointed the first Senator from Florida.

Florida participated in its first presidential election as a state in 1848. The Whigs were the winners in that year, electing Thomas Brown as governor, a Whig congressman, and taking control of the legislature which assured the election of a Whig Senator. The State even cast its three electoral votes for a Whig President, Zachary Taylor.

Toward Civil War

Politics, economics and sociology combined in the decades from 1850 to 1880 to change the political structure of Florida and the nation, for almost 100 years. Sectionalism became more important than nationalism.

Economically, the southern states were in trouble. Most of the economy was based on one cash crop, cotton, and that crop depended on slave labor. When the price of cotton fell, planters had to borrow money, and most often from northern banks. The planters had to borrow to purchase more land because cotton wore the soil out rapidly. New cropland had to be used. The North gained more control of the economics of the South. Cotton was carried in boats from the North and the North's mills processed it into cloth.

Slavery itself was becoming an issue. Northern abolitionists wanted to do away with slave labor. Southern planters needed to expand it and obtain new western lands. In the middle were those who felt that the South could keep slavery, but not expand westward.

Economics and slavery caused people to drift toward political parties which reflected their veiws. The Whig Party almost disappeared in 1852 after losing both the Florida and the national election. State's rightests in the old Whig Party became Democrats. Others drifted to various short lived parties, finally becoming Republicans in 1860.

The Democrats of Florida became more and more involved in the defense of slavery as a political issue. Much of the strong defense was due to the strong attacks by abolitionists in the North against slavery. Governor Edward Perry in 1858 wanted to form a state militia and he favored "...eternal separation from the Union." Perry believed that the North had violated federal law by not returning runaway or fugitive slaves. He believed that if the North was not bound by law, then neither was Florida bound by the statehood law.

In 1859, John Brown's raid on the Federal Arsenal at Harpers Ferry, Virginia sent shock waves through Florida. Brown had intended to start a slave rebellion, and this caused fear in Florida that the same thing could happen there. Slave regulations were strictly enforced, with "night riders" being formed to put down any suspicious slave activity and attack whites suspected of "Yankee" or antislavery beliefs.

Lincoln's Election

All the problems of the nation and the young state of Florida climaxed in the election of Abraham Lincoln as President in 1860. Lincoln did not receive one vote from the citizens of Florida.

The legislature voted to call a People's Convention to vote on secession or withdrawal from the Union. The convention held in Tallahassee on January 7, 1861, voted to secede with only five "no" votes from Walton County. An Ordinance of Secession was prepared and approved 62 to seven. On January 11, the Ordinance was signed at the capital. After almost sixteen years as a state, Florida was independent.

Florida remained an independent state, until it joined the Provisional Government of the Confederate States of America of January 28, 1861. It formally joined the Confederacy on April 22, when the Confederate Constitution was approved.

Governor John Milton was a vigorous state's-righter and encouraged the seizure of federal properties during the early secession days. He served during the entire war, promoting Florida as a food and salt supplier for the south. Political parties as known before the war did not exist. Everyone who spoke up was a Democrat and those who did not support the Confederacy kept quiet. Milton did not have to run for governor in 1864, because a Constitutional change eliminated that election.

Florida Currency

With seccession, Florida needed money to function as a government, to pay soldiers, to pay Confederate war taxes and for general purchases. Gold and silver became very scarce, and the Floridians doubted the worth of Confederate currency, which became worth less and less as the war progressed.

Florida began to produce its own Treasury Notes in 1861 and ceased in 1865. During the war, the notes held their value because of Florida's stable economy and lack of battles. When the war ended, there were about $1,800,000 in notes in circulation, but they had lost their value as the war came to an

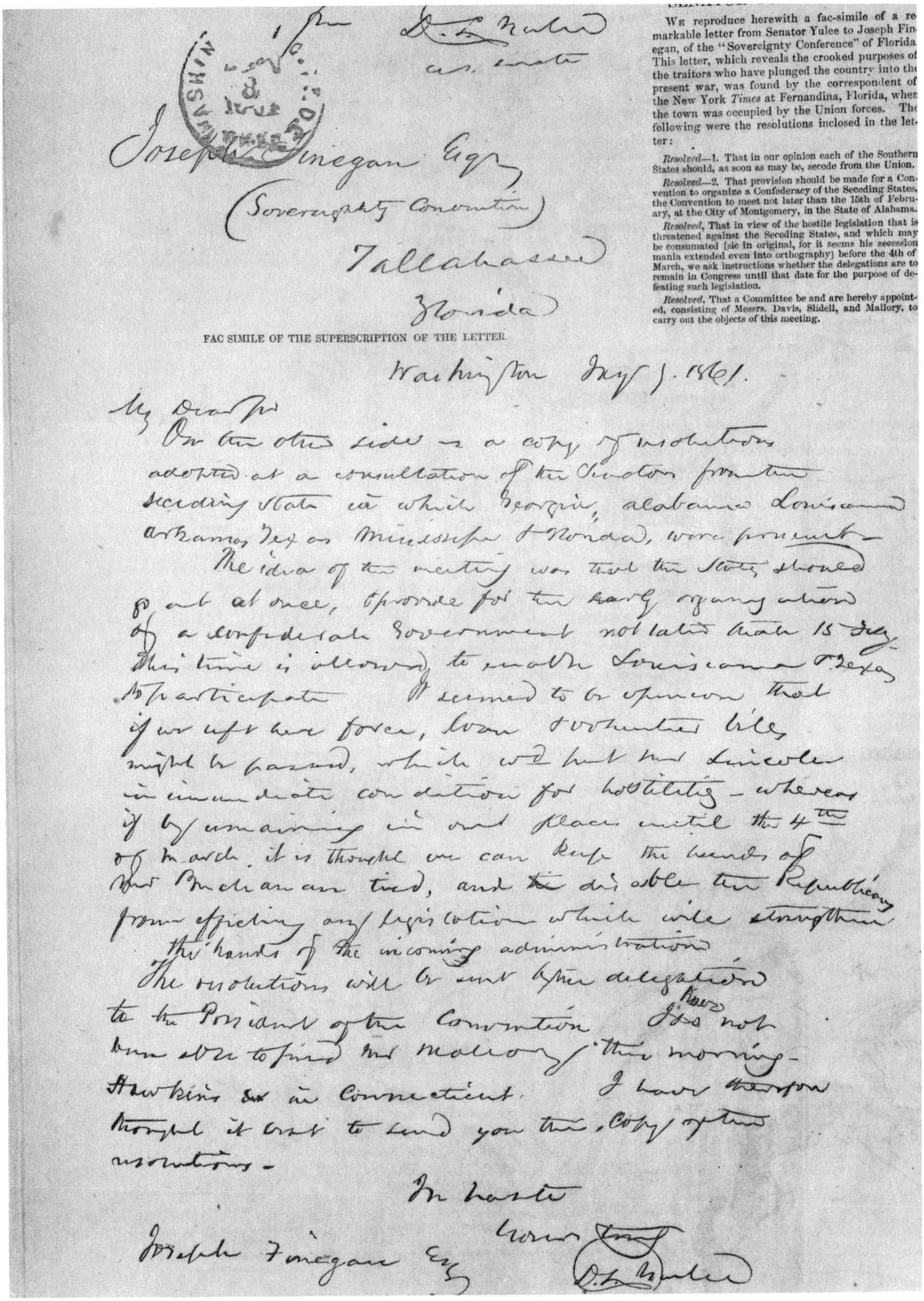

WE reproduce herewith a fac-simile of a remarkable letter from Senator Yulee to Joseph Finegan, of the "Sovereignty Conference" of Florida.
This letter, which reveals the crooked purposes of
the traitors who have plunged the country into the
present war, was found by the correspondent of
the New York *Times* at Fernandina, Florida, when
the town was occupied by the Union forces. The
following were the resolutions inclosed in the letter:

Resolved—1. That in our opinion each of the Southern
States should, as soon as may be, secede from the Union.

Resolved—2. That provision should be made for a Convention to organize a Confederacy of the Seceding States,
the Convention to meet not later than the 15th of February, at the City of Montgomery, in the State of Alabama.

Resolved, That in view of the hostile legislation that is
threatened against the Seceding States, and which may
be consummated [sic in original, for it seems his secession
mania extended even into orthography] before the 4th of
March, we ask instructions whether the delegations are to
remain in Congress until that date for the purpose of defeating such legislation.

Resolved, That a Committee be and are hereby appointed, consisting of Messrs. Davis, Slidell, and Mallory, to
carry out the objects of this meeting.

Joseph Finegan Esq.

(Sovereignty Convention)

Tallahassee

Florida

FAC SIMILE OF THE SUPERSCRIPTION OF THE LETTER.

Washington Jany 3. 1861.

My Dear Sir

On the other side is a copy of resolutions adopted at a consultation of the Senators from the seceding States in which Georgia, Alabama Louisiana Arkansas Texas Mississippi & Florida, were present—

The idea of the meeting was that the States should go out at once, & provide for the early organization of a Confederate Government not later than 15 Feby. This time is allowed to enable Louisiana & Texas to participate. It seemed to be opinion that if we left here force, loan & volunteer bills, might be passed, which would put Mr Lincoln in immediate condition for hostility — whereas if by remaining in our places until the 4th of March. it is thought we can keep the hands off Mr Buchanan tied, and to disable the Republicans from effecting any legislation which will strengthen the hands of the incoming administration

The resolutions will be sent by the delegations to the President of the Convention. It has not been able to find Mr Mallory this morning. Hawkins is in Connecticut. I have therefore thought it best to send you this copy of the resolutions —

In haste

Yours truly

D. L. Yulee

Joseph Finegan Esq

Senator Yulee's letter. Notice the opinion of the Northern press.

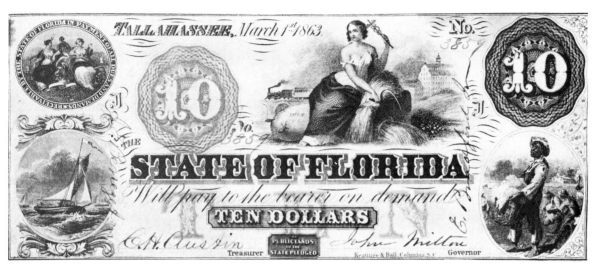

Florida Photographic Archives

Florida Civil War currency

Florida Photographic Archives

Florida Civil War currency

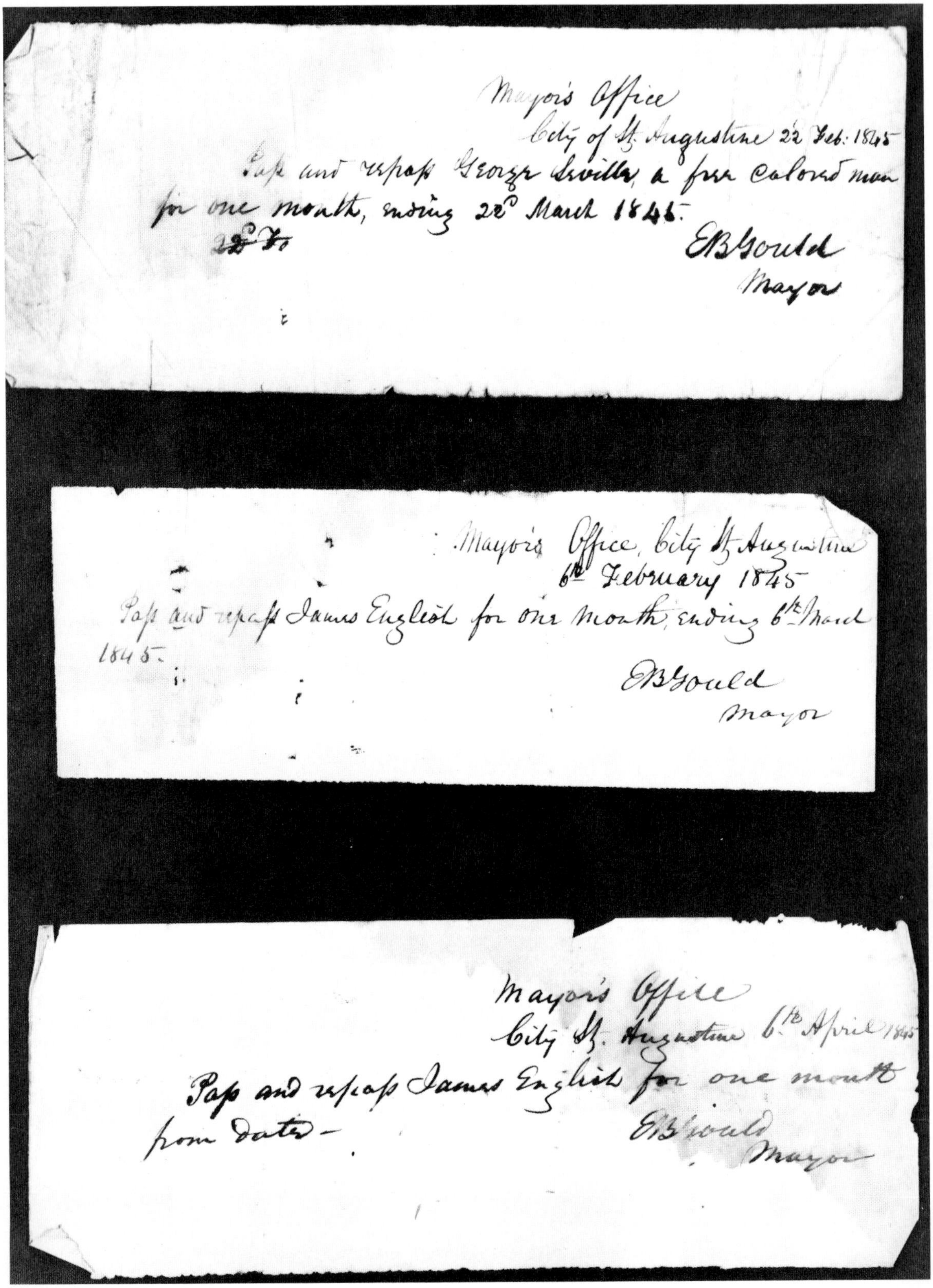
Mayor's Office
City of St. Augustine 22 Feb. 1845
Pass and repass George Sevilla, a free colored man for one month, ending 22d March 1845.
~~22d Do~~
E B Gould
Mayor

Mayor's Office, City St. Augustine
6th February 1845
Pass and repass James English for one month, ending 6th March 1845.
E B Gould
Mayor

Mayor's Office
City St. Augustine 6th April 1845
Pass and repass James English for one month from date —
E B Gould
Mayor

Florida Photographic Archives

Freedman passes

JONATHAN C. GIBBS (1826-1874)

Jonathan Gibbs was one of the first black members of the Florida Cabinet, serving as Secretary of State for four years (1865-1873) and as Superintendent of Schools from 1873 to his sudden death at age 48 in 1874.

Mr. Gibbs was born in Philadelphia, Pennsylvania to free black parents. His father was a Methodist minister who died while Jonathan was very young. As a boy, he was apprenticed to a carpenter and learned that trade. With the support of the Presbyterian Church, Gibbs attended Dartmouth College in New Hampshire and Princeton University in New Jersey. As a Presbyterian minister, Rev. Gibbs served a church in Philadelphia, and then opened a school in North Carolina.

After the Civil War, he came to Florida where he helped to write the new Constitution of 1868. He was appointed Secretary of State, and then, Governor Ossian B. Hart appointed him Superintendent of Schools. Rev. Gibbs improved education by requiring the development of school courses of study and buying better textbooks. He worked for better teacher education. His efforts were recognized by the National Education Association when he gave a speech on "Education in the South" before their convention in 1873.

Unfortunately, Rev. Gibbs died suddenly in 1874, just as his educational improvements were beginning to make their mark.

---

end. The Constitution of 1868 declared the notes null and void.

Reconstruction

Florida was to see its political life change with the end of the Civil War. Change actually began with the Emancipation Proclamation by President Lincoln. This proclamation freed all slaves in those states in rebellion against the Union. This proclamation was to be made the law of the land with the enactment of the 13th Amendment to the Constitution which abolished slavery throughout the nation.

Florida entered the period after the Civil War with most of the control of government to be led by federal laws. Florida was under a military governor from April 1, 1865, until July 4, 1868. Colonel John Sprague possessed more power than the elected governor, David Walker. Sprague said he served as "military commander, civil governor, judge, jury, and doctor and lawyer."

Lincoln's Plan

President Lincoln proposed that the former Confederate states not be punished. His plan for the states to reenter the Union was called the ten percent plan. If only ten percent of a state's registered voters in 1860 would take an oath of allegiance to the Union, the state would be restored to full status. The only other major condition was the writing of a new state constitution. The Constitution had to recognize the 13th Amendment, repeal the Ordinance of Secession and repudiate war debts. This nonpunishment plan never had a chance to be put into effect because of the assassination of President Lincoln.

Andrew Johnson

Vice president Johnson assumed the presidency after Lincoln's assassination. His reconstruction plan was modeled after Lincoln's, but he was not able to overcome opposition by radical Republicans in the U.S. Congress who wanted to punish the South.

Johnson did appoint a provisional governor for Florida, William Marvin, of Key West. Marvin was able to get a Constitutional Convention to agree to the requirements of the Lincoln/Johnson Reconstruction plan. There was much debate over the idea of giving equal rights to blacks.

Black Codes

The State Legislature set out to define the status of the freed blacks. Social custom did not allow the planter class legislators to give equality to the blacks even though they accepted the 13th Amendment.

Laws for the blacks, called Black Codes, were passed to control the former slaves. The Codes were a reaction of fear as to what the freed blacks might do against their former masters. They were a reaction to the widespread wanderings of the freed blacks. Blacks before the war had not moved about freely, but now they were on the roads enjoying their new found freedom. This was a shock to the whites.

Legal restrictions on the blacks under Black Codes included the following items:

1. Vagrancy and loitering laws with whippings or jail for being unemployed.

2. Death penalty for rape of a white woman. (There was no punishment for rape of a black women.)

3. Restrictions on the use of firearms.

4. Sunset Laws which required blacks to be off the streets before sunset.

5. Contract labor laws which required blacks to continue working for the person with no provision to leave their employment.

The sharecropping system also restricted the blacks. Under this labor arrangement, a black would work a landowner's farm in return for a third of the harvest. The owner provided seed and tools since the blacks had no money. If there was a bad crop, the blacks could not pay for the seeds and equipment. Over a period of time they got deeper in debt and the law did not allow them to leave the land if they owed anything. It must be stated, though, that similar systems existed in the North for laborers. This was especially true in coal mines where the miners were paid in company money or scrip, which could only be spent in company stores. Miners went into debt to their employers. White property owners in the South were somewhat justified in their anger over Northerners saying how bad the South was, when the Northern businessmen were practicing the same idea.

Violence and Reaction

Many whites, upset by the new status and attitude of the freed blacks, reacted with violence. Blacks were beaten and whipped for exercising their new found rights. Florida and other states elected ex-Confederate leaders to the U.S. Congress. This, along with the Black Codes and violence, caused Congress to react.

President Johnson's plans were completely discarded, and he was impeached, but not convicted by only one vote. Congress was now free to punish the rebellious states. In 1867, military rule was established in Florida, and a new Constitutional Convention was called. Congess required that states allow blacks to register and vote for delegates.

The Convention occurred at the same time Congress was passing the 14th Amendment to the Constitution. This gave citizenship to blacks and barred former Confederate officials from holding high state and federal offices. This amendment had to be approved by a state seeking readmission to the Union.

The Constitutional Convention give blacks the right to vote in elections and established tax-supported schools. This Constitution of 1868 was approved by the citizens of Florida, and Florida was readmitted to the Union on July 25, 1868. A Republican Governor, Harrison Reed, along with a Republican Legislature was elected at the time of the Constitutional approval.

Secret Societies

The federal troops were supposed to protect the newly acquired rights of blacks, but many times were helpless against secret organizations. The Order of the White Camellia and the Ku Klux Klan were organized to stop blacks from voting.

Blacks were beaten, lynched and terrorized for attempting to vote. It made no difference that the 15th Amendment to the national Constitution made it illegal to deny male blacks the right to vote. They were effectively stopped, if not by threat, by death. Since the government protected the blacks, the secret societies took the law into their own hands. They were not elected, but in some areas they were in power. Blacks were at first ordered not to vote, or to vote Democratic. Later, they were simply ordered not to vote.

Republican Era

Many accounts of the Reconstruction Period have tried to prove that the government following the war was totally bad. This was not completely true. The Constitution written in 1868 was one of the

Florida Photographic Archives

Senator David Levy Yulee

best in the United States at that time. It had universal male suffrage, meaning that all men could vote, including Indians and blacks. It provided for circuit courts, public education and homesteading on public lands. All state and county officers were appointed by the governor to prevent one group from taking over a county.

Republicans were called by various names depending on their background. Carpetbaggers were Northerners who had come south to take advantage of the unrest and make money. Scalawags were Southerners who allied themselves with the Republicans.

When the first legislature met in 1868, its members consisted of 13 carpetbaggers, 21 scalawags and 19 blacks on the Republican side. There were 23 Democrats making up the minority. The Governor was Harrison Reed who was called a carpetbagger, but he had lived in Florida for several years. He filled many offices with "old lines" southern planters. No blacks were in the first cabinet, but he did appoint several to county offices. The Lieutenant-Governor was William Gleason of Dade County.

Reed had enemies on all sides. He had been a Freedman's Bureau agent which aided blacks in their new citizenship, this caused the cotton planters to dislike him. He tried to run the government for the benefit of all, so the radical Republicans wanted him out of office. Gleason tried to impeach Reed in 1868 and declared himself Governor. The Supreme Court disagreed with Gleason and declared Reed was still Governor. Gleason and Reed then helped impeach the Secretary of State for stealing the State Seal. Then, Reed had Gleason thrown out as Lieutenant-Governor, because he had not lived in Florida the required three years, even though he owned land on Biscayne Bay.

Reed appointed Jonathan C. Gibbs to replace the impeached Secretary of State. Gibbs had helped write the Constitution of 1868, and then served in the Cabinet for four years as the Secretary of State. He then was appointed Superintendent of Schools. Gibbs was a problem for many southern whites. He was educated, a minister, performed well in office, and a black.

Another black in the first government after 1868 was Josiah T. Wells, who served in the

145

**Secretary of State
Jonathan C. Gibbs**

Legislature and then was elected to the United States Congress. Wells, like Gibbs, saw the necessity of education for Florida to advance.

Republicans began to lose their control in 1872. Although Ossian Hart was elected Governor, it was by a slim margin over the Democrat candidate. Times were changing. Republican rule in the South and Florida had depended on strong support from the radical Republicans in the North. Some of the old line radicals had left office or died, and the Republicans in the North were losing interest in the South.

Election of 1876

The election of 1876 was probably one of the most dishonest national and state elections to be held. Republicans voted blacks over and over by taking them from poll to poll. Democrats tried to stop blacks from getting to the polls and often were successful. On both sides, ballots were stuffed.

Florida citizens elected Democrats to state offices including Governor George Drew. More important to Florida and the South was the closeness of the election for the President of the United States. The vote for President in Florida was so close that no one could tell who had won. There were two sets of ballots existing, one showing the Republican, Hayes, as victor and the other showing the Democrat, Samuel Tilden, as winner.

An election commission was appointed to decide the winner in the state. One Democrat and two Republicans were to decide the correct ballots. William Cook, the Democrat, voted for Tilden; C.A. Cowgill, the black Republican, voted for Hayes. The election was up to Secretary of State Samuel B. McLin. Hayes and Tilden both promised many things to get Florida's four votes. Finally, Hayes promised that federal troops would be pulled out of the South if he won. McLin voted for Hayes. The ballots were challenged, but the U.S. Supreme Court said Florida's ballots had to be counted for Hayes.

McLin, later, disappointed because he personally did not receive much from Hayes, said he had lied and that Tilden had actually won. It was too late. The South was now in the hands of Southern politicians.

Bourbon Rule

The period of blacks in politics ended for a period of time with the election of 1876. Many former Whigs, who thought the whites had to ban together to keep blacks from voting, joined the Democrat Party. The bourbons, or Democrats who favored industry over the blacks, began their rule under Governor Drew. A serious effort to attract businesses was started. Other southern states would continue trying to exist on agriculture while Florida sought to widen its economic base. Governor Drew reduced state taxes to make Florida more appealing to immigrants and investors. During his term, salaries for state officials were reduced to lessen the state debt.

Governor Bloxham was still confronted with a large state debt when he took office in 1880. The state had borrowed money during the Civil War to aid railroads in the state. Public land had been used as security for the money. When the railroads went bankrupt, Bloxham ordered their land foreclosed to help pay the debts. More money was needed, and Bloxham made a deal with Hamilton Disston to sell him 1.6 million hectares/four million acres of land for $1,000,000. The money paid off the debt, butDisston owned a large tract of what was to be very valuable land in Florida.

Constitution of 1885

The Democrats were able to hold control of the state and federal offices in the 1884 elections, but they received a scare from within their own party. A liberal Democrat, Frank Pope, was supported by Republicans against the Democrat candidate, Edward Perry. Perry won because the Republicans were unable to form a strong coalition with black votes. White supremacy won but was badly shaken.

Fear of losing public office and dislike of the "Republican Constitution" of 1868 led the Democrats to write a new Constitution. The Constitution of 1885 created a one term governor, eliminated the office of Lieutenant-Governor, created a six member Cabinet and made county offices elective except for the County Commissioners. There was a provision for county tax-supported schools and for the creation of a state medical board. Almost everything was progressive in the new constitution except for the provision allowing a poll tax.

The poll tax was legislated in 1889 and effectively eliminated blacks from voting. A fee was charged before you could register to vote and a receipt was given. The tax eliminated blacks because many times they did not have the $2.00 to pay the tax, or if they did pay it, they were not given a receipt. If a black did pay the tax, got a receipt and tried to vote, the poll workers would challenge the receipt as being invalid. Poor whites who joined the Democrat Party were never asked to show their receipts and most never paid the tax. They just voted.

A One-Party State

The poll tax eliminated what political base the Republicans had, and they did not even field candidates in the 1892 elections. "Primary" elections began being held. These primaries only allowed Democrats to vote and nominate candidates. When the general election came, the election was over because there was no opposition. The peculiar thing was that the primary was an attempt to restrict voting, but over the years became a democratic process for citizen control of the restricted party conventions.

Return to the Two-Party System

One-party politics remained dominant in Florida and throughout the South for many years. Florida was the first state to break the mold. Blacks in the 1930's and '40's switched allegiance from the Republicans to the New Deal Democrats. President Franklin Delano Roosevelt openly courted black votes in his

Replica of Florida's first capitol, built in 1942 for Florida's Centennial

Florida's second capitol as drawn by Francis de Castelnau in 1838

Earliest known photograph of Florida's capitol. Sometime between 1845 and 1891

Capitol in 1902, shortly after addition of dome and North and South wings

Florida Photographic Archives

Capitol in 1951

Florida Photographic Archives

Capitol Complex in 1965

Florida's new capitol and surrounding state office buildings

defeat of the Republicans four times in a row. The Florida Legislature removed the poll tax in 1937, four years before the United States Supreme Court declared it unconstitutional. Florida Republicans began to seriously run for state offices once again. Many local offices became Republican with Dwight D. Eisenhower's victory in the Presidential election. Florida voted Republican in 1956 when Eisenhower won his second term and for Richard M. Nixon when he was defeated by Democrat John Kennedy in 1960.

The Florida Democrat Party wanted to disassociate itself from the national elections. They voted to hold elections for

Governor and Cabinet during off Presidential election years. A Constitutional Amendment achieved this after the 1964 election.

Governor Claude R. Kirk, Jr. became the first Governor elected after the change to the off year election. In 1966, he became the first Republican elected Governor of Florida since 1872. He ended 94 years of Democrat dominance. Proof of the two-party system came four years later, when a Democrat became Governor again. In 1980, Florida voted for Republican President Ronald Reagan and sent Republican Paula Hawkins to the U.S. Senate.

Florida's blacks resorted to demonstrations in the 1960's to protest discrimination and the government's failure to do anything about it. Demonstrations in Tallahassee and Daytona were defended by Governor Farris Bryant as a right of the citizens of Florida, but he declared he would not tolerate violence or destruction of property.

In 1964, Martin Luther King, Jr. was jailed for charges relating to attempts to desegregate public facilities in St. Augustine. King called off the protest when an interracial council was appointed to work out the problems. Governments in Florida, resisted federal attempts to end segregation during the 1960's, but Florida did make significant changes with less violence than other southern states. Blacks fully reentered the political arena with the Voting and Civil Rights Acts of the 1960's.

Constitutional Change

During Governor Kirk's term, the 1885 Constitution was revised. The executive branch was strengthened, and the office of Lieutenant-Governor was re-established. The Cabinet was officially stated in the revision of 1968. The Cabinet includes the Secretary of State, Attorney General, Comptroller, Treasurer, Commissioner of Agriculture and Commissioner of Education.

Florida's Government Today

Floridians today are citizens of cities, counties, Florida and the United States. They are affected by all and effect all if they choose to do so. The bases for government in Florida today is the State Constitution of 1885 as amended in 1968. The state government is divided into three branches: the executive, the judical and the legislative.

Executive Branch

The executive branch of government in Florida consists of: the Governor, Lieutenant-Governor, Cabinet and various departments. The Governor is the "supreme executive," but some power is shared with the Cabinet. Powers exclusively under the Governor are as follows:

1. enforcement of laws
2. be commander-in-chief of all military forces of the state not in active U.S. service
3. initiate judicial proceedings against state, county or municipal officers
4. give a state of the state message to the Legislature
5. appoint persons to vacancies in elected offices
6. appoint persons to head executive departments, commissions and boards in state, county and municipal governments
7. suspend public officials
8. remove public officials

The heads of agencies appointed by the Governor are considered to be in the "Little Cabinet." These include: The Senior Executive Assistant, Transportation, Business Regulation, Health and Rehabilitative Services, Pollution Control, Professional and Occupational Regulation, Community Affairs and Citrus.

The Governor of Florida at the time of election must be at least 30 years of age and have been a resident of Florida for seven years. The Governor must swear to uphold the Constitution of Florida and the United States. The elected Governor cannot be a

Governor's Mansion

convicted felon nor judged to be mentally incompetent.

Governors of Florida serve four year terms and can serve a consecutive term. A Governor can be removed from office by the Legislature if two-thirds of the House votes for impeachment and two-thirds of the Senators present vote for conviction. Four members of the Cabinet may request in writing for the Supreme Court to declare the Governor mentally or physically incapable of performing governmental duties.

Impeachment proceedings can also be brought against the Lieutenant-Governor, members of the Cabinet, the Supreme Court and lower courts.

Lieutenant-Governor

The Lieutenant-Governor of Florida is first in line of succession to the office of Governor.

Qualifications for being Lieutenant-Governor are the same as Governor. Only one vote is cast for Lieutenant-Governor and Governor, and they must run as a team.

Following the Lieutenant-Governor in succession of office are the Secretary of State, the Attorney General, Comptroller, Treasurer, Commissioner of Education and Commissioner of Agriculture.

The Cabinet

All members of the Cabinet have the same terms and qualifications. They must be 30 years of age, and they serve four year elected terms.

Secretary of State.

This office is in charge of the Department of State and as such is over all elections in Florida. The Secretary of State certifies eligible candidates for state and federal offices.

There are numerous other functions of the office including publishing rules and regulations of state agencies, issuing charters to instate corporations and certificates of authority to operate in Florida for out of state corporations. All documents of the legislative and executive branches are kept by the Secretary of State's office. Notary publics are commissioned by the Secretary of State's office.

The Secretary of State licenses employment agencies, private detectives, security officers and all organizations soliciting funds. Library Services, Archives and History, and the Division of Cultural Affairs are under this office.

Attorney General

The Attorney General is the chief legal officer of Florida. Powers of the Attorney General come from common law, the State Constitution and laws of the Legislature. Common Law of England as of July 4, 1776 is still in effect in Florida, except where it has been superceded by the Florida or United States Consitutions.

The Attorney General appears in behalf of the state in the District Courts and the Supreme Courts. Opinions are also given on questions of law, which are binding until reserved by a court.

Comptroller

The Comptroller is the chief fiscal officer of the state. This office is the "watchdog of the public treasury" in that it approves and settles accounts. The Comptroller's office will write five million checks a year and keep Florida operating financially.

Banks and financial operations in the state are controlled by the Comptroller as head of the Department of Banking and Finance.

Insurance Commissioner and Treasurer

When the office of Treasurer was reorganized in 1969, the title of Insurance Commissioner was added. Now the treasurer keeps all state monies and regulates all insurance operations in the state. As Insurance Commissioner, he/she is also State Fire Marshall and in charge of investigating fire and arson. The State Fire College at Ocala is part of this office.

Commissioner of Agriculture

In 1969 this department was renamed the Department of Agriculture and Consumer Services. The department has numerous responsibilities including these: making sure labels and ingredients match; inspecting accuracy of fuel pumps; analyzing feeds, seeds, fertilizers and pesticides to see they are not harmful; control of animal and plant diseases; reforestation and conservation.

Commissioner of Education

The revised Constitution of 1868 changed the Superintendent of Public Instruction to Commissioner of Education. The Commissioner supervises Florida's entire system of public education, from kindergarten through graduate school. There are five divisions: Public Schools, Vocational Education, Community Colleges, University, and Blind Services.

This department at one time was just a record keeping agency. Today, it is the leadership of education in Florida.

Judicial Branch

There are four divisions of courts in Florida. In 1972 the courts were reorganized, eliminating municipal courts. The divisions are The Supreme Court, District Courts of Appeal, Circuit Courts and County Courts. The first two are appellate courts and the latter are trial courts. The appellate or appeals courts hear cases that have already been tried.

Supreme Court

There are seven Justices on this court, elected for six year terms. They each must be a qualified voter, live in Florida and have been a lawyer for 10 years. The Chief Justice is elected by a majority vote of the Justices and rotated every two years. The Supreme Court meets in Tallahassee.

GOVERNMENT

This court under the Constitution hears appeals on death penalties, rulings on state laws, and state debts. It may also review any decisions of the District Courts. The Supreme Court administers and disciplines all the other Florida courts and justices.

District Courts of Appeal

District Appeal Justices meet the same in all requirements as the Supreme Court Justices, there are five district courts with 41 judges, seven in each district. They hear appeals in groups of three judges. The districts are as follows: 1st District - Tallahassee, 2nd District - Lakeland, 3rd District - Miami, 4th District - West Palm Beach, 5th District - Daytona Beach.

These courts hear almost all appealed cases, because the Supreme Court can refuse to hear an appeal.

Circuit Courts

There were 20 Circuit Courts in Florida in 1981, with 309 judges. The number of judges in each circuit varies with the population and caseload. The judges serve six year terms but should have practiced law for five years, before serving a term.

Cases in these courts are of general jurisdiction and usually are jury trials. Types of cases include: civil disputes over $1500, juveniles, criminal prosecution of felonies, tax disputes, titles of property, and injunctions against unlawful acts.

County Courts

The average citizen in Florida rarely comes in contact with any court except the County Court. These courts are referred to as "people's court" because they deal with traffic offenses, disputes less than $1500, and less serious law violations or misdemeanors. There is a County Court in each county and in 1981 there were 198 judges.

Florida Department of Commerce & Tourism

Supreme Court Building

Requirements for County judges changed in 1978. Before then it was not necessary to be a lawyer, if the county had a population of less than 40,000. Any new judge now must be a lawyer. The judge must be a resident and voter in the county served.

Legislative Branch

This branch of government makes the laws of the State of Florida. It is bicameral or has two Houses, the House of Representatives and The Senate. Representatives serve two years and Senators serve four. Legislators must be 21 years of age and residents of the district they serve.

Each House of the Legislature has its own officers. The presiding officer of the Senate is called the President of the Senate and the Speaker presides over the House of Representatives.

Committees are organized in each House in order to filter out unnecessary or frivolous bills. This saves time in floor debate and keeps a legislator from having to know the content of every bill introduced. The important committees of the Senate are as follows: The Rules, Judiciary, Ways and Means, Transportation, Education, and Health and Welfare. Major House of Representative Committees include: Rules, Appropriations, Finance and Taxation, Elections, Health and Welfare, and Education. Each of the Houses is equal to the other and any legislation may be introduced in either House.

Both Houses have leaders based on political power. These are appointed positions and reflect which party is the majority party. The Majority Leader and Minority Leaders try to push legislation which their party favors. The Senate and the House elect non-members as record keepers. All members of the House or Senate must file their bills with either the Clerk of the House of Representatives or the Secretary of the Senate. These record keepers publish daily "calendars" of proceedings and "journals" of floor actions.

The Legislature meets annually since 1972, and the second Tuesday after a regular general election. Special sessions can be called by the Legislature under the joint authority of the Speaker and President.

Florida Department of Commerce & Tourism

House of Representatives

Local Governments

Floridians lives are directly affected by local governments. There are several which affect the daily lives of the State's citizens, including: City, County, Metropolitan, Consolidated, or Special District. Each of these is organized under a "charter." That means the Legislature has given them authority to govern.

Cities

There are three types of city governments: the Mayor/Councilperson, Commissioner, and Council/Manager. The Mayor/Council-person government consists of elected officers running on a city wide or district basis. The Mayor is the executive branch and the Council is the legislative branch. There are appointed positions in the city: police chief, fire chief and recreation head. This is the most common city government in Florida.

The second most popular form of city government is the Commissioner type. This is a Council of Commissioners who are the only elected officials, which exercise both executive and legislative functions.

In the Council/Manager type of government, the Council holds both executive and legislative powers, but hires a City Manager to run the city.

Metropolitan

This is a loosely knit organization of cities and communities to provide services to the area. They are concerned with growth and the zoning of land. Miami, North Miami Beach, Coral Gables and other communites are organized like this, but they still maintain their own services apart from the others.

Consolidated

Consolidated government allows cities and a county to join together to avoid duplication of expenses and services. This form has only achieved success on a large scale in the Jacksonville-Duval County consolidation.

Florida Department of Commerce & Tourism

Senate Chamber

The government is a Mayor/Council government overseeing one fire department, one law enforcement agency and other services. A few Atlantic Beach communities have not joined the consolidated government.

Special Districts

Special Districts are legislated authority areas dealing with one or more services to people living in a district. This could be water control or any local interest area.

The most widespread Special Districts are school districts. In Florida, school districts are the same as counties in area and borders. Each district has a School Board which governs the district. The board handles executive and legislative functions, but has a superintendent to administer the district. All board members are elected and are responsible for the school budget, property tax rates for school support and administering the curriculum.

Counties

County government in Florida have many members who are elected. The County Commission handles most of the administration in a county. There are five to seven commissioners for each county. The Board of Commissioners is the legislative body in the county. Elected officials such as: Sheriff, Tax Collector, Property Appraiser, the Supervisor of Elections and the Clerk of the Circuit Court are independent of the County Commission.

Federal Government

The Federal Government has representation in Florida. In 1981, this included: two Senators elected for six year terms, and 15 Congressmen elected for two year terms. The number of Congressmen will increase due to the increase in Florida's population in the 1980 census. Florida's Claude Pepper has had 14 years service in the U.S. Senate through 1980 and has been elected to the House of Representatives since 1962.

The Story of Florida House

Travel is a part of the northern Floridian lifestyle. When traveling to Washington, D.C. Floridians can visit their very own house - Florida House. Florida House is the first "State House" in the nation's capital. It was established in 1973 to be a home away from home for visiting Floridians. At Florida House, Floridians can relax, get information about touring the capital and have a glass of real Florida orange juice!

Florida House is a three story brick building just one block away from the grounds of the Capitol. It is a good example of historic preservation. Before it was purchased for use as Florida House, it was a rundown apartment building. It has been completely restored and decorated in the style of the late 1800's. The furnishings have all been donated or paid for by Floridians.

The idea for Florida House came from Senator and Mrs. Lawton Chiles. Florida House is very popular. Thousands of visiting Floridians use it each year. Florida House has been so successful that several other states are thinking of following Florida's example.

How a Bill Becomes A Law in Florida

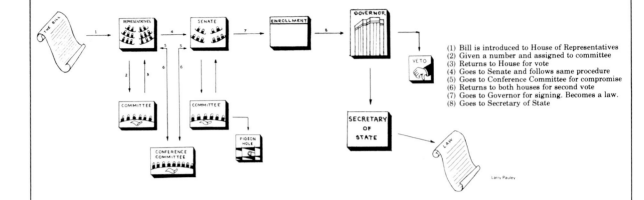

(1) Bill is introduced to House of Representatives
(2) Given a number and assigned to committee
(3) Returns to House for vote
(4) Goes to Senate and follows same procedure
(5) Goes to Conference Committee for compromise
(6) Returns to both houses for second vote
(7) Goes to Governor for signing. Becomes a law.
(8) Goes to Secretary of State

Larry Pauley

Lawmaking in Florida is the responsibility of the State Legislature. This body is comprised of two houses, the House of Representatives and the Senate. Members of the House are elected every two years while Senators are elected every four years. The House has 120 members and the Senate has 40.

The Legislature meets every year to consider the proposed budget and needed changes in laws of the state. Many of the ideas that the legislators propose are from the citizens of the area which they represent.

Suppose you have an idea for making a law to eliminate the tax on gasoline. How do you, as a citizen, get this change into effect? Your first step is to go to your Representative or State Senator and propose it to him/her. If he/she thinks it's beneficial to the state, she/he begins the process of lawmaking.

Introducing The Bill*
Your Representative has the legislative staff write the proposal into legal language. It is now a bill! The Representative then introduces it into the House of Representatives. After the bill is introduced, the Speaker of the House refers it to a committee.

Committees
The two houses are divided into committees which study bills. There are so many bills introduced each year that all of them could not be discussed by the entire legislature while in session. Also, many bills are too unimportant to take up the time of all the members.

When the bill is assigned to a committee, it is discussed and the committee takes one of these actions: (1) approves it, (2) rejects it, or (3) changes it and then approves it. After taking action on the bill, the committee decides whether or not to "report it out of committee." This has to be done before the whole house votes on it. The committee will report a bill out with either a recommendation to approve the bill, defeat of the bill, or no recommendation at all. The committee can decide not to report your bill out and this effectively "kills it" or "pigeonholes" the bill.

Voting
After being reported to the house, the whole house discusses the bill and changes it, if the Representatives want to do so. Then they vote on it. If approved, it is still not a law because the Senate now must act upon it.

After the introduction of the bill, the Senate President refers it to a committee. The bill then follows the same procedure in the Senate as it did in the House of Representatives. If the Senate passes it with some differences from the House bill, it is then sent to a conference committee.

Conference Committee
The conference committee is composed of members of both the House and Senate. Their purpose is to **compromise** the differences in the bills which the two houses have passed. When this is done, the compromised bill is sent back to both houses for approval. This bill is still not a law because now it is sent to the Governor.

Governor
The governor now has the bill and can sign it, allow it to become a law without his/her signature, or veto it. If he approves it, we have a new law. If he vetoes the bill, it goes back to the legislature. The legislature can make it a law, but only if two-thirds of the House of Representatives and Senate vote to override the veto. If the veto is not overridden, no one in Florida would have to pay the tax on gasoline. The law is placed in the state code by the Secretary of State. Once the bill becomes a law, it is then the duty of the Governor to enforce it.

This procedure may seem lengthy and complicated, but making a law is a serious act and must not be done hastily. There remains one more safeguard within the state concerning lawmaking, and that is, of course, the State Supreme Court. If another citizen feels the new law is contrary to the Constitution of Florida, he/she may take it to court where the Supreme Court decides the point. However, the Court cannot decide on a law's legality until a citizen decides to go to court.

*The bill may be introduced into either house, but we will follow the bill as if it were entered into the House of Representatives. The procedure remains the same if the bill is entered into the Senate.

There are Federal judges with jurisdiction in Florida. They are appointed by the President of the United States and usually follow the political beliefs of the President who appointed them. These Federal Judges are appointed for life. Florida is included in the Fifth Federal Circuit Court. This Court includes the states of Florida, Georgia, Alabama, Mississippi, Louisiana and Texas.

In 1981 Florida was divided into three Federal Court Districts: Northern with three judges, Middle with nine judges, and the Southern with 12 judges.

The government and formation of Florida has been unique in American History.

Shaped by its people, history, geography and culture, it serves all the people within the state. The Spanish would have difficulty recognizing their discovery now as powers and offices have changed hands. We do not know what the future holds for our state government.

> *Perhaps a changed county government... consolidated counties... a year-round legislature... a new court system... or some other strengthening of our democratic system.*

Whatever it is, Floridians will shape the government as times change.

GOVERNMENT

Industry

Florida Department of Commerce & Tourism

Orange Production

INDUSTRY

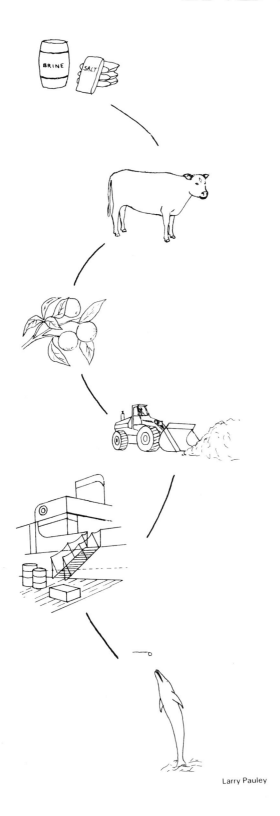

Larry Pauley

Introduction

Everywhere you look in Florida there is evidence of a growing state. Citrus groves, processing plants, phosphate mining, paper plants, fishing, printing, electronics, space related production, house construction, cattle, tourism and many more industries are located within the borders of the state.

Florida was the seventh largest state in population in 1980 and projections indicate that by 1990 will have increased to fourth. The state is located in the Southeast area of the "sunbelt," one of the fastest growing regions in the United States. In 1980 Central Florida was within 804.5 kilometers/ 500 miles of one-fourth of the population of the United States.

Florida is well suited for industrial growth. The state has a large skilled work force, a variety of transportation facilities, excellent climate and a good location. Foreign and domestic markets are easily accessible from the state. South America, which lies entirely to the east of Florida, is closer to the state than any other state in the Union.

Indians

Industry has not always been large manufacturers or hectares/ acres of groves producing goods for consumption by other people. The word manufacture comes from Latin meaning, "to make by hand." Before the Europeans entered present day Florida, the native Americans were manufacturing many items. Clothing, dugouts, tools, pottery, hunting weapons and other items were handmade to help in the daily struggle for survival. Most items were made from the resources found close by, but some importing of goods did occur. The Indians used timber, animal hides, seashells, clay, flint, animal bones and even extracted salt from sea water.

Early Settlers

When the Europeans arrived in Florida in 1513, they were more advanced in manufacturing and agriculture than were the Indians of the peninsula. They did not, however, proceed to industrialize the area immediately, but two of their imports, oranges and cattle, served as a basis for those industries.

Agriculture was to be the basis of Florida's economy until after the American Civil War. The most important crops were to be cotton and indigo. There was some construction, but it was not a major part of the economy. Two types of labor existed in Florida, slave and individual. Slave labor was based on work being done by an owned class of people without wages. Individual labor was mostly on small farms where the owner and family did all the labor themselves.

At the start of the Civil War, industry in Florida consisted of cotton, oranges, sweet potatoes, corn, sugar cane, cattle, lumber and turpentine. There were two small iron foundries, a shoe factory, a cloth mill, a wool carding factory and a tannery. A few salt evaporators, grist mills and sugar mills were scattered around the territory. Almost 50 percent of the population was black slaves. This was all to change rapidly.

Salt

The salt industry played a brief but important role in Florida's early history. Early Indians obtained salt by simple evaporation. Sea water or brackish water was placed in jars and allowed to evaporate leaving a residue of salt. The Spanish and English had imported it from Europe and only used Florida salt when supplies were late.

During the territorial period Americans still imported the majority of salt from England. Then with the coming of the Civil War and the Northern blockade of Southern ports, salt production became imperative. Confederate troops needed it as a food preservative and their animals required it in their diet. Florida began to supply it from the Tampa Bay area.

Seawater was boiled in large kettles, the residue was spread on planks to dry and then packed to ship. The salt industry gave rise to other industries. Wood had to be cut into staves and coopers made barrels to ship the salt. Wagon masters arrived to haul the important mineral to the railroads for further shipment.

Within one year the price of salt rose from three dollars for 30.2 liters/ bushel to $20.00. Saltworkers were exempted from being drafted by the Confederate Army and many men flocked to the area. The importance of Florida's saltmaking industry can be seen by the fact that the Union Navy raided saltworks all along the coast. The southerners began placing them in tidal swamps. For every one destroyed, two were built. The price rose so high that speculators started buying the tidal land and building brick salt works. Smugglers made fortunes by slipping past the blockade and taking salt to the Carolinas.

The industry flourished until the end of the war when other supplies became available. Speculators who had made fortunes in Confederate currency had nothing but worthless paper.

Tourism

After the Civil War a new industry came to Florida and would completely change the state. This was tourism. Beginning at that period, about 1875, Florida's leaders began to "sell" Florida. These individuals saw Florida's sub-tropical climate, miles of wide, sandy beaches, and abundant lakes and rivers as a selling point to people from the northern states. Florida was to be an escape from the harsh cold, ice and snow which dominated their existence four to five months of every year. Florida offered a paradise to people in the large, industrial centers such as Boston, New York, Pittsburgh, Cleveland, Detroit, and Chicago. They now had the opportunity to get away from the rush of people and traffic, the noises and smells of large cities.

Prior to the development of the railroad and highway systems, steamboats operated on several of Florida's rivers. The St. Johns was very heavily traveled from Jacksonville to the south, and the Oklawaha to Silver Springs beckoned many travelers. It was,

however, the development of the railroad in the 1880's which set the pace for future years. Two men, Henry Plant and Henry Flagler, were in large measure responsible for opening the state to tourism. They built the railroad lines throughout the state and expanded their interests to hotels. These hotels, located in St. Augustine, Ormond Beach, Palm Beach, Tampa, and Miami, to mention a few, offered luxurious accommodations in their day. Indeed, several are still in operation in one form or another. For example, in St. Augustine and Tampa the old Flagler hotels are now colleges.

By the 1920's, Florida was winter residence for many of the nations wealthiest individuals. Miami and Palm Beach were centers of the most sophisticated forms of entertainment. Huge mansions began to dot the landscape along the beaches, and more hotels were being built. Land in south Florida sold sight-unseen and land speculators made huge profits. In central Florida, automobile racing on the beach became a world famous event in the city of Daytona Beach. In the late 1920's and early 1930's, tourism declined as two devastating hurricanes hit south Florida and the nation plunged into an economic depression. By the 1940's, despite World War II, prosperity returned and with it Florida's tourist industry.

A dramatic change was brought to Central Florida's tourist economy by Walt Disney. In 1971 he opened Disney World to the public. This single facility brought millions of visitors to the area and spawned development of other attractions in the area. The impact can be seen in the airport in Orlando. Before 1971, one million passengers flew in and out of old McCoy Air Force Base, the only airport. In 1980, six million passengers went through Orlando International Airport. Sixty-eight percent of those passengers arrived to visit Disney World. The new $300 million Orlando Airport, *"...the prettiest terminal in the world,"* is projected to handle 12 million passengers by 1987.

1980 — VISITORS TO FLORIDA

	Number	Expenditures in Florida	Avg. Stay (Nights)	Per Person Dollars Spent
Domestic (auto)	20,618,000	$8,901,054,680	16.0	$439.00
Domestic (air)	11,904,000	$6,102,354,230	9.4	$528.00
Domestic (other modes of travel)	1,300,880	N/A	N/A	N/A
Foreign	2,100,000	$2,077,572,000	N/A	$989.00
Total	35,922,880	$17,080,980,910	N/A	$1956.00

1980 TOURIST IMPACT

Tourist - Generated Expenditures in Florida	$17,080,980,910
Tourist - Generated Business Receipts (Total travel expenditures less taxes)	$16,056,122,056
Tourists - Generated Employment	580,200
Tourist - Generated State Tax Revenues	$786,725,122

In 1980 almost thirty-six million tourists visited the state and spent almost sixteen billion dollars. The largest percentage of tourists came from New York, Illinois, New Jersey, Pennsylvania, Canada, Georgia, Ohio, Massachusetts, Michigan and Virginia. Seventy percent of our visitors come by automobile. Why did they come? According to one survey, visitors came for rest and relaxation, beaches, to see attractions, fishing, boating, and to see historical sights.

What areas of the state attracted most visitors? According to a 1979 survey by the Department of Transportation, the most popular areas of the state were Orange, Osceola, Volusia, Pinellas, Escambia, Broward, Hillsborough, Okaloosa, Dade, Bay, and Palm Beach Counties. Of the state's 5,788 licensed hotels and motels in Florida, 3,625 were located in these eleven counties.

As a result of the natural features which attract people to Florida, many organizations have constructed commercial attractions which draw large crowds of visitors. Among the most popular are Disney World, Busch Gardens, Sea World, Cypress Gardens, Kennedy Space Center, Silver Springs, Marineland, Circus Hall of Fame, Stars Hall of Fame, Miami Seaquarium, and Sunken Gardens.

Miami's tourist industry received some bad publicity in the late 1970's and '80's and was hurt financially. During the period from 1920 until 1970 Miami was the tourist center of Florida. The wealthy of the world congregated for fun in the sun. This tapered off with reports of crime and drugs in southern Florida on national news. Northerners went elsewhere in Florida on vacation.

This slack period started turning around in 1981 when Europeans and South Americans proclaimed it the in-place for foreign travelers. Miami responded with the establishment of restaurants with foreign cuisines. Some hotel bars even converted to English style pubs.

Tourist cottages in Pensacola in 1941

Modern tourist facilities at Panama City. Notice the changes which have occurred in tourist facilities.

W.D. Chipley

Hamilton Disston

Henry Morrison Flagler

Henry B. Plant

Four early developers of Florida

Florida Photographic Archives

Tourism and the related service industries, generate tremendous incomes in Florida and provide much of the revenue of the state. Tourism brings many advantages, but also creates problems. Florida's fresh water resources are limited, and the number of visitors create a drain on this resource. In addition, as we attempt to meet the needs of incoming tourists, we must constantly repair highways and build new roads. This is a very expensive proposition. Thirdly, as more and more hotels, motels, gas stations, restaurants, shopping centers, and attractions are developed, much of our prime agricultural land is being turned into masses of concrete. Fourth, we must consider the cost of energy. Our tourist facilities and attractions are all climate controlled; huge air conditioning units burn billions of BTU's of energy, most of which is generated by the burning of fossil fuels.

Florida now attracts visitors from all over the world. The state's location and good air service makes it convenient for visitors from South America, Europe, Asia, Africa and Australia.

The tourist industry provides millions of dollars for support jobs from motel cleaning staffs to pilots of jumbo jets. These support personnel provide comfort and information for the millions of visitors to Florida.

Manufacturing

Manufacturing is the transformation of the natural products of our farms, forests, and fisheries, into new products. We call these natural products raw materials. The place where raw materials are changed into new products is called a manufacturing establishment or factory.

In 1977 the total value of manufactured products in Florida was just over 9 billion dollars. The chief products were food and kindred products; apparel and other textiles; lumber and wood products; paper and allied goods; stone, clay, and glass products; fabricated metals; machinery other than electrical; electric and electronic products; and transportation equipment. Of those included in the list, electric and electronic products, transportation equipment, and food and kindred products account for over

---

LIGHTS, CAMERA, ACTION, DOLLARS

Florida has been associated with the film making industry since 1908 when "A Florida Feud" was produced in Jacksonville. By 1915 Jacksonville was equal to Hollywood, California in movie production. Over the years Hollywood won out, but in 1980 filmmaking was on the upswing in Florida once again.

A diversity of films and television shows have been shot "on location" in the state. Some of Florida's many springs have been used because of their crystal clearness. Some movies filmed in Florida between 1940 and 1980 included "The Creature From The Black Lagoon" and James Bond scenes. Television shows included Lloyd Bridges in "Sea Hunt" and the underwater scenes from "240 Robert." The Miami Sequarium served as the location for an ABC-TV series "Jennifer's Journey."

Governor Bob Graham in 1981 stressed the importance of filmmaking to Florida when he said, *"The movie industry is important in our overall program of economic development, and it has the secondary benefit of continual film exposure to Florida as a quality place to live and visit."* The economic impact has grown tremendously since 1974, when Florida established a film office. In that year, filmmaking generated $12 million in the state. Six years later the gross amounted to $125 million. There were 19 major productions shot in Florida totaling $78.5 million.

Moviemaking is almost a total profit making adventure for the state. With an average budget of $6,000,000 per film, a great deal of money is brought into a community. Usually, 40 percent of the budget is spent in the community of the filming. When "Jaws II" was filmed in Navarre, the financial impact was phenomenal. The cast and crew spent $750,000 on hotel rooms, $200,000 at a lumber yard, $170,000 for local extras in scenes, $250,000 to a car dealer for vehicles, $200,000 for boats and a hardware store received $18,000 for paint. In 1980 Mount Dora's economy received one million dollars in receipts from "Honky Tonk Freeway." Two thousand local extras were hired and paid a daily wage. The high school band was hired, the members paid and $1,500 was given to the school.

one-third of the total value of manufacturing in Florida. Manufactured goods amount to 64 percent of the goods produced in the state.

In 1977, there were 12,366 manufacturing establishments registered in the state. Of these, 10,884 were located in the large urban centers of the state which would include Ft. Lauderdale, Hollywood, Jacksonville, Miami, Orlando, Pensacola, Tampa, St. Petersburg, and Lakeland. This fact is not surprising as a large company looking for a new location has certain priorities in selecting a site. Among these would be a sufficient labor force, good transportation facilities, institutions of higher education for training and recruiting purposes, and access to cultural activities.

Food Products

The largest group of manufactured products in Florida is food products. A large percentage of the value of food processing comes from citrus products. The growing of citrus products has been encouraged by innovations in packaging and shipping. Citrus fruit only had a short shipping time before it was unusable.

As new methods were developed, the markets for Florida citrus increased. Three early inventions helped in this market: the metal can, mechanical refrigeration, and machine blown glass bottle. The two means of packaging allowed vast quantities of citrus parts and juices to be shipped and stored over a long period of time. The major invention causing the ability to ship further was mechanical refrigeration with the basic patent being held by Dr. John Gorrie of Florida. The disadvantage of this type packaging was bulk. It took a lot of space to ship squeezed orange juice to northern markets.

The most important advance in processing citrus came by an innovation, or combination of already known ideas to create a new idea, by Clarence Birdseye. Birdseye visited Labrador in 1915 and observed that the Eskimos placed fish out to be frozen, then thawed it and had fresh tasting fish. He realized that freezing slowed down bacterial growth and retarded spoilage. In 1925 Birdseye, using Gorrie's refrigeration idea, marketed quick frozen fish. Twenty-four years later Birdseye invented a food

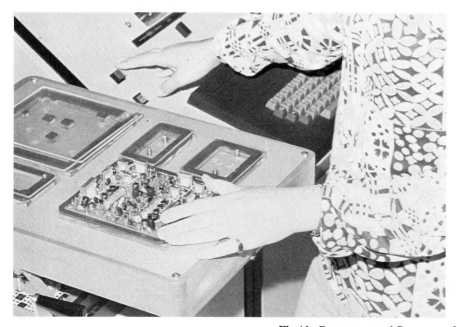

Florida Department of Commerce & Tourism

The electronics industry in Florida is growing rapidly.

Florida Department of Commerce & Tourism

Phosphate shipping from the Port of Tampa

dehydration process, and frozen concentrated orange juice was created. By dehydration, taking out the water, the cost and volume of shipping orange juice decreased. By freezing the remaining pulp, the shelve life increased.

Frozen concentrated orange juice went on the market in 1945-46 and sold 854,280 liters/ 226,000 gallons. In 1976, Florida produced 703.08 million liters/ 186 million gallons of this product.

Citrus by-products include stock feed, citrus molasses, peel oils, alcohol, wines, marmalades and jellies. The most important of these by-products is stock feed. With the increase of citrus production there has been more peel, pulp and seeds. These are converted into stock feed by grinding and adding of lime. The annual production is over 907,200 metric tons/ one million tons per year.

Related food processing industries include the packaging of frozen vegetables, shrimp and crabmeat.

Other Manufactured Products

Chemicals account for over one billion dollars a year of all Florida's manufactured products and rank second to food processing. The chemical industry is centered in Dade and Polk counties. Floridians produce agricultural chemicals like fertilizer, plastics, drugs, paints, varnishes, soaps and detergents.

The manufacturing of electronic equipment is increasing in Florida. It has an added value of $740,000,000 per year. This area should grow rapidly as the "Information Revolution" grows.

Other major areas of manufacturing in the state include production of transportation equipment; printing and publishing; paper products; garment making; and stone, clay and glass products.

Agriculture

Florida seemed destined from the beginning of European visits to be a great agricultural area. The Frenchman, Jean

Ribaut, described the Florida landscape in 1563 with glowing terms.

"(We) entered and veud the cuntry (Florida) theraboute, which is the fiarest, frute fullest and pleasantest of all the worlds ... it is a inspeakable, the commodities that be sene there and shalbe found more and more in this incompreable lande, not yet broken with plowe irons, bringing fourthe all things..."

Agriculture in Florida in the 1980's reflects the observations of Ribaut. In 1979, the receipts from Florida's agriculture totaled more than $3.9 billion and retail sales were $12 billion. There were 35,000 farms covering about 6.1 million hectares/ 15 million acres or two-fifths of the state. These farms averaged 164.7 hectares/ 407 acres in size.

Citrus

Citrus came to Florida by a long route. It was brought to Spain from the Orient and then to Florida by the Spanish. It appears that Columbus brought with him the sour orange and lemon. Sweet oranges had been limited to royalty and came to America after Columbus. Pedro Menendez, a Spanish soldier, reported abundant groves around St. Augustine in 1565.

The Spanish took the plantings with them everywhere they went. By 1800, trees were growing along the St. Johns River, Tampa Bay and St. Augustine. The planting expanded but a severe freeze in 1835 killed many trees. The grapefruit was introduced by Count Odet Phillipe around 1820.

As the population grew and expanded to new areas, citrus trees spread also. Railroads allowed groves to be planted in the interior away from rivers. This expanded the hectares/ acres planted. Markets began to open in New England for oranges and other citrus fruits. The fruit was shipped in barrels with Spanish Moss for packing. In 1886, there were 1,000,000 boxes of oranges produced and by 1894 production reached 5,000,000 boxes, twice as much as California. The freeze of 1894-95 almost ruined the industry and only 150,000 boxes were packed. The industry moved southward into warmer areas of Florida, but it was 1910 before production reached the prefreeze level. Production tripled in the next 10 years and has grown steadily up until 1979-80, when production was 283,550,000 boxes. Three

Citrus fruits were introduced to Florida over 400 years ago.

Cigar rollers in Tampa in 1920's

Strawberry harvesting

Have working conditions improved over the years?

severe freezes damaged citrus crops in Florida prior to the 1982 season. These occurred in 1963, 1977 and 1981.

Citrus crops in Florida include oranges, grapefruit, tangelos, tangerines, limes and lemons.

Nuts and Tropical Fruits

Jackson County produces more peanuts than the rest of the state. Jackson, Walton and Santa Rosa Counties lead the state in pecan production. In southern counties, Florida farmers raise tropical and semi-tropical fruits including avocados, bananas, guavas, mangoes, papayas, and pineapples.

Other Crops

A big part of the agricultural picture in Florida has to do with field crops. Vegetables, melons, and strawberries are grown in large quantities. Farmers planted almost 202,350 hectares/ a half million acres of these in 1980, valued at over 600 million dollars.

Some of the vegetables grown are snap beans, cabbage, tomatoes, sweet corn, cucumbers and watermelons. Nationwide, Florida ranks first in production of fresh, sweet corn and second in the production of celery.

Farms throughout the northern and western parts of Florida produce many crops for the market. Some of these are tobacco, soybeans, oats, cotton and hay for livestock. Some wheat is grown here, also.

Two kinds of tobacco are grown in Florida. The first tobacco was introduced from Cuba in the 1800's. It has become a valuable crop to Florida's agriculture. Growers earned 30 million dollars from a 9.98 million kilograms/ 22 million pounds crop in 1978.

When the early explorers came to Florida, they didn't find all of these fruits and vegetables. The only crop that was being grown and eaten was corn or "maize," as the native Americans would call it. The Spanish brought many of these vegetables with them from Spain and the West Indies. These plants

172

adapted very well to the environment, in Florida, and have become an essential part of Florida's economy.

Sugarcane

For many years Florida imported most of its sugar from Cuba. Cuba is an island nation very close to South Florida. In 1961, our country stopped trading with Cuba. This was due to a strained relationship between the two countries.

Florida began growing more sugarcane commercially at that time. The farm area grew from 14,569 hectares/ 36,000 acres in 1961 to 133,956 hectares/ 331,000 acres in 1979. Sugarcane is grown mostly in south Florida, near Lake Okeechobee, in the mucklands. Sugarcane has become the number one field crop, in dollar value, grown in Florida. In 1978, the seven mills of Florida produced over 198.9 million dollars worth of sugarcane.

Flowers

On any given winter morning in the northeastern part of this country, a family could sit down to a table filled with Florida products. A glass of Florida orange juice or Florida grapefruit with Florida sugar could begin the meal. Cereal with Florida strawberries or some Florida eggs would be nice. In the middle of the table, a beautiful bouquet of yellow pom poms would brighten a dreary winter day.

The production of fresh cut flowers is becoming a profitable industry, in our state. Some of these flowers are carnations, chrysanthemums, poinsettias and lilies. Nationwide, Florida is first in production of gladioli and second in pom poms. It is first in production of foliage plants and second only to California in flower production. Each year more Florida hectares/ acres are being used to develop this growing industry. The Apopka growing area produces 33 percent of Florida's foliage and 51 percent of sales.

Florida Department of Commerce & Tourism

Sugarcane harvesting at Clewiston

Florida Department of Commerce & Tourism

A modern greenhouse

Cowboys wrestling a bull by Frederic Remington in 1895.

Farm Animals

Animals are everywhere in Florida. Many can be seen in the wild, in the Everglades, the forests or the state parks. Others can be enjoyed in zoos, such as Busch Gardens in Tampa or Crandon Park in Miami.

Farm animals play an even greater role in Florida's welfare. They have a big impact on the economy of our state. Farms throughout Florida provide eggs for our breakfast tables, beef for our backyard barbeque and milk for our school lunches.

Cattle and horses were first brought to Florida in the early 1500's by Ponce de Leon. Hernando De Soto spread hogs throughout the state. Later, Spaniards brought sheep, goats and poultry. By 1700, large numbers of cattle, horses and hogs roamed the state.

The first cattle were scrawny and tough. During the 1700's, the cattle were driven to the coast in cattle drives. The "vaqueros" or cowboys used long whips to drive the cattle. English settlers called them "crackers" because of the sound of the whips. The

Seminoles and Miccosukees were the best cattlemen in the early 1800's but were driven south during the Seminole wars.

Many people think of cowboys and range wars as being out west, but Florida had both in the 1890's. Frederic Remington, the famous western painter, painted scenes of the Florida frontier cattle range.

Florida cattle did not improve in quality until almost 1900. Then, Brahman cattle were crossbred to give resistance to heat and disease. Later, Angus, Hereford, Shorthorn and Charolais improved the meat quality.

Research aided in eradicating tick fever and worms in the cattle. In 1920, the Texas tick infected Florida cattle so badly that southeast Georgia erected a double barbed wire fence. The fenced area was patrolled to keep out Florida cattle. Some counties placed a quarantine on tick infested cattle.

Cattle were dipped in vats of insecticide to halt the infestation. Cattlemen at first resisted, but cooperated after seeing the price of tick free cattle increase.

Florida Photographic Archives

Fighting over a stolen herd by Frederic Remington in 1895

Florida Photographic Archives

In wait for an enemy by Frederic Remington in 1895

Modern cattle roundup

Hogs and pigs of high quality are produced in Florida.

All of these factors combined to increase the beef cattle industry in our state. By 1980 Florida ranked ninth in production of beef cattle in the United States. There were 20,500 cattle farms in Florida in 1980.

The dairy cattle industry has continued to grow in Florida. Milk production has steadily increased each year. The number of dairy farms and dairy cattle throughout the country have been decreasing in the past years. Florida's numbers have only increased. By 1980, the state's dairies produced almost 908,000,000 kilograms/ two billion pounds of milk. These dairies provide virtually all the milk that is consumed here in Florida.

Other kinds of farms are important to agriculture, also. In 1980, there were approximately 8,200 farms in northern Florida that produced over 425,000 hogs and pigs. Though it is not the biggest industry in our state, it does produce high quality pork for our dinner tables.

Horses have always been important to Florida, even in the days of the early explorers. Today, the breeding of horses has become a very profitable business. Most horse farms are in central Florida, around Marion County. Our climate makes it desirable for raising thoroughbreds, and breeders are having great success, also. Championship horses have won at the Kentucky Derby and other famous tracks around the world.

Poultry farms in Florida are more like poultry factories. Chicken farms around the state have machines that collect and package the eggs without the touch of human hands. Floridians eat most of the chickens and eggs that are produced within the state. Some eggs are shipped to other states.

Hillsborough County, on the west coast of Florida, is the largest producer of eggs in the state. To advertise the area as one of the nation's leading poultry producers, there is a chicken plucking contest held each year in nearby Spring Hill. People come from miles around to try to set a new world record in chicken plucking.

Honey

Sometimes people run the other way when there are bees around, but in Florida they are important. We produce most of the honey in the United States. Florida with over 360,000 hives in 1979 had more bees than any other state. Honey production reached 12,748,320 kilograms/ 28,080,000 pounds in 1979. Two special favorites are orange honey and the rare tupelo honey, which is produced in West Florida.

Bees are important to citrus and various vegetables. Farmers depend on bees to pollinate those plants and trees.

Florida Department of Commerce & Tourism

Florida raised and bred thoroughbred horses are becoming known throughout the world.

The Papermaking Process

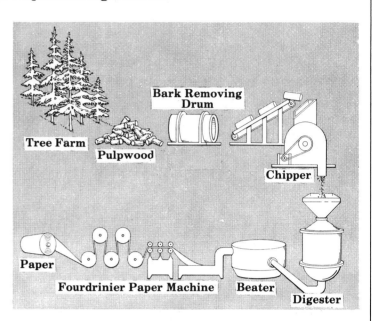

Pines to Paper

1. Trees are selected.
2. They are cut down and taken to mills.
3. Bark is removed.
4. The logs are ground up for easier handling.
5. This is cooked in chemical and steamed.
6. The material is strained to remove impurities.
7. The pulp is washed and put on a roll.
8. It has become a roll of paper.

Forestry

Whether it is a forest in Michigan, California, or Florida, trees are a renewable resource everyone needs. Florida's 20 million acres of forests are some of the largest in the country.

Forests have always been important to the people who lived here. The forests were used by native Americans to build homes and for various kinds of food.

The importance of forestry in Florida reaches far back in our history. There are records showing that the Spanish exported some lumber in the early 1700's. In the late 1700's, when Florida was temporarily under British rule, the British built the first sawmill near Pensacola. Shipbuilding became important during this period and the British harvested the Live Oak tree and shipped it to Pensacola, St. Augustine, and Jacksonville for this purpose. Early forts were built by the Spanish and English, using timber from Florida's forests. Some of the earliest sawmills, in Florida date back to the 1700's. Florida's first highway from St. Augustine to the St. Marys river was built by the English using timber.

Florida's great potential in the development of the forestry industry was hampered by the lack of transportation facilities. This problem was largely overcome by the 1880's with the expansion of the railroad. Three individuals deserve the credit for this achievement. They are: William D. Chipley, Henry Plant, and Henry M. Flagler. By 1891 there were 4,128.7 kilometers/ 2,566 miles of Florida railroad in operation and lumber production had increased to 192,000,000 board feet.

Before 1925 most people did not worry about losing the forests. The only known example of forest management was in 1828, when the U.S. Navy purchased 12,141 hectares/ 30,000 acres of land on Santa Rosa Island near Pensacola. Oak trees were planted for use in building ship hulls. Other than this, trees were slowly being destroyed. The government stepped in and began a program to replenish Florida's forests. Since 1928, over three billion seedlings have been planted.

There are over 300 species of trees in Florida. Some of these are cypresses, oaks, cedars and magnolias. The most common harvestable trees in the state are the Longleaf Pine, also known as the Slash Pine, Cypress, and Cedar. The multi-million dollar industry includes products such as: pulpwood, plywood, structural materials, furniture, paper, paperboard containers and boxes. Paper products are the main result of this industry. There are nine large paper mills in Florida that keep paper flowing to places throughout the nation and the world. Other products such as: plywood, utility poles and fuel wood are made from these trees.

Due to the increase in industries that produce wood and wood products, Florida's forests generate a large income for our state. The overall economy of Florida is three million dollars a year richer due to our forests and related products.

Trees are not only valuable for the products we make of them, but they have a value just standing in the forest. Forests provide a home for wild animals, many of them endangered species. The roots of these trees prevent the erosion of the soil. That means the soil will wash away without them.

Over 404,700 hectares/ one million acres of Florida's forest lands are protected by the Federal Government in National Forest Preserves. This land is administered by the

U.S. Department of Agriculture, Division of Forestry. There are three National Forests in the state. These are the Apalachicola, Ocala, and Osceola National Forests. All are located in the northern section of the state. The Forest Service maintains numerous camping areas in both the Apalachicola and Ocala National Forests, and many visitors come to these areas each year. Two of the major springs in the state are located in the Ocala National Forest. These are Alexander and Juniper Springs. The Forestry Service does offer leases for lumbering in these areas but strict controls regarding re-forestation and clearing are required. In addition, the state of Florida maintains four State Forests. These are the Blackwater River in Santa Rosa and Okaloosa Counties; the Withlacoochee in Citrus, Hernando, Pasco and Sumter Counties; and the Cary and Pine Log State Forests in Bay and Washington Counties.

Florida's only National Park, the Everglades National Park, located in Dade, Monroe, and Collier Counties, is administered by the National Park Service of the U.S. Department of the Interior. Many endangered species of trees are protected in this preserve including royal palms, mahoganies and mangroves. The Big

Suwannee River Cypress, ringed to kill the trees before cutting in 1929

Polk and Hillsborough Counties have been the main mining locations for Florida's phosphate industry. Today, as these counties are nearly empty of their phosphate, the companies are turning to new fields in Hardee, Manatee, and Sarasota Counties.

Phosphate is a mineral. Florida supplies forty percent of the world's phosphate. It is used in fertilizer, for without phosphate no food crops can be grown.

Manatee and Sarasota County governments are not pleased with their future in phosphate mining. Huge shovels are used to strip away the earth and to dig out phosphate. Thousands of acres of land are disturbed and, if reclaimed, still are barren for years. The natural vegetation is disrupted, as are farms and wildlife. The issue in Sarasota and Manatee Counties seems to be: Should the mining companies who own the land be allowed to strip mine it of a valuable natural resource, or should local people control their resources and the quality of their lives?

County governments want strong controls. They want to save some phosphate for the future -- not using it all today or selling it today to other nations. They want to protect the land and see that it is levelled and plants are restored. They want to protect the water supplies which mining disrupts. And they want to give short-term mining permits (five years) to see that the land is restored and water quality protected. All of the drinking water in these counties flows under or over land owned by the phosphate companies.

The phosphate companies want long-term permits and fewer controls on their mining operations.

The problems are many. Phosphate mining uses millions of liters/ gallons of fresh water to mine and to process the mineral. Deep strip mining will affect underground water supplies as well as surface water in rivers and streams. These are the supplies of drinking water upon which life in these counties depend. There are air pollution problems from the dust blowing out of the mines and increases in natural radiation. The processing yields great masses of slimy clay goo which must be contained by large and expensive dams. In the 1970's, a dam at a Cities Service mine broke and the slime killed off all living things for 128.7 kilometers/ 80 miles of the Peace River.

Florida faces a classic dilemma. Should government favor the rights of phosphate companies and the economic prosperity that their industry brings to Florida today? Or should government restrict these companies to protect the environment and persons living in these areas? Is there a way to satisfy every one who is a party to this conflict?

Cypress Swamp, also located in this area is one of the few remaining preserves for the beautiful cypress trees.

People need these forests for recreation. Some of the best camping, fishing and canoeing in Florida all begins in one of these forests.

One of Florida's most famous trees is probably its oldest. "The Senator" is over 3500 years old. It is a cypress tree near Winter Park, in Central Florida. It is 38.4 meters/ 126 feet tall and can make someone standing next to it fell very small.

Trees continue to aid prosperity in Florida. In 1978, income from the sales of trees and tree products reached 3,849,474,400 dollars. We must continue to encourage reforestation. The need for wood products will only increase as we approach the next century. The need to stand in a forest and see the strength and beauty of the trees will probably always be with us.

Minerals

Minerals are a non-renewable resource. This means that the earth does not rebuild minerals as it does soil, trees, and vegetation.

Minerals are the basic raw materials for our energy sources, industrial products, and many building materials. These resources may be divided into two groups: metallic and non-metallic. Non-metallic minerals include fossil fuels such as: oil, gas and coal as well as: sand, gravel, phosphate and limestone.

Most of the mineral resources under our surface are classified as non-metallic. These include phosphate, limestone, dolomite, rutile and ilmenite, zircon, staurolite, clays including Kaolin and Fuller's Earth, sand, gravel, sulfur, and petroleum. Of this list, Florida ranks first in the United States in reserves of phosphate rock, Fuller's Earth clay, staurolite, titanium and zircon.

Phosphate

Phosphate was first found in Florida in 1881. Early operations used picks, shovels and wheelbarrows to break up and load the phosphate after it had been dynamited. Some of the labor was by convicts who had been "leased" by the state to the mining companies. Steam shovels were later used and then the electric dragline.

Phosphate is stripped mined and many times destroys the terrain and top soil. New laws have required the return of the land to a usable surface.

Around 80 percent of the nation's phosphate is produced in Hamilton, Polk, Marion, Gilchrist and Citrus Counties. These five counties account for 33 percent of the world's production of the mineral. Phosphate is used primarily in the production of fertilizer. Other uses include baking powder, water softeners, rustproofing compounds, photographic supplies, and fireproofing compounds. In addition, a by-product from phosphate, uranium oxide, is in early stages of development. This by-product is used in the production of nuclear energy and it is estimated that Florida may eventually produce up to 454,000 kilograms/ one million pounds of uranium oxide each year.

Limestone

Limestone is used in road construction and cement manufacturing. In addition, our high grade limestone is used in the building industry to make plaster and mortar. One type of limestone, coquina, was used in construction by the Spanish in the 1500's. If you visit St. Augustine, you will see Fort San Marcos which was built out of coquina. Clay, especially Koalin and Fuller's Earth, are used for whitewares, cement, fungicides, absorbers, filters, and cat litter. Sand and gravel is a base material in the production of concrete, mortar, and asphalt.

Fuller's Earth

Fuller's Earth is mined in Gadsden and Marion Counties. It is marketed as cat litter and mixed with fertilizers. It has a high value in the petroleum refining industry because of its filtration qualities.

Petroleum

Petroleum development in Florida has been underway for the past 40 years. In 1977 Florida was listed as ninth in the nation among oil-producing states. Most of our oil is used as gasses of various types. These gasses include propane, butane, methane and natural gasoline. Sulfur, a by-product of petroleum production, is becoming increasingly important. In 1977 sulfhur production was valued at $15,000,000.

Petroleum resources have been developed primarily in northwest Florida in Escambia and Santa Rosa counties. There is much research in progress by oil companies in both the Atlantic Ocean and the Gulf of Mexico in locating and developing new oil fields offshore. In the early 1970's, a number of test wells were drilled off Florida's Gulf coast. These wells did not produce and were abandoned. Many of Florida's citizens do not want wells drilled off-shore because of the fear of "blow-outs" and "spills" which might pollute Florida's beaches.

Electric Power

Florida is a large consumer of electric power, from the light bulb or hairdryer in your

Florida Photographic Archives

Florida Power and Light Ice Wagon in 1927

home to the launch pad at Cape Canaveral.

The history of electricity has been closely associated with the state. Thomas A. Edison had his winter home in Fort Myers where he conducted experiments in his laboratory. Edison's residence in Florida spurred interest in the new source of power and lighting.

Before 1900 small businesses began generating electricity for their own use. If they produced too much, it would be sold to another business which saw the advantage of electric. These small "electric companies" were the predecessors of major companies of today.

The tourist and railroad industries played a part in the rapid use of electricity and the incandescent light bulb in Florida. In 1893, only four years after Edison invented the light bulb and one year after the first central generating plant opened in New York, Jacksonville's St. James Hotel had lights installed. There were 16 outlets, eight inside and eight outside.

Henry Flagler built a generating plant in Miami to service his Royal Palm Beach Hotel in 1896. He had a line strung to the Florida East Coast Railway a few blocks away. Private users along the line were allowed to tap into the line for a fee. Flagler built another generator in 1904. Ice companies and hotels were the prime users of electricity before 1910. However, during that time a commercial generator was built in Miami at the mouth of the Miami River. The first customer was a three horsepower motor at what is now the Miami Daily News.

Electricity produced by small private firms spread throughout the state. Between 1891 and 1900, Lake City, Palatka, Monticello, West Palm Beach, Titusville, Key West, St. Petersburg and, of course, Fort Myers all had electricity in addition to Jacksonville and Miami.

The ice making industry, based on Dr. Gorrie's patent, became a large producer and user of electricity. As more companies needed reliable power, a change took place in the

Florida Power and Light

Turkey Point, Dade County. This power plant helps generate electrical power for Florida's growing population. The large structure to the right were Florida's first nuclear generating units.

182

industry. The American Power and Light company in 1924 began purchasing smaller companies and properties to form the Florida Power and Light Company. This began a period of reliable service to wide areas. Lineman still rode horses or paddled boats to string and repair lines but the modern use of electricity was spreading throughout the state.

Electric power in the early years was generated by coal fired steam generators which later changed to oil fired in the 1950's. Florida Power and Light brought the state into the "Nuclear Age" in 1972 and 1973 with two nuclear generating units at Turkey Point in Dade County. By the mid 1980's, there were to be five nuclear generators in Florida, producing 3,711,000 kilowatts of power. These five will save an estimated 142.9 billion liters/ 1.2 billion barrels a year in oil. Nuclear generated power accounted for about 15 percent of Florida's power in 1981. Steam generated was 84.5 percent and only one-half percent was hydroelectric. By 1988, Florida's electric production should be 35,245 megawatts.

Fishing

Florida is one of the nation's leading commercial fishing states. A large amount of seashore and freshwater areas have long made Florida's fishing industry popular. Over $80,000,000 in commercial fish are caught annually in Florida waters or brought to the state's many harbors. More than one-half of the annual catch of 76 million kilograms/ 168 million pounds are shrimp and lobster. Florida provides 10 percent of the nation's shrimp catch.

The most important catches are catfish, grouper, mackerel, pompano, red snapper, clams, oysters and scallops. Two-thirds of the nation's red snapper comes from Florida.

Two specialty commercial fishing products are caught in Florida's waters. Sponge fishing in the Tarpon Springs area provides most of the natural sponges in America. Menhaden and shark catches are converted to fertilizer, oil and poultry feed.

Construction

"Buy land." "Get real estate." These are indeed two very short sentences; sentences which are repeated over and over to anyone who has money to invest in the state of Florida. As our population increases and more people visit the state each year, the need for structures to house these individuals increase. In addition, providing services such as shopping facilities, gas stations, restaurants and the like must keep pace. All of this comes under the broad umbrella of the Construction Industry. Take a drive around your city. How many structures are visible this year which were not there just two years ago? In many places in Florida it would be difficult to make an accurate count.

The firms engaged in this tremendous amount of building are called construction firms. When you consider it, there are many facets to putting up a building. One needs an architect to draw plans, people to clear the site, electricians, plumbers, carpenters, steel fitters, concrete pourers, landscape artists and many more. Buildings are usually divided into two categories: residential and nonresidential. Residential construction may be two varieties: single-family structures and multi-family structures such as apartment buildings and condominiums. As the population of an area increases, land for building becomes more scare. Generally, this means a change from single-family residences to multi-family residences. The assessed value of new construction in Florida for 1979 was almost five billion dollars with over one quarter of a million workers in the state engaged in the construction industry. In order to construct a new building, contractors must secure a building permit from the local government. According to the statistics, 173,345 building permits were issued in Florida in 1979.

The condominium or "condo" for short, is the latest fad in residential ownership. A condo is an apartment in a multi-story building which is purchased and owned just like a single-family dwelling. Condos are

Florida Department of Commerce & Tourism

Shrimping is an important part of Florida's commercial fishing industry.

Florida Department of Commerce & Tourism

The shipping industry employs thousands of workers in Jacksonville.

springing up all over the state and many apartments which once were for rent are switching to condo status. The "condo" craze has led to a number of interesting problems. Some of these include service fees for grounds and maintenance, re-structure of home-owners insurance rates, and the population density on various pieces of land. In recent years, state, county and municipal governments have been wrestling with these problems in attempting to establish laws and regulations which protect both the owner and the governments involved.

In several counties according to 1979 figures, the number of multi-family residences under construction was greater than the single-family dwellings. These counties included Alachua, Broward, Collier, Dade, Manatee, Palm Beach and Pinellas. If we look at the figures for individual cities, we get an even better idea of the changing nature of our housing facilities. For example, in Tallahassee the number of multi-family structures under construction in 1979 was three times that for single-family structures. In Ft. Myers there were fifteen times as many multi- and single-family permits and Key West had an amazing twenty-five times more multi-family buildings than single-family dwellings.

Needless to say, the trend in the state toward apartment and condominium living is resulting in great social changes. The philosophy of owning ones own home on a quarter of an acre is dwindling. We must consider very carefully the positive and negative elements involved in this change. For example, many communities have found it necessary to establish "density caps" for multi-story dwellings. This means that only a certain number of apartment or condo units may be built per hectare/ acre of land. Density caps tend to limit the number of floors that a structure may contain. Our government leaders are trying to balance the resources that are needed on the land such as water use, transportation and parking facilities, sewage control facilities, and other such problems.

A new form of housing construction gained importance in the early 1980's. This was manufactured housing. The once bus like

1979 CONSTRUCTION COSTS

Metropolitan Area	Marshall Valuation Service Index	Cost Per Square Foot 50,000 Sq. Ft.	100,000 Sq. Ft.	150,000 Sq. Ft.
Akron, Ohio	1.04	$37.39	$37.00	$36.83
Atlanta, Georgia	.93	32.86	32.52	32.37
Birmingham, Alabama	.92	33.08	32.73	32.58
Dallas/Ft. Worth, Texas	.97	34.88	34.51	34.35
Ft. Lauderdale, Florida	.95	33.57	33.22	33.06
Houston, Texas	1.02	36.67	36.29	36.12
Jacksonville, Florida	.92	32.51	32.17	32.02
Milwaukee, Wisconsin	1.08	38.83	38.42	38.25
Orlando, Florida	.91	32.15	31.89	31.67
Pensacola, Florida	.92	32.51	32.17	32.02
Pittsburgh, Pennsylvania	1.07	37.81	37.41	37.24
Richmond, Virginia	.95	34.16	33.80	33.64
Rockford, Illinois	1.03	37.03	36.64	36.48
San Francisco, California	1.20	43.14	42.69	42.50
South Bend, Indiana	1.05	37.75	37.35	37.18
Tallahassee, Florida	.87	30.74	30.42	30.28
Tampa/St. Petersburg, Florida	.95	33.57	33.22	33.06

Source: Marshall Valuation Services, The Marshall and Swift Company, October 1979.

Mahogany veneer is made in Pensacola.

Mobile home construction is increasing in importance in Florida.

mobile home has achieved acceptability and new style across the state. Cardinal Industries of Sanford has developed many styles for manufactured houses. The components are manufactured in a plant, trucked to the building site and assembled.

Space

The space related industries have grown since 1919, when the first U.S. guided missile was fired at Carlstrom Field in Arcadia. Cape Canaveral became the center for the space industry beginning in 1950. In that year, a German V-2 rocket was launched with a U.S. Army missile attached. The U.S. Government purchased 35,517.7 hectares/ 87,763 acres for a space complex in 1961. The State of Florida gave the usage of 21,672.9 hectares/ 53,553 acres to the federal government.

Thousands of space industry employees add to the economy of Florida. The federal government adds millions of dollars to the state's economy.

Labor

Perhaps the most important phase of industry is labor. Those who make the products, pick the citrus, operate the theme park ride, herd the cattle, gather the honey, pot the flowers, pick the strawberries, dig the phosphate, check the power lines, catch the fish and thousands of the things to supply goods and services are an integral part of industry. The large population of Florida has created a melting pot of diverse skills. These people provide experiences in every phase of business, commercial and industrial activity in the state.

Florida has workers of all ages. In 1980 there were 3.2 million people in the prime working ages of 18-44. This ranked eighth in the entire United States. Ages 45-70 gave Florida a skilled and experienced work force which was first in the nation.

The Constitution of the State of Florida provides that no one shall be denied the right to work because of membership or non-membership in a labor union. This provision gives an individual the right to choose whether to be a member of a union or not. Union membership in 1978 amounted to 11.7 percent of the total work force in Florida.

The combination of climate, natural resources, financiers and laborers have developed Florida's industries

from the first Indian dugout... to salt evaporators... to citrus groves... to phosphate mines... to nuclear energy.

Florida's industries will continue to change as the economy demands.

Unit 8   Education

Dr. Mary McLeod Bethune

Florida Photographic Archives

EDUCATION

McGUFFEYS
READER

Larry Pauley

Introduction

Today, there are many opportunities to learn in the State of Florida. Children, youth, and adults have opportunities to develop their skills and learn new careers. They can learn new hobbies and ways to improve their lives. The public school system provides an education for students from kindergarten through college and doctors' degrees. There are classes for students and adults in community colleges throughout the state. Private schools offer educational opportunities for children and adults. Public libraries and television stations offer other ways to learn. Education in Florida is part of our way of life.

Public education is extensive. Florida has 1,996 elementary and secondary schools, 219 adult education centers, 47 vocational training centers, 28 community colleges, nine state universities, and one school for the deaf and blind.

Public schools in Florida are growing in numbers of students served and improving in quality. As the population of Florida increases, more and even better schools are built to serve students. Since 1968, Florida has operated free public kindergartens in elementary schools. Students are enrolled in a standard curriculum in elementary schools. When they reach middle school, or junior high school, more choices of subjects are available. At the high school level, students pursue the courses which will help them most in later life. Some take courses to prepare them for college. Others take courses preparing them for a vocation, or career. State education officials have developed tests to improve the quality of education in Florida and to see that students getting diplomas measure up to what are called State-wide Minimum Competency Levels.

Florida's public schools are complemented by private schools. Twelve percent (one-eighth) of Florida's children and youth attend private schools. These schools offer grades kindergarten through the senior year of high school. Some are small, while others are large schools. Many are operated by religious groups and offer their students courses in religion and moral education. In most of these schools, parents pay tuition to cover the cost of their children's education.

Although the state operates many vocational centers, there are over 200 state-licensed vocational and technical schools. By paying tuition and meeting the entrance requirements, students young and old may learn anything from typing to airplane flying.

Beginning in 1957, Florida built a statewide community college system. This system is growing. Now, almost all of Florida's people live within driving distance of a community college where they can take courses, so that they can go forward to a university, or can learn a new career. Many adults drive to community colleges just to learn about things which interest them or help with hobbies.

Florida has public universities throughout the state. The nine state universities stretch from Pensacola to Jacksonville, and down to Orlando, Tampa, and Miami. In 1979, the state's universities awarded students over 20,000 bachelor's degrees, some 5,000 master's degrees, and almost 1,500 doctoral and professional degrees. The universities also conduct research on important state problems. Farmers get up-to-date research from universities. The Florida Solar Energy Center tests solar water heaters and new ways to use sun-power in the Sunshine State. Universities study the state's rivers, ponds, and seacoast. Some do research on education to improve the way we learn. You cannot think of a big problem in Florida which is not being studied by scholars and students in a State university.

Florida has 69 accredited private colleges and universities. Many students attend these private schools and pursue their vocations. These private colleges are involved in research on topics ranging from history and medicine to urban air pollution and poetry.

Of course, education is more than schools. Florida has over 150 public libraries where citizens can borrow books and other media.

EDUCATION

Many libraries offer courses and special programs on topics of interest to citizens, young and old. Books, magazines, newspapers, government documents, films, and historic records are available at libraries.

Public broadcasting is important in our educational system, too. Florida has nine public television and six public radio stations sending programs for entertainment as well as learning. Florida's system uses earth satellites to beam programs to all citizens.

Floridians are aided in learning by the oldest of books and the latest of space technology!

Early Cultures

All of these opportunities to learn were not always available. The early cultures in Florida had some system of educating the young. Native Floridians (Indians) and those native Americans from other areas had to pass on knowledge and competencies to their children. If children did not learn how to fish, hunt, grow food, and defend the villages, their group and its culture would vanish. Strong villages and groups required strong education.

Children in early cultures did not go to a school to learn. They learned from their friends, parents and other adults. Children learned their language and the traditions of the group by talking, listening and participating in group life. Storytelling and ceremonies were educational. Household practices and group celebrations taught beliefs, values, and religion. Hide and seek games taught skills in camouflage and quietness. Wrestling taught quickness and developed strength. Other skills were taught in a "learn by doing" manner. Hunting, making clothing, cooking food, preserving food, tending crops, making baskets and pottery, trading, and skinning animals were jobs done by children side-by-side with adults. They learned as they gew older.

Native Floridians knew directions and studied the stars and the lands around them.

They could travel hundreds of kilometers/ miles through the forests, swamps, and grasslands and know exactly where they were and where they were going.

Tribal history and a sense of pride in one's group were taught by storytelling and group celebrations. Older members of the group taught the younger members. In this way, everyone was a teacher and any place where the group camped or settled was a "school."

Early Schools

European settlers who first came to Florida had to educate their children in similar ways. They taught their children at home, as they lived and worked. As the children grew up and if the parents had the money, they sent the children off to school and college in other, more settled places. Few Florida children got the advantage of going away for formal education. Franciscan friars were the first Florida school teachers. In 1605, they were conducting a primary school in the convent of the Immaculate Conception. The children of St. Augustine were instructed by a *maestro de gramatica.*

Under the Spanish, mission schools were established where European and native youth learned religion and Spanish from the priests who served as teachers. Under later governments, the wealthier settlers hired private teachers (tutors) to teach their children, when tutors were available in their communities. A Roman Catholic parochial school, supported with taxes and free to all children is St. Augustine, was opened in 1789 and continued until 1821. An earlier schoolhouse had been constructed in 1778 and still stands today. But before 1800, schools could be found only in the towns of Florida. Even then, the schools were one-room common schools with all grades taught together. The schools only operated when a teacher was available and when money was available to pay the teacher, and keep the schoolhouse repaired. Some schools had taxes to pay the costs. Others received money from churches. But most operated as parents paid fees to the teachers. Formal education was not available to many children, most of the time. At best, children would receive the three r's -- *readin', ritin', and 'rithmetic.*

After Florida became a United States Territory, in 1822, at the first meeting of the Florida Legislative Council, an act was passed to set up an apprenticeship system. Orphans and poor children could be "bound" to a master who was required to teach them a trade, how to read and to write. Apprentices lived with their masters who fed and cared for them while they were learning a trade. Learning was by doing -- apprentices worked long and hard for their masters. They were bound to their masters from two to seven years. Usually boys served until age 21 and girls were bound to age 21 or until marriage.

Under the Territorial Government, federal lands were leased and sold to raise money to support schools. The territorial council gave permission for towns and counties to conduct lotteries to raise money for schools. Tickets were printed and sold, with the winning ticket holder to receive a money prize, and the profits going to the town or county school fund. The federal lands were a greater source of support for schools than were the lotteries.

There were no common schools for all children, male and female, white and black, as we have today. One of the big educational issues was whether the government had a

---

Legislative and Court Acts of Early Florida
An Act Concerning Guardians and Wards, Masters, and Apprentices

2. Be it further enacted that every poor orphan who has not estate sufficient for his maintenance out of its profits shall by the order of the courts aforesaid, be bound out as an apprentice until he arrives at the age of twenty one years, if a boy and the age of sixteen, if a girl, to some master or mistress who shall covenant to teach and said apprentices, some art, trade, or business, to be particularized in the indenture, and also to teach them reading, writing, and arithmetics, and to give them a new suit of clothes when they shall arrive at age.

Edmund Law
President pro tempore of the Legislative Council
(Approved 31st. August, 1822)
Wm. P. DuVal
Governor of the Territory of Florida
Acts of Florida, 1822, p. 11

· · · · · · · · · ·

At a special session of the county court of Leon County on Friday the 3rd day of April A.D. 1831
    Present for Leon
    David P. Macomb P. Justice
Upon the application of Hercules R. W. Andrews It is ordered that John Brashear a minor be bound apprentice to him to learn the art and mystery of cordwaining* until said John Bradshear shall have arrived at the age of twenty one years, which will be on the 10th day of April in the year one thousand eight hundred and thirty-three
    And the Court Adjourned
    David B. Macomb

* Rope making

Leon County Court Records — Microfilm, Florida State Library.

**Games and exercises were really
education for early Indians
by Le Moyne**

Old schoolhouse at St. Augustine

Interior of old schoolhouse

**One room schoolhouse in Dade County
in 1889**

Florida Photographic Archives

Horse drawn wagonettes were used as school buses in Duval County in 1898

Florida Photographic Archives

Hialeah school room in July, 1924

195

responsibility for the education of all children in Florida, or just for the education of poor children. The various towns and counties which had elementary schools varied in their policy. Some charged all students, while some charged only those who could pay. Still, others had private schools open to paying customers only.

Fewer towns had secondary schools, which were then called academies. At the academies, a student could learn English literature, modern languages, mathematics, science, and other subjects, depending upon the talents of the teacher employed to instruct at the academy. In the 1820's, there was an academy at Webbville (in Duval County) and one in the Panhandle region, the St. Andrews' Bay Academy. In the 1820's and 30's academies opened for various lengths of time in: Tallahassee, Jackson County, Quincy, St. Augustine, and Pensacola. A few received public tax support. Most were open to students for tuition payment. For almost all of Florida's children after elementary school, there was very little formal education available to them.

The census of 1840 reports that there were only 69 schools and academies in Florida, and some were free only for the very poor. Further, the census showed that there were 9,303 youth between the ages of five and 20 in Florida (4,722 boys and 4,531 girls), but only 732 were reported to have been enrolled in school. These facts show the limited nature of formal educational opportunity.

Statehood and Education.

Once Florida joined the Union and became a State in 1845, the people again thought about formal education for their children. People needed to read deeds and sign legal papers. Arithmetic skills were needed for buying and selling goods. Schooling was needed to do everyday things. The ability to read and write was a personal matter of community status. Therefore, educated persons in Florida encouraged the development of educational systems for others. The churches wanted better education for all Floridians. Church leaders believed that all people should be able to read the Bible. People needed to be able to write, so that they could record births, deaths, and marriages in their family Bibles. This was often the only record on earth of a family existence and its traditions.

In 1849, the legislature established common schools and the office of the State Superintendent of Schools. Counties were to elect school superintendents and school boards to oversee county operated schools. Money from the sale and lease of federal lands was set aside to support county schools. By 1850, a free school opened in Tallahassee for white children, and tax-supported schools opened in Key West, Apalachicola, Jacksonville, Marianna, and Pensacola.

In 1850, Florida passed a free school law and became the fourth state in the nation with free public schools. David Walker, the State Superintendent of Schools in 1858, said *"...In our common schools and State Seminaries (colleges), we may well hope that the time has almost arrived when all the children of Florida may and will be educated in her own institutions."*
Superintendent Walker worked long and hard to improve Florida's schools, but the Civil War interrupted his efforts. The war drained money for education. Attention was focused elsewhere.

After the Civil War, great strides were made in education, especially for black children and adults. As governor, David Walker created a state common school system for blacks. If students could afford it, they paid tuition. If they could not, the schooling was free. A special tax of one dollar was levied on all blacks, ages 21 to 55, to pay for the schools. A black man, the Rev. E.B. Duncan was appointed superintendent of the black schools. In 1867, there were 34 day schools for blacks and 22 night schools. The State and the Freedmen's Bureau had made a significant beginning at opening educational opportunity for children and adults in the black community -- which had

JAMES WELDON JOHNSON (1871-1938)

James Weldon Johnson was born in Jacksonville, Florida, on June 17, 1871. His mother was a school teacher at the Stanton Institute, a high school for black students. He studied at Atlanta University and taught in a rural school in Georgia for awhile. After his graduation in 1894, James Weldon Johnson returned to Jacksonville to teach. He was a successful teacher and became principal of the Stanton Institute.

James Weldon Johnson was truly motivated as a student. While serving as principal, he studied law and was the first black man to pass the Florida Bar examinations which allowed him to practice law. Always a learner, he wrote music and poetry. He moved to New York where he was freer to develop and express his talents. There, with his brother, Johnson wrote songs for vaudeville, minstrel shows, and light operas. He performed on the stage in the United States and Europe as a musician, and served his country as a diplomat in Venezuela and Nicaragua.

In 1912, James Weldon Johnson put his feelings and ideas on paper in a book entitled: Autobiography of an Ex-Colored Man. This book and other activities brought him to a leadership position in the National Association for the Advancement of Colored People (N.A.A.C.P.) in 1916. He worked to bring about racial harmony and justice, and to improve educational opportunities for blacks and poor persons. From 1930 to his death in 1938, James Weldon Johnson taught at Fisk University and wrote articles on racial issues and his cultural heritage. He was a nationally famous Floridian who was a leader for quality education.

been seriously neglected.

The new state Constitution in 1868 set forth the promise that it was *"the duty of the state to make provision for the education of all the children residing within its borders."* Yet, a law passed in 1869 maintained segregated schools: separate schools for blacks and whites. Educational progress had been made in Florida, but education was not equal for all children.

In 1869, the white and black schools were placed under one state superintendent of schools. Progress continued and it was reported that over 16,000 children were enrolled in school in 1871, one-fifth of the youth in the state. The Superintendent of Schools in 1873, was Jonathan C. Gibbs, a black. By 1884, the state had only eight white and three black secondary (high) schools. The black secondary schools were Lincoln Academy in Tallahassee, Douglass High School in Key West, and the Stanton Institute in Jacksonville.

Expansion and Improvement in Public Schools.

As Florida's population increased, the number of schools increased. Every town had a "common school," or an elementary school where children could learn to read and write. Most often, these were one-room school houses with a single teacher to teach all ages. But in the larger towns and cities, the many private academies and tuition schools for older students were becoming tax-supported high schools. State tax money and local taxes provided funds for these high schools, which offered students courses in: English, government, history, Latin, mathematics, science, and geography. Jacksonville had the first high school, under the leadership of Albert J. Russell, Duval County Superintendent of Schools. He opened Duval High School in 1877 and got the county to support the first unified school program from elementary school through high school. Orlando had added a high school section to its elementary school in the 1870's. The Melrose Union Academy served three rural counties, namely: Alachua, Clay, and Bradford. They pooled their tax moneys to support a high school. The Alachua Institute of Hawthorne was built where two railroads crossed, to serve its population more conveniently.

In 1884, the State Superintendent of Schools ordered some changes. "Industrial arts," or vocational training was to be added to the school curriculum, and schools were to become graded. To organize education better for students, the superintendent demanded that schools offer curriculum for different age children. Especially in the larger schools, Florida saw students organized by "grade level" -- first grade, second grade, and so forth. A child in a one-room schoolhouse may have studied the same thing six times by the time he was in the sixth grade. Under the graded plan, he would advance by grades. Tests would be given at the end of each year for promotion to the next higher grade. Each class level would have different skills and subjects for students to master.

Students attended schools only if the school was available, and if they and their parents desired an education. In 1883, Florida was reported to have had 1,429 schools with 51,449 students enrolled. By 1901 there were 2,336 schools. While it is not known how many students graduated from elementary school, it was reported that 136 students received high school diplomas that year.

High school attendance was not expected or required of everyone. There were no laws requiring any school attendance in Florida, before 1919. In that year, the state legislature passed a "compulsory education law." After

that, all parents had to send their children to elementary school. Still, high school was not required and even today, students must attend school only until the age of 16.

Schooling in Florida was not an easy or an inexpensive matter. Parents and students had the problem of transportation to school and the costs of clothing and supplies. Even in free public schools, books and supplies were not provided. In 1911, free school books were provided only to the poor. In 1928 free school books were loaned to students in grades one through six. It was not until 1935, in the middle of the Great Depression, that the state decided to provide all textbooks in basic subjects from elementary through high school.

Integration

The Great Depression of the 1930's and the years of World War II had an impact upon Floridians' thinking about education. In 1944, Governor Spessard L. Holland appointed a Citizens' Committee on Education. Governor Millard F. Caldwell

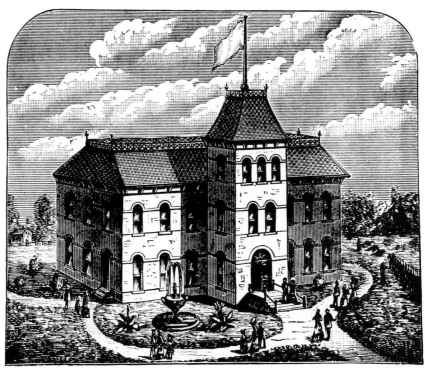

Florida Photographic Archives

East Florida Seminary at Gainesville, 1883

Students in 1981

reappointed the committee and the legislature approved the idea in 1945. This committee presented a 400-page report on Education and the Future of Florida. The report came just as thousands of soldiers and sailors were returning from the war to pick up their lives, education, and families. Florida was on the eve of its great growth in population. The time was ready for action and the legislature passed the Minimum Foundation Program. More state money was to be spent on schools and colleges, better qualified teachers were to be educated and hired in the schools, and a more equal system of educational funding was started. Rich and poor, urban and rural youngsters were to get better schooling.

It was in this climate of educational improvement that a great change came. In 1954, the United States Supreme Court ruled that segregated schools were unconstitutional in a ruling known as Brown vs. Board of Education of Topeka, Kansas. Florida had maintained a dual system of education dating back at least to 1869. With rare exceptions, black students had attended black schools and white children attended white schools. Federal court orders to desegregate schools were not popular ones in all social circles, and many of Florida's political leaders were slow to say, "We will obey the law."

Jan Hartle

Students in Orlando in 1981

LeRoy Collins, Florida's 33rd Governor (1955-1961), a lawyer from Tallahassee, tried to lead efforts to integrate peacefully Florida's schools. Florida experienced less turmoil and violence than most other southern states, because desegregation came along with the improvement and modernization of education in Florida. Governor Collins won the acclaim of leaders in the white and black communities for his courageous speeches and actions. He was a leader on the Southern Regional Education Board and attempted to provide the same leadership to the whole region as the South experienced a radical shift in educational and social customs.

Collins' successor, Farris Bryant, the 34th Governor of Florida (1961-1965) was an accountant from Marion County. He continued Governor Collins' educational improvements in Florida. After five terms in the state legislature, Governor Bryant appreciated what quality education could do for Florida and Florida's children. He improved teacher salaries and helped to improve teaching. He opened the way for more students to go to college and the universities.

Federal Money

Another change in education occurred during the 1960's, which was the increased influence of the federal government in state school systems. Vast amounts of money came from Washington, D.C., for certain school programs. Educators used this new source of funds to start new programs.

By 1978-79, federal aid paid over 11 percent of operating Florida's public schools. The state paid 51.6 percent and local property taxes paid a little over 37 percent.

In the 1980's federal regulations about mainstreaming handicapped students, multi-cultural and bilingual education, school bussing, and similar policies have been resisted. Many parents thought that control of local schools was slipping from their elected school officials to office holders in Washington for whom they had not voted. Many times this feeling was expressed about federal decisions to ban Bible reading, prayer, and religious celebration from public schools. Other times the complaints are masks for unhappiness over desegregation. But, responsible parents and local officials are concerned that the education of children should reflect local values and customs. There seems to be a voter backlash against

Osceola County School Board

Reedy Creek Elementary School near Kissimmee is designed to conserve energy by using solar energy and being partially earth-sheltered.

federal regulations in favor of a return to more local control. Conficts over federal money, regulations and meaning of justice in educational opportunity for all children will continue for a long time. Citizens, political leaders, and educators in Florida will be working out their answers to these conflicts.

Growth and Quality

In 1979 there were fewer schools in Florida than in 1901. However, the schools today are much larger. As the population of Florida increases, the numbers of students will increase. This means there is a need for additional state and county tax revenues. The quest in Florida's schools for the rest of the 1980's is not handling more students. It is improving the quality of education.

Commissioner of Education Ralph Turlington instituted a Minimum Competency examination which is in the process of becoming a requirement for graduation from Florida's high schools. Students are expected to have mastered the reading, writing, and math skills necessary for survival in the 20th and 21st centuries' social life. With this assessment in place, Commission Turlington has plans to raise Florida's educational system to the top twenty-five percent of the nation's schools. Educators, parents, students, and citizens across Florida are developing plans to improve the quality of education -- and the quality of life -- for Florida's students. The quest for better education is eternal. But, the plans for Florida education in the 1980's are bold and exciting.

Private schools provide education for one-eighth of Florida's FSU school children.

Private Elementary and Secondary Schools

The first schools in Florida were private schools. These schools were conducted by Spanish Roman Catholic leaders. Today, Roman Catholic churches and religious orders operate schools for Florida's children. They have been joined by other religious groups who now operate schools. In addition, there are many private schools which are not associated with religious organizations.

The private schools now enroll one-eighth (about 12 percent) of Florida's students in grades kindergarten through 12. This is a dramatic increase since 1950 when only about four percent of Florida's students were in private schools. The Roman Catholic Church in Florida operates about 180 elementary and secondary schools with a total enrollment in 1980 of 73,254 students. These schools are found in each of the five Florida dioceses of the Church: The Archdiocese in Miami, the Diocese of Orlando, the Diocese of St. Augustine, the Diocese of St. Petersburg, and the Diocese of Pensacola-Tallahassee.

The Florida Association of Christian Colleges and Schools reported in 1980 some 49 accredited and 50 provisional schools, K to 12, across the state. These schools range in size from a few hundred students to well over a thousand students. Like the Roman Catholic Schools, they offer their students a curriculum which is based upon the religious beliefs and values of the supporting religious group. Parents pay tuition fees so that their children may attend and receive religious and moral teachings along with the regular curriculum of history, English, science, physical education, and so forth.

There are other religious schools which are not associated with state or national organizations. There are also many private schools which are not religious in affiliation or orientation. They are day schools, where parents send their children each day, and boarding schools where children live in dormatories while pursuing their education. Bolles School in Jacksonville and Howie-in-the-Hills Academy are examples of boarding schools. MacClay School in Tallahassee is one of the many private day schools in

U.S. Dept. of Labor

Students with hearing disabilities are receiving special help.

Florida. The different kinds of schools in Florida give parents and students some freedom of choice about education, especially if they are able to pay tuition charges, in addition to the taxes which support the public schools.

The Florida Sheriff's Association operates three education and care facilities for youth who have lost parents or who cannot be cared for at home. The Boys Ranch is a home for neglected or homeless boys which was opened in 1957 at Live Oak, Florida. The Girls Villa for needy and worthy girls was opened in 1970 at Bartow, Florida. In 1978, near Clearwater, Florida, the Association opened a Youth Ranch for brothers and sisters who are neglected or homeless. Most of these children attend public schools during the day, but eductional programs are offered, including vocational education. The programs are funded entirely through private contributions.

Special Schools

In 1884 the Florida Institute for the Blind, Deaf, and the Dumb was opened in St. Augustine. Tuition was free, for indigent Florida residents between the ages of six and 21. Today the school is called the School for the Deaf and Blind. It offers students from grades kindergarten through 12, a full curriculum. Children with defective hearing and sight who cannot make adequate progress in regular schools can live and study at this facility in St. Augustine. The school has a medical staff to work with teachers.

The Florida Department of Education has a Division of Blind Services which develops programs for blind students in educational programs across the state. As more students with learning disabilities are placed in regular classrooms, this division and state programs in the Florida Department of Health and Rehabilitation Services are

203

FROM ELDERBERRIES AND CHARCOAL TO BETHUNE - COOKMAN

MARY McLEOD BETHUNE (1875-1955) was born in Mayesville, South Carolina, to parents who were poor, former slaves. She was one of 17 children. She had an opportunity to attend school when one was built near her home. Later a white dressmaker in Colorado paid for a scholarship which permitted her to attend Scotia Seminary in North Carolina. Later, Dr. Bethune attended Moody Bible Institute in Chicago, Illinois. She wanted religious training since her first plan was to be a missionary in Africa, spreading the word of Jesus Christ. But Dr. Bethune decided to stay at home and serve black people who needed educations.

May McLeod taught school in Augusta, Georgia, and in Palatka, Florida, for over eight years. During this time she married Albert Bethune. In 1904 she decided to move to Daytona Beach, Florida and open her own school. Dr. Bethune is said to have had only $1.50 when she got to Daytona Beach! She later wrote that she burned sticks to make charcoal to be used as pencils. The students gathered elderberries and made their own ink. Together, Dr. Bethune and her students went around Daytona collecting old chair, desks, and other needed materials. The Daytona Educational and Industrial Training School for Negro Girls, which Dr. Bethune opened with five students, had 250 students in two years. Her students learned and the school survived!

In 1923, Dr. Bethune's school merged with the Cookman Institute to become Bethune-Cookman College. The Cookman Institute had been founded in Jacksonville in 1872 by the Rev. Dr. S.B. Darnell with aid from the Freedmen's Aid Society. It was named after Alfred Cookman, a Methodist minister who gave money for the first building. In 1875, it had two teachers and 50 students. When Dr. Bethune's girls school merged with the Cookman Institute, the College became co-educational (enrolling both girls and boys). It was supported by the Methodist Church in Florida. The Jacksonville campus was closed and the College was established in Daytona Beach, where it is located today.

In 1924, Dr. Bethune was elected president of the National Association of Colored Women's Clubs. In 1936, she founded and served as president of the National Council of Negro Women. She was an advisor to President Franklin Delano Roosevelt and to the founding conference of the United Nations. Dr. Bethune rose from her poor background to live a life of helping others. Her school lives on as one of Florida's most important colleges.

working closely with teachers of children, youth, and adults.

In 1900, the Florida State Reform School was opened in Marianna. It was to serve wayward boys and restore these law breakers to their communities "with purposes and characters fitting them for good citizens and with a trade fitting them for self-maintenance." In 1915, the Florida Industrial School for Girls was established. It opened in 1917 at Ocala, with a curriculum of mathematics, reading, story telling, history, and industrial work (trades). Later another boys' school was opened north of Okeechobee to serve South Florida.

These schools for wayward youth are for severe cases. The Florida Division of Youth Services and local public schools offer educational programs in county youth detention centers and in START Centers. Students may continue their education while being held for court decisions and for decisions by youth workers. After conviction,

to prevent all children from having to go to a correctional center, the state operates halfway houses. Youth live at these centers while serving the court-imposed punishment. These centers have educational facilities and teachers. Many youth on good behavior can go to public schools in the area. The Criswell House in Tallahassee was the first of many state-operated halfway houses. They are attempts to keep students out of jails and from becoming hardened criminals.

State and federal correctional institutions offer educational programs to inmates. Inmates can pursue elementary and high school diplomas. They can, in many cases, take community college courses and earn A.A. (Associates of Arts) Degrees while in prison. Since 1949, the Apalachee Correctional Institution at Sneads has had a full educational program for first felony offenders to age 25. Glades Correctional Institution in Belle Glade has a full program for Spanish speaking inmates.

Vocational Education

Tax supported vocational education had its beginning in Florida during the late 1800's in Jacksonville. Today about one-half million people are taking courses leading to improved skills for new and better jobs. The citizens of Florida are supporting vocational education with their tax dollars at community colleges and at vocational education centers in county school systems. Per capita expenditures for vocational education in Florida exceed those of any other state in the South. In the United States, only Massachusetts spends more than Florida.

In 1981, the total vocational labor force supplied by state programs will exceed 100,000 workers. Of these workers, almost 25,000 will be trained in special trades and industrial jobs. Many will have been in apprenticeship programs where students learn on the job working as carpenters, plumbers, auto mechanics, solar installers, and many other occupations.

Private schools offer occupational training in addition to those state operated programs. There are over 200 licensed vocational-technical schools in Florida. Students who meet the requirements and can pay tuition may learn anything from typing to air conditioning, from welding to airplane flying and mechanics.

Vocational education is important to Florida. It keeps our citizens employed and productive, and it attracts new industries. For these reasons Florida has established a fine vocational system available to all students, young and old. In 1981, Commissioner of Education Ralph D. Turlington said: *"No Florida citizen should have to miss his or her connection to a successful career. Almost every Floridian lives within 30 miles of a job training center. Your first stop (to a successful career) is just around the bend from where you live."*

FLORIDA PUBLIC SCHOOL SYSTEMS

Six Largest School District 1979		Six Smallest School District	
Dade County	223,740	Lafayette County	880
Broward County	136,648	Liberty County	910
Hillsborough County	110,908	Glades County	1,071
Duval County	105,385	Union County	1,398
Pinellas County	89,746	Gilcrist County	1,444
Orange County	81,271	Dixie County	1,685

These systems have 49.5 percent of all public school students in Florida. Dade County alone has almost 15 percent of the public school students in Florida.

These systems have less than half of one percent of all public school students in Florida.

Community Colleges

Two year "junior" colleges were operating in Florida as early as 1927 when St. Petersburg Junior College opened as a private institution. In 1933, Jacksonville University opened as a private college, but it became a University with a four year program. It was Palm Beach Junior College, opened in 1933, that set a pattern for tax-supported education in communities across Florida. In 1947, the Citizens' Committee on Education recommended that junior colleges be established in all population centers. The state legislature responded and the junior college movement was off to a start.

St. Petersburg Junior College became a public college. Chipola Junior College which opened in 1947 as a private school, became public in 1948. Pensacola Junior College and Washington Junior College for blacks in Pensacola were public schools. By 1964, there were nineteen junior colleges, including six junior college centers which had originally been established for black students.

Today there are 28 fully integrated community colleges. The name "junior college" has been dropped because the community colleges today are doing more than teaching the first two years of a college education. They offer a range of vocational-technical courses and provide many courses, for credit and without credit, to meet community interests. You can even go to community college to take hobby courses in subjects ranging from flower arranging to bee keeping.

The community colleges vary in size, depending upon the size of the communities served. Miami-Dade Community College had over 40,000 students in 1981, while North Florida Community College at Madison had less than 1,000. Each community college serves a district and all of Florida's 69 counties participate in a community college district except for four counties. Miami-Dade Community College has four campuses to serve its students, and offers additional courses in off-campus centers (e.g., high schools, community centers, etc.). St. Petersburg Community College has three campuses and is building a fourth.

Students at Chipola Community College in Marianna can study for careers in; welding, business, drafting, electric wiring, cosmetology, agriculture, auto mechanics, and appliance repair, as well as college subjects which can be transferred to a university. Students at Broward Community College, a large college, can study for careers in: day care, landscaping, data processing, pest control, air traffic control, real estate, hotel administration, radiation therapy, and many more careers. The community college system is growing and improving the lives of Floridians.

Colleges and Universities in Florida

For many years Florida was without a college or a university. To get an education beyond the academy, students had to leave the state. Finally, in 1851 a state law provided funds for two seminaries (colleges). Two years later the East Florida Seminary opened in Gainesville, and in 1856 the West Florida Seminary opened in Tallahassee. After the Civil War, the state created the Florida Agricultural College in 1870. Under the Morrill Land Grant Act of 1862, the federal government provided 36,423 hectares/ 90,000 acres of public land. These lands were sold or leased to provide money for colleges teaching agricultural and mechanical skills. The Florida Agricultural College was first located at Eau Gallie, but is was moved to Lake City in 1884. Later it was moved to Gainesville and became part of the University of Florida.

The state government was also concerned about teacher training. In 1887 it established a training school for white teachers (a "normal school") at De Funiak Springs and one for black teachers in Tallahassee. The black school in Tallahassee received land grant funds from the federal government under the terms of the "Second Morrill Act in 1890" and it later became the Florida Agricultural and Mechanical University.

206

University of Tampa, former Plant Hotel

Despite federal funds and state government concerns, funds were very limited. By 1905 the legislature passed a law proposed by H.H. Buckman of Duval County. A state system was organized which included a school for white women west of the Suwannee River in Tallahassee, another for white men east of the Suwannee in Gainesville, and a coeducational school (for males and females) to serve blacks in Tallahassee. In 1909 they were named The Florida State College for Women, the University of Florida, and the Florida Agricultural and Mechanical College for Negroes.

During this same period of time, religious organizations and persons of wealth were also concerned about the lack of higher education in Florida. The Methodist Church opened several colleges which were short-lived. The Florida Conference of the Methodist Church, which included South Georgia, opened a college in Thomasville, Georgia, and later in 1852 opened a college in Micanopy, Florida. They failed during the Civil War. After several attempts following the Civil War, a seminary was established in Orlando. It moved to Leesburg in 1886 and in 1902 moved to several locations in Clearwater. Finally, in 1923 it was moved to Lakeland and later became known as Florida Southern College.

Bethune-Cookman College at Daytona Beach resulted from the merger of two black schools. Mary McLeod Bethune's Daytona Normal and Industrial Institute for Girls, established in 1904, and the Cookman Institute of Jacksonville, started by Rev. D.B.S. Darnell in 1872, came together in 1923 under Methodist support. Later the Daytona-Cookman Collegiate Institute became Bethune-Cookman College. By 1941 it had dropped high school and junior college courses and offered four year degees.

Edward Waters College in Jacksonville was opened in 1872 by the Rev. Charles H. Pierce of the African Methodist Episcopal Church in Florida. It opened in Live Oak,

Florida, as Brown Technical Institute, and later became Brown University, but had money problems. By 1892 it was operating again, this time in Jacksonville as Edward Waters College. The famous Jacksonville fire of 1901 destroyed its buildings but the college was rebuilt and continued serving students until this day.

Rollins College in Winter Park was opened in 1885 by the Congregational Church (now the United Church of Christ). Winter Park contributed land and money to the college. Alonzo W. Rollins of Chicago gave $50,000, so the college was named after him. The college opened with five faculty members. Today, it remains a small, coeducational liberal arts college. It stresses its pre-medical and pre-law program, and has a five-year business administration program.

Stetson University at DeLand, Florida, was opened by the Baptist Church. In 1883 it was called DeLand Academy after Henry A. DeLand from Fairport, New York, who founded the town. By 1885 it was a college. In 1886, John B. Stetson, the famous Philadelphia hat manufacturer, began donating important sums of money to the college until his death in 1906. The college took the name of the hat-maker in 1899, becoming Stetson University. Its athletic teams are known today as the "Hatters." Stetson University pioneered in music education and business education. In 1900, it opened the first law school in Florida, which in 1954 moved to St. Petersburg.

Jacksonville University was opened in 1934 as Jacksonville Junior College, offering courses at night. After the Second World War, it moved to a beautiful location in Arlington on the St. Johns River, offered day classes, and in 1956 granted four-year degrees as Jacksonville University. Today it has over 3,000 students and stresses business administration as well as liberal arts courses of study.

The University of Miami was only an idea during the real estate boom of the early 1920's. George E. Merrick, the developer of Coral Gables, got the sponsors of the University to locate in his new city. A hurricane struck before the first building was up and the boom was over. The school struggled during the Great Depression of the 1930's. But today it is one of Florida's great universities. It has famous programs in medical and marine sciences, inter-American studies, law, and business administration.

Like the University of Miami and Jacksonville University, the University of Tampa is a private school. In 1931, citizens in Tampa opened Tampa Junior College as an evening college. In 1933, during the Depression, the college moved to Henry Plant's famous Tampa Bay Hotel which became Plant Hall of the University of Tampa. Four-year degrees were offered and the university grew.

At the end of the Depression in 1940, Barry College was established as a Roman Catholic

Florida Photographic Archives

Stetson University in 1904

women's college. Sister Mary Gerald Barry, Mother General of the Dominican Sisters of Adrian, Michigan, and her brother, Bishop Patrick Barry of St. Augustine were the leaders in its opening. Today, the school is a small college with an outstanding reputation.

After the Second World War, Florida grew rapidly and so did its colleges and universities. The G.I. Bill allowed veterans to receive funds to go to college and to approved trade schools. Many veterans took advantage of this opportunity and attended Florida colleges. Federal grants and loans to colleges and universities opened even more opportunities to students in Florida. Finally, the integration of education after 1954 and financial aid opened the way for poor and minority students to obtain higher education.

The State University System expanded rapidly after the war. The enrollments at Florida A & M University, the University of Florida, and what became Florida State University soared. Soon civic leaders wanted universities -- public universities -- in their cities for their children. The state began to expand the number of universities in response to these demands.

The University of South Florida opened with a freshman class in 1960, at Temple Terrace north of Tampa. It has expanded rapidly with thousands of part time students in the Tampa area and with branches in St. Petersburg, Ft. Meyers, and Sarasota. New College in Sarasota, which opened as a private school in 1960 under the United Church of Christ, became an innovative educational branch of the University of South Florida in 1975. Today, the University of South Florida is one of the largest universities in Florida.

In the fall, 1964, Florida Atlantic University opened on 485.6 hectares/ 1,200 acres in Boca Raton, Florida. The University of West Florida opened on a 404.7 hectares/ 1,000 acre campus in Pensacola in 1967. Florida Technological University (now the University of Central Florida) opened in Orlando during 1968, and Florida International University in Miami opened in September, 1972. The latest university in the nine-member state university system is the University of North Florida. It opened in Jacksonville in October, 1972, on a 404.7 hectares/ 1,000 acre campus.

These new state universities offered students lower tuition than private colleges

E D U C A T I O N

Florida Photographic Archives

Anastasia Hotel in 1926, now part of The University of Miami

Knowles Memorial Chapel at Rollins College, Winter Park

and universities. They offered students a chance to learn closer to their homes. Students responded by enrolling in great numbers, especially by transferring from their community colleges to take junior and senior courses and earn their Bachelor of Arts and Science degrees.

The growth of public universities has not slowed the growth of private colleges in Florida. Jones College, which was founded as a private business college in Jacksonville in 1918, now has branches in Fort Pierce, West Palm Beach, and Norfolk, Virginia. The Florida Institute of Technology, founded in 1959 at Melbourne, has prospered. It offers degrees from the Bachelor of Science to the doctorate in many science and engineering fields. Flagler College opened during 1968 in the historic Ponce de Leon Hotel in St. Augustine as a fine liberal arts college with an outstanding cooperative program with the Florida School for the Deaf and the Blind. In 1963 Archbishop Coleman F. Carroll opened the Seminary of St. Vincent de Paul in Boynton Beach for the education of

priests. Its program stresses bi-lingual, bi-cultural education for priests from Hispanic backgrounds or preparing to serve Hispanic peoples. St. Leo College, north of Tampa, began offering four-year degrees in 1959, and continues as a small college. Webber College in Babson Park is a business and secretarial college. Other colleges have developed from religious communities in recent years. Shelton College in Cocoa Beach is a Christian evangelical school. The Miami Bible College opened in 1962 and offers degrees in Bible education. Other Bible colleges are found in many Florida communities. Other religious groups have opened small colleges such as Southeastern College in Lakeland which is operated by the Assembly of God Church. Florida Presbyterian College, now Eckerd College, in St. Petersburg opened in 1960. Marymount College in Boca Raton is a small liberal arts college for women, operated by the Religious of the Sacred Heart of Mary. The Embry Riddle Aeronautical Institute moved to Daytona Beach in 1965 and continues its specialized educational program.

It is impossible to imagine much that a student cannot learn at a private or public college or university in Florida. The courses and subjects taught are many. Today's student has a world of skills and knowledge available which would have dazzled a child growing up in Florida in 1900. Educational opportunity in Florida today is plentiful for all -- white or black, male or female, rich or poor. A student is only limited by lack of a desire to learn. In the future there will be advances. Perhaps...

> ...computerized schools,...
> television classes taught live,...
> specialized high schools,...
> decentralized schools,... classroom
> with parent assistants or

whatever the citizens of Florida decide is best for their citizens.

**E
D
U
C
A
T
I
O
N**

Recreation

Florida Division of Commerce and Tourism

John Pennekamp Underwater State Park

RECREATION

Larry Pauley

Introduction

Florida is a fun state! There are so many things to do in Florida that one visit is usually not enough. Every part of Florida has its own special attraction. Fresh and salt water fishing is a relaxing pastime, for any visitor. There are miles of beaches for swimming and boating. The state parks and the national forests are a beautiful setting for a family vacation. Besides the fun that nature provides, Florida offers many commercial attractions. Disney World, Busch Gardens, and Sea World are just a few that are enjoyed by adults and children alike.

Floridians and visitors have many other types of entertainment to choose from. Professional sports such as football and soccer are developing rapidly in Florida. Modern dinner theatres, fairs, amusement parks, museums, and art shows are available continuously.

Many of these activities are fairly new to tourists in our state. Some of them, such as: swimming, fishing, and hunting were enjoyed as far back as 1513, when Ponce de Leon stepped on the sands of Florida.

Early Recreation

Native Americans enjoyed living in Florida long before Europeans explored and claimed it. They hunted, fished and hiked many areas of Florida for food to feed their people.

Recreation for these early people included foot races for boys and young men. A favorite game was "chunkey." A small stone hoop was rolled on the ground and spears or sticks were thrown at it. Scores were based on where the hoop was hit. Dancing and singing were ways of relaxing and rejoicing. Sometimes the dance was part of a religious ceremony.

Whatever the activity, it was usually related to survival. The recreation of the native Americans helped them learn how to deal with their environment. A young hunter had to be quick to kill a deer or a wild turkey. Early Florida Indians engaged in: races, wrestling, animal calls, and throwing of

Florida Division of Commerce and Tourism

Florida Caverns at Marianna

knives and tomahawks. One can easily see that foot races would serve as good training for engaging in battle. Wrestling developed strength and agility. Being able to imitate animal sounds was used both for obtaining food and for warfare. Target shooting with the bow and arrow served to entertain and to develop a survival skill for the young brave. Hide and seek, played by both young girls and boys, taught quietness and the ability to camouflage. The ability to use a knife and a tomahawk were developed by contests of accuracy in throwing at targets. In this way, recreation was survival training and not just entertainment. This freedom of movement would not continue as settlers took over the lands of the native Americans.

Life for the native American changed as the Europeans came to Florida. The English, the Spanish and the French each brought some of their own culture to our state.

Children's Games

As the people of Florida advanced with the rest of the nation toward the Civil War, the people still enjoyed some forms of recreation. Marbles became popular and remained popular in Florida. Games with pocket knives gave hours of pleasure to the neighborhood boys and "tomboys." In a knife game like "mumblety peg," the skilled knife handler would flip it off the fingers, wrist, elbows, or even the head and have it stick straight up in the ground. The girls enjoyed making and playing with cornhusk and dried apple dolls until the "newfangled" China ones became available.

Early Outdoor Sports

Fishing and hunting were also popular and have remained popular to the present day. In the 1800's, these were still survival recreation. Fishing is both recreational and

Florida Division of Commerce and Tourism

Pensacola Beach

commercial. Hunting has become almost entirely recreational. As the state became more populated and the economy changed life styles, the recreation changed. When cattle became a major industry, the skills of cowboys became popular sports and recreation. Roping, shooting and steer wrestling tested the skills of these cattlemen. More importantly, it provided a way to relax after a hard week's work.

Horseshoe pitching was always a favorite and every town had its champion. That person was, of course, the "greatest shoe thrower in the whole country." Horseshoes were a big thing at week-long revival camp meetings. The camp meeting itself became a form of relaxation from vigors and struggles of daily life.

Parlor and Running Games

For the less wealthy, parlor games were very popular before the beginning of radio and television. In the late 1800's and early 1900's, families would visit together in the evenings. Games like "charades," "twenty-questions," and "I spy" provided hours of fun and mental exercise. Playing cards was popular except in areas where it offended the religious attitude of the people.

Outdoor games for children provided much exercise. Ever popular was "kick-the-can," "tag," "hide and seek," and "chase." One recreational activity for competition between boys and girls was "skipping rope." More than once, a young male hung his head in defeat to a girl in jumping "hot pepper."

Tourism

The latter part of the 1800's was a period of rapid growth for Florida. It soon became one of the fastest growing areas in our nation, and still is today.

Tourism is the largest industry in our state. It really began back in the 1800's after the Civil War. Many people came to Florida looking for cheap land.

One of those early tourists was Hamilton Disston. In 1881, he paid one million dollars for 1,618,800 hectares/ 4,000,000 acres of

land. What he bought was mostly swampland and had to be drained. He tried to built a canal system, to drain his land. He was not successful.

Two early developers of Florida met with greater success. Henry Flagler built hotels along Florida's east coast. Then, he built a railroad to transport his customers. Henry Plant opened up the west coast of Florida with his railroad, in the 1800's, also.

The railroad became a very important part of the tourist industry in Florida. Before that time, steamboats were very popular. Steamboating along Florida's waterways was an exciting way to travel. You never knew if there would be an alligator around the next corner. The steamboat lines lost their customers to the railroad, since the train was a faster and more convenient way to travel.

Today, the railroad has lost that popularity. The airlines speed visitors from every state and many countries around the world. The interstate and state highway systems help visitors crisscross the state in a few hours, in their own automobile. In this way, modern methods of transportation have greatly increased the tourist industry in Florida.

Throughout its history, Florida has been a favorite place of some of our presidents. They came to relax, enjoy fishing or just the warm climate. Among these were Teddy Roosevelt, Grover Cleveland, Herbert Hoover and Franklin D. Roosevelt. Several of our past Presidents had winter homes in Florida. Harry Truman resided in Key West, John Kennedy in Palm Beach and Richard Nixon in Key Biscayne.

Wealthy

Travel was and is the main entertainment for the wealthy of Florida. Many of these people would spend winters in Florida, summers in New England and holidays in Europe. Havana, Cuba attracted tourists until the Castro revolution closed down that popular gambling spot. Puerto Rico and the Bahamas became short vacation spots for many Floridians. Others stayed in Florida year round and visited the many different facilities, especially the springs.

Tourists and developers will continue to bring millions of dollars and many changes to Florida. Even though this is very good for the economy, Floridians must be sure that the beautiful features of Florida are protected for the generations ahead. The state has much to offer its visitors as well as the people who work and play here.

Radio

The radio, short for "radiate out" has an interesting history of development. The most important step occurred in 1895. Guglielmo Marconi sent dots and dashes by sound waves to a receiver. Then, in 1900, an American physicist, Reginald Fessenden, made the first radio-voice transmission. Soon afterwards, the radio phenomenon began. In 1919, President Woodrow Wilson broadcast from a ship to World War I troops on other ships.

This new form of entertainment rapidly spread across the United States. Florida entered the radio era in 1921. Station WQAM began broadcasting from Miami to Floridians within listening distance. The first licensed station in Florida was WDAE of Tampa in 1922. Today, no person in Florida is out of touch with radio waves.

Radio changed many things. Floridians picked up new pronunciations and changed speaking patterns. New words entered into the vocabulary. Evenings were spent by a whole family sitting around the radio listening to performers from faraway. The radio helped to de-isolate the people in rural areas. News, which had taken weeks to hear or read about now came almost instantaneously. Walter Winchell gave his opening statement of, "Mr. and Mrs. America and all the ships at sea, let's go to press," and all ears listened. Comedy and mystery were at the turn of a dial. Everyone knew Jack Benny, Burns and Allen, Fibber McGee and Molly, The Lone Ranger, The Shadow, and The Green Hornet.

Music from the best singers in the nation was heard in Floridian living rooms. Who could not recognize Bing Crosby, Kate Smith, or Al Jolson? Every citizen could hear their President speak to them personally. Dramas and mystery shows were listened to regularly along with soap operas. Listeners had to use their imagination to picture the character and scenes. Radio also brought products to the listener's ear. Just as the traveling peddlers had tempted the pioneer, the latest "radio offer" tempted many listeners. "Commercial" became a new word in the language of Floridians. Along with this, came the latest words from those "slickers" from New York.

Local stations began to develop their own style. Some became stations for popular music, shortened to "pop" music. Others became "hillbilly" music stations. Some even played classical music.

In 1981, there were over 200,000,000 radios in America. The radio has become an important part of all our lives. Florida in 1980 had about 325 radio stations.

To avoid thinking that cultural changes were only one way, it is important to recognize Florida's cultural exports to the rest of the nation. Residents in the northern states began to hear about beaches and a land where there was no winter. Land was sold by way of commercials to land hungry northerners who had never seen Florida. Even words like "gator," short for alligator, became part of the northern vocabulary.

Southern music was beamed northward and became a part of crossing cultures. Gospel music which had been a part of Florida's culture for years began to be heard all across the nation. Today, groups like The Florida Boys sing to standing room only crowds across the country.

Movies and Television

Entertainment for Floridians was enlivened by the new moving pictures or movies as they were known. Movies created a form of entertainment where the viewers could distract themselves from the rigors of

Florida Division of Commerce and Tourism

Balloon Race at Orlando

Florida Division of Commerce and Tourism

Scuba diving

daily life. They could see famous stars on the screen and watch the good guy beat the bad guy. Every town in Florida had its movie house and the price in the 1930's was five cents. During the 1950's, it went up to 25 cents for adults. From the 1920's, until 1960, the movie theaters were often filled to capacity. Then, that new form of entertainment, the television, became a strong competitor. People quit going to movies and began staying home to watch TV. Many movie houses closed down, and television personalities became as widely known as the earlier radio ones had been. In fact, some of them were the same people.

Today, almost every family in Florida has a television and many households have two or more. But television did not destroy the other two entertainment media.

A major factor caused all three electronic media to survive, and increased recreation and entertainment facilities. Floridians have experienced a reduced hourly working period. It was not uncommon to work 70 to 80 hours a week at the turn of the century. Today, the average worker in Florida averages less than 40 hours per week. This, plus vacation time, has given more time for entertainment. In addition, most radio stations changed to music formats and movie theaters upgraded their facilities, thus allowing all three media to coexist. In 1980, Florida had 40 television stations.

Florida has been the setting for some major films. Several have been filmed in Miami Beach and surrounding areas. One was a Burl Ives film about the Everglades and the other a James Bond movie called, "Thunderball." Several movie stars have homes in Florida and spend some of their spare time here. Many underwater films are filmed at Silver Springs. You can see the remains of old sets there.

Burt Reynolds, an actor, is probably the most known resident of Florida, at the present time. Mr. Reynolds is famous, to Floridians, for another reason. He has opened a dinner theatre in Jupiter, Florida, near his home. Movie and television stars such as: Dom DeLuise, Sally Field, Brian

Florida Department of Commerce & Tourism

Orange Bowl Festivities

Keith, and of course Burt Reynolds perform there. The season runs from January to May.

As a past student of Florida State University, Mr. Reynolds wanted to do something to help the school. In early 1981, he donated a large sum of money to the theatre department of that university. His donation made the theatre department one of the richest in the country. Floridians are proud of Burt Reynolds. He has accomplished a great deal as a performer in movies and television and has contributed much to Florida.

Television is as important in the lives of Floridians as it is in everyone else's in our country. When television began, many people thought it would replace movies. It didn't. It is a different form of entertainment. Television is informative. It can teach us to cook, to read, or to exercise. Television gives us news, some good and some bad. It allows us to see and hear events as they are happening. Television has become a very important part of life.

Television in Florida began in Miami. The first station, WTVJ, went on the air in January, 1949. We now have more than 30 commercial television stations and several educational channels. Cable television is bringing even more choices for viewing pleasures.

Spectator Sports

Fun in Florida sometimes includes watching others play. Most cities in Florida offer amateur sports in college, high school and little league. Some cities have professional sports to enjoy. For many years, active sports were the province of males. Today, female sporting events include almost every facet of sporting life.

Football

Professional football has developed into a multi-million dollar industry in our state. The Miami Dolphins began competing in the American Football League in 1965. The team was at its best during the 1972-73 football season, because Miami won 17 straight games, which included the Super Bowl in January, 1973. The Dolphins were champions the following year, also.

Tampa Bay Buccaneers appeared on the football scene in the fall of 1976. The Bucs have received great support from the fans in the Tampa Bay area. Football "fever" has taken over the cities on the west coast of Florida.

The major college football teams, in Florida, are Florida A and M, Florida State, University of Florida, and University of Miami. The annual excitement for college football teams is the bowl game. The Orange Bowl game has been played in Miami since 1933. That year, the University of Miami beat Manhattan 7 to 0. There are three other college football bowl games, namely: the Tangerine Bowl in Orlando, the Orange Blossom Classic in Miami and the Gator Bowl in Jacksonville.

Most of these young people began playing football in high schools around the state or in one of the hundreds of little league football organizations available.

Baseball

When baseball first appeared in Florida, it was a "rough and tumble" sport. The game was played without gloves and was not organized like today. The sport had been a popular game between battles during the Civil War. Returning veterans probably first introduced it into Florida.

The popularity of the game spread rapidly and it became one of the major entertainments of the late 1800's and early 1900's. There were sand lot, semi-pro, and professional teams scattered throughout the state. It may be difficult for you to believe, but there were no "Little League," "Babe Ruth Leagues," or "Pony League" to try out for. The "kids" in the neighborhood would have "pick-up" games. Sometimes a team from one town would play another. A factory would occasionally pay some of its workers extra if they were good ball players and would play on weekends.

Florida is a favorite place for many of the major league baseball teams. This is where they have spring training. While the weather is still harsh in other parts of the country, baseball teams like to practice and prepare for the new season, in a warm climate. High school and college teams can play a longer season in Florida than many other places. This gives Floridians more experience at the sport.

Tampa is the winter home of the Cincinnati Reds, while Miami gives a warm welcome to the Baltimore Orioles. Clearwater, Fort Myers, Winter Haven and many other Florida cities play host to the various major league teams around the country. These spring training teams participate in what is known as "The Grapefruit League." Here they prepare for the regular season.

Florida has minor league professional teams, also. These teams help train players for the major leagues. Florida colleges have become known for preparing many young men for professional baseball careers.

Little league baseball is the beginning of many careers. Almost every town and city offers young people a chance to play in a league. The Belmont Heights little league team, of Tampa, went to the World Championships in August, 1980, but lost to the team from Taiwan. They made Florida, especially Tampa, proud of them.

Basketball

Basketball is truly an American sport. Baseball had its origin in the cricket of England, and football can be traced to the Greeks and Romans. Basketball was invented in the United States by James Naismith in 1891. He wanted a game that could be played indoors at the Y.M.C.A. The first games were played with cone-shaped peach baskets for goals and jump balls after every goal.

In Florida, basketball has become a very popular college sport. Major colleges and universities throughout Florida compete with other schools in the southeastern part of the nation.

Florida Division of Commerce and Tourism

Toronto Bluejays' spring training camp at Dunedin

Basketball is a popular sport for both boys and girls at the high school level. State championships are held each year to decide the best team throughout Florida. Many people in Florida play basketball for church leagues, Y.M.C.A.'s and neighborhood pickup games. What started out as a winter indoor sport is now played year round, indoors and out.

Jai Alai

Jai Alai is an exciting, fast-moving game, something like handball. The players use a "cesta," or basket, to throw the ball against the wall at speeds of 150 miles per hour. It can be very dangerous.

This danger and excitement brings thousands of visitors to the Jai Alai frontons all over Florida, each year.

Track and Field

Floridians have always run, jumped and thrown things. From the earliest Indians, to the Spanish, French, English and Americans, competition in what is now known as Track and Field has existed. Florida's climate allows year round participation in these activities. Elementary students through college athletes enjoy this type of physical fitness. Middle schools, junior highs and high schools compete throughout the state. College track and field athletes compete nationally, and even internationally. Many Floridians dream of winning a gold medal in the Olympics.

Soccer

Another professional sport that attracts large crowds is soccer. The Tampa Bay Rowdies and the Ft. Lauderdale Strikers have been "winning" teams since they started playing. Pele, the famous Brazilian soccer star, played against the Tampa team several times to a crowded stadium. The Tampa team usually won.

Soccer is a rapidly growing sport in Florida. What is really making soccer grow, is young people. Thousands of them are playing soccer in little league and high school soccer teams across the state.

Florida Division of Commerce and Tourism

Surfing in the Atlantic

Water Sports

"Let's go to the beach." Now that's a common expression heard along Florida's coastline. The beaches of Florida have always been its greatest attraction. The white sands, warm water, and beautiful sea shells have drawn visitors since Florida's earliest years.

The Atlantic Ocean on the east coast and the Gulf of Mexico on the west offer more than swimming, to its visitors. Boating and water skiing in the waters off the coast of Miami or St. Petersburg are a common sight to see. Scuba diving is an exciting way to explore the brightly colored coral reefs around the Florida Keys. Daytona Beach is the place for you to bring your surfboard and find a high wave. Collecting sea shells can be fun, on Sanibel Island, near Ft. Myers. It is world famous for the unusual varieties of shells that wash ashore.

Swimming has become a competitive sport. Young swimmers compete in meets, in both Olympic styles and long distance swimming. With its abundance of water, Florida is a natural training area for this sport.

Fishing

There are more kinds of fish in Florida's fresh and salt waters, than any other place in the world. Some of the fresh water fish, from lakes and rivers, are bass, trout, and catfish. These can be found in Lake Okeechobee, Loxahatchie and Lake George during most of the year. There are thousands of lakes in Florida, for the avid fisherman. You must buy a fishing license to fish in fresh water.

Salt water fishing along Florida's coasts does not require a license. Over 600 varieties of fish can be found in different regions along the coast. Deep sea fishing, in the Atlantic, can be an exciting day. A fisherman could come home with: grouper, snook, redfish, sailfish, marlin, dolphin, pompano, red snapper, and many more. The great tarpon can be found around Homestead or Tampa Bay.

Many cities such as: Clearwater, Ft. Lauderdale, and Fernandina Beach provide piers extending into the ocean, for fishing close to home. For the beginner or the veteran fisherman, Florida has a variety of ways to enjoy this relaxing sport.

Dog and Horse Racing

Further excitement is found at the many greyhound race tracks, in our state. Visitors may bet on their favorite dog or just enjoy watching them race.

For those who are interested in larger animals, horse racing can be viewed, in our state. There are five tracks for regular races, one for quarter horses and two tracks for harness racing. All of these race tracks offer pari-mutual betting. The most famous of these tracks is the Hialeah Race Track, near Miami.

The raising of race horses, in central Florida, has become a thriving business. The warm sunny days and the short winters have brought more people to our state for that purpose.

Rodeos

Horses in Florida are used in the exciting world of rodeo. In one day at the rodeo, you could see riding, roping, bronco busting and more. The Big Silver Spurs Rodeo, in Kissimmee, is held in February, each year. The All Florida Championship Rodeo can be seen in July, in Arcadia. Both of these rodeos, as well as a few others, bring many cowboys and cowgirls into the state each year. This has become a popular attraction which is seen by thousands of spectators each year.

Golf

It is almost impossible to go anywhere in Florida without finding a golf course or tennis court. These sports have become increasingly popular due to the year round sunshine and warm climate. The southeastern area of Florida has close to two hundred facilities for golf and tennis. There are hundreds more throughout the state.

The months of February, March, and April are busy with professional golf tournaments, around the state. In February each year, spectators flock to the Jackie Gleason Golf Classic, in Lauderhill, Florida. Another popular tournament is in Tallahassee. The PGA Open is held in April. Miami, Sarasota, and Jacksonville host other tournaments throughout the year. November is the time for the National Team Championship Golf Classic. The setting for this yearly event is Walt Disney World, in central Florida.

Besides being a spectator at the professional tournaments, the average golfer can have fun playing. There are public and private golf courses around the state.

Tennis

As an amateur sport, tennis is enjoying as much popularity as golf. It is hard to find an empty court. Althea Gibson, a former Florida A & M student was an outstanding tennis player. Tennis has been growing as a professional sport over the years, in our state. There are several professional tournaments held each year, in Florida. The mild climate and sunny days will surely increase these tournaments, as years pass. There are now several "tennis schools" in Florida, which teach young players the sport. Most hope to participate as a professional.

Auto Racing

Another spectator sport that draws attention is auto racing. Daytona Beach has been famous for auto racing since the early 1900's. One of the most exciting times at Daytona Beach came in 1935. That year, Sir Malcolm Campbell broke all records for speed. He drove "Bluebird" down the hard sandy beach at speeds over 442.5 kilometers/ 275 miles per hour.

Eventually, Daytona became so popular, a speedway was built. Car and motorcycle classics are held every year. The 4th of July weekend brings thousands of people to Daytona for the Firecracker 400.

Sebring hosts the Grand Prix Sports Car 12-hour endurance race, in mid-March, each year. Though auto racing is a dangerous sport with hundreds of miles per hour speeds,

it is an exciting way to spend the day for many visitors and residents of Florida.

Commercial Attractions

Florida was the choice for many vacationers even before Disney World or Busch Gardens opened their doors. Tourists have always been attracted to Florida's warm climate and sunny beaches. Now, commercial attractions have made Florida an ideal place to take a family vacation. It would be very difficult and expensive to see all of Florida in one visit. Most tourists come again and again.

The first commercial attraction in Florida was Cypress Gardens created by Dick Pope, Sr. The gardens opened in 1936 and immediately became world famous. Pictures of Cypress Gardens appeared in major magazines around the world. MGM movie studios used the gardens in two movies. Nearly forty million visitors have seen Cypress Gardens since Mr. Pope opened it.

Walt Disney World has become Florida's number one attraction. Millions of people have visited this central Florida amusement park since it opened. Walt Disney bought 10,926.9 hectares/ 27,000 acres of land in central Florida in the mid 1960's and began building this place of fun and fantasy. Eventually, it will include an experimental city of the future. The unusual part, Walt Disney never saw this multi-million dollar venture. He died before it was completed, however, his brother Roy Disney, opened the park in October, 1971.

The presence of Disney World in central Florida attracted other amusement activities such as Sea World. Here you can see dolphins and killer whales perform unbelieveable feats. You can actually feed and touch the dolphins, if you wish. There are enough activities and shows to entertain a family for more than a day.

Circus World has been another successful tourist attraction. Visitors not only watch, but may participate in circus events. There are rides and clowns and even an elephant ride.

Florida Division of Commerce and Tourism

Cypress Gardens

Busch Gardens, in Tampa, has become the second most popular commercial attraction in our state. It was built around the Anheuser-Busch brewing company. Busch Gardens offer bird and animal shows, beautiful gardens, exciting rides and a tour of the brewing company. Many people like to see how beer is made. A really unusual feature is the cageless zoo. Animals are allowed to roam on an open plain while visitors pass on a monorail.

South of Tampa, in Sarasota, you will find the Circus Hall of Fame and the Ringling Museum. When John Ringling died, he gave his estate to the state of Florida. This included the $1.5 million mansion which has been converted into a museum.

Since Florida became the home of the space program, Cape Canaveral has been added to the vacation plans of many visitors. Here you can take a tour of Kennedy Space Center and view the educational exhibits. It has became a popular place for tourist, as well as, a favorite field trip for school children.

Marine research attractions are a fun way to spend the day and learn about fascinating animals. Among these are the porpoises, sharks and killer whales. Marineland in northern Florida, was the first animal feature of this kind in our state. The Sequarium, in south Florida, has been the home of Flipper, the television star. Here you can see these mammals give astonishing and sometimes comical performances.

There are certain animals featured in our state. Lion Country Safari allows people to drive their cars through a park with lions roaming free. Others feature monkeys, birds, alligators and snakes.

Some of the gardens in Florida have become very popular. It was no accident that Ponce de Leon gave the name Florida to our state. Florida, in Spanish, means flowery. The flowers and plant life, are enjoyed in many private and public gardens around the state. Cypress Gardens and Busch Gardens are the best known. Sunken Gardens, in St. Petersburg is the oldest. They opened in 1924, and today have over 7,000 varieties of tropical plants and flowers.

The Japanese garden in Miami and Thomas Edison's botanical gardens in Fort Myers, his winter home, provide service to the tourist industry.

Commercial ventures have been an economic boon to Florida. The tourist industry gives thousands of jobs to people across Florida. Many industries and businesses benefit from the money that is spent. The natural beauty of Florida was enough to bring visitors to our state, but commercial attractions have turned tourism into a billion dollar industry.

Resort Cities

The resorts at Fernandina Beach and Jacksonville Beach were popular spots even before the railroads of Flagler and Plant reached far into south Florida. Now, there are many resort cities along both of Florida's coasts. Daytona Beach, Ft. Lauderdale, Hollywood and Key West are resort cities on the east coast. The most famous resort city in Florida is probably Miami Beach. With its thousands of hotel and motel rooms along the Atlantic Ocean, Miami Beach has been a favorite of tourists from around the world. Here something for everyone can be found. Sports such as swimming, water skiing, boating, shuffleboard, tennis, and golf are found in great abundance. Nightclubs and fine restaurants are a large part of the resort life in Miami Beach.

The beaches along the Gulf of Mexico have become known for their resort facilities. St. Petersburg, Clearwater, Pensacola, Fort Walton, Naples and Sanibel Island are some of the most visited resort beaches. Innisbrook, in the northern part of the Sun Coast, has recently become an exclusive resort area.

In the early days of Florida, there were not as many resorts to choose from. In the late 1890's two of the most famous old resorts, the Royal Poinciana in Palm Beach and Royal Palm in Miami, were built by Henry Flagler. Since that time, hundreds of resorts have been built all over Florida. This has made it even more desirable for visitors to extend their stay.

Springs

The hundreds of springs found in Florida are an important source of water. Some of the larger springs have been developed into tourist attractions. Silver Springs, Homosassa Springs and Weekiwachee Springs have much to offer a visitor. Glass bottomed boats allow viewers to see brightly colored fish beneath the surface. Most of these places offer swimming, picnicking and boating. A visit to one or more of these beautiful springs is a pleasant addition to a family vacation.

Historical Attractions

Some people come to Florida for the beaches and sunshine. Some come to enjoy the various commercial attractions. Others are interested in the history of Florida. There are many places in Florida that date back several hundred years.

St. Augustine is a city that goes back 500 years. It is the oldest city in the nation. In St. Augustine, you can see the oldest house (1599) and the oldest wooden schoolhouse. The historical part of the city shows life as it was in the 1700's. The state play "The Cross and The Sword" is performed here.

Most of the history of Florida is found in the northern part of the state. Forts, built by the Spanish and the British can be found in St. Augustine and Fernandina Beach, as well as, other areas in northern Florida. The battlefields of Natural Bridge and Olustee can be seen in this area. Both were battles of the Civil War.

Further south in Florida, visits can be made to Key Biscayne and the Cape Florida Lighthouse. It is one of the oldest structures in Florida. This area was once a coconut plantation, but has condominiums and apartments now.

Various museums, other old homes, Indian burial mounds, and monuments throughout Florida can be seen as a part of its long history.

Gasparilla Festival

Rodeo Riding.

State and National Parks

The largest and most famous park in Florida is the Everglades National Park. Visitors come to the park each year by the thousands, to see the unusual birds, the tropical plants, and maybe an alligator.

A visit to the park could include a canoe trip to a mangrove forest or an air boat ride through the "river of grass." Many people just like to walk the trails and enjoy the beauty of an unspoiled place. The Everglades is the last place in our nation that some of these animals or birds can still be found.

Visitors to Florida interested in camping, fishing and hiking have a choice of many state parks and three national forests. Hunting is allowed in the national forests by special permit.

The Apalachicola National Forest is the largest of the three, with 225,215.6 hectares/ 556,500 acres located in northwest Florida. This park has a canoe trail along the Sopchoppy River. Many other canoe trails exist throughout the state.

The most unusual park in Florida is the John Pennekamp Coral Reef State Park. It is the first underwater park in our nation. A glass bottom boat allows you to view the only living coral reef along the North American coast. Scuba diving is the adventurous way to see the brightly colored fish and rock formations. Scuba is an acronym meaning self contained underwater breathing apparatus.

Florida's parks and forests are a beautiful attraction to visitors looking for sunshine, water sports, fishing and camping. Visitors and Floridians must do everything possible to preserve the beauty in our state.

Fun In Florida

There is so much to do in Florida that many people have trouble deciding what to do first. A day, a week, or months of fun can be enjoyed by the visitor and resident alike.

What should we do today? The choices are endless... swimming... sunning... boating... football... soccer... a week at Disney World... the Everglades... birdwatching... and more.

Whatever fun you are looking for, you are sure to find it in Florida . . . The Sunshine State!

Lifestyles

Florida Photographic Archives

Billy Bowlegs III and fellow chief leaving a church service

LIFESTYLES

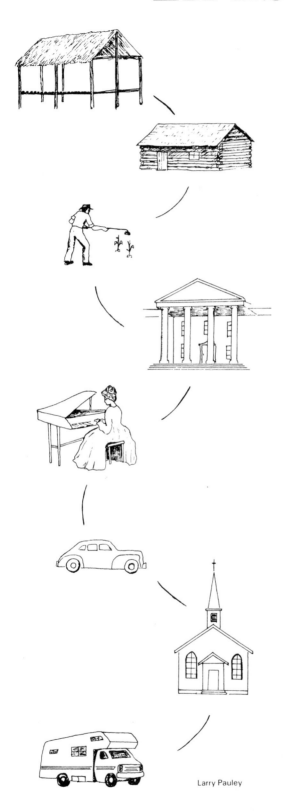

Larry Pauley

Introduction

How do you describe a Floridian? A group of students were asked this question. Their responses varied.

"...was born here."

"...is friendly."

"...is an individual."

"...is creative."

"...would not like to live anywhere else."

"...says 'Boca' instead of Boca Raton and 'St. Pete' rather than St. Petersburg."

"...always has a tan."

"...goes North for a vacation."

"...respects our state."

"...isn't surprised to hear Spanish, Japanese, German, Arabic, French, Greek or any other language at Disney World."

"...loves sports."

"...a person from Florida."

"...is like a kaleidoscope.

All of these describe some characteristics of being a Floridian. It is impossible to pinpoint exactly what a Floridian is. Each and every person has her/her own idea of what makes a true Floridian. We are going to look at the heritage, culture, religion, and location of the people who make up this state. This study could be called many things, but we have chosen to label it "Lifestyles."

When we look around, we see many different cultures. They range from the immigrant taking the oath of citizenship to the American Indian living and working here. Between this newest citizen and the one with the oldest claim to citizenship comes a variety of people. All are Floridians.

Floridians drive cars, eat at fast food restaurants, work in factories, attend church, go camping, pick oranges, and do many other things which make up their lifestyle. What people do today, though, may be different from what was done a few years ago or will be done a few years in the future.

Students of today find it difficult to imagine the past. If you were a teenager in 1950, your family would not have had a television set, let alone color. In 1960 you would not have flown in a commercial jet in Florida or ridden on an Interstate Highway.

Before 1945, there were no drive-in movies. In 1960 you would have paid only fifty cents to attend a first run movie. During the same year, you could not have done "wheelies" on your skateboard nor ridden your 10-speed bicycle.

Looking further back, a teenager in 1900 had never ridden in an automobile, seen an airplane, nor seen a movie. In 1875 you would not have eaten ice cream in a cone. Your family would not have had a sewing machine. One hundred years ago you would not have called your friends on the telephone or gone to a roller skating rink. You would not have used the words "scuba" nor ecosystem.

Eating habits have also changed. You could not have gone to a fast food hamburger restaurant in 1950. In 1900 your breakfast could not have been dry cereal in a box. It would not have been sugar-coated cereal in 1950.

Clothing styles and materials have changed greatly. Girls could not have worn bikinis to a swimming pool or beach in 1940. It was impossible to buy a polyester suit in 1950 or nylon hose in 1930. T-shirts were only underwear in 1940. Jeans were worn for working on the farm or in the groves in 1950 and neckties had to be worn to be well dressed.

You could not have made many purchases on Sunday in 1950. Gas stations had people to pump your gas in 1970 and they even cleaned the car's windshield. During the early 1960's you did not wear pants to school if you were a girl.

We all have difficulty picturing life during earlier times. When each generation looks at those which have preceded it, the lifestyles may seem strange or amusing. In order to better appreciate our ancestors and our heritage, it is necessary to consider that future generations will look back on life today and find some of our actions peculiar. It is important to remember that because something is different, it does not mean it is necessarily bad or funny. Lifestyles are continuously changing.

L
I
F
E
S
T
Y
L
E
S

It should also be remembered that lifestyles of present day Floridians have been strongly influenced by the past. Each generation of Floridians has learned from previous generations who lived before them. In this way, cultural traditions have been handed down. Today as yesterday, Floridians are influenced by the arrival of new cultural groups. Each new group has brought different customs and different ways of doing things. As native groups have mixed with newcomers, cultural exchange has taken place. This is a very old process, and it is still going on today.

Cultural exchange takes place very quickly today. Through modern means of transportation, Floridians use products that come from almost every country in the world. In the same way, goods from Florida travel abroad. We can turn on a television set and observe activities among cultural groups in places that are half way around the globe. This is a form of cultural exchange that can help us learn more about other people.

Indians

Life in what is now Florida was quite different when the early Indian civilizations lived here. Many times these early people did not leave written records, or we cannot interpret the records they left. What we know about these people comes from studying artifacts. These are man-made remains such as: bits of pottery, clothing, tools and weapons. Archaeologists study artifacts and "read" the clues about the way prehistoric people obtained their food, how they built their houses, what they ate, how they dressed and how they worshipped.

Life

The Indians of America probably came across a land bridge that once connected Asia to Alaska, over what is now the Bering Strait. They probably followed animals southward and slowly over thousands of years covered North, Central and South America. They were all Mongoloid peoples and we call them Paleo-Indians, meaning old or ancient Indians.

Some of these Indians were highly civilized, like the Aztecs and Mayas. Others remained primitive, like those in the Amazon River basin. Most, however, became hunter-cultivators with strong family and tribal ties. They all had similar appearances: bronze skins, strong arms and legs, wide skulls, high cheek bones, and straight black hair.

St. Johns People

The St. Johns people were hunters and nomadic wanderers. When they arrived at the St. Johns River around 5,000 B.C. they found enough food to remain in one area. They started constructing shelters for protection from the more dangerous animals. Their houses were on stilts. Animals and fish provided their food, of which they simply threw the remains down to the ground. Sometimes they would move to another location, but most of the time they would spread a layer of sand and soil over the trash. Slowly, the trash dumps built into mounds, which placed the people higher and safer. Mound building was common to the Paleo-Indians as can be seen in the Ohio Valley and Mexico.

Tools at first were the ready made items, animal bones, shells, sticks and hands. Their clothing was simple skin, breechcloths and moss skirts. Little is known of their religion, but they probably did not believe in life after death. Human bones have been recovered from the "middens" or trash heaps. Apparently, when a person died, they were simply shoved in with other animal remains.

These people found fallen trees and hollowed them out for dugout canoes. This means of transportation has not changed in design since pre-historic times. This allowed them to travel greater distances, faster. It helped spread their culture across the peninsula.

These people slowly learned to use flint and make simple pottery. The earliest pottery was "fiber tempered," with vegetable fibers mixed in with the clay to prevent shrinkage while firing or heating the pottery. Some designs lead to the belief that the idea of fiber pottery came from South America around 2,500 to 2,000 B.C. This leads to the belief that as the first Florida Indians spread across the peninsula they encountered boat travelers from South America. Some may have come from the Caribbean Islands.

Slowly, the Indians developed the pure clay, fired pottery and decorated it with an important design, maize. They learned that maize placed in the ground would grow more maize. This discovery changed these Indians from hunters to farmers, now they could establish permanent villages.

A society began to develop as stronger men became chiefs and their children were prepared to succeed them. The growth of villages developed into tribes and families stayed together longer. This gave them protection. The villages were built higher and higher on mounds. Sometime during the development of the tribes and villages, religion began to develop. The mounds began to play a part in the religion and the beliefs in a life after death. Captives were sacrificed to the sun on mounds, and burials were made in them.

Mounds

Indian mounds in Florida were built in many different shapes. There were circular mounds like snakes or shells, spider like mounds, and even the nine breadloaf mounds of Taylor River. Some were temples, such as the one found at Fort Walton and others had varied uses.

Those in the northern glades area were not only ceremonial, but functional. They had earth ridges, canals and artificial ponds. The ridges served as terraces for corn planting, and the canals for draining the land. Some were burial mounds, others were temple mounds, but all of them had middens.

The burial mounds contained two types of burials. Primary burials had the bodies placed in specific positions. They were usually bent at the knees in the fetal position. Secondary burials were less organized. First, the bodies were allowed to decay, and then the skeleton or parts of it were wrapped in a small bundle or placed in an urn. The wrapped bones or urn were then buried. Sometimes the bones were not wrapped but scattered around the mound.

Mounds were numerous in some areas. Over 40 mound sites have been found around Tampa Bay. They are 9.15 meters/ 30 feet or higher. Sometimes a single mound would cover several hectares/ acres.

Calusa

The Calusas lived south of the Caloosahatchee River. They expanded and dominated the Everglades area. The Calusas conquered the Tequesta of the Biscayne Bay area and the Ais and Jeaga of the East Coast. They spread their culture by conquest. Their houses with open sided and thatched roofs were adapted by the Seminoles and called "chickees."

Northern Tribes

The northern tribes were not united by any strong tribe, like the Calusas. They developed under different chiefs. However, there was a common thread in the area, an artistic culture. The first remains of this culture were found on Weeden Island in Tampa Bay. Because of this, it was called "Weeden Island Pottery." The culture extended from Charlotte Harbor around the Gulf Coast to the Mississippi River. These Indians excelled as pottery makers, jewelers, and figurine makers.

The greatest center of culture was at the Fort Walton Mound, where Indians used conch shells, shark teeth, bones and other teeth to carve for jewelry. They made copper headbands and bracelets, and pierced and strung fresh water pearls. These Indians traded as far north as the Ohio Valley for quartz and other semiprecious stones to be used for jewelry. Deerskins were hand painted with beautiful designs.

These northern people were the best pottery makers of Florida. Pots, jars, drinking vessels, and bowls were made in multiple shapes and designs. They were decorated in a variety of colors, some with handles shaped like birds, animals and humans.

Timucuans

The "Weeden Island" people controlled northern Florida until around 300 A.D. The last prehistoric people that swept across Florida were the Muskhogeans, a warlike uncultured people. They replaced the fine pottery of the conquered people, with crude pots decorated only with corncobs.

This group became known as the Timucuan, numbering about 14,000 of the 30,000 Florida Indians. While the members of this tribe were to perish within 200 years of the arrival of the Europeans, we have a remarkable record of their culture. With pictures and words, the French artist Jacques LeMoyne preserved for us the lifestyles of the sixteenth century Timucuans. LeMoyne traveled throughout Florida with the explorer Rene de Laudionniere.

LeMoyne described the Timucuans as tall, healthy and handsome. They were good farmers, though their tools were very simple. Their main crops were beans and corn. Part of their harvest was kept in storehouses for use in the winter. On special occasions, feasts were a main part of the celebrations.

The clothing of the Timucuans was fashioned from whatever was available from the environment: animal skins, feathers and Spanish moss.

Exercise was highly valued by the Timucuans. The young men and boys participated in races, and played a game in which a ball was thrown at a target. Timucuan men were skilled at hunting and fishing, and they were excellent warriors.

Pre-European Period

The exchange of culture between Indian groups and tribes began to accelerate around 1,000 A.D. These Indian groups had different languages; in many cases they seem to have had similar lifestyles and customs.

When a child was born, it was usually carried on a cradleboard until able to walk.

Indian burial mound pottery from Bird Island in Lake Weir

OFFERING THE SKIN OF A STAG TO THE SUN

Florida Photographic Archives

Timucuans offering a sacrifice to the sun by Le Moyne

Young children ran and played. The method of punishment was one of shaming the child. Around seven or eight years of age, boys began training for hunting and fishing. The girls began training for cooking and family work. When they were ready for marriage, the families chose the person who would become the spouse.

Food consisted of berries, meat, beans, squash, and maize. Maize, beans, and squash are important as this shows that these Indians were changing from gathering to farming. Pumpkins and gourds were also raised. The agricultural activities were done in clearings which had been burned. The Europeans called these clearings "old fields." The Indians preserved meat by salting or smoking it. Vegetables were preserved by drying. The Indian women cooked their food in holes in the ground. At mealtime everyone ate with their fingers and threw the garbage aside.

Shelters and clothing were practical. Adornment was worn in the form of jewelry. Housing was the Indian wigwam or chickee. The wigwam and chickee differed from the teepee used by the prairie Indians. Clothing was made mainly from tanned deerhide or buckskin. The women were clothed in Spanish moss aprons. Leather moccasins were used as footwear.

Before the Europeans arrived in North America, the Indians had no large beast of burden. The only domesticated animal was the dog. Because there was no animal for carrying, the Indians did not make use of the wheel. We recognize that they knew the principle of the wheel because they played a game of rolling hoops and throwing things through the hoops. When they transported goods, they either used the dugout canoe or carried them.

Education was "learn by doing." Boys and girls were taught separate skills. Each skill served a necessary part in the village or tribal life. History, or an appreciation of the past, was taught through a form of free verse poetry. The stories, often sung, related the past deeds of the tribe. The poetry was a mixture of myths, legend, and deeds. Sometimes the singing was accompanied by bone flutes, rattling dried gourds, or drum beats.

The musical instruments were also used for celebrations. Most of the celebrations or feasts were related to religion. The harvest feast is an example. There was much eating, dancing, and praising the gods for a good harvest. They believed in life after death. All living things were considered important in their religion.

Fire was made by two processes. The first was by friction. A stick was placed in a block with a hole notched in the block. Wood shavings were placed around the turn stick. The stick was rotated rapidly by pulling back and forth on a leather thong looped around the stick. When the shavings reached the kindling point and ignited, they were transferred to small twigs and a fire was built. The second method was the spark method. Wood shavings were placed on the ground. Then the fire maker would strike a piece of flint against a metal stone, usually iron pyrite. When struck together, a spark would fly, igniting the shavings.

These Indians had a variety of tools and weapons. The items were made of wood, stone, bones, shells, and metal. Weapons included bows and arrows, tomahawks, and spears. Tools included axes, hammers, digging implements, and needles for sewing. Sharpened rocks were attached to sticks for weapons and tools by an ingenious method. The stick was split for a few centimeters/inches and the rock was placed in the splits. Leather thongs or sinews were soaked in water and tied around the stick and rock. It was then placed in the sun to dry. As it dried, the leather shrunk and held the rock tightly to the wooden handle. Almost all tribes made baskets and pottery. They did not have the potter's wheel, but were still able to produce artistic pottery.

Indian Contributions

The 1500's were to bring a great change to the Americas. Europeans were to begin their great migration to America. Many times they would not give credit to the native Americans for their contributions in lifestyle and culture. Leather clothing, moccasins, and canoes were Indian inventions readily adapted by the Europeans. Indian agricultural methods were adopted by the Europeans, planting in the "old fields" left by the Indians.

New food items became a part of the Europeans' life. Maize, turkey, popcorn, pumpkins and tobacco were a few of the items added to the diet of Europeans.

Indian names and words were added to the vocabulary of the Spanish, French and English. The cultures blended until sometimes, it is difficult to find the origin.

The Spanish

The Spanish arrived on the Florida peninsula in 1513 and viewed it as a land to be conquered. They thought of the natives as "uncivilized" and believed it their duty to civilize them. This "civilizing" of the Indians was actually an attempt to destroy the Indian culture and supplant it with the Spanish culture.

Religion was to become the most lasting part of the Spanish culture to be brought to America. The Spanish attempted to convert the Indians to Catholicism. They built missions across northern Florida from St. Augustine to Apalachee. The Spanish approached the Indians differently than the English. They were souls to be saved. There were over 50 missions by 1650 including places like San Francisco, San Diego de Salmatoto, and San Juan.

The Spanish considered the missions more important than the soldiers because the Catholic Pope wanted the King of Spain to Christianize Florida. Life in the missions centered around the mystery of the Mass. Indians from surrounding villages trekked to the mission when the bell was rung. The Indians were baptized, married and buried in Catholic ceremonies. In a visit by the Bishop of Havana to St. Augustine, 2,074 Indians were baptized along with 370 Spaniards.

A serious result of the European migration was the importation of disease. Thousands of Indians died from diseases like measles. They had not developed any immunity to European diseases and once a village became infected, sometimes the entire population would die.

The Spanish gave freedom to Indians and black slaves escaping from Georgia. This created hostility toward the Spanish. It also gave slave traders an excuse to raid Florida, where they took more slaves. Captain Thomas Nairne took slaves from the Ais and Jeaga and almost eliminated the Tequestas and Calusas. He drove them northward to slavery which changed the lifestyle of the Indians dramatically. In some villages they were adapting the Spanish ways and as slaves were exposed to English customs. A small percentage escaped both cultures for a while by migrating to the Everglades.

Spain's soldiers and missionaries brought other cultural changes to Florida. They brought a beast of burden and transportation, the horse. They brought oranges, cattle, metal tools and the gun, also.

The French

France's influence on the culture of Florida was limited. This was due to the short time they actually occupied modern day Florida. However, if you include the area of what was West Florida, the French Mardi Gras still exists today in Mobile.

Perhaps the most significant transfer of culture was not from the French to the Indians, but vice-versa. The culture of the Timucuans was recorded by the French artist Le Moyne de Morgues. He drew the best presentation we have today of undisturbed Indian life.

The French accepted the Indian lifestyle more than the Spanish and English, and therefore made little attempt to change the Indians.

The English

When the English received Florida in 1763, the Spanish had been there over 200 years. Many of them were second generation Floridians, never having seen Spain. It was a sad day for the 3,046 citizens of St. Augustine who sailed for Havana in small boats. They were refugees from Florida to Cuba along with many Catholic Indians, who feared the Protestant English. Some Indians retreated into the Everglades or to the Keys, which the Spanish still claimed.

A change was to come rapidly to Florida with English occupation. The governor of East Florida gave 40.5 hectares/100 acres to each head of a family coming to Florida and 20.2 hectares/50 acres were added for each member of the family and slaves. As they came into St. Augustine and other villages, the English did not like the Spanish architecture and proceeded to change it. They tore down shutters, which allowed cool evening breezes in and kept the sun out and replaced them with solid glass. The courtyards or patios seemed unnecessary and they roofed them over. Outdoor kitchens on the patios were replaced by chimneys and fireplaces inside the houses. New houses were built of wood instead of the coquina of the Spanish. Fruit trees were cut for firewood and lumber. The English seemed intent to completely replace the despised Spanish way of life.

In East Florida there were attempts to bring in the genteel English society. Dances or balls were held and intellectuals discussed local and world affairs. The upper class men wore wigs and satin coats. The ladies wore fancy gowns, wigs and sprinkled themselves with jewelry.

Governor Grant had a mansion called "The Villa" with 40 slaves and 2,428.2 hectares/6,000 acres. Colonel Robert Bisset owned 3,844.7 hectares/9,500 acres on the

Mosquito River. This included five settlements and a slavetown with 70 inhabitants. Numerous other large estates were located in East Florida, all of them designed in the English style.

Literature was developed during the British control of Florida. The "East-Florida Gazette" was published during this period until 1784. The first two books published in Florida were brought out, The Case of the Inhabitants of East-Florida and Essay II, On the Nature and Principles of Public Credit.

The Indians had to come to terms with the English. A treaty was signed in East Florida pledging the Spanish idea of land ownership. All land belonged to the Indians except that which they had given to the Spanish. The English were to occupy a small region bounded by the Atlantic Coast, St. Johns River and the St. Marys River. All the rest of East Florida was Indian territory.

Landless Englishmen, however, saw the successful cattle areas of the Indians and the vast territory in central Florida as land for occupation. Soon the Indians were being driven southward.

The fifteenth English Colony, West Florida, was little more than a frontier when compared with the fourteenth colony of East Florida. Roads were inadequate and social comforts almost unknown. Pensacola was the Indian center for Southern British North America. Therefore, it was always crowded with Indians and traders. It was a rough and tumble atmosphere, with fights and duels being common.

New Smyrna

A different type settlement was developed during the British period in East Florida. This was "New Smyrna" on the East Coast. Dr. Andrew Turnbull had been a British consul at Smyrna in Asia Minor and had married a Greek girl. He saw Florida as an area having a climate similar to the Mediterranean area and a place for refugees from Turkey to begin a new life. Turnbull received three grants of 8,094 hectares/ 20,000 acres on the Hillsborough River. Here he had 500 houses built by means of slave labor. Turnbull sailed to the Mediterranean and brought Greeks, Italians and people from the island of Minorca to Florida. These people were indentured servants. By this system a person agreed to work for a set period of years in America in exchange for passage to the New World. The indentured servants at New Smyrna received clothing, food and housing; in return their heavy labor made a prosperous settlement for Turnbull. At the end of the period of indenture, usually seven years, they became free and were sometimes given property.

The indentured servant system did allow people to start a new life in America. There are families in Florida today who can trace their heritage to this system. One bad aspect of the system was that many blacks sold as indentured servants were never released. This helped to establish a slavery system based on race. The greater number of Europeans provided them an opportunity to impose this unfair extension of the indentured system upon the Africans.

The indentured servant system in New Smyrna was successful. There were complaints of abuse of the servants by Turnbull's overseers, but the settlement survived. Internally, there were cultural problems of the New Smyrna people, and the English did not trust any of them because most were Catholic.

The Americans

With British control, settlers poured into Florida. The land was fertile, especially in the region that came to be known as Middle Florida (between the Suwannee and Apalachicola Rivers). The big cash crops were cotton, tobacco, sugar cane and rice. Food crops included corn, beans, sweet potatoes and collard greens. Farm families also produced their own eggs, milk, butter and cheese. Many families had at least a few cows, hogs, and chickens.

In the forests, game was abundant. Pioneer dinner tables were well supplied with venison, rabbits, squirrels, wild turkey and quail. Fresh fish were plentiful in the rivers, lakes and coastal areas.

For those necessary foodstuffs that were not produced at home or made available by nature, the frontier people could travel to a general store or trading post. At such facilities they could stock up on salt, coffee, flour, grits and dried beans.

Special Occasions

Food was often the focal point for parties, festivals and other special occasions. On the frontier, big celebrations often accompanied a house-raising. A house-raising involved the building of a house - often in one day - by a settler, his friends and neighbors. After the work was done, there was dancing to the music of fiddlers. Food was served in a picnic setting.

The plantation set and wealthier town folk enjoyed large dinner parties at which each guest would bring a specially prepared dish. Supper was usually preceded by an evening full of dancing, accompanied by the music of fiddles and banjos.

The Christmas season was an especially festive occasion. The celebrations lasted for a week, and included parties, feasts and gift giving. Slaves were included in some of these activities (including gift-giving), and were excused from their duties during the holiday week.

Clothing

Florida frontier families also produced much of their own clothing. Dresses for women featured long, floor length skirts. These were usually made of simple homespun fabric. For special occasions, brightly colored calico was popular. Those who couldn't afford "storebought" colored fabrics sometimes used indigo or dyes made from tree bark to color their cloth. Wealthier ladies favored silk dresses with wide, padded skirts.

Men of the frontier wore pants and coats of jeans materials. These were usually home made, and were worn for almost all occasions. The "designer" jeans of the day

came from Kentucky, and were sometimes available in Florida stores. Fashionable gentlemen wore suits made of broadcloth or, especially in the summer, of linen or gingham. Shoes for men and women were made from the tanned hides of cattle and from deerskin.

An interesting example of cultural adaptation can be seen in the classic dress of the Seminole women today. While the colorful designs are distinctly Seminole, the fullness of the skirt and the ruffled blouses were adapted from styles worn by pioneer settlers of the mid 1800's.

Religion

Religion was a powerful force in territorial Florida. Churches were established very quickly in frontier communities. Circuit riding preachers often served communities that did not have a resident minister. Most of the settlers belonged to one of the major Protestant denominations: Baptist, Methodist, Presbyterian or Episcopalian.

The Roman Catholic religion, which had been the major denomination during the Spanish period, declined sharply in membership during the first part of the territorial period. By the time of statehood, it had begun to regain some of its former strength.

A few Jews were among Florida's territorial pioneers, but no synagogues were established until after the Civil War.

Seminoles

A new culture was developing among the Indians of Florida and the southeast. This was the Seminole Indian group. The name had derived from the Jamaican word "Cimarrones," for Indians and blacks who had escaped slavery and run away to the mountains of Jamaica. In Florida, the term was used to describe all the Indians who were migrating away from the white areas. The pronunciation of the word, at first, was "Seminolies" and came to mean "runaways." The Indians did not call themselves this at first, but referred to all

Indians in Florida as "People of the Peninsula." These people were a mixture of tribes including Creeks, Choctaws, Chickasaws, Cherokees, Catawbas and other smaller tribes. There was also a percentage of blacks who had run away from slavery living with the Seminoles.

A group which many times is placed with the Seminoles is the Miccosukee. This Hitichi-speaking group settled around Tallahassee in the Spanish days, but later migrated south to the Everglades. The Seminoles, including the Miccosukee, became good farmers and cattlemen, but their lifestyle and land ownership would cause problems for them when the Americans obtained Florida.

Second Spanish Period

England lost Florida after only 20 years of ownership. Spain attempted to reinstitute her culture, but it really was a substitution. Most of the English fled when they found out that Spain regained Florida. The Indians adjusted somewhat, but kept migrating to the Everglades. Some of the Spanish Floridians who had left for Havana returned and the Catholic Mass once again was celebrated. The Spanish did not have time to completely reestablish control because of a new energetic nation to the north, the United States.

The Frontier

During the territorial period Florida was a paradox. This marked the simultaneous beginnings of: the upper class southern planter, the dirt farmers, the slaves, and the proud Seminoles. Each contributed to the culture of Florida.

The southern plantation had its origin from two areas, the "Old South of the Carolinas and the English estates of the British occupation of Florida. Life for the white plantation owner was very good. This society respected education and culture, while frowning on those who labored.

At the other extreme were the black slaves. The slaves were denied freedom, citizenship and education. Their labor was looked upon

---

THE SEMINOLES AND THE BLACKS

An interesting part of Florida's history is found in the relationship between Indians and blacks during the first half of the 19th century. Before Florida became a U.S. possession, it was a place of refuge for runaway slaves from nearby southern states. The escape routes of the runaways often brought them in contact with Seminole Indians. While relations with the Indians were not always good, it often happened that the Indians and blacks helped each other.

Slaves who escaped sometimes set up independent villages. On other occasions they became the slaves of Seminoles. They were purchased by the Seminoles, also. As masters, Seminoles were kinder than whites or other Indian tribes that kept slaves. Seminole slaves were allowed to raise their own crops and livestock. In return, a portion of the crop or herd was taken by the Seminoles as payment or tribute.

The blacks imitated the Seminoles' dress and learned to speak their language. Many of them spoke Spanish and English as well, therefore becoming more valuable to the Indians in their dealings with whites.

White settlers feared that the presence of blacks among the Seminoles would set a bad example for their slaves. Indeed, some slaves did escape and cast their lot with the Seminoles.

The blacks fought alongside the Seminoles in battles against white settlers and soldiers during the Seminole wars. They were able warriors, military advisers and served as spies for the Indians. When the war drew to a close, several hundred blacks went with the Seminoles who were transferred to western lands. Most of the runaways were returned to their former owners, others captured were sold into slavery.

Seminole man and boy in dugout canoe

as a duty to make the life of the wealthy planter comfortable. The lives of the slaves were carefully controlled. Owners were afraid the slaves might try to escape; they feared revolts, also. Slaves depended on the owner for everything: clothing, food, living quarters, religion and sometimes even life itself.

Within the slave community there existed a caste system. Those who worked as house servants usually had a better life and a higher rank than those who labored in the fields.

Treated worse than blacks in the territories of Florida were the Indians who had been treated as human beings by the Spaniards. The English saw them as markets, but the Americans saw them as savages who hindered them from obtaining land. The Americans wanted the Indians out of the way by any means possible.

A semblance of legality was maintained by signing the Treaty of Camp Moultrie. Its main purpose was to hide from the Indians the fact that the new government planned to move them across the Mississippi River as soon as possible. This treaty changed the lifestyles of the Seminoles. These once proud people who had been farmers and cattle owners were reduced to begging. Their children went hungry and were ridiculed when they went any place.

In 1838, several Seminole chiefs were tricked into signing an agreement to move west to Oklahoma. The agreement was resisted by young braves, causing the outbreak of war. After five years of war the Seminoles were either relocated or driven deep into the Everglades. Their culture had been permanently altered.

A group of Floridians who fit neither the upper nor lower class were frontiersman. They lived in the north and were typical American frontiersman of English background. They generally owned no slaves and disagreed with the idea of forced labor.

243

These proud people believed in hard work and God. Their houses were log cabins, consisting of two rooms with the same roof and a space in between. This was apparently a cross between the American frontier log cabin and the Spanish patio. Almost everything was done outdoors, including cooking. Food consisted of: game animals, hogs, chickens, corn and berries. Corn provided not only food, but the shucks were used for mattress stuffing, making brooms and toy dolls.

Life was hard work for the whole family. On the frontier, large families were an advantage, and families with eight to ten children were not uncommon. School consisted of the boys learning to do outside jobs and the girls learning household chores. Play for the children was hide and seek, running and jumping.

Ante Bellum Florida

The period between statehood in 1845, and the Civil War saw a more rigid structure in the society of Florida. The society was like a pyramid. On top was the planter class with set rules of social conduct. An unwritten code required men to be extreme gentlemen, courageous and honorable. A challenge to one's honor more often than not resulted in a duel. Men were expected to engage in oratory, politics and professions which required no labor. The ladies were to be beautiful and pure. They were expected to read, paint and be defended by the men.

Professionals were the second level of society and they were acceptable at events of the planters if they or their families owned slaves. Lawyers, doctors and Episcopal ministers were in this class. The third level was the "working white" class such as: overseers, slavetraders, and storekeepers. They were spoken to by the planter class but never invited to social events.

Below this was the lower class of whites, the farming families. This group felt they were equal to the first class but the planters did not think so. Slightly less than this was a subclass of actors and innkeepers.

At the bottom of the pyramid were the slaves. Though at the bottom, their labor supported the whole system for they were the basis of everything. The planter class saw them as a total group and not as individuals with emotions. Some were well trained, while others were uneducated field hands, but all used their intelligence to survive in a world they could not control. Some were loyal to their masters, others were bitter against the system. Most were religious, finding a comfort in the hope for eternal life. They had two lives, one in front of the whites and another when they were alone during the evenings or holidays. Here they would laugh, sing, fall in love, cry and comfort each other. But, slaves were aware that they did not control their own lives.

Slavery found its way into the lives of those who did not own slaves. Ministers defended the system from the Old Testament and lawyers cited the Constitution as to its legality.

Housing

Most houses in Florida at the time of statehood were made of wood. On some of the plantations and in the larger towns such as St. Augustine, Tallahassee and Pensacola, there were large, fine residences of frame construction. These homes were made of sawn boards and had glass windows.

Most Floridians, however, lived in much smaller dwellings. As in other frontier areas during this period, many of the houses were log cabins. Some of the larger log houses had front and back porches, and a separate log kitchen where the cooking was done.

Families who could afford it purchased "storebought" furniture. Wealthy planters prided themselves on their expensive furnishing, which often included imported silverware and china. For most pioneer families, furniture was usually homemade. Beds, tables and chairs were fashioned from pine or oak. Pillows and mattresses were stuffed with grass, moss or feathers.

Frontier families helped beautify their homes with a wide variety of ornamental plants and trees. Among the most popular varieties were crepe myrtles, periwinkles and four o'clocks. Such plantings can be seen in yards and gardens throughout Florida today. Wealthier families grew fancy roses, oleanders and planted stately magnolia trees.

As the plantation economy prospered, brick and masonry homes became popular with the wealthier class. Some of these mansions have been preserved and can be seen as museums today. One of the most famous of these is the Gamble mansion, located near Bradenton. Dating from this era, but of a somewhat different architectural style are the picturesque two story frame homes that were built in Key West. These homes were modeled after homes in New England, and were often made by ships' carpenters. Typical of this style is the Oldest House in Key West, built in 1829. This house is now maintained as a museum.

For travelers, housing could be obtained very reasonably, compared to today's standards. In 1845, the City Hotel in Tallahassee (which was the largest hotel in Florida) charged $1.00 a day for a room and meals! There was no telephone when Florida became a state. The electric telegraph had recently been invented, but it had not reached Florida. News traveled by word-of-mouth, through the mail or was printed in newspapers. Ten Florida newspapers were being published in 1845, including two in Tallahassee.

Food and Farming

Floridians, in 1845, were much more directly involved in producing and obtaining their food than are present-day residents. Over 90 percent of the population lived on farms or rural areas. In order to plant crops and cultivate gardens, the land usually had to be cleared. Some fortunate farmers

Ronald Cold

Oldest house in Key West

Farming house with mud chimney in 1886

obtained land that was already open. Sometimes this land consisted of the "old fields" that had been cleared earlier by Indians. However, much of the land was forested, and the trees had to be removed before crops could be grown.

The wealthy planters had slave gangs to do this work. The small landowner who had no slaves had to clear the land himself with the aid of his family and sometimes, his neighbors. Whoever did the job, it was long hard work.

Civil War

The period of the Civil War brought great social changes to Florida. Disuse during the war had led to the general wear of buildings and plantations in Florida. The wealthy had spent much of their money on the war effort or converted it to now worthless Confederate currency. Only one mansion remained unburned on the St. Johns River.

Poor people suffered more than the plantation owners. White farmers returning to their land found overgrown areas they had sweated and toiled to clear. Their stock of cattle, pigs and fowl were all gone.

Former black slaves, now freed men, clogged the roads in rural areas and streets of cities. They were at the same time confused, frightened and happy. Confused, because the plantation economy had not prepared them for freedom. Frightened, because they did not know what was going to happen to them. Happy, because they were free to go as they pleased, even though without a prior destination.

A Readjusting Society

The period following the end of the Civil War created a need for readjustment of society. The government in Washington decreed that the old pyramid society was dead, but it would take many years for it to happen. Many former plantation owners just picked up what was usable, headed south into unpopulated areas of Florida and started over. Others resented that blacks were able to vote and participate in government.

Blacks began to exercise their new citizenship. They ran for public offices, voted and served on juries. Poor whites had to compete for jobs with blacks. There were more people looking for work than there were jobs available.

The old society began to be idolized and glamourized by many whites. The problems of the slave society were forgotten and only the good remembered. Even the whites who had not owned slaves began to resent the blacks' freedom. New secret societies like the Order of the White Camellia and the Ku Klux Klan arose to take away the rights of blacks.

Rumors, fear, and violence were the weapons of these secret groups. Stories were told of secret African rituals being practiced with sacrifices and blood rites. These stories caused fear in law abiding whites and caused them, if not to support, at least not to oppose the White Camellia and KKK. Fear was instilled in blacks with threats. Night riders wearing masks and sheets burned crosses in front of blacks who tried to practice their citizenship. Violence like whippings and lynchings drove the blacks into secondary citizenship.

All of these events were coded into a system called "Jim Crowism." Blacks, who briefly had experienced citizenship, were made to ride separate streetcars, go to separate parks, and eat in separate dining places. Blacks retreated to their own society under this segregation.

Literature

Not all of the period from 1865 to 1900 was spent depriving the blacks of citizenship. This was a period when literature about Florida became popular. Abby M. Brooks wrote: Petals Plucked from Sunny Climes; Sidney Lanier contributed, Florida: Its Scenery, Climate and History. William Cullen Bryant wrote a series of newspaper articles for the "New York Evening Post." Harriet Beecher Stowe moved to Mandarin, where she wrote: Letters From Florida and Palmetto Leaves. All of these works discussed the advantages of life in Florida.

The first articles on the beauty of Lake Okeechobee were written by Fred A. Ober for "Forest and Stream Magazine." Charles J. Maynord wrote: The Birds of Florida in 1872-78. These writings developed an interest in the state by northerners and others, who began looking to Florida as a place for beginning a new life.

Tours and vacations in Florida were becoming the "in thing" for wealthy northerners. Steamboat cruises up the St. Johns and Oklawaha Rivers to Silver Springs gave the rich and famous a look at vegetation and animal life seen nowhere else. The thrill of seeing alligators on the shore was told and retold by tourists.

Immigration

The wealthy were not the only people to have an interest in Florida. Land hungry northerners of the working class saw an opportunity to better their lives and circumstances. Many Europeans and people from other areas also saw the chance for freedom and opportunity. All brought elements of their cultures, adding to the diversity and color of Florida.

Cubans

One of the first groups to come to Florida after the Civil War were from only 144.8 kilometers/ 90 miles away. In 1867, problems in Cuba caused thousands of Cubans to flee their homeland to the nearby Florida Keys. This would be the first of many refugee flights from Cuba. Once again, the Spanish speaking people were on the peninsula. Most of these Cuban people concentrated in Key West and then in Tampa. There, they found work in the cigar industry. They were 25 percent of the work force of the Key West Extension of the East Coast Railroad. Railroad officials wanted the Cubans and Spanish because they were the most "efficient and industrious."

Swedish

Henry Sanford, in 1871, brought more than 100 Swedes to work in his citrus groves. A heavy immigration of Swedes never

Live Oak Plantation in Leon County, once the home of Governor John Branch. Shown in 1889

occurred, but a few families formed the community of New Uppsala. Others came to the area over the years, and many of their descendents still live in the area.

A Swedish promoter, Olaf Zetterlund, and the Florida East Coast Railway started a land development scheme using Swedish language appeals. This resulted in the start of the Lutheran community of Hallandale in 1897.

Dutch

Promotions in their native language drew immigrants from the Netherlands to Florida. Many were attracted by the similarities in terrain. Others saw the chance to obtain land more easily than waiting for land to be drained in Holland. A colony in 1883 settled at Fernandina, but soon moved to near Tallahassee.

Danes

White City became the first settlement for settlers from Denmark. They were also enticed by promotions written in their own language. Louis Pio saw the advertisements and brought several hundred Danes to White City in 1893. The community almost failed because Mr. Pio died and the manager embezzled funds. The Florida East Coast Railway stepped in and aided them financially. The Danes prospered and by 1900 were advertising for "young marriageable ladies" to immigrate to White City.

Another Danish community aided by the Florida East Coast Railway was Dania. The railroad appointed A.C. Frost as land agent for the settlement. By 1908, there were over 1,000 Danes raising tomatoes and pineapples for a living in Dania.

Russians

A small number of Russians came to Florida around 1900. They had fled internal troubles and hard times in Czarist Russia. There were settlements of over 4,047 hectares/10,000 acres where vegetables were raised. The Russian communities were closely knit groups. During the Great Depression some returned to their native land while others scattered throughout Florida.

Jews

Persecution in Europe and in many countries led Jews of different nationalities to emigrate to Florida. Restrictions on land ownership in Europe had led many into the business world where they excelled. A large Jewish community developed in the Miami area. Many became leaders in the community.

Japanese

Henry Flagler's promotions of Florida brought a group of Japanese settlers to the East Coast. Flagler and Joseph Sakai arranged for the purchase of a settlement north of present day Boca Raton in 1903. The community was called Yamato and the settlers raised tea, tobacco, rice and pineapples. They also tried to develop a silk industry by raising silkworms, but the project failed. By 1907, there were 200 Japanese living in Yamato, where they had the most successful pineapple plantation in southern Florida.

The growth of Yamato brought a United States Post Office and a station on the East Coast Railway. Prosperity lasted until other pineapple growers became more efficient and profits declined. Many settlers moved to other areas, some returned to Japan and a few remained. Many were victims of the internment of Japanese during World War II, when President Franklin Roosevelt ordered all Japanese and Japanese-Americans imprisoned in the Midwest. Many had their property confiscated.

One of the Japanese settlers, Mr. George Morikami of Delray, gave the state of Florida 16.2 hectares/ 40 acres for an Agricultural Experimental Station. He also gave West Palm Beach the same amount of land as a recreational park for a memorial.

Greek diver in 1944 at Tarpon Springs

Greeks

Climate, geography and vocation brought one of the most successful groups to Florida. John Cocoris, a sponge dealer, realized that the area in Tarpon Springs had the basis for a large sponge industry. He knew the best sponge divers in the world came from Greece. He brought a group of experienced Greek deep sea divers to Florida in 1905. Cocoris bought diving equipment and developed the sponge industry.

Many Greeks followed the original immigrants and a large Greek community grew in Tarpon Springs. Originally sponge divers, the Greeks have became fishermen, restaurant owners, and business men. The large Greek community brought their Eastern Orthodox Catholic Church to West Florida along with their culture and customs. The annual Epiphany celebration draws tens of thousands of visitors to Tarpon Springs.

Poles

Political and social unrest in Poland caused many Poles to emigrate to the United States in the early 1900's. A group of 50 Poles from Warsaw settled south of Jacksonville. Another group settled near Bunnell in Flagler County. Both communities flourished for a while, but most residents moved to other towns. Their strong Catholic faith is reflected in churches in the area.

Railroads, Automobiles and Airplanes

Major changes in the character of Florida were brought about by changes in transportation. Families could travel further and see more. Cities grew at the end of each rail stop, as railways were laid across the state. As highways were constructed, rural areas opened up. It was no longer necessary for a worker to live close to where he was employed.

In 250 years of Spanish occupation little more than the St. Augustine area and the Pensacola region had been occupied. During the next 150 years towns and cities sparsely dotted the state. Since 1900, Florida has been occupied statewide. It now takes no more than an hour by jet to go any place within the state.

Improvements in transportation have brought millions of residents to the state since 1900. Most migration in America has had a westward trend since colonial days. Florida is one exception. Migration to Florida has been predominantly from the north. The cultural makeup in the 1980 census showed 60 percent of the residents of Florida were not natives of the state.

Another migration has occurred from the Carribean Islands. Governmental problems and economics have forced thousands of Cubans and Haitians to sail for freedom to the Florida Peninsula. In 1980 alone, 125,000 Cubans migrated to southern Florida as refugees. This has caused cultural problems in Miami and other Florida cities.

Women

Citizens born in 1900 would see major changes occur in the lives of women. Women could not vote in 1900, but by 1921 they had gained suffrage. It would be 1970, though, before women could borrow or have credit on their own ability. Relegated to housework or menial tasks in 1900, two World Wars began to change their dress and jobs. With a shortage of men as teachers and factory workers in 1918, women entered the teaching profession and started working the assembly lines in factories. Again, it would be the 1970's and 80's, before women became administrators in either factories or schools at the secondary level.

Clothing and hair styles changed rapidly with the turn of the century. Few women had short hair before 1900, but soon afterward short hair became the style. Long dresses to the ankles shortened during World War I and by the '20's "Flappers" were the rage. Since 1940, dresses have regularly lengthened and shortened from "mini" to "midi" to "maxi." Beaches in 1900 had women covered from neck to ankle, but in the 1980's bikinis were predominant. Movie stars began wearing slacks in films, during the 1940's, and by 1960

Picnic in the 1890's

women in every part of society were wearing pants. During the late 1970's dresses once again became very fashionable. Shorts gained acceptability almost everywhere.

Men had slight changes in clothing during the same period. Pants changed from slacks to knickers and then back to slacks. A change which created an uproar was hair styles for men. During the 1960's, male students were sent home from school for having long hair or attempting to grow beards. By the mid 1970's, the men teachers sported beards and long hair.

Work Week

The reduced work has allowed more time for relaxation. At the turn of the century only the wealthy took vacations. Farm labor or factory workers worked 70 hour weeks and had no vacation time. Today, almost every person working in Florida expects and gets a vacation with pay. The reduced work week of 40 hours and sometimes as low as 32 hours has given more time for leisure activities. Games such as golf and tennis, once the activities of the wealthy, are played today throughout Florida by all levels of society.

Food

One of the greatest changes in lifestyle has been the change in eating habits. From the earliest settlers through the 1800's most Floridians grew and provided their own food. Canning and drying food was an agonizing chore. In the later part of the 1800's and early 1900's, markets supplied freshly killed meat and fresh vegetables. Bakeries had route wagons and delivered fresh baked goods to the door. Dairies did the same, the milkwagon was a common sight. Food was kept fresh in cellars or in ice boxes. The iceman made daily deliveries of blocks of ice. The ice was put in the ice box to keep food cool. Preparing meals was a long hard task. Hours were consumed each day in cooking.

Changes occurred when food was put in metal cans and factory blown bottles. Less time was spent in preparation. Cooking stoves changed from open hearths, to wood burners, to gas, to electric, and to the modern microwave oven. It only takes minutes now to cook the same item it once took hours to prepare at the turn of the century.

There are sociologists who predict that by the year 2000 over 90 percent of all food will be prepared by restaurants. During the 1980's, one of the fastest growing industries in Florida was the restaurant and the fast food business. Foods do much to help us understand the lifestyle of Floridians. Food plays an important part in every culture, from the way it is obtained to the way it is prepared, to the way it is consumed.

For earlier generations of Floridians, diets consisted mainly of what could be grown near the place where one lived. With modern means of transportation and food packaging, foods from all over the world find their place to the dinner tables of Floridians. In the same way, foods produced in Florida travel around the globe.

Despite the wide assortment of foods available, many Floridians still favor the "special" foods that are part of their cultural heritage. Imagine a Florida picnic table spread with foods donated by various cultural groups represented in the state. There might be grits, cornbread and blackeyed peas from those reared in the traditions of the Old South; arroz con pollo (chicken and rice), frijoles negroes (black beans) and platanos (fried plantains) from those of Cuban heritage; and stuffed grape

leaves and Mousaka from those of Greek ancestry. Jewish Floridians might add bagels and lox and cream cheese. Floridians with roots in the Bahamas might contribute some tasty conch fritters. These specialties and many more are prepared daily in homes throughout Florida. They can also be found on the menus of many fine restaurants around the state - along with such standard American dishes as steak and potatoes! Florida's position as a leading tourist state has given rise to many outstanding restaurants, some of which are famous around the world.

Floridians on the go have readily adopted fast-food restaurants as part of the modern lifestyle. These popular establishments dish up everything from hamburgers and hotdogs to fried fish and pizza.

Music

Music is still another element of lifestyle that helps define the culture of a people. Florida has been the setting for several well known songs. Perhaps the most famous is Stephen Foster's "Suwannee River," the State Song. During the 1920's, "Moon Over Miami" was a nationwide hit. The lyrics of

Florida Photographic Archives
Author Marjorie Kinnan Rawlings

Florida Photographic Archives
Author Ernest Hemingway

several Jimmy Buffet songs refer to South Florida locations. Florida inspired the classical composer Frederick Delius. Delius was an Englishman who lived near Jacksonville from 1884-1886. Florida folk songs were the basis for some of his works.

Gospel singing has a large following in Florida. Many gospel groups perform throughout the state and some, like the *Florida Boys* have a national audience. Musical tastes in Florida have been shaped in part by the musical heritage of arriving settlers and national trends. Popular music forms enjoyed by present-day Floridians include country-western, rock, gospel, bluegrass and jazz. Musicians from nearby islands of the Caribbean have sent the rhythms of calypso, reggae and Afro-Caribbean beats to Florida's shores.

Floridians are not only consumers of music, they are producers of it. Many important recording studios are located in the state, especially in South Florida. Among the artists who have recorded performances here are the *Bee Gees*.

To please tastes of classical music lovers, symphony orchestras perform in at least eight cities, including Miami, Ft. Lauderdale, Jacksonville, Orlando, St. Petersburg, Sarasota, Miami Beach, and the Greater Palm Beach area. Major Opera companies include the Asolo Opera Company in Sarasota; the Civic Opera of the Palm Beaches; and the Greater Miami Opera Association. The state legislature placed the "Florida State Symphony" and "Florida State Opera" under the Florida State University School of Music.

Art and Literature

Floridians can enjoy fine works of art at many art museums and galleries throughout the state. There are numerous art exhibitions conducted throughout the year. Often, these take the form of sidewalk art festivals. Some of the larger sidewalk exhibits, such as those in Coconut Grove and Winter Park, attract many thousands of visitors.

The pages of literature contain many colorful descriptions of lifestyles in Florida down through the years. Sometimes these descriptions have been written by native Floridians. On occasions, they have been written by visiting writers who came to the state and were fascinated by its charm. Probably the most famous author to live and work in Florida was Ernest Hemingway (1899-1961). Hemingway owned a home in Key West. Here he wrote some of his best known works, including For Whom the Bell Tolls and The Snows of Kilimanjaro. One of his novels, To Have and Have Not, described life in Key West during the 1930's. Hemingway's Key West home is now a museum and a National Historic Landmark.

A native Floridian who did much to advance the cause of black culture in the United States was James Weldon Johnson (1871-1938). Johnson was born in Jacksonville. This gifted man was a poet, teacher, musician, attorney and diplomat. Johnson wrote or edited many books about black poetry, music and religion. His most famous book was called God's Trombones, but he is better known as the author of the song, "Lift Every Voice and Sing." During the early 1900's, this song became known as the Negro National Anthem.

Another author who earned fame for herself and for the state was Marjorie Kinnan Rawlings (1896-1953). Mrs. Rawlings came to Florida in 1928. She soon developed a strong feeling for the state, which she shared in her writing. Her works include beautiful passages that describe the landscape and people of rural Florida. Her most famous work is The Yearling, which tells the story of a young boy growing up on the Florida frontier. The Yearling won the Pulitzer Prize for literature in 1939.

Where Floridians Live

Since the territorial period, Florida has changed from a rural society to an urban society. In 1845, over 90 percent of the people lived in rural areas. Today, over 90 percent of the people live in or very near urban areas.

James Weldon Johnson, author, song writer and diplomat

Jacob Summerlin, "King of the Crackers," established the county seats of Polk and Orange Counties.

Harriet Beecher Stowe (in black) being greeted by Governor- Stearns in 1874

Thomas Edison at Key West Navy Base during World World I.

Swimming at Palm Beach in 1904

Miami Beauty Parade winners in 1920

Jacksonville Western Union boys in 1913

Lake City Fire Department in 1914

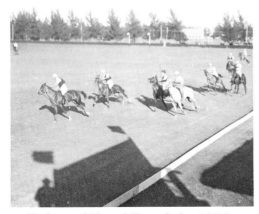

Polo at Miami Beach in 1922

Coral Gables baseball team in 1924

Florida Photographic Archives

The Census Bureau defines urban areas as places which have 2,500 or more inhabitants. Eight of Florida's cities have over 100,000 residents.

Several of Florida's cities are among the fastest growing urban areas in the United States. The Fort Myers - Cape Coral area was ranked number one in rate of growth by the U.S. Census Bureau. Its population grew 94.2 percent between 1970 and 1980. Among the top ten fastest growing urban areas were Sarasota (67.5 percent), Ft. Lauderdale-Hollywood (62.5 percent), and West Palm Beach - Boca Raton (58.2 percent).

At the same time Florida's cities are gaining in population, many large cities in the northeastern and midwestern United States are declining in population. Some demographers (social scientists who study population) think that people are leaving the big cities in other parts of the country to come to Florida in search of a better lifestyle. Such people are trying to escape from pollution, overcrowding, crime and high taxes.

With Florida's population growing so fast, it is easy to get the impression that the state is getting very crowded. In some places this is true. But many parts of Florida are very sparsely settled. If one flies the length of the state in an airplane, it is amazing how much of the land below appears to be uninhabited. There are huge areas of forest, farm and pastureland, and other open spaces. This is because 90 percent of Florida's population lives on less than 10 percent of the land. Again from an airplane, one can see that much of the urban development is concentrated in the coastal areas.

Life in and Around Cities

As Florida's urban areas increase in size, much of the residential growth occurs in areas surrounding a central city. These surrounding areas are known as suburbs. Suburban living has done much to shape the lifestyles of Floridians who live in and around cities. A typical suburban dwelling consists of a single-family home - a home for

Florida Photographic Archives
Central Avenue in St. Petersburg in 1901

one family on one piece of property. This home will usually have two or three bedrooms, and one or two bathrooms. In many cases, it will have a room that helps describe lifestyle in the state - the Florida Room.

As the decade of the eighties began, the price of a single-family home had become too expensive for many Florida families to afford. This was especially true for young families. By mid-1981, the average price of a new home in Florida had risen to $75,000.

Because the purchase price of homes is so expensive, many Floridians rent the places where they live. This may be a single family house, a duplex (usually designated for two families) or an apartment in a building with several other families. Large apartment buildings have become very widespread in Florida's cities and suburbs.

Many apartment buildings in Florida have been converted from rental units to condominiums. With a condominium arrangement, a person buys the apartment or dwelling unit instead of renting. Some buildings of this type are constructed originally as condominiums. The condominium has become popular with many Floridians who feel it provides more convenience and less maintenance than a single family home.

While the suburbs continue to expand with single-family homes, apartment buildings and condominiums, many urban residents still live in the main parts of the cities. Since the central city is usually the part that was developed first, it often contains older houses and other buildings. Some of these sections contain housing that is badly in need of repair and is inadequate for a number of reasons.

In several Florida cities, older, inadequate housing is being replaced to provide better living conditions for people. Sometimes this takes the form of public housing. Through public housing projects, low-income families are given financial assistance to buy or rent a home. Construction of new housing and other buildings can help renew the main parts of cities that have become rundown.

Florida Photographic Archives

1926 Florida land auction

Life Outside the Cities

The lifestyle of rural areas in Florida is quite a bit different from life in the cities. Rural areas have more open space than the cities. The pace of life is slower, and there are fewer vehicles and less pollution. There is also less serious crime. For these and other reasons, a number of urban dwellers are being attracted to Florida's rural areas. But, there are fewer cultural activities available to rural residents such as: theatres, movie houses or sporting events. A wide range of shopping does not exist and there are fewer job opportunities.

Dwellings in rural areas are usually single-family residences. The barn may still be a part of farm life, but otherwise the modern farm or ranch house looks much like a home in the city or suburbs, and has the same modern conveniences.

Whether or not a residence is rural or urban, single-family or multi-family (apartment or condominium), Floridians place great value on a waterfront location. Homesites on lakes, rivers, canals, or the ocean are very popular. Some Floridians like waterfront living so much they actually live on the water in houseboats or live aboard boats. With this type of lifestyle, a person can go fishing, surrounded by all the comforts of home!

Another kind of "portable home" popular with many Floridians is the mobile home, or trailer. Modern mobile homes have most of the features of a fixed dwelling, usually at a much lower price. In mid-1981, there were over 400,000 mobile homes registered to Florida owners.

A mixture of housing styles is found in Florida's five Indian reservations. Here, members of the Seminole and Miccosukee tribes try to preserve ancient tribal customs while adapting to modern society. This is often a difficult thing to do. Some Indians live in the traditional "chickees," while others live in modern concrete block or wooden frame homes.

Seminole village in 1946

Preservation

While homebuyers, builders and planning officials concern themselves with ways to provide new housing, some other people have joined together to preserve some of the best homes and building styles from the past. Several Florida communities have set up historic preservation districts in which old structures are restored and preserved. Such areas help us keep a living link to our past by letting us see how our ancestors lived.

Preservationists are not always successful. Sometimes the pressures for modernization are too great, and valuable older buildings are torn down to make way for new ones.

Mobility

The modern Floridian can move easily from place to place around the state. Florida's cities are connected by a network of state roads and interstate highways, railroads, and the routes of several airlines. Within the cities, mobility is aided by automobiles, buses, and in some areas, rapid transit systems.

Floridians depend heavily on the automobile. Most of Florida's cities have grown outward from the central city into the suburbs. People regularly commute from their homes to their place of work by automobile. This pattern is highly developed in Dade County, which in 1980 had more cars per capita than any large urban area in the country, including Los Angeles. Floridians also rely on the automobile for recreational travel and other trips.

Rising fuel prices have caused many Floridians to buy smaller, more efficient cars. A number of residents have turned to other means of personal transportation. Motorized two wheel vehicles, including mopeds and motorcycles, have become very popular. An even greater number of people have returned to an even older form of personal transportation - the bicycle. The bicycle has been thought of mainly for its recreational use. Now it is being seen as a significant transportation vehicle that does not use fossil fuels. The bicycle is quiet and doesn't pollute. Since 1972, the bicycle has outsold the automobile in Florida.

Florida is an especially good place to use a bicycle because of the state's generally flat land and its excellent year round climate. To accommodate cyclists, several Florida communities have installed bicycle paths along some of their roadways. In 1980, the Governor appointed a Bicycle Coordinator for Florida to help plan for improved use of bicycles throughout the state. Unfortunately, as bicycle usage has increased, so has the number of accidents. Florida has an unusually high rate of accidents involving bicyclists. An even more basic form of transportation than cycling is running. Running and jogging have become very popular activities among Florida's modern lifestyles. Floridians run not only for recreation, but to improve their health.

Clothing and Grooming

Floridians dress in a variety of styles. Fashions in the Sunshine State are influenced by the climate, cultural backgrounds and the persuasive suggestions of modern advertising.

While Florida's sub-tropical climate encourages informal styles, the widespread use of air conditioning permits the wearing of more formal attire for many occasions. Office workers in Florida cities often dress in much the same manner as office workers in northern cities.

Styles introduced by one cultural group often spread quickly to other parts of the population. The guayabera shirt, of Hispanic origin, is a stylish and popular alternative to a shirt and tie for many Florida men. Cowboy boots are worn not only in ranching and farming areas, but also by many city residents. The "Afro," a hairstyle developed by blacks, has been the inspiration for a variety of hairstyles worn by whites.

Among teenagers of both sexes, the 1980's began with the dominant uniform consisting of the T-shirt and jeans (designer or otherwise).

One curious phenomenon occurred during the 1970's. Many older people (including some parents) adopted certain dress and grooming habits of young people, including longish hair styles for men and jeans for men and women. Perhaps only one thing is certain about Florida fashions: they will be sure to change.

Senior Citizens

A group in Florida increasing in number and visibility is that of the senior citizens. Florida's population in 1980 included more than 17.5 percent of people over 65. Cities, counties, and the state have adopted laws and regulations to fit the needs of Florida's senior citizens.

Teenagers

A new classification of age arose in the 1940's. It is called the "teenager." Early in Florida's history children went from being a child to being an adult. If they attended school they often ended their education at the eighth grade and entered the working world. With compulsory school laws, more and more students graduated from high school. Teenagers had an impact on the lifestyle during the second half of the 20th century.

The telephone became a necessity to them, not a luxury. A major point in their lives became their sixteenth birthday, the day they were eligible to obtain a driver's license. Their taste in music changed the whole industry. In the 1950's, when "Rock Around the Clock" came out, parents were aghast. Rock and roll and its offshoots were here to stay. Teenagers buy millions of dollars of records and tapes each year.

Television

Television has brought the entire world into Florida's living rooms. Satellite transmission has allowed today's citizens to see events thousands of kilometers/ miles away instantaneously. Prime time shows, specials, game shows, and soap operas are a part of daily life. To see just how different lifestyles are today, look at the TV vocabulary used above. If you could go back just to 1900 and speak of prime time, soap operas, or game shows, you would receive a blank stare from your listeners. If you were going to watch the "special" tonight, people would think you were going to stand by the railroad track and watch the "special" go by.

Television has become a major force affecting the lifestyles of many Floridians.

TO GRANDMOTHER'S HOUSE WE GO

Grandchildren going to grandma's house for a visit in today's world had better not expect the stereotyped little old gray haired woman of the past. When grandchildren prepared for a visit years ago, any day was fine. Grandma was always there, ready to cook a big meal, and talk to them all day.

Today, when they call on the telephone to tell grandma of their plans, there are a few surprises. Because of her career as a buyer for a large company, she has to fly to New York for two days. However, she tells them, Saturday would be a fine day to visit. "Don't be too early, though I am playing golf at 7:00 a.m., but I should be home by 10 o'clock."

The grandchildren arrive at ten with their parents. Grandma's not there! As they are waiting, a silver Corvette pulls into the driveway, and "grandma" steps out to greet them. They hug and kiss each other and enter grandma's condominium. She tells them to get ready for a swim in the pool. When everyone is ready, grandma walks out in her swimsuit carrying a tennis racquet, ready to play in case anyone tires of swimming.

Later at mealtime, grandma suggests hamburgers and french fries at a fast food place instead of wasting the visit cooking. Of course, she will pay. After seeing a movie, the grandchildren pile into their parents' car and start thinking—It sure is fun to visit grandma!

Almost all Florida households have at least one television set of which is used an average of six hours a day. For many Floridians, television is the main source of news and entertainment, and is an especially strong influence on young people. It has been estimated that by the time the average Florida teenager is 18 years old, he or she will have spent 20,000 hours watching television.

Floridians have changed greatly over the years since settlement. Just as no one knew of the changes that would take place by 1981, we do not know how life will change in the future:

> *...perhaps rocket travel... an increase in leisure time... telephones with televisions... robot housecleaners... a pill that supplies all the nutrition needed for a week.*

But with these changes, lifestyles will continue to be guided by the evolving traditions of the many cultural groups that make up Florida.

**L
I
F
E
S
T
Y
L
E
S**

NASA

The space industry provides many jobs in Florida including one for Astronaut John Young

CAREERS

Larry Pauley

Introduction

A student in Florida has many opportunities to try a variety of careers. Florida offers jobs in almost every field possible. Training can be done in: public schools, private schools, vocational schools, community colleges, specialized academies, business schools, colleges, universities, on-the-job training, and apprentice programs.

Career development can begin with jobs performed around the house. This then expands to neighborhood self-employment. Jobs like paper routes, babysitting, cutting grass, and even pet sitting will let you explore the world of work. At the age of sixteen students can have a part-time job. Grocery stores, fast food restaurants, service stations, restaurants, delivery services, ice cream parlors, limited kinds of help on construction work, and a variety of other "first jobs" await the teenager.

As students enter high school, many have already decided on a life's vocation. Others make the decision during high school or at a later time. They have been receiving guidance from parents, teachers, and friends. Each person will make a decision about which occupation or occupations to follow.

Today's teenager has the chance to enter a working world that gives opportunity to everyone. Females or males can be employed in any job they are capable of doing. Any person can rise to as high a position as desired. This was not always true. Throughout most of the history of Florida and America, boys were expected to do certain jobs and girls learned household skills.

This pattern was true even before the Europeans arrived in America. The Indian system limited women to tasks related to preparing food, making clothing, and doing other homemaking tasks. The male was expected to be the hunter and warrior. In many cases, the female had to wait upon the male. Usually only men rose to positions of leadership.

As the pioneers from Europe moved into the southeastern U.S., they brought their ideas about jobs with them. When building a house, the men and boys worked on the house while the women and girls prepared food. The men were the providers and the women were the homemakers.

A young man in the 18th and early 19th centuries had few choices as far as a vocation. Many followed in the footsteps of their fathers. This provided on-the-job training. If the family had a farm, the sons would work along with their father, learning all of the tasks. The daughters would work with their mother, learning cooking, sewing, quilting, and doing other "feminine" chores.

The major change in employment came with the growing effect of the "Industrial Revolution." Young people were no longer limited to farming, home industries, or merchandising. Road building, railroad construction, mining, timbering, boat building, saltmaking, and other industries increased the area of employment in the 1800's.

When the automobile became popular, new jobs started and others ended. As a career, blacksmiths almost disappeared while auto mechanics came into being. This is a major problem which you will have to consider. Will the career that interests you still exist in the future? Will new developments in computers or new inventions affect you?

As the choices created by the Industrial Revolution have increased so has the difficulty in making a career decision. In the U.S. Government book, **Dictionary of Occupational Titles**, over 20,000 different jobs are listed as available in the United States. Most of these exist in Florida. Today's students must consider these questions. What fields match your interests and skills? What type of education or training is needed? What fields are expected to offer good prospects for a job? What are the expected earnings? What are the working conditions? Does the job offer year-round employment, or is it affected by weather or the economy?

There are answers to these questions, but it must be remembered that the answers change as the economy changes. The demand for workers in any occupation depends on the desires of consumers. If a product or service is unwanted, either by public or private consumers, no workers will be needed. Barbers would not be needed if people decided not to cut their hair. Astronauts would be out of work if the federal government did away with the space program.

In addition to product demand another factor is technological innovation. In the 20th century, technology has both created and ended hundreds of thousands of jobs. Alexander Graham Bell's telephone gave birth to an entire industry. At the same time Henry Ford's low cost automobile put stable owners, blacksmiths, and carriage makers out of business. Changes in businesses cause other changes. When supermarkets came into being, the number of small self-owned groceries were greatly reduced.

The U.S. Department of Labor estimates that in 1985, 104.3 million people will be in the civilian labor force. This is a 19 percent increase over the 1976 level of 87.5 million. The size of this labor force increased rapidly after 1960, largely due to the increased number of women entering the working world. No one can forecast for sure the changes in occupations. However, most changes take place in an orderly and predictable way. Students who are thinking about a career can obtain information about jobs up to five years in advance. To aid students in researching a career, the U.S. Department of Labor has divided all jobs into 15 clusters. These career clusters are Agri-Business and Natural Resources; Business and Office; Communication and Media; Construction; Environmental Control; Fine Arts, Humanities, and Athletics; Health Services; Homemaking and Consumerism; Hospitality and Recreation; Manufacturing; Marine Science; Marketing and Distribution; Personal Services; Public Services; and Transportation.

Agri-Business and Natural Resources

There are many occupations in agri-business and natural resources in Florida. Vegetable (truck) farming, citrus fruit, livestock raising, dairy farming, forestry, and phosphate mining provide most of the jobs in this cluster in Florida. By 1980, Florida was 12th of all 50 states in its sale of farm products. It is first in the southeast. This includes the sale of: fruits and vegetables, livestock and livestock products, and dairy products.

Citrus fruit is Florida's most valuable agricultural product. Florida is the world's leading producer of oranges and grapefruits.

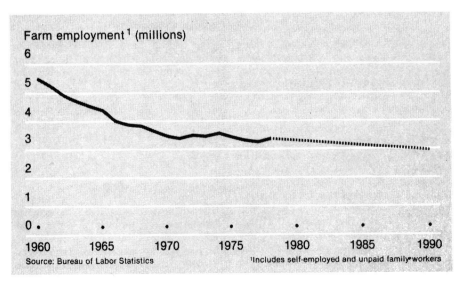

Farm employment[1] (millions)

Source: Bureau of Labor Statistics [1]Includes self-employed and unpaid family workers

Although farm output has increased significantly since 1960, employment has dropped by two-fifths and is expected to continue to decline.

We also supply other citrus such as: lemons, limes, tangerines, and tangelos. Most citrus is grown in the central and southern part of the state.

Livestock is our second most valuable agricultural product. Not only are cattle raised, but hogs, thoroughbred horses, turkeys, and chickens. Some cattle ranches are quite large and have several employees. Others are small and run by families. Most of the dairy farming is done to provide milk and dairy products to Florida's residents.

Of Florida's agricultural products, truck crops are third in value. Truck farms are located all over the state. Some areas are famous for their crops. Plant City is the Strawberry capital of the world. Other crops grown in Florida include: snap beans, cabbage, celery, sweet corn, cucumbers, eggplant, escarole, lettuce, green peppers, potatoes, squash, tomatoes, and watermelons.

There are many jobs related to farming. Some of these are meat inspectors, farm managers, farm product salespeople, auctioneers, slaughterhouse workers, and veterinarians. These farm related jobs require a high school diploma or special training. Veterinarians have as much training as physicians.

Farming techniques are changing rapidly. To keep up with the advancements, many farmers have become college graduates. The best way for a young person to enter farming is to take over a family farm. Overall, farm employment will be decreasing due to new technology.

Forestry is an important industry in Florida. Most of the forests are located in the northern part of the state. Our major forest product is pulpwood, used to make newsprint and paper products. Forestry offers various jobs for people who enjoy outdoor work. Many young people can enter forestry as an unskilled laborer during the summer.

Phosphate is Florida's largest mining industry. About 90 percent of the phosphate is used in fertilizer. The phosphate mines are large employers in central Florida. They hire workers with many different skills and educational backgrounds.

Many Floridians have made successful careers in agri-business. Wayne Mixson built a cattle ranch and is a farmer. He was elected as Lt. Governor in 1978. Ben Hill Griffin, in 1981, was one of the most successful citrus growers in the state.

Business and Office

The business and office career cluster includes office, computer, banking, insurance, and administrative occupations. Business and office workers perform many tasks that are needed to make businesses and other organizations operate. Clerical workers keep files, type, and operate office machines. Professional and technical employees give legal advice, prepare and analyze financial reports, design computer systems, and arrange bank loans.

Jobs in office work exist for people with different educational backgrounds. Some jobs can be entered with a high school education. Others require, technical schools or college education. Many clerical workers do detailed, repetitive tasks such as filing. Many professional office workers work with ideas and problem solving.

In 1980, about 16 million people worked in clerical office jobs. These included secretaries, bookkeepers, cashiers, typists, shipping and receiving clerks, receptionists, bank tellers, telephone operators, and file clerks. The largest number, 20 percent, are secretaries and 10 percent are bookkeepers. Some of these workers are highly skilled. These include title researchers in real estate firms and executive secretaries. Messengers and file clerks are relatively unskilled.

Clerical workers need a high school education. They should also have skills in: reading, spelling, grammar, and arithmetic. Most beginning clerical workers receive on-the-job training. Clerical workers must also be flexible. As more computers are used in business, some jobs will no longer be needed. New jobs will be created.

Bureau of Labor Statistics

Programmers write detailed instructions that list the steps the computers must follow to solve a problem.

Job opportunities for clerical workers should increase through the 1980's. Salaries usually start at minimum wage, but increase with skill and ability. The average income for experienced secretaries in 1980 was $250 per week.

Key punch operators, systems analysts and programmers are three jobs which did not exist in 1950. All of these people work with computers. Most computer careers require a college degree or special training. As the use of computers grows, so will computer job opportunities. Salaries range from an average of $175 per week for beginning keypunch operators to an average of over $450 per week for experienced systems analysts.

Banks use all of the clerical workers described above, plus tellers. Tellers must have a high school educational and show accuracy with numbers and details. Job opportunities should increase through the 1980's for banking jobs. However, banking salaries generally are not as high as those in some other industries.

Insurance companies hire actuaries, claim representatives, and underwriters. They must have college degrees and be good with mathematics. They may average over $18,000 per year.

Administrative occupations include: accountants, lawyers, and personnel managers. These jobs require a college education. Competition is stiff in these areas because salaries are usually high.

There are many other business and office careers not described here. They all have one thing in common with the careers mentioned above, though. Employers like for office workers to dress neatly and to be friendly.

Communication Media

The act of communication is an important part of being human. People have always looked for ways to pass on knowledge. For this purpose, the communication field has a broad range of occupations. The focal points are research, writing, editing, making productions, and transmitting information. There are several communication careers. Some of the career choices are interpreters, writers, newspaper reporters, radio and television announcers, technical writers, printers, camera operators, and technical assistants.

Most of these jobs require much education and skill in observing. Skill in thinking clearly and logically, and an excellent use of the language is needed. Competition for media jobs is keen. More people seek jobs in this field than are available because of the "glamour" appeal.

Writing as a career requires self-discipline and communicating clearly. Most writers also have or have had a second career. This enables them to write and still make a living. Florida has produced many successful writers including: Allen Morris; Marjorie Kinnan Rawlings; James Weldon Johnson;

Robert G. Sherrill; Dr. Frank G. Slaughter; and John D. MacDonald.

Interpreters help people of different cultures overcome language barriers by translating. The job opportunities are limited in this area. In the United States in 1979, less than 1,000 people worked full-time as interpreters. Most of those worked for the United Nations or the U.S. government. However, the salaries are excellent. A good interpreter can earn more than $40,000 per year. Florida has excellent opportunities for interpreters. Many foreign language speaking people live in the state.

Newspaper reporters gather information and write stories about current events for printing in the daily or weekly newspapers. Large daily newspapers in Florida assign some reporters to "beats" such as the police department. Some reporters may specialize in science, education, politics, business, labor, or sports events. On weekly papers, reporters may handle several other jobs, such as photography or selling advertisements.

Most newspapers require a college degree for employees. A degree in journalism can be earned from several universities in Florida. Students interested in journalism should start by working on the school newspaper.

Bureau of Labor Statistics

Programming and engineering workers often are under great pressure to meet broadcast deadlines.

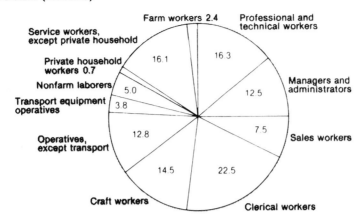

Workers (millions)

Projected distribution of employment by occupation in 1990.

Source: Bureau of Labor Statistics

You should practice good English and writing in every class. A knowledge of such subjects as: history, economics, political science, speech, and science is needed.

Many young people entered the journalism field during the 1970's. This led to an overcrowding of the career, but by 1985 there should be an increase in demand for reporters. Beginning reporters usually start in small town newspapers and work up to larger newspapers. Salaries in 1980 ranged from $8,000 to $25,000, depending upon experience and size of the newspaper.

Radio and television announcers bring the outside world to all of us. Most radio announcers work as disc jockeys. They introduce music, give the news, do commercials, and "ad lib." Announcers working for television and large radio stations usually specialize in sports, news, weather, or other areas. They must know their specialty. If a written script is needed, the announcer will write it. Announcers are paid to appear at banquets and dances. Some announcers become well-known and highly paid.

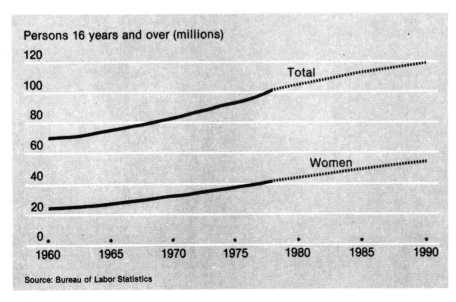

Although labor force growth will slow during the 1980's, the proportion of women will increase.

270

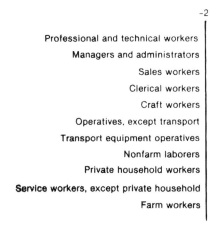

Projected change in employment, 1978–90 (millions)

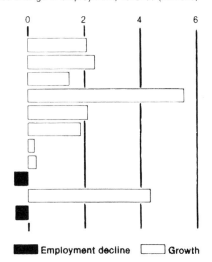

Through the 1980's, changes in employment will vary widely among occupational groups.

Professional and technical workers
Managers and administrators
Sales workers
Clerical workers
Craft workers
Operatives, except transport
Transport equipment operatives
Nonfarm laborers
Private household workers
Service workers, except private household
Farm workers

Source: Bureau of Labor Statistics

■ Employment decline ☐ Growth

Announcers must have a pleasant and well-controlled voice. They need a good sense of timing and excellent pronunciation. Correct use of English or the language of the intended audience is very important. A knowledge of dramatics, current events, music, and sports improve chances for success. School courses in: English, public speaking, drama, foreign languages, and electronics will help the future radio or TV announcer. Hobbies in: music, sports, and writing are helpful. Many announcers begin by working part-time at small stations.

Salaries are usually higher at larger stations.

Another career choice in communication is that of the writers. Writers prepare materials for almost every personality seen or heard on TV or radio, among these are commercials, dialogues, words for songs, and other written materials. Many TV and radio personalities began as writers for other people. Writers must have an excellent use of language and an understanding of world events.

There are many other behind-the-scene jobs in communication media. Engineers make sure the right song or commercial is

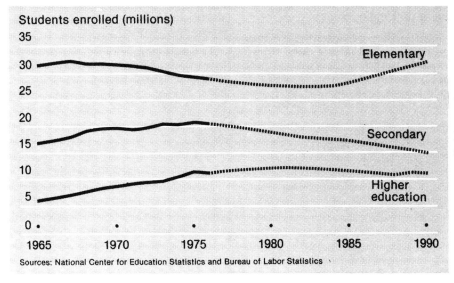

Changing enrollment levels will be the primary factor affecting employment of teachers

Sources: National Center for Education Statistics and Bureau of Labor Statistics

played at the right time, while camera operators make the pictures possible. Directors fit everything together correctly.

The number of careers in communication media is expected to increase as Americans demand to know more about the world around them.

Construction

Construction craft workers are the largest group of skilled workers. There are more than a dozen skilled construction trades that vary greatly in size. The major trades - carpenters, painters, machinery operators, plumbers, and electricians have more than 200,000 workers each. There are over a million carpenters alone. In contrast, there are only a few thousand marble settlers, terrazzo workers, and stone masons.

Construction work may be divided into three groups: structural, finishing, and mechanical. Structural workers include: carpenters, machinery operators, bricklayers, iron workers, cement masons, stonemasons, and boilermakers. Finishing workers include: lathers, plasterers, marble setters, terrazzo workers, painters, paperhangers, glaziers, roofers, floor covering installers, and insulation workers. Those in mechanical work are plumbers, pipefitters, construction electricians, sheet metal workers, elevator constructors, and millwrights.

Most jobs in the construction industry are with small contractors. They usually employ less than 10 people. A few large contractors, however, employ thousands. Large numbers of construction workers work for other industries. Phosphate mining needs workers to construct facilities and maintain them. Chemical manufacturers need plumbers and pipefitters to maintain the pipe networks in their processing plants. Government agencies hire workers to construct and maintain highways, buildings, and sanitation systems.

Nearly one out of six construction trade workers are self-employed. They contract with homeowners and businesses for small jobs. Self-employment is most common in paperhanging, painting, and floor covering.

Most construction workers learn their trade through an apprenticeship program. This is a set period of on-the-job training. In addition, there is classroom work. Another way to learn construction skills is to work as laborers or helpers and observe the experienced workers. Some people learn by attending vocational, technical, trade, or correspondence schools.

Employment in the construction industry should continue to be excellent during the 1980's. However, construction work depends upon the weather and economy. An increase in building will not need the same percentage increase in workers. Better technological developments in construction methods, equipment, and materials will raise output per worker. One factor which adds to this is the use of pre-fabricated units.

There are many problems in the construction trades. Although you can work outdoors nearly year round in Florida, rain can cause delays or lay-offs. A problem in the economy can stop the building trade entirely. A strike in one trade may stop work in another. These workers have more injuries than other occupational clusters. However, these trades offer more chances for earnings, advancements, and outdoor work for the non-college graduate than other fields.

Wires must be positioned and connected with care.

Architects spend many hours at the drawing board.

Environmental Control

The newest career cluster is environmental control. It grew out of a need to protect the environment from pollution and other abuses. Oceans, forests, air, and rivers must be used widely. Natural resources are limited. So, a new group of scientists, called environmentalists, came into being. Their job is to work for a balance between nature and industry.

Most people in environmental control have a very special background in science. Some are environmental engineers. They design factories and equipment that control air and water pollution. Geologists study the structure and history of the earth's crust while geophysicists study the earth's electric, magnetic, and gravitational fields. Meterologists study the atmosphere and try to forecast the weather. Oceanographers study the ocean. This is very important because two-thirds of the earth's surface is covered by ocean. Oceans also provide food, fossil fuels, and other minerals.

Almost all jobs in environmental control require a college degree. Usually, the more education you have in this area, the more money you can make. Job opportunities should be good all through the 1980's. Some of these jobs will be as teachers in universities. Other jobs will include travel and outdoor work. Students interested in working in environmental control should begin taking science classes in high school.

Fine Arts, Humanities, and Athletics

The glamour career cluster includes performing arts, social sciences, sports, and design. Everyone dreams of being on stage, catching the winning touchdown pass, or snapping the greatest photograph. Besides these, there are many more careers in this group. The "stars" all have supporting or behind-the-scene personnel.

Because training, earnings, and opportunities vary, each of the four career areas will be looked at separately. There is one important point to remember about these careers, all of them require years of training and in many times natural abilities.

The performing arts include instrumental music, singing, acting, and dancing. The performing arts have the goal of affecting the emotions of the audience. Using music, speech, and movement, the artists interpret human experience.

Within the performing arts, there are usually more talented people than there are available full-time jobs. As a result, many performers add to their incomes by teaching or other occupations.

Young people should remember how difficult it is to earn a living as a performer. They should consider making their art a hobby rather than a profession. To be successful they need talent, determination, and luck.

Only a few actors and actresses become stars of stage, movies, television, or radio. A few more become supporting performers. Most struggle for a place in the industry and are glad to pick up a part whenever they can. Many work as extras without speaking parts, while others find jobs as: drama coaches, directors, or teachers. The total employment in this area in 1980 was 15,000 people.

Young people who want acting careers should take part in high school and college plays or work with little theater groups.

Drama schools have become a more important way to begin acting.

Salaries for actors vary greatly. However, in 1980, between two-thirds and three-fourths of the members of the Screen Actors Guild earned less than $2,500 per year. Less than five percent earned more than $25,000.

Three other types of performing artists are dancers, musicians, and singers. In America during 1980, there were a total of 8,000 dancers, 127,000 musicians, and 23,000 singers. Most of them work long, hard irregular hours. Many of these workers had to add to their incomes by teaching or doing other jobs.

Floridians with successful acting careers include: Ben Vereen; Patrick O'Neal; Esther Rolle; Jo Anne Pflug; Faye Dunaway; and adopted son, Burt Reynolds. Other performing artists with successful careers in music and singing include: Jimmy Buffett; Mel Tillis; Pat Boone; Jim Stafford; and Anita Bryant.

Humanities, a completely different field from performing arts, have social scientists studying all areas of human society. Whatever their specialty, they are concerned with some part of society, culture, or personality. Anthropologists study primitive tribes, modern communities, and

Actor, Burt Reynolds

civilizations of the past. They study the physical characteristics, cultures, and languages of all people, past and present. Economists study capital and the production, distribution, and consumption of

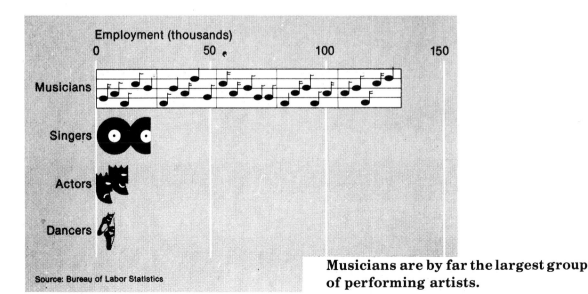

Source: Bureau of Labor Statistics

Musicians are by far the largest group of performing artists.

goods and services. Geographers deal with the relationship between geography and economics, politics, urban problems, and culture. They seek to explain why and how people live where they do. Historians describe and interpret the people, ideas, institutions, and events of the past. Political scientists study the theories, goals, and organization of all types of government. Psychologists observe the behavior of humans and other animals in order to understand their actions. Sociologists study the behavior and relationships of groups such as: the family, communities, and minorities.

Earnings in the social sciences vary depending upon the chosen area within the cluster. For example, a geographer who teaches makes less than one who works for a petroleum company in search of fuels. Generally, more education a social scientist has, the more money earned. Psychologists have the highest average salary in this career area.

Employment in the social sciences is expected to grow in all areas except three. These three areas are historians, political scientists, and sociologists. There will, however, be openings in all areas due to death or retirement.

All careers in the social sciences area require a college education. Most people in these professions continue university studies and obtain higher degrees. Training can be obtained in these careers at colleges and universities throughout Florida.

The job of people in design occupations is to make products or places more useful and appealing. Good design can improve the appearance of the products we use, where we live, where we work, and our recreation areas. Different design careers require different levels of training and education. Floral designers often learn by on-the-job training. Many times they do not need a high school diploma. Architects, on the other hand, must have at least five years of professional education. The most important things in

Daytona Beach Raceway

Nascar Intl. Speedway Corp.

Tampa Bay Buccaneers versus the Miami Dolphins. Professional athletes' careers are usually short.

design occupations are creativity and the ability to communicate ideas through designs and displays. There are many design occupations, among these are architects, commercial artists, display workers, floral designers, interior decorators, landscape architects, and photographers.

Many young people today see professional sports as a career for them. However, it is very difficult to become a "star." Although there are more openings today than a few years ago, the chances of getting a professional contract are very limited.

There are many sports played by Floridians. The most popular are football, baseball, and basketball. Sports which could possibly provide a career are auto racing, billiards, boat racing, archery, bowling, boxing, figure skating, golf, horse racing, motorcycle racing, racquetball, soccer, softball, jai-alai, surfing, tennis, track and field, volleyball, water skiing, and wrestling.

The "big three" sports have many things in common. They all have limited opportunities. In America in 1980, there were 1500 professional football players, 4000 baseball players, and only 400 basketball players. Each sport has very few openings during the year. Football has about 75; baseball, 120; and basketball, 60. A person is able to participate for only a short span of their lifetime. Most athletes finish their sport "career" at an average age of 31. Some last longer, but few play past the age of 40.

There are common factors which make these sports attractive to young people. First, of course, is the high salary. Minimum salaries may range from $20,000 to $30,000. In 1981, Dave Winfield the highest paid baseball player, earned $1,200,000. Bob Griese earned $400,000 when he retired in 1981. Basketball's Magic Johnson received $600,000.

Basketball and football players receive most of their training through college play. Baseball players usually play in "minor" leagues. There are a few exceptions, but they are rare.

Most careers in sports are found in related areas. Coaches, trainers, managers, and officials are found throughout the U.S. These people have a longer period of participation than athletes. Many pursue this career all of their working lives. Some work beyond age 65.

Most coaches and managers have a college education. A coach must have qualities of leadership. One thing always concerns a coach - if he loses too many games, he may lose his job. Most coaches have been involved in sports before entering coaching. There are many job opportunities. A coach may work for a professional team, a university, a high school, a junior high, or a middle school.

The athletic trainer is in charge of preventing and treating injuries. This position is becoming more common and requires advanced schooling.

Officials are required at all levels of athletics. Most receive on-the-job training. Umpires in professional baseball, however, must attend umpire's school. This is available in Florida. Most officials work part-time at officiating and have other careers. They officiate because they enjoy sports.

Another popular job in the world of sports is the sports journalist. Jobs in this area range from the local newspaper sports writer to the nationally known television announcer. The salary ranges vary with careers in this area, however most let you work closely with athletes. Writers usually have a college degree in journalism.

Announcers may have a college degree, but many get the job because of their past participation in sports.

Many careers are closely related to athletics. Front office personnel include such careers as: general manager, public relations director, ticket manager, scouts, accountants, and clerical workers.

Many Floridians have had a successful career in athletics. Football players include Fred Biletnikoff and Steve Spurrier. In baseball there are Steve Garvey and Lou Piniella. Dave Cowens went to professional basketball from Florida State University. Althea Gibson and Chris Evert Lloyd became tennis stars. Jack Nicklaus is one of the "all time great" golfers. Bob Hayes, known once as "the world's fastest human" was a champion Olympic sprinter in 1964. He later played professional football. Pat Summerall became a sports announcer for CBS.

Architects plan buildings and involve themselves in all developmental stages of a construction project. Since duties of an architect require a number of skills, their salaries are far above average. There will be a need for more architects through 1989. There is a possibility that too many will be trained, this may lead to an oversupply as the decade ends.

Commercial artists design layouts for magazines, newspapers, and catalogs. Many people enter this field, therefore, competition is keen and advanced training is becoming necessary. The highest incomes in 1980 averaged around $400 per week. Most employers expect a commercial artist to have two to four years of specialized training beyond high school.

Display workers and floral designers often learn their trade through on-the-job training. Both jobs usually begin at minimum wage. Opportunities in display work are declining, while floral design opportunities are increasing. Many floral designers take advanced training.

Industrial designers combine artistic talent with knowledge of marketing,

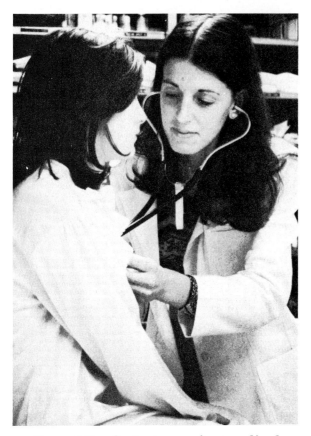

One of the fastest growing medical specialties is family practice.

materials, and methods of production. Training can be obtained in art or technical schools. Job opportunities and salaries are increasing. In 1980, the average salary was $20,000.

Interior decorators make areas more useful and attractive. Many learn while on-the-job, but a college education can help in obtaining a job. Most interior decorators are self-employed, therefore, incomes vary greatly.

Everyone enjoys attractively planned residential areas, public parks, and commercial areas. Landscape architects design these areas and help in many types of projects. They plan and arrange trees, supervise grading, construction, and planting. The training requires a college degree plus advanced schooling. There is a need for more landscape architects. The salaries are increasing as the demand for this work grows.

A photography career may begin as a hobby. Photographers use their cameras to record events, places, and people. Some specialize in scientific or medical photography. Training of a photographer is available in college, but many learn by doing. The chances of a successful career in photography depends on one's ability. Those in newspaper work earn an average of $15,000 while self-employed photographers can earn higher salaries. Nixon Smiley and Hampton Dunn have used photography to show Florida's past in books.

Health Services

When people are sick or injured, having health services readily available becomes very important. The availability of these services depends on the number of people employed and on geography. Urban areas have more health facilities than rural areas. The number of health personnel has grown very rapidly in recent years, but the location of health care centers remains a problem in Florida, the South, and America.

In 1980, about 4.3 million people worked in health related occupations. The jobs included doctors, nurses, dentists, therapists, technologists, technicians, administrators, and assistants. Registered nurses, physicians, pharmacists, and dentists make up the largest professional health occupations. The number ranged from almost one million nurses to almost 115,000 dentists.

Other professional medical persons include: osteopathic, physicians, chiropractors, optometrists, podiatrists, veterinarians, physical therapists, speech pathologists, audiologists, and dieticians. Technicians of various types are included as health service workers. X-ray technicians, dental hygienists, and laboratory technicians are a few of these. A large number of people, 1.5 million, worked as practical nurses, nursing aides, orderlies, and attendants.

Hospitals employ about half of all workers in the health field. Others work in: clinics, laboratories, pharmacies, nursing homes, public health agencies, mental health centers, private offices, and patient's homes.

The education and training requirements for work in the health field vary greatly. Professional health workers like physicians, dentists, pharmacists, and others must complete a number of years of training in college and beyond. They must also pass a state licensing exam. On the other hand, some health service occupations can be entered with little specialized training. Many community colleges offer courses to prepare students for various health jobs. In many non-professional jobs, on-the-job training allows workers to learn the needed skills. At present, many employees prefer those who have completed some formal education. This may be obtained in one of Florida's vocational schools or colleges.

Earnings of health workers range from those of a physician, which is the highest paid occupation, to those of a nursing aide, who earn minimum wage. People in health occupations that require graduation from college earn about twice as much as the average wage.

Employment in the health field is expected to grow much faster than the average growth for all occupations through 1989.

Population growth and the public's increasing awareness of the need for good health add to an increased demand for health care careers. Other openings will be created each year by increased funds from federal, state, and local governments for health care. The employment outlook is excellent.

Training is available in Florida for many health fields. Medical schools are located at the University of Florida, University of South Florida, and the University of Miami. Nursing and technician training are available at several universities, junior colleges, and vocational schools throughout the state.

Homemaking and Consumerism

A career as a homemaker is a challenging one that requires much skill and has many duties. No other single occupation has more influence on the economy. Homemakers make decisions about where to shop for groceries or clothing. They decide which brand of toothpaste, bread or blue jeans to buy. They choose doctors, dentists, banks, and dry cleaners. Over 90 percent of all

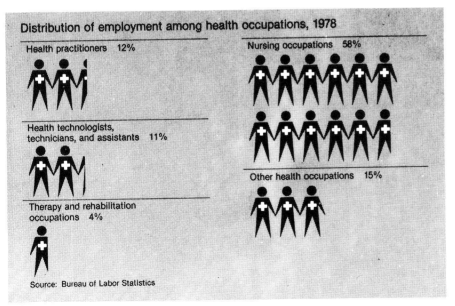

Distribution of employment among health occupations, 1978

Health practitioners 12%

Health technologists, technicians, and assistants 11%

Therapy and rehabilitation occupations 4%

Nursing occupations 58%

Other health occupations 15%

Source: Bureau of Labor Statistics

About five nurses are employed for every health practitioner.

television commercials are directed at them.

Homemakers become mathematicians during the time they prepare a budget or practice comparison shopping. They are scientists when plans for nutritious meals are made or cleaning supplies carefully stored. They are counselors when they solve family problems and teachers when dealing with children. When making their homes more energy efficient, they become engineers. When giving first aid, they are health care workers.

Most homemakers learn by on-the-job training. Others take special classes in school. Many homemakers are college graduates with degrees in home economics. There is no salary for homemakers since the reward is a feeling of accomplishment. For many persons, this career is the most satisfying of all.

Some homemakers have combined homemaking with another career. Since it is no longer necessary to choose between homemaking and another occupation, it is possible to have two careers and be good at both.

A career related to homemaking is a home economist. Many home economists are school teachers. They teach cooking, sewing and the skills necessary to operate a home and care for a family. Home economists work for business firms or trade associations. Their job is to promote certain products or equipment.

Consumerism is a field related to homemaking. Most of the people in this field work for the government. Their job is consumer protection. In Florida the Department of Agriculture and Consumer Services hires many consumer experts.

Specialists outnumber general practitioners by 5 to 1.

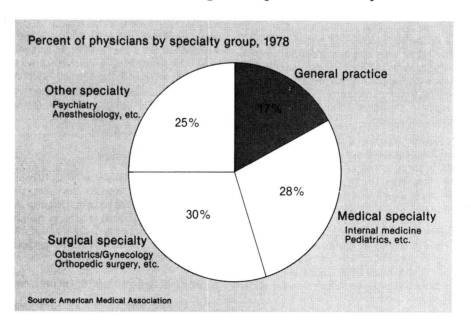

Percent of physicians by specialty group, 1978

General practice 17%

Medical specialty
Internal medicine
Pediatrics, etc. 28%

Surgical specialty
Obstetrics/Gynecology
Orthopedic surgery, etc. 30%

Other specialty
Psychiatry
Anesthesiology, etc. 25%

Source: American Medical Association

City of Miami, Office of Information and Visitors

Norway at Port of Miami

Hospitality and Recreation

Hospitality and recreation is one of the fastest growing career clusters. It is concerned with entertainment for the public. As Americans gain more leisure time, they seek more entertainment. Florida's many tourists look for recreation during their vacations.

Many workers are employed in Florida's state and national parks. Millions of people visit these parks each year for camping, canoeing, fishing, and hiking. Workers, such as park managers, maintenance personnel, and fishing and hiking guides, assist the public.

Private attractions are large employers. A wide range of jobs are available at large amusement parks such as Disney World and Busch Gardens, These jobs include: maintenance personnel, ride operators, security officers, and park managers.

Many of Florida's recreational jobs involve water or the beach. There are jobs available as: swimming, life guard or diving instructors, pool maintenance personnel and sailing or skiing instructors.

For those with special skills, there are jobs as instructors in several other areas. These include: golf, tennis, racquetball, and gymnastics.

An exciting area in hospitality and recreation is working on a cruise ship. Cruise ships operate out of Florida. The port of Miami has several sailings weekly. A variety of jobs exist on cruise ships. They extend from recreational director to captain of the ship. There are sailing jobs as well as service jobs.

People who enter these career areas should like working with people. Some of these jobs require little or no training, others require special skills or higher eduction. Salaries for specialists or managers are above average. The wages for routine jobs such as ride operators or maintenance personnel are usually minimum wage. It is possible to start work in this career area at age 16 and advance through on-the-job training.

Manufacturing

Almost everything we use whether work, play, or sleep is manufactured. Factories produce materials from simple pencils to complicated computers, or tiny electronic parts to huge aircraft carriers. Manufacturers employ more workers than any other career cluster. In the U.S., nearly one-fourth of all workers are employed by industry, while in Florida nearly one-third of the workers have industrial jobs.

On small printing presses, adjustments are made by the operator.

Many different products are manufactured in Florida. Factories process citrus fruits and vegetables in central Florida, paper products in the North, and clothing in Miami. We build ships, produce electronic equipment, publish and process chemicals. It would be difficult to name Florida's many industries.

A relatively large number of jobs exist related to manufacturing. Most require at least a high school diploma, however, some jobs need a college education. Many companies prefer employees with vocational or technical training. Most employees can advance to higher and better paying positions with on-the-job training programs.

In 1980, workers in Florida averaged over $250 per week. They worked slightly above 40 hours per week.

Through the 1980's, the demand for manufactured products will become greater, but employment will increase slowly due to improved means of production. Some industries such as plastics, computers, and medical equipment, will increase more rapidly.

Marine Science

As the population of the earth increases, we will turn more and more to the oceans for food and fuels. The people who study the oceans and our ability to use them are marine scientists. There were few marine scientists in 1980 and the need for more is growing. There are oceanographers, meteorologists, cartographers, marine geologists, life scientists, ecologists, aquanauts, and support personnel engaged in this type of study.

This career gives the student a chance to explore a frontier area. Although water covers more than two-thirds of the earth's surface we know very little about the oceans. Ocean study is a good career for the curious and investigative type student.

Oceanography is one of the branches of marine science. These people study many aspects of marine life. Some study ocean movements, plant life, animal life, chemical makeup of the ocean, and even temperatures. There were less than 10,000 oceanographers in 1980. It is one of the fastest growing professions in the world. They must have a college degree plus other skills such as mathematics. Several college degrees are available in marine science from Florida's universities.

Florida, a peninsula state, is surrounded by the Atlantic Ocean, the Gulf of Mexico, and the Caribbean Sea. It has more coastline than any other state except Alaska. Job opportunities for marine scientists are excellent in Florida.

Meterologists study how the ocean affects the atmosphere and vice-versa. Meteorologists spend much of their time studying tropical storms. Others work in laboratories interpreting facts and figures for use by fisherman. Cartographers are geographers who specialize in map making. Marine cartographers map the bottom of oceans. This aids in a better understanding of ocean currents and fish movements. Marine geologists study the mineral wealth of the oceans. Life scientists and ecologists

Oceanographers use specialized instruments in their studies.

study plant and animal life and man's effect on them.

There are many technical assistants and support personnel in the marine sciences. Divers, sailors, clerks, cooks, and many others help in the long voyages at sea. Almost all careers in this cluster require advanced training.

Marketing and Distribution

In 1980, 20 percent of all workers were employed in wholesale and retail trade. The largest number - about three-fourths - worked in retail trade. Wholesalers buy goods in large amounts, distribute, or resell them to retail stores, industries, and public or private institutions. Retailers sell goods directly to consumers by mail, in stores, or door-to-door. Most sales occur in stores.

As a consumer, you may buy goods in department stores, supermarkets, specialty shops, restaurants, or fast food places. These retailers purchase their goods from wholesalers.

There are a wide range of skills needed in this career cluster. Some jobs demand a college degree. Many require a high school diploma or vocational training. Others provide on-the-job training.

More than half of all workers in marketing and distribution are white collar workers. These include professionals, managers, clerical workers, and sales workers. Managers supervise the work force and must make the decisions. They make up about one-fifth of the work force and clerical workers are one - sixth. Cashiers, bookkeepers, secretaries, office clerks, or office machine operators make up the clerical staff. Many shipping and receiving clerks work in wholesale and retail trade. Sales workers make up one-fifth of all workers in this cluster. Sales workers are very important because these are the people that meet the public. They must be neat, clean and very polite at all times.

Most white collar jobs require a high school diploma or vocational training for full-time employment. Many managers and professionals need a college degree.

Blue collar workers hold 25 percent of this cluster's jobs. Many work as mechanics, repairers, gas station attendants, drivers and delivery workers, meat cutters, and material handlers. Some of these jobs provide on the job training, while others need special vocational training.

One specialized career in marketing and distribution is in advertising. There are writers, photographers, designers, and promoters who want to help you decide what to buy. Several universities in Florida offer college degrees in marketing or in advertising.

Service workers make up one-sixth of the workers in this industry. Most of these are food service workers such as waitresses and cooks. Others are janitors, cleaners, and

Some restaurants cater to customers who wish to eat a leisurely meal in pleasant surroundings.

guards. Many of the jobs in this area may be done on a part-time basis.

As the population grows in the 1980's, employment in this industry is expected to increase. The need for certain jobs will decrease, however, due to new labor saving devices. For example, the use of computers will limit the need for clerical workers because they allow one person to do more work than before.

Many Floridians have been very successful in marketing and distribution. In 1977, Eckerd Drugs, founded by Jack Eckerd, had the sixth largest net income of any company in the state. George Jenkins opened the first Publix Market in Winter Haven in 1930. Today, there is a chain of 235 supermarkets.

Personal Services

Workers in personal service occupations perform a wide variety of jobs. Many of the occupations are not considered glamourous but they are all easy to enter. Although most of these jobs do not require higher education, they do offer a good opportunity for advancement. These workers help other people in their daily lives. Basically, there are seven groupings in the personal service cluster. These are domestic services, lodging services, barbering and cosmetology, laundry and apparel services, attendant services, domestic animal care, and food and beverage preparation services.

Domestic service personnel perform necessary tasks. There are housekeepers, yard workers, cooks, maids, nursemaids, butlers, and chauffeurs. All of these employees usually work for individuals or families. Workers receive minimum wages at first. These wages increase as years of service increase. Many employees become very close to their employers in this type job.

In the lodging services, the workers help people who are away from home enjoy where they are staying. Many people are needed to provide comfort for the traveler away from home. Jobs in this area range from the maid at a hotel or motel to the manager. Other jobs are bellhops, room clerks, desk clerks, maintenance people, janitors, elevator operators, parking lot attendants, and advertisers. This job area allows many opportunities for advancing to a better paying job.

During the 1960's, many barbers went out of business because of changes in hair styles for men. Then, in the late 1970's hair styling became popular, and a more specialized type of barbering came into being. This job is closely related to working in beauty salons as a cosmetologist. Workers in these areas help people to improve their appearance. Many barbers and cosmetologists own their own businesses.

People in the laundry, dry cleaning, and clothing services help other people to dress better. A variety of jobs exist including: clerks, cleaners, pressers, shoe repairers, launderette attendants, tailors, and dressmakers.

Attendant personnel serve in many ways. Chaperones accompany people on trips to educational or recreational facilities. Checkroom attendants store and protect clothing of people attending a place or event. Locker room attendants work at health resorts, swimming pools, and gyms. They keep the area in good condition and help users. Guides help visitors to better understand what they are seeing.

A growing occupation is that of pet care. People want their pets to be well-groomed and fed. Kennel keepers attend to pets that must be boarded while the owners are away. Dog and cat groomers keep the pets attractive looking. Pet shop attendants feed, water, clean, and handle animals so that customers purchase healthy pets. Animal trainers teach the pets to perform certain tricks, tasks, and to behave better. One specialized animal trainer is the horse trainer.

The largest employment of all the personal services is in the food and beverage preparation group. This area is the largest employer of young people in America. Fast food restaurants provide an excellent starting place in the world of work. Jobs include counter persons, cooks, order clerks, and waiters. More advanced careers include wine stewards, butchers, chefs, caterers, and supervisors.

Although some people look upon the personal service careers as just a beginning job, many others make a career of it. A good example of this is Andrew Reiss. As a child he observed the food service system at Miami's Carillion Hotel, where his father was the maitre d'. Reiss started in the food service business at the University of Florida because the food was poor in the fraternity dining hall. He transferred to Florida State University's restaurant program and in 1981 owned four restaurants in Tallahassee.

Personal service workers are very important in Florida. Tourism is one of our largest businesses. Personal service workers, especially those in lodging services and food and beverage preparation, make vacations pleasant for our visitors. Many visitors return for another vacation.

Public Services

In the past, people who entered work in the areas of public services knew their earnings would be below average. This has been changing recently. The public has become aware of their valuable services. Most workers perform governmental services, others are in private industry regulated by governmental agencies. Public service careers can be divided into the following groups: education, health services, postal services, highway services, protective services, social services, rehabilitation and correction, and military service.

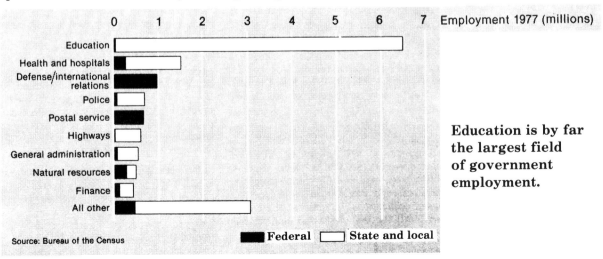

Education is by far the largest field of government employment.

Source: Bureau of the Census

■ Federal ▢ State and local

Government in the United States is the largest single employer in the country. Federal, state, and local governments need thousands of workers each year. In 1980, there were 16 million workers in public services. This included more than two million men and women in the military services. Some of these careers require a high school education while others require college training.

A large group of public service people are lawyers. This profession requires a specialized college education. A new lawyer in Florida must pass the state bar examination to practice law. Many enter politics. Governor Bob Graham, a lawyer is in politics. Former Governor Reuben Askew worked for President Carter's administration in the area of international trade. Representative Claude Pepper of Dade County has been in politics since 1929. He has served in the Florida House of Representatives, the U.S. Senate and the U.S. House of Representatives. In 1980, he turned 80 years old and served as chairman of the House Committee on Aging. Mrs. Gwen Sawyer Cherry, a graduate of Florida A & M was elected to the Florida Legislature in 1970.

Many citizens have served in government. Paula Hawkins was elected to the United States Senate in 1980 after serving on the Florida Public Service Commission. The first black to serve on Florida's Little Cabinet was Mrs. M. Athalie Range. She was appointed Secretary of the Department of Community Affairs in 1971.

The importance of education continues to grow. Once a farming economy, we have become a highly technical and urban society. New machinery and products are constantly being invented. These call for new skills to manufacture and operate them. As a result, more educated workers are needed to fill many new positions.

People today have more time for personal developments and leisure than in the past. Adult education and craft courses have large

Window clerks must be courteous and tactful.

numbers of students looking for personal enrichment.

In 1980, more than three million people were involved in jobs at all levels of the education. Teachers work with people of all ages in many subjects. Some teach youngsters during their first years away from home. Others work mostly with adults.

Kindergarten and elementary school teachers introduce children to the basic concepts of learning. Middle school, junior high, and senior high teachers serve during the period from childhood to young adulthood. The main job of the secondary teacher is to teach students specific subjects. College and university teachers present specific materials in depth. Jobs at the college level are highly competitive, therefore, teachers must have advanced degrees. College teachers usually have flexible schedules and some do special research. All teaching positions require a college degree. The outlook for employment as a teacher shows a decline in all areas with the exception of elementary. One of Florida's outstanding educators was Mary McLeod Bethune, who founded Bethune-Cookman College.

Other occupations closely related to teaching are teacher aides, librarians, and counselors. Aides assist teachers in the classroom, while others work outside the classroom. The pay is about one-half that of a beginning teacher. Most teacher aides receive on-the-job training.

Librarians stock informative materials for people. They work with books and with audio-visual materials. Most familiar are the ones that work in the school library. Others work in city, state, or university libraries. Librarians have a specialized college degree.

School counselors help students make career plans and choose courses. They help with personal or school problems, too.

Other educational employees are maintenance personnel, bus drivers, and computer personnel. These generally do not require a college education. The computer workers need a technical education. The advanced jobs in public education are principals and other administrators.

Public health services employ a large number of people in Florida. The Department of Health and Rehabilitative Services provides mental, physical, and emotional health services. Employees in this area closely follow those in the Medicine and Health Cluster.

The United States Postal Service employs over 80,000 people in America and several thousand in Florida. All jobs are classified as civil service. Prospective employees must obtain a high score on the civil service examination. The pay is based on the score received. In 1981, the minimum salary was $13,500. Jobs include: mail deliveries, window clerks, mail separators, route supervisors, truck drivers, and many more.

Highway services, in Florida, are a part of the State Department of Transportation. There are jobs for the high school graduates as well as the graduate engineer. Truck drivers, road repairers, design personnel, and many others help construct and repair Florida's roads and highways.

There are many agencies which help protect the citizens of the state. These are called regulatory services. Meat inspectors, building inspectors, weight and measure personnel, food and restaurant inspectors, and truck weighers make sure the public is safeguarded.

Almost every child dreams of being a firefighter. This career comes in the protective services group. Law enforcers such as: a city police officer, a county deputy, a state highway patrol officer, or even a federal marshal, are found in Florida. Most law enforcement personnel receive some type of formal training. The student thinking of entering law enforcement should consider several things. Often, there is danger involved, it is not as exciting as pictured on television, and most of the work is routine.

Other occupations in the protective services include: judges, court clerks, conservation officers, and civil defense workers. Some of these need a college education, others a high school diploma.

Social services include members of the clergy. Whether Jewish Rabbis, Protestant ministers, or Catholic Priests, they council other people of their faith. They provide spiritual leadership within their communities and help people to worship according to their faith. Members of the clergy are widely regarded as models.

Rehabilitation workers serve to help handicapped persons adjust to their personal lives. They help others make vocational plans. Employment opportunities in this area will grow during the 1980's, since more federal funds are being spent to educate and rehabilitate the handicapped. Educational requirements vary, however, most workers need advanced education. In many cases some medical knowledge is necessary.

Gas, electric, water, sewage, telephone, and other public utilities employ large numbers of Floridians. There are employment areas in production, transmission, and office personnel. This career area allows an employee to work outdoors or indoors, depending upon desire and skill. Outdoor jobs include: telephone line workers, pipeline workers, meter readers, and power line

Most jobs in the public utilities require a high school diploma, along with a pleasant personality. Workers must enjoy working with the public. There are advancement opportunities with on-the-job training. In Florida in 1980, public utility workers averaged 42 hours per week with an average wage of $8.00 per hour.

The Armed Forces offer young people career opportunities in many areas. Jobs include almost every job found in civilian life. Each year the armed forces train thousands of men and women. The military services - Army, Air Force, Navy, Marine Corps, and Coast Guard - compare with civilian employers. They offer job benefits and training programs that make military service attractive.

In 1980, over 2.1 million persons were on "active duty" in the Armed Forces. They were stationed throughout the U.S. and the world.

Transportation

The transportation industry offers a wide range of career opportunities. Some require little education while others demand a college degree. There are many jobs in this field, over two-fifths of the workers drive buses, trucks, or cabs, fly aircraft, or operate trains and ships. The rest of the workers provide the support services. Some employees deal directly with customers. Flight attendants and reservation agents help airline passengers. Railroad station agents arrange for the transportation of cargo. Airplane mechanics, truck mechanics, and railroad shop workers keep equipment in good working order. As our economy grows and the population in Florida and the U.S. increase, more transportation workers will be needed. With greater emphasis on fuel conservation, the need for mass transportation workers should increase. Employment in most air and highway transportation jobs will increase, at least through 1989. However, jobs in the merchant marine and the railroad industry will decline.

Bureau of Labor Statistics

Seamen stands lookout watch aboard a destroyer.

electricians. Indoor jobs include all the clerical and office staffs plus specialized jobs such as telephone operators. Much of this industry depends on computer technology.

Bureau of Labor Statistics

About 584,000 long-distance truckdrivers were employed in 1978.

Even in these areas, new workers will be needed to replace those who retire, die, or transfer.

Many careers in transportation require post high school training or college. Among these are air traffic controllers, airline pilots, and airline attendants. Some careers require special skills learned on the job or as an apprentice. Examples of these are merchant marine officers, locomotive engineers, and telegraphers. Most transportation careers are non-college trained. These include taxicab drivers, parking attendants, truck drivers, bus drivers, railroad station agents, conductors, merchant marine sailors, and reservation agents. Salaries range from minimum wages to as high as $110,000 for captains on the largest aircraft.

Some of these jobs are available only in certain geographical areas. Tug boat captains or harbor pilots are located in areas with a port, such as the Port of Tampa. Air traffic controllers and airline pilots are found at airports such as Miami International. Bus drivers and truck mechanics can work almost anywhere.

Training for most of these careers is available in Florida, either in the universities, vocational schools, or as on-the-job training.

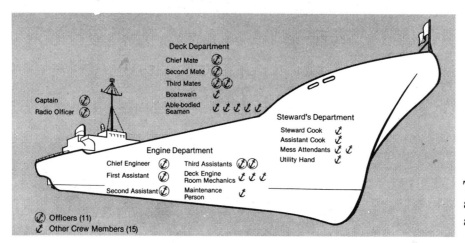

Deck Department
Chief Mate
Second Mate
Third Mates
Boatswain
Able-bodied Seamen

Captain
Radio Officer

Steward's Department
Steward Cook
Assistant Cook
Mess Attendants
Utility Hand

Engine Department
Chief Engineer   Third Assistants
First Assistant   Deck Engine Room Mechanics
Second Assistant Maintenance Person

Officers (11)
Other Crew Members (15)

Typical crew aboard a modern, automated ship.

Conclusion — Sources of Career Information

Much information on careers is printed by government, industry, trade unions, professional association, private guidance, services, and other organizations. You should be careful in using any single piece of career guidance material. Earnings statements more than five years old may need to be adjusted. You need to consider the source of the material. This will tell you the purpose of the material. Some career material is produced only for objective guidance. Others are for the purpose of recruitment. Biased information may leave out important items. It may glamorize the job, overstate the earnings, or exaggerate the demand for workers.

Excellent sources of career guidance materials are your parents, your school counselor, your teacher, your school library, your friends, neighbors, and the Florida State Employment Service.

A high school diploma by itself is not enough training for many jobs, but sometimes, neither is a college degree. Different fields of work require different types of training. Employers always wish to hire the best qualified persons available. This does not always mean choosing the one with the most education. The type of education and training a person has had is important. An important part of career planning is deciding on the type and amount of training which is needed.

People who have chosen career goals may not find the decision difficult. Physicians, for example, must complete four years of college, four years of medical school, and one year of residency. Cosmetologists must complete a state approved cosmetology course. For most people, the decision is more difficult. They may not have chosen a career or the field they have chosen may be entered in a variety of ways. Some may not know whether they want a job that pays high or one which they would enjoy. For example, a person may wish to be an auto mechanic. The decision is whether to leave school and learn on-the-job or to graduate and attend a vocational school.

People thinking about dropping out of school should realize that a high school education has become standard. The educational level of the work force has risen. In 1952, the average worker had completed 10.9 years of school. By 1980, this had risen to 12.9 years. Thus, nongraduates are at a disadvantage when seeking jobs that offer higher pay or advancement. The unemployment rate is much higher for drop outs than graduates. The unemployment rate drops as the amount of education increases. Average yearly income rises with the number of school years completed. In 1980, college students earned over 33 percent more than high school graduates.

As the opportunity to earn a college degree has become more widespread, more high school graduates have attended college. In

290

1952, only 7.9 percent of the work force had four years of college. This amount increased to almost 20 percent by 1980.

Although college graduates do earn more on the average than high school graduates, there are many well-paying jobs for the high school graduate. Workers in construction, mechanics, and repairer occupations earn as much or more, in some cases, than college graduates.

Whatever one's goals and aspirations, it is time to start planning now. This will allow plenty of time for you to investigate, prepare, and if necessary, change to another career.

The future belongs to you as a citizen of Florida and the United States of America. Careers abound in the world of work. It could be:

> *...an airplane pilot... park ranger... writer... TV star... teacher... storeowner... motel worker... performer or any job that will satisfy your needs.*

CAREERS

Unit 12   **Future**

Metrorail, Metro-Dade County

Metrorail rapid transportation in Dade County

FUTURE

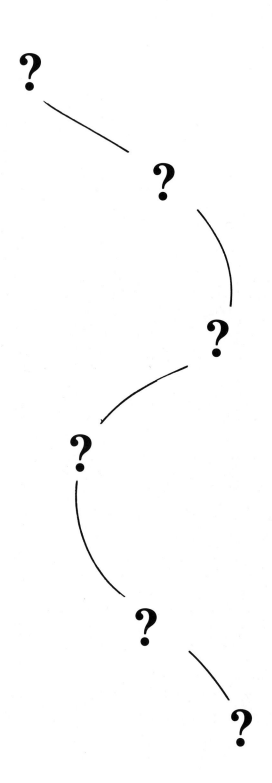

Introduction

What is Florida? Florida is over 1609 kilometers/ 1,000 miles of coastline, only Alaska among the fifty states has more. Florida is over 16,090 kilometers/ 10,000 miles of rivers and streams. It is over 7,000 lakes and springs, from very small ones to the vast body of water known as Lake Okeechobee. It is over 3,000 species of plants and hundreds of animals. Florida is over 38 million tourists each year. With almost 10 million population, Florida is seventh largest among the states. Seven thousand to 15,000 people move to Florida every week to set up housekeeping. By 1990, Florida is expected to be the fourth largest populated state in the United States of America.

In good years and bad, Florida grows in population and development. The quality of life is high. Florida holds its own citizens and attracts the citizens of other states and nations.

But what does the future hold? That is uncertain. Will the future bring a crisis? Or will the future mean a better life for all Floridians?

No one has a crystal ball to see into the future. But we know that people have a great deal to do with making their own kind of future. How we deal with today's problems and opportunities influences what our future will hold. In A PANORAMA OF FLORIDA we have read about many of those opportunities and problems. But before we close our study, let's reflect upon some major issues.

Population Growth

Florida's population growth is a major issue which affects all other issues. From 1950 to 1980, the United States population as a whole grew by 45 percent, while Florida's population more than tripled. Florida went from twentieth most populous state to the seventh most populous. All indications are that this population growth will continue into the future, especially with people moving into Florida from other states.

Florida also continues to draw new residents from other countries. Some of these people are very wealthy, and are attracted by the many investment opportunities in the state. Other new arrivals are very poor, in search of a better life in Florida.

Wherever these additional residents come from, Florida will experience more development and a greater demand for services. New residents can help the economy, since they are customers for the goods and services Florida produces. But new residents arriving in great numbers can put a strain on the resources of the state and of local communities. Some local governments have attempted to establish population limits for their communities. Such proposals have been difficult to carry out.

A more realistic approach to population growth is to plan for it. In the past, many Florida cities have experienced rapid growth with no real "master plan" to serve as a guide. Today, most large communities and many counties in Florida have planning departments. People who work in these agencies try to look into the future to estimate the need for specific services. One way they do this is by examining statistics to discover patterns in population growth and in the cost of services.

As communities expand outward, the cost of delivering services becomes greater. Roads, water and sewer lines and other utilities must be extended. Police and fire protection must be provided over a wider area. All of these things are very expensive.

Some planners think a solution to this problem is to encourage greater density within existing cities. This usually means concentrating houses and other buildings in a smaller area. This approach often results in multi-story or high rise buidings for residents and offices.

With increased density, there is the threat of congestion, or overcrowding. Planners who recommend greater density must make sure that they include a sufficient amount of open space in their plans for parks and recreation.

Whether Florida's cities grow outward or upward, the housing units themselves are likely to be smaller. Not only is land becoming scarce, but housing costs have risen so much that many people cannot afford to buy a house. As a result, many developers are building smaller houses on smaller lots to reduce costs.

With more people, Florida will experience more development and a greater demand for services. In the private sector, we will need more housing, medical facilities, shopping centers, and recreational opportunities. In the public sector, governments will be asked to supply: schools, hospitals, highways, sewers, water supplies, and so forth. These services will cost money, especially in our time of rising prices. Florida's low tax rates will have to be increased to cover these additional expenses.

More people means more workers who will need jobs to support themselves and their families. Jobs in the service industries, such as those workers who serve tourists, and jobs in agricultural and extractive industries (mining and forestry) are generally low paying jobs when compared to industrial pay scales. Some Floridians hope to see industry expand in the state to provide jobs and higher paying positions for workers. State officials expect more manufacturing jobs, as well as more jobs in insurance, finance and real estate fields. Governments expect to hire more workers to provide services for the growing population. Construction and real estate development will provide even more jobs. But still there is concern about employment opportunities for all Floridians, new and old.

More people means more children and youth who will need schools and colleges. In 1979, 25.2 percent of Florida population was between the ages of zero and seventeen. By 1989 this percentage will have dropped to twenty-three percent, but the actual number of Floridians, aged zero to seventeen, will have grown larger. These persons will require the construction of more schools, recreation facilities, an so forth.

More people means more elderly in Florida. In 1960, persons over sixty-five years of age made up 11.2 percent of our population. In 1979, they made up over 17 percent. It is predicted that Florida's senior citizens will make up over 19 percent of the population by 1989. Florida's population is old and is becoming older. Most of these older Floridians will be on modest and fixed incomes, yet they will require extensive public services such as: transportation, medical/health, housing and nursing care. Not only will the private sector grow to provide some of these services, but the public sector with tax revenues will have to do far more than it does today.

More people means more pressure upon Florida's cities. Growth in national and international trade has increased the size of our cities. People are attracted to cities from other states and from other nations. Of the twenty-five most rapidly growing cities in the United States, ten are in one state -- Florida. Growth requires more housing, roads, public transportation from taxis and buses to

---

TOURIST CAPITAL OF THE WORLD

In the year 1990 Central Florida will be the tourist capital of the world!

This prediction was made by Walter Roberts, the editor of "Florida Trend" magazine. Roberts based his prediction on several factors. First, he concluded that Disney's new EPCOT or Experimental Prototype City of Tomorrow will increase visitors to Disney World to 24 million. If you eliminate repeat visitors and local patrons, the net tourists would be 14 million per year. Secondly, he concluded that Spain hosted 31 million visitors in 1980, most of them foreigners. Florida on the other hand hosted over 36 million visitors, most of them from the U.S. With foreign tourism to America growing at a rate of 40 percent, Roberts concluded that Florida would be the most visited place in the world.

No one knows what EPCOT will do, just as in 1971 no one could confidently predict the result of Walt Disney's purchase of land in rural Florida. The only question now is, "Where is that rural area?"

Lake Okeechobee Spillway Construction in 1935. Why is there still controversy about this lake?

airports, sewers, police, and firepersons. Growth strains and the services provided in the public sector and generally results in higher taxes. Congestion seems to breed crimes of property and violence. In 1980, Dade County reported an all-time high of 580 murders. These crimes and those associated with the illegal drug trade place greater burdens on law enforcement agencies -- the costs upon taxpayers.

Florida has been a state most dependent upon imported energy resources. With the energy shortages of the 1970's now the energy shortages and higher priced energy of the 1980's, Florida faces problems. Generating even more electricity to power homes, farms, factories, and cities, Florida relies upon imported oil more than most states. To switch to coal or nuclear energy means greater environmental problems, and controversy about air quality and nuclear wastes and dangers. Florida also consumes more energy in its transportation sector than other states. The tourist industry and getting Florida's crops to market in northern cities

require vast amounts of gasoline and diesel fuel. As these fuels gallop upward in costs and downward in supply, Floridians will have to discover alternative ways to move people and goods.

The energy issues of the 1970's and the 1980's will be repeated with water. Water will be the great issue in Florida's future. There is no comprehensive state plan for the water resources. The state is divided into water management districts which have attempted planning, but the burden of tremendous population growth has overwhelmed planning thus far. South Florida faces water shortages in the near future. As cities spill over into the Everglades and as farming interests develop the Glades and the Kissimmee River-Okeechobee region, conflicts over water will be severe. Already Dade and Pinellas Counties have exhausted their water resources and "borrow" water from nearby counties. How long will other counties be willing (or able) to share water?

Development creates greater demand for water, on the one hand, and tends to

GROWING CITIES

In 1980, three out of every four Americans lived in a metropolitan area. This is, in a place in or near a city of at least 50,000 population. Of the 25 fastest growing metropolitan areas in the nation, ten are in Florida.

CITY	PERCENTAGE GROWTH, 1970 to 1980
1. Fort Myers - Cape Coral, FL	94.2
3. Sarasota, FL	67.5
5. Fort Lauderdale, FL	62.2
8. West Palm Beach - Boca Raton, FL	58.2
14. Orlando, FL	53.3
17. Bradenton, FL	50.4
19. Daytona Beach, FL	43.6
22. Tallahassee, FL	43.6
24. Tampa - St. Petersburg, FL	42.4
25. Lakeland - Winter Haven, FL	40.9

For a long time Americans thought that bigger was better. Today, residents of Florida are wondering about that. Is bigger better? Should we be proud of our growth? Is it a matter of civic pride that our city is growing faster than another city?

adversely affect the quality of natural water systems, on the other hand. Water quality seems to be a limit on the growth of Florida's population, farms and cities.

As Floridians venture into the future, they will have to be careful about destroying the beautiful and life-sustaining environment which is so delightful and lends so much to our lives. More people, more farms, more jobs, more housing, more factories, more hospitals, more highways and airports, more parks, and so forth are required. In recent years, Floridians have met the challenge of population growth with a sensitivity to the needs of people and with a concern for environmental quality. We no longer believe in "Growth at any price." But the issues of the future -- especially energy and water -- will be more severe than those of the past. Will we as Floridians be able to meet the challenge with fairness?

The New Promised Land

"If only I can make it to America, my troubles will be over." This feeling is expressed by thousands of immigrants who come to this country in search of a better-life. For many immigrants, "America" means "Florida." Throughout Florida's colorful history, immigrants from many lands have contributed to the state's growth and development.

But people from other countries have never come in such great numbers as in recent years. In 1980 alone, 130,000 Cubans came to Florida. In the same year, 13,000 arrived from Haiti. Large numbers of people also arrived from Colombia, Venezuela, and Nicaragua.

Most of these new arrivals to Florida have been accepted by the United States as immigrants. An immigrant is one who has been admitted to establish permanent

Florida Photographic Archives

Cuban Revolutionary Society in 1938. Why has Florida been attractive to Cubans fleeing internal strife in their homeland?

MIGRATION MIGRAINE

"Floridians are the direct recipients of the failure of the United States to establish a sane, reasonable, coherent and workable approach to immigration," said Governor Bob Graham. He warned that the flow of illegal aliens into Florida was one of the state's most serious problems. *"Dade County jail is now estimated to have a total population of approximately 950 to 1,000 persons. It is estimated that 20 percent to 25 percent of that population are refugees,"* he said.

"The federal judges are enforcing maximum numbers in the jails and, in one case, threatened to force the Dade County jail to release two persons from jail for every one admitted in order to reduce the jail population. And yet, the federal government will not take steps to enforce this immigration policy because it may cause a confrontation with Castro." Graham warned that the migration of refugees is rooted in the overpopulation, economic backwardness, lack of adequate food and housing and political strife that exists in Latin America. He said the problem is augmented by the images of the American life that are beamed across the world through television, causing people to try to reach America's shores.

The situation will not abate, Graham stressed, until the federal government enforces the immigration laws currently on the books, in addition to articulating a comprehensive immigration policy for the 1980's. Graham also called on the Florida business community to help the agricultural development of the Caribbean basin nations. *"One of the things that Florida has to offer these countries is a tremendous wealth of knowledge and experience in the practical application of agricultural techniques,"* he said.

residence. Under the best of conditions, it would be difficult for the communities of Florida to absorb so many new residents. But many of the newcomers from Cuba and Haiti came to this country to escape from poverty, or from a form of government which they did not like. They became known as refugees.

These people had little or no money and very few possessions. They were in need of food, clothing, housing and medical care. Employment was difficult to find, and refugees competed with Americans for scarce jobs. Refugee children crowded into schools that were low on funds. To make matters even worse, the Cuban government sent criminals and mentally ill persons along with the rest of the refugees. Some of these people committed crimes or created disturbances upon their arrival in Florida.

Many Floridians were very upset by the problems created with the arrival of the refugees. They thought there should be more restrictions regarding the entry of immigrants. They further felt that the federal government should have provided more help in caring for and educating the refugees.

Others pointed out that the United States is a nation of immigrants, and that the newcomers should be given a chance. Despite all the problems, many of the refugees have obtained jobs and are learning to speak English. They are also learning about American customs and laws. Like many immigrants before them, many will become good citizens of the United States.

But the economic and political problems that caused these people to come to Florida still exist. Refugees and other immigrants will continue to make the journey to Florida, often risking their lives. Is there a better way to deal with this situation?

Illegal Immigrants

Besides the thousands of foreigners who enter Florida legally, there are many others who enter the state illegally. If they are caught, they can be deported, or sent out of the country. Like the legal immigrants, many of the illegal immigrants have come to Florida to find work and a better way of life.

Illegal immigrants are a serious problem in Florida. They often become victims of dishonest people who take advantage of their illegal status. Frequently, illegal immigrants must pay large sums of money to persons who smuggle them into the state. Once they arrive, they must avoid being caught by the authorities. If they find work, it is usually for wages that are below the legal minimum. If jobs are scarce, there is sometimes conflict between the illegal immigrants and American workers who are competing for the same jobs.

No one knows how many illegal immigrants there are in Florida, but authorities of the U.S. Immigration and Naturalization Service estimate that the number is in the thousands. Officials do not have enough agents to catch all of the illegal immigrants in Florida. When illegal immigrants are caught, it is very expensive to deport them.

Migrants

The problem of migrant laborers is often related to illegal immigration. Migrant laborers are usually farm workers who move from state to state. Florida is one of the states that has many migrant workers during certain times of the year. In many cases, migrants may be immigrants, either legal or illegal. Other migrants are American citizens. Whatever their background, the lives of migrants are usually very difficult. When they do work, they spend long hours in the fields and orchards. But the chances for steady employment are slim. As seasonal workers, they may pick apples or cherries in Michigan during the summer, and tomatoes and cucumbers in Florida during the winter. In between, they may harvest crops in Indiana or South Carolina.

Because of this pattern of migration, migrants do not have permanent homes in any one place. When they work in Florida, they usually live in camps that have been set up for migrants. Some migrants rent rooms in private homes or apartment buildings.

When housing is scarce, some migrants end up sleeping in their cars or trucks.

Migrants do very important work. They harvest crops that cannot be picked by machines. Their work is hard and tiring. It usually involves much bending, stooping or reaching. Most migrants receive very low wages by American standards. But for a migrant who has just come from Haiti or Mexico, the wages may seem very high. Such a worker may earn more from a few weeks of work in Florida than he could from an entire year's work in his homeland.

In recent years, living conditions for migrants have improved. But the lot of a migrant is still difficult and uncertain. Wages are better, but they are seldom above the legal minimum. For illegal migrants, wages are usually well below the minimum. Housing is better, but it is often scarce and expensive. Health care and educational services have improved, but do not always reach those who need them. Under certain conditions, migrants are eligible for food stamps and emergency assistance.

Through education, ambition and the opportunity for better jobs, many people escape from the migrant stream. But in every generation , there always seems to be more poor people to take the place of those who leave. Migrants do the jobs nobody else wants to do. Their work is very important. They help produce the food that is consumed by millions of people in Florida and other parts of the country and the world.

Are there better ways to harvest our vital crops while at the same time helping the migrants to achieve a decent way of life?

War On Crime

Crime against persons and property is one of Florida's more serious problems. During 1980, the violent crime rate (the rate for crimes such as murder, robbery with violence, and assault) increased 27 percent throughout the State. At the opening of the 1981 session of the legislature, Governor D. Robert Graham declared war on criminal activities in Florida. He urged legislators to pass laws that would help convict criminals

Florida Photographic Archives

Migrant worker's family and campsite in 1939. How have conditions improved?

and stop crime. The governor vowed that "We will not turn Florida over to the criminals."

Much of the talk today is about crime in South Florida involving the drug trade and recent immigrants into Florida. But people who think about the good old days as crime free should think with historical facts. Crime is not new to Florida. In 1840, five years before Florida became a State, troops were stationed in Tallahassee because of lawless conditions in the capital city. A visitor from New England wrote home from Tallahassee that it was not safe to walk the street at night "without being armed to the teeth."

Florida's last territorial governor, John Branch, addressed the problem of crime in a message to the legislative council in 1845. This message was very similar to Governor Graham's remarks to the legislature in 1981. Governor Branch complained that the Criminal Code was not accomplishing its purpose. He thought that there were not enough jails. He also suggested that not enough funds had been provided to enable police to enforce the law. Whatever the cause was, Governor Branch urged the council members to "trace it out and apply the remedy."

Today, as in 1845, a large part of the "remedy" for fighting crime involves money. Money is needed to hire more persons who deal with crimes and criminals -- police, judges, corrections officers, investigators, prosecutors, and public defenders. Money is also needed to modernize and build jails and correctional facilities.

Some of Florida's leaders argue that if more money is spent to fight crime, less will be available for schools, roads, and other State needs.

Other legislators and leaders say that part of the solution to crime in Florida lies in tougher laws. They want to increase penalties for convicted criminals.

Still other leaders think that more resources should be applied to conditions which lead to crime. They want to spend money on correction facilities, youth workers, and improved programs for younger lawbreakers. Juveniles are responsible for many of the crimes committed in Florida. Unless their behavior can be corrected or prevented at an early age, juvenile offenders are likely to develop into adult criminals. Those leaders who share this point of view favor programs that prevent crimes and rehabilitate the offenders.

The war against crime in Florida will not be an easy one. It will require the best efforts of State and local authorities. Because many of the crimes in Florida are linked to national and international problems (such as drug trafficking and illegal immigration), Florida will require more assistance from federal law enforcement authorities.

Individuals are confronting crime in their neighborhoods in some parts of South Florida. Many people are participating in crime watch programs, reporting strange "goings on" to their police departments. Support for law and order legislation and for law enforcement officials is on the upswing in the State.

A combined effort of all levels -- individuals, local and state law enforcement, and federal law enforcement officers -- can help to keep Florida a safe place for future generations of residents and tourists.

Air Pollution

A clean, attractive environment is one of the main reasons visitors and new residents come to Florida. Compared to many large industrial cities throughout our nation, Florida's communities are relatively free from air pollution. Wind currents across the state keep Florida's air clear. Generally the winds disperse pollutants which are released into the air from cars, factories, and farms. Florida does not have large numbers of factories which release smoke and gases into our air.

There are some locations in Florida where air pollution is a problem. The major source of air pollution in Florida is automobiles, buses, and trucks. By 1981, there were over

Governor Bob Graham led Florida into the 1980's.

seven million of these vehicles in our state. In cities where motor vehicles are found in greater numbers, there are concentrations of pollutants coming from their exhaust pipes. These exhaust fumes contain gases including dangerous carbon monoxide.

If the winds stop blowing and certain weather conditions occur, the pollutants can build up in the air trapped near the ground. When this happens, a city's air might look smoky and brownish. This air is not only unpleasant to breathe, it is dangerous to our health.

Florida has other sources of air pollution. The mines and plants which produce phosphate cause certain pollutants. Pulp and paper mills, chemical plants, aircraft exhaust, and electric power plants release pollutants into our air. Forest fires can be a major source of pollution during dry periods.

Many laws have been passed by Congress and by the State legislature to control the sources of air pollution. Some of these laws have been very effective. Cars today burn cleaner fuels. Power plants are required to control smoke stack exhaust. Paper mills and chemical plants are required to operate with less pollution going into the air. But some laws and rules are not followed. To keep Florida's air clear and bright, it will require better enforcement by the Florida Department of Environmental Regulation. In addition, citizens in Florida need to be informed about the dangers of air pollution and the need to support the efforts of the Department of Environmental Regulation.

Solid Waste Disposal

More people means more solid waste. The amount of garbage produced in Florida each day averages out to about 2.7 kilograms/ six pounds per person! This adds up to over a metric ton/ ton a year for each person in Florida -- and the amount is steadily rising as each year goes by.

In most of Florida's communities, garbage is hauled away and either burned or buried in land fills. Both methods can cause pollution problems. Burning garbage in incinerators or open dumps can create air pollution. Burying garbage, if not done properly, can cause offensive odors. It can also pollute surface waters, like our streams and lakes, and pollute ground waters where we get our drinking water. Hauling masses of garbage consumes energy and that is very expensive, causing higher taxes.

All citizens can reduce waste by practicing conservation and recycling materials which can be used again. Paper, aluminum, and glass bottles can be recycled into new products. Communities can improve waste disposal techniques by installing air pollution devices on incinerators. If a community buries its garbage, it can do so in plastic-lined pits. That way harmful chemicals will not seep into our water supplies. Each day the garbage should be covered with soil. If a soil cover is used and if a plastic liner is used, the disposal site is called a "sanitary landfill."

Some of Florida's communities are beginning to encourage recycling in the household and at the landfill. Dade County has a Resource Recovery Facility at its landfill. This modern plant can dispose of 907,200 metric tons/ one million tons of garbage each year. It recovers metals and glass for recycling into new products. Energy is produced by burning the garbage, producing electricity for 40,000 homes.

Garbage is a growing problem in Florida. But with proper citizen conservation and recycling, we can preserve our farm lands from becoming landfills. And, we can preserve the fine quality of our water and air resources. Floridians are discovering that by hauling less garbage we save energy. But by carefully burning garbage, we can produce electricity for our homes. By recovering aluminum, paper, and glass we can produce new cans, bottles, and paper at lower costs! Garbage is a problem, but it has its uses in Florida.

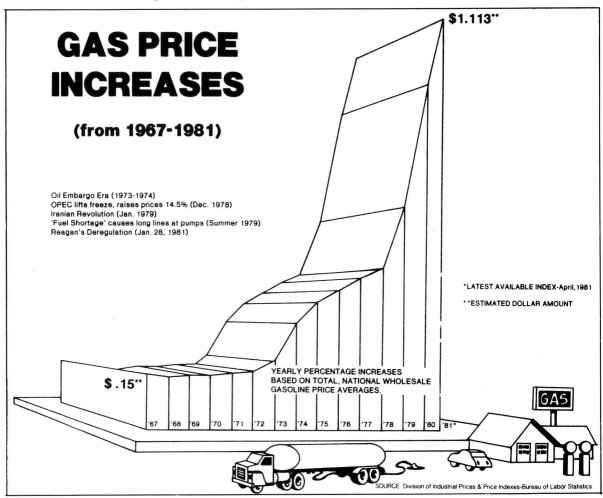

GAS PRICE INCREASES

(from 1967-1981)

Oil Embargo Era (1973-1974)
OPEC lifts freeze, raises prices 14.5% (Dec. 1978)
Iranian Revolution (Jan. 1979)
'Fuel Shortage' causes long lines at pumps (Summer 1979)
Reagan's Deregulation (Jan. 28, 1981)

$1.113**

*LATEST AVAILABLE INDEX-April, 1981

**ESTIMATED DOLLAR AMOUNT

$ .15**

YEARLY PERCENTAGE INCREASES BASED ON TOTAL, NATIONAL WHOLESALE GASOLINE PRICE AVERAGES.

'67 '68 '69 '70 '71 '72 '73 '74 '75 '76 '77 '78 '79 '80 '81*

GAS

SOURCE Division of Industrial Prices & Price Indexes-Bureau of Labor Statistics

Metro Dade photo by Jean Marie Massa

Waste Recovery Plant

The Promise of the Future

Florida faces many tough challenges in its future. At the same time, there are many fascinating developments taking place that may be useful in meeting some of those challenges.

Some of the most exciting developments are taking place in the field of communications. With the aid of space-age inventions, scientists and engineers are combining the telephone, computer, and television to microchips, multiplying greatly the ways we give and receive information. communities the kinds of television programs can be increased. There will be many channels to choose from. Some will carry one subject such as: sports, news, weather, religious programs, old movies, stock market and financial information, or college courses. Some people are predicting that newspapers will not be printed and delivered by bicycle, but will be beamed into homes by way of the cable and the T V screen.

Perhaps the most promising aspect of some of the new systems will be the ability to provide two-way communication. With this feature, it will be possible for people to work at home rather than go each day to an office. Tasks such as typing or computer operation could be done from a den or a living room. You could go to school with a TV and a computer terminal right in your living room. No buses and no more walks to school in the rain!

With two-way communication, viewers could order merchandise from their homes after seeing products on their TV screens. Several cities now have all-shopping channels. This reduces trips to shopping malls and stores.

These developments could change the way we live and interact with other people. It might help to solve some of our environmental problems. With some people working, studying, and shopping at home fewer trips by motor vehicles would be needed. Energy and air pollution would be saved. People would spend more time at home interacting with other family members. But these developments would tend to reduce the time spent interacting with other community members. Do you think that this could be a problem?

FLORIDA ENERGY PROFILES

Florida is unique among the states in regard to energy.

• In 1978, the state depended on petroleum and natural gas for almost 85 percent of its energy needs; petroleum constituted 70.1 percent of the total consumption of primary energy. This contrasted with the United States as a whole, which used petroleum and natural gas for approximately 70 percent of its energy needs, with less than 50 percent of primary energy consumption being petroleum.

Percentage of Total Energy Consumption By Primary Energy Source
Florida and the U.S., 1978

Total Consumption:
Florida .... 2,266.5 trillion BTU
U.S. .... 78,474.9 trillion BTU

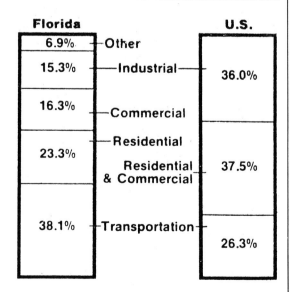

	Florida		U.S.
Hydroelectric	0.1%		3.8%
Nuclear	7.6%		3.8%
Coal	7.6%		17.8%
Natural Gas	14.6%		25.5%
Petroleum	70.1%		49.1%

• The consumption of energy in Florida differs from that of the country as a whole. The transportation sector is the largest energy consuming sector in the state. In 1978, transportation accounted for 38.1 percent of energy use in Florida, but only 26.3 percent of the nation's. While 36 percent of the country's total energy consumption was in the industrial sector, industry accounted for only 16 percent of energy use in Florida.

Percentage of Total Energy Consumption By Sector
Florida and the U.S., 1978

	Florida		U.S.
Other	6.9%		
Industrial	15.3%		36.0%
Commercial	16.3%		
Residential	23.3%		Residential & Commercial 37.5%
Transportation	38.1%		26.3%

Source: Governor's Energy Office, Tallahassee

TO BE OR NOT TO BE, LAKE OKEECHOBEE?

Lake Okeechobee is South Florida's greatest fresh water reservoir and a key to balancing periods of flood and periods of drought. It is a habitat for wildlife, an industry with commercial fishing, and a tourist industry with its swimming, fishing, and boating.

The lake was formed about 5,000 years ago and it is part of a larger system. The lake gets its water from rain and from rivers and streams bringing water down from as far as Orlando. The Kissimmee River, Taylor Creek and Nubbin Slough supply water to the lake.

Once these rivers brought sweet, fresh water to the lake. Today, they bring pollutants from cities and farms. The lake may die before another quarter century passes -- due to pollution.

How does pollution enter the lake? First, in the old days, a meandering 151.2 kilometer/ 94-mile Kissimmee River discharged nutrients as it flowed through 20,235 hectares/ 50,000 acres of marsh on its way to the lake. The marsh and marsh grasses filtered out the nutrients. But the river was channelized -- turned into a 83.7 kilometer/ 52-mile ditch. The marshes went dry and the marsh grass died. The river's nutrients were no longer filtered and flowed into the Lake. The growth of towns at the headwaters of the river (Orlando, Kissimmee, etc.) put more nutrients into the water. Orlando and other cities dump wastes and sewage. These make their way to the lake.

Second, ranchers and dairy farmers who sold out farms for urban development in Broward and Dade Counties moved to Okeechobee County. Huge dairy farms and ranches around the lake discharge pollutants into the lake. Fertilizer from citrus groves washes into the lake. Sugar cane growers have discharged field water, with fertilizers, into the lake. There are about 200,000 head of cattle in the Kissimmee River Valley and discharge their wastes into the river and down to the lake.

These nutrients cause algae to grow rapidly – to "bloom." As the algae die they use the oxygen, and nothing else can live. After several cycles of algae bloom and death, a slime covers the bottom of the lake, destroying plants which add oxygen to the water. In short, nothing can grow except species of worms and some trash fish.

The beauty of the lake and its natural systems are destroyed. This, in turn, affects all life in Florida below the Lake, since its waters assist the eco-systems of the Everglades and all towns and cities in South Florida.

The lake, the Everglades, the farms and the cities are all part of a large system. Each depends upon the other for quality and survival.

Florida's future is very bright. One only has to look around to see a state with people who have solved serious problems in the past and will do so in the future. There will be problems, but there are solutions. As President Ronald Reagan said in 1981, we may have to sacrifice some but the states and nation will prosper because we are strong.

Florida's citizens can look forward to living in a state which will help lead the nation into the 21st century.

Because of interstate migration, changes in population will vary among States

Percent change in population, 1975 to 1990

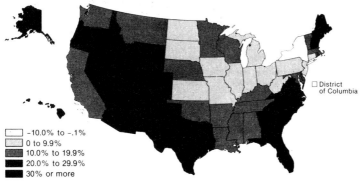

-10.0% to -.1%
0 to 9.9%
10.0% to 19.9%
20.0% to 29.9%
30% or more

Source: Bureau of the Census

307

BIBLIOGRAPHY

Andrews, Evangeline, Ed. **Jonathan Dickinson's Journal.** New Haven, CT: Yale University Press, 1961.

Bailey, T.A. **A Diplomatic History of the American People.** Boston: D.C. Heath and Company, 1964

Baldwin, John L. **Climates of the United States.** Washington: U.S. Department of Commerce, 1973.

Balseiro, Jose Agustin. **The Hispanic Presence in Florida.** Miami: E. A. Seemann Publishing, Inc., 1976.

Bamford, Hal. **Florida History.** St. Petersburg: Great Outdoors Publishing Company, 1976.

Benedict, Ruth. · **Patterns of Culture.** Boston: Houghton Mifflin Co., 1934.

Bennett, Charles. **Laudonniere and Fort Caroline.** Gainesville: University of Florida Press, 1964.

Bice, David A. **A Panorama of West Virginia.** Charleston, WV: Jalamap Publications, Inc., 1979.

Browne, Jefferson. **Key West: The Old and the New.** St. Augustine: The Record Company, 1912.

Bullen, Adelaide. **Florida Indians of Past and Present.** Gainesville, Florida: Kendall Baooks, No Date.

Carson, Ruby Leach. **Fabulous Florida.** Dallas, Texas: Manfred, Van Nort & Company, 1942

Cox, M. and Dovell, J. **Florida: From Secession to Space Age.** St. Petersburg, Florida: Great Outdoors Publishing Co., 1974.

Census of Population, Bureau of the Census, U.S. Department of Commerce, 1981.

Ceram, C.W. **The First American: The Story of North American Archaeology.** New York: Harcourt, Brace, Jovanovich, Inc. 1971.

Climate of Florida. Silver Springs, MD.: U.S. Department of Commerce, 1972. (From series **Climate of the States)**

Comparative Climatic Data Through 1976. Asheville, North Carolina: U.S. Department of Commerce, 1977.

Conch Cooking. Key West, Florida: Florida Keys Printing and Publishing, No Date.

Cooke, C. Wythe. **Geology of Florida.** Tallahassee: The Florida Geological Survey, 1945.

Cooke C. Wythe. **Scenery of Florida, Interpreted by a Geologist.** Tallahassee: The Florida Geological Survey, 1939.

Craighead, Frank. **The Trees of South Florida.** Vol. 1, The Natural Environments and Their Succession. Coral Gables, Florida: The University of Miami Press, 1971.

deBlij, Harm. **The Earth: A Topical Geography.** New York: John Wiley and Sons, Inc., 1980.

Dasmann, Raymond. **No Further Retreat: The Flight to Save Florida.** New York: Macmillan Company, 1971.

Dean, H. and Spears, P. **Florida: Pathways to Progress.** Tallahassee, Florida. Graphic Language Corporation, 1979.

Douglas, Marjory Stoneman. **Florida: The Long Frontier.** New York: Harper & Row, 1967.

Downs, Robert B. **Books That Changed America.** New York: Mentor, 1970.

Florida Becomes a State. Florida Centennial Commission. St. Augustine, FL: The Record Press, 1945.

The Florida Bicentennial Trail: A Heritage Revisited. The Bicentennial Commission of Florida, 1976.

Florida Department of Transportation, Annual Report, 1979 Tallahassee

"Florida." **Encyclopaedia Britannica Macropaedia,** Vol. 7. Encyclopaedia Britannica, Inc., 1977, pp. 424-429.

Florida 10 Million. Tallahassee: Florida Department of Administration, 1973.

Frisbie, Louise. **Peace River Pioneers.** Miami: E.A. Seemann Publishing, Inc. 1974.

The Green Plan. Tallahassee: Bureau of Comprehensive Planning, 1975.

A Half Century of People Serving People. A History of the Florida Power and Light Company. Florida Power and Light Company, 1975.

Hawkes, Alex. **Guide to Plants of the Everglades National Park.** Coral Gables, Florida: Tropic Isle Publishers Inc., 1965.

Hoffmeister, John. **Land from the Sea.** Coral Gables: University of Miami Press, 1974.

Irving, Theodore, M.A.. **The Conquest of Florida by Hernando De Soto.** George Putnam & Son. 1869.

Key West Woman's Club. **Key West Cook Book.** New York: Farrar, Straus and Company, 1949.

Lawson, Edward. **The Discovery of Florida and Its Discoverer Juan Ponce De Leon.** Edward Lawson, 1946.

Lewin, Ted. **World Within a World: Everglades.** New York: Dodd, Mead and Company, 1976.

Long Daniel. **The Power Within Us. Cabeza de Vaca's Journey.** Duell, Sloan & Pearce, New York, 1939.

Marcus, Robert & Fernald, Edward. **Florida: A Geographic Approach. Dubuque, Iowa:** Kendall/Hunt Publishing Company, 1975.

Marth, Del and Marth, Martha. **The Florida Almanac, 1980-81.** A.W. Barnes and Co., 1980.

McCarthy, Joseph **Record of America.** New York, Charles Scribner's Sons Volume 2, 1974.

Monthly Normals of Temperature, Precipitation, and Heating Cooling Degree Days 1941 - 70. Asheville, North Carolina: U.S. Department of Commerce, 1973.

Morgan, Nancy. **Aunt Nancy's Suwannee Country Cooking.** White Springs, Florida. Mrs. Nancy Morgan, 1971.

Morris, Allen. **The Florida Handbook, 1981-82, 18th ed.** Tallahassee: The Peninsular Publishing Company, 1981.

Morris, Richard. **Encyclopedia of American History.** New York: Harper, 1953.

Neyland, Leedell W. **Twelve Black Floridians.** Tallahassee, Florida. Florida Agricultural and Mechanical University Foundation, Inc., 1970.

Occupational Outlook Handbook. Washington, D.C.: Bureau of Labor Statistics.

Parker, Gerald and Cooke, C. Wythe. **Late Cenozoic Geology of Southern Florida, with a Discussion of the Ground Water.** Tallahassee: The Florida Geological Survey, 1944.

Patrick, Rembert W. **Florida Under Five Flags.** University of Florida Press. Gainesville, 1955.

Puetz, C.J. **Guide to Fun in Florida; Florida Wildlife Federation,** 1974.

Pritchard, Peter C. H. ed. **Rare and Endangered Biota of Florida.** Gainesville: University Presses of Florida, 1978.

Puri, Harbans and Vernon, Robert. **Summary of the Geology of Florida and a Guidebook to the Classic Exposure.** Tallahassee: Florida Geological Survey, 1964.

Raisz, Erwin. **Atlas of Florida.** Gainesville: University of Florida. Press, 1964.

BIBLIOGRAPHY

Randall, J.G. and Donald D. **The Civil War and Reconstruction.** Boston: D.C. Heath and Company, 1966.

Rawlings, Marjorie Kinnan. **The Yearling.** New York: Charles Scribner's Sons, 1939.

A Report on Urban Waste Disposal. Washington: National Center for Resource Recover, Inc., 1971.

Resource and Land Information for South Dade County, Florida. Washington: U.S. Department of the Interior, 1973.

Sand, George. **The Everglades Today.** New York, Four Winds Press, 1971.

Simpson, Robert & Riehl, Herbert. **The Hurricane and its Impact.** Baton Rouge: Louisiana State University Press, 1981.

Skinner, W. and Gaines, W. **Adventures In Florida History.** Pensacola, Florida; Town and Country Books, 1974.

Smith, Julia Floyd. **Slavery and Plantation Growth in Antebellum Florida 1821-1860.** Gainesville: University of Florida Press, 1973.

State Transportation Plan: Bicycle Element. Florida Department of Transportation, 1980.

St. Augustine Cookery. St. Augustine: The Flagler Hospital Auxiliary, 1965.

Tannahill, Reay. **Food in History.** New York: Stein and Day Publishers, 1973.

Tebeau, Charlton. **A History of Florida.** Coral Gables: University of Miami Press, 1971.

Toner, Mike. **This Land of Ours.** Miami: The Miami Herald, 1976.

Thompson, Ralph B. (editor). **1980 Florida Statistical Abstract.** University Presses of Florida, Gainesville, 1980.

Tropical Cyclones of the North Atlantic Ocean, 1871-1977. Asheville, NC: National Climatic Center, U.S. Department of Commerce, 1978.

Veri, Albert, Jenna, William and Bergamaschi, Dorothy. **Environmental Quality by Design.** Coral Gables; Florida: University of Miami Press, 1975.

Vest, B.B. Florida: **Historical and Contemporary Life in the Sunshine State.** Tampa: Beach Products, Inc., 1974.

Whitson, Skip. **Old Florida 100.** Albuquerque, NM: Sun Publishing Company, 1977.

Woodward, C.V. **The Strange Career of Jim Crow.** New York: Oxford University Press, 1955.

The World Almanac & Book of Facts, 1981. New York: Newspaper Enterprise Association, Inc., 1981.

The World Book Encyclopedia. Chicago: Childcraft International, Inc., 1980.

World Weather Records 1961-1970. Volume. 1, North America Asheville, NC: U.S. Department of Commerce, 1979.

Newspapers:

The Miami Herald, Miami.

The Miami News, Miami.

The Charleston Gazette, Charleston WV.

Sentinel Star, Orlando.

Magazines:

"Florida Trend." Tampa: 1980-1981

"Pace." Charlotte 1980-1981

APPENDIX
Lakes

Natural fresh-water lakes of 16.09 square kilometers/ 10 square miles or more in Florida:

	County	Area (sq.mi.)	(sq. kil.)
Okeechobee	Hendry, Glades, Okeechobee, Martin, Palm Beach	700	1,812.7
George	Putnam, Marion, Volusia, Lake	70	181.3
Kissimmee	Osceola Polk	55	142.4
Apopka	Orange	48	124.3
Istokpaga	Highlands	43	111.4
Tsala Apopka	Citrus	30	77.7
Tohopekaliga	Osceola	29	75.1
Harris	Lake	27	69.9
Orange	Alachua, Marion	26	67.3
E. Tohopekaliga	Osceola	19	49.2
Griffin	Lake	14	36.3
Monroe	Seminole, Volusia	14	36.3
Jessup	Seminole	13	33.7
Weohyakapka	Polk	12	31.1
Talquin	Gadsden, Leon	11	28.5
Eustis	Lake	11	28.5
Blue Cypress	Osceola, Indian River	10	25.9
Hatchineha	Polk, Osceola	10	25.9
Lochloosa	Alachua	10	25.9

First-Magnitude Springs of Florida

	Average Cubic Feet per second	Average Cubic Meters per second	Water Temperature °F	Water Temperature °C
Alachua County				
Hornsby Spring	163	4.6	73	23
Bay County				
Gainer Springs	159	4.5	72	22
Citrus County				
Chassahawitska Springs	139	3.9	74	23
Crystal River Springs	878	24.9	75	24
Homosassa Springs	192	5.4	73	23
Columbia County				
Ichatucknee Springs*	358	10.1	73	23
Hamilton County				
Alapaha Rise	508	14.4	—	
Holton Spring	482	13.6	—	
Hernando County				
Weekiwachee Springs	176	5.0	74	23
Jackson County				
Blue Springs	190	5.4	70	21
Jefferson County				
Wacissa Springs Group	374	10.6	69	21
Lafayette County				
Troy Spring	166	4.7	72	22
Lake County				
Alexander Springs	120	3.4	74	23
Leon County				
Natural Bridge Spring	106	3.0	68	20
St. Marks Spring	519	14.7	69	21
Levy County				
Fannin Springs	102	2.9	72	22
Manatee Springs*	181	5.1	72	22
Madison County				
Blue Spring	123	3.5	70	21
Marion County				
Rainbow Springs	788	22.3	73	23
Silver Springs	823	23.3	73	23
Silver Glen Springs	112	3.2	73	23
Suwannee County				
Falmouth Spring	125	3.5	70	21
Volusia County				
Blue Spring	162	4.6	73	23
Wakulla County				
Kini Spring	176	5.0	70	21
River Sink Spring	164	4.6	70	21
Spring Creek Springs	2,003	56.7	73	23
Wakulla Springs	375	10.6	70	21

*Florida State Park

Rivers

Stream	Length		Drainage	
	Miles	Kilometers	area in sq. miles	area in sq. kilometers
Alafa River	25	40.23	335	867.51
Apalachicola River	*94	151.25	17,200	44,541.00
Aucilla River	*60	96.54	747	1,934.43
Blackwater River	*49	78.84	860	2,227.05
Chipola River	89	143.20	781	2,022.47
Choctawhatchee River	*100	160.90	4,646	12,031.25
Econfina River	43	69.19	239	618.91
Escambia River	*54	86.89	4,233	10,961.95
Fisheating Creek	51	82.06	436	1,129.06
Hillsborough River	56	90.10	690	1,786.82
Kissimmee River	94	151.25	2,945	7,626.35
Little Manatee River	38	61.14	149	385.85
Manatee River	35	56.32	80	207.17
Myakka River	68	109.41	235	608.55
Ochlocknee River	*102	164.12	1,720	4,454.10
Oklawaha River	79	127.11	2,970	7,691.09
Peace River	106	170.55	1,367	3,539.97
Perdido River	58	93.32	925	2,395.37
St. Johns River	273	439.26	8,840	22,892.00
St. Marks River	36	57.92	535	1,385.43
St. Marys River	127	328.88	1,480	3,832.60
Sante Fe River	76	122.28	1,520	3,936.18
Shoal River	37	59.53	499	1,292.21
Suwannee River	*177	284.79	9,630	24,937.78
Withlacoochee River (south)	86	138.37 138.37	1,710	4,428.20
Withlacoochee River (north)	*23	7.01 7.01	2,120	5,489.94
Yellow River	*61	98.15	1,365	3,534.79

*Distance from mouth to Florida State Line; other mileages are from mouth to point where the stream name changes or to the headwaters.

Source: U.S. Geological Survey, Water Resources Division, Ocala

311

Counties of Florida

County	County Seat	Date Formed	Origin of Name
Alachua (9)	Gainesville	December 29, 1824	From either the Spanish "La" for "the" and the Timucuan "Chua" for "Sink" or the Seminole-Creek "luchuwa" for "jug."
Baker (38)	Macclenny	February 8, 1861	James McNair Baker, Confederate Senator and judge.
Bay	Panama City	April 24, 1913	St. Andrew Bay
Bradford (36)	Starke	December 21, 1858	Originally New River County. Renamed for Captain Richard Bradford, the first officer killed in the Civil War in the Battle of Santa Rosa Island.
Brevard (25)	Titusville	March 14, 1844	Originally named St. Lucie. Renamed for Theodore Washington Brevard, a North Carolinian who became state comptroller.
Broward (51)	Fort Lauderdale	April 30, 1915	Governor Napoleon B. Broward
Calhoun (20)	Blountstown	January 26, 1838	John C. Calhoun of South Carolina. A major proponent of State's Rights.
Charlotte (57)	Punta Gorda	April 23, 1921	Charlotte Harbor. It may have originated as the Spanish "Carlos" or "Calos" a corruption of the Indian tribe "Calusa." The English changed it to Charlotte for the wife of King George III.
Citrus (44)	Inverness	June 2, 1887	Florida's main agricultural product.
Clay (37)	Green Cove Springs	December 31, 1858	Henry Clay of Kentucky, Secretary of State under John Quincy Adams.
Collier (62)	East Naples	May 8, 1923	Barron G. Collier, land developer in southern Florida and advertising tycoon.
Columbia (16)	Lake City	February 4, 1832	The poetical name of the United States, based on Christopher Columbus.
Dade (19)	Miami	February 4, 1836	Major Francis Langhorne Dade, commander of troops in the Dade Massacre.
De Soto (42)	Arcadia	May 19, 1887	Hernando de Soto, Spanish explorer. One of two counties named for him.
Dixie (59)	Cross City	April 25, 1921	The poetical and lyrical name of the South.
Duval (4)	Jacksonville	August 12, 1882	William Pope DuVal, first territorial governor of Florida.
Escambia (1)	Pensacola	July 21, 1821	Possibly from the Spanish "cambiar" for "to exchange or barter" or from unknown Indian origin. Also for an Indian village called by the Spanish "San Cosmo y San Damian de Escambe"
Flagler (53)	Bunnell	April 28, 1917	Henry Morrison Flagler, railroad builder and businessman.
Franklin (17)	Apalachicola	February 8, 1832	Benjamin Franklin, scientist, writer and diplomat.
Gadsden (5)	Quincy	June 24, 1823	James Gadsden, aide to Andrew Jackson in Florida campaign and diplomat who arranged the Gadsden Purchase.
Gilchrist (67)	Trenton	December 4, 1925	Governor Albert Walter Gilchrist.
Glades (58)	Moore Haven	April 23, 1921	Everglades
Gulf (66)	Port St. Joe	June 6, 1925	Gulf of Mexico
Hamilton (15)	Jasper	December 26, 1827	Alexander Hamilton, first United States Secretary of Treasury.
Hardee (55)	Wauchula	April 23, 1921	Governor Cary Augustus Hardee.
Hendry (63)	LaBelle	May 11, 1923	Captain Francis Asbury Hendry, the "Cattle King of South Florida."
Hernando (22)	Brooksville	February 24, 1843	Hernando de Soto, Spanish explorer. One of two counties named for him.
Highlands (56)	Sebring	April 23, 1921	Reflects the geographical hilliness of the area.

County	County Seat	Date Formed	Origin of Name
Hillsborough (18)	Tampa	January 25, 1834	Named for Wills Hills, the Earl of Hillsborough from Ireland. He was Secretary of State for the English colonies and received a land grant in Florida.
Holmes (27)	Bonifay	January 8, 1848	Named for Holmes Creek which was named for the Holmes Valley. This name came from either an Indian chieftain with the English name Holmes or a settler named Thomas J. Holmes.
Indian River (65)	Vero Beach	May 30, 1925	Indian River
Jackson (3)	Marianna	August 12, 1822	Andrew Jackson, soldier and U.S. commissioner and governor of the territories of East and West Florida. He later was the seventh president of the United States.
Jefferson (13)	Monticello	January 20, 1827	President Thomas Jefferson
Lafayette (33)	Mayo	December 23, 1856	The Marquis de Lafayette, a French nobleman who aided the cause of American independence from England. He received a land grant in Tallahassee but never saw it.
Lake (43)	Tavares	May 27, 1887	Named for the large number of lakes within its boundaries.
Lee (41)	Fort Myers	May 13, 1887	General Robert E. Lee
Leon (7)	Tallahassee	December 29, 1824	Juan Ponce de Leon, Spanish explorer who named Florida.
Levy (26)	Bronson	March 10, 1845	David Levy Yulee, member of Florida's first constitutional convention and U.S. Senator.
Liberty (36)	Bristol	December 15, 1855	Named for ideal of the United States.
Madison (14)	Madison	December 26, 1827	President James Madison.
Manatee (31)	Bradenton	January 9, 1855	Manatee or sea cow.
Marion (24)	Ocala	March 14, 1844	General Francis Marion, American Revolutionary War hero, nicknamed "the swamp fox."
Martin (64)	Stuart	May 30, 1925	Governor John W. Martin.
Monroe (6)	Key West	July 3, 1823	President James Monroe. He was president when Florida became part of the United States.
Nassau (10)	Fernandina Beach	December 29, 1824	Named for the "Duchy of Nassau" a former state in western Germany. The name was in an English line of royalty and brought to the area by the English. The county was named for the Nassau River and Nassau Sound.
Okaloosa (52)	Crestview	June 13, 1915	From the Choctaw "oka" for "water" and "lusa" for "black." It probably refers to the Blackwater River.
Okeechobee (54)	Okeechobee	May 8, 1917	From the Hitchiti Indian words "oki" for "Big" and "chobi" for "water."
Orange (11)	Orlando	December 29, 1824	The many orange groves in the area.
Osceola (40)	Kissimmee	May 12, 1887	The Seminole Indian chief, Osceola.
Palm Beach (47)	West Palm Beach	April 30, 1909	Palm trees along the Atlantic Ocean.
Pasco (45)	Dade City	June 2, 1887	Samuel Pasco, Speaker of the Florida House of Representatives. He later was a United States Senator.
Pinellas (48)	Clearwater	May 23, 1911	From the Spanish "Punta pinal" for "point of pines."
Polk (39)	Bartow	February 8, 1861	President James K. Polk
Putnam (28)	Palatka	January 13, 1849	Benjamin Alexander Putnam, Speaker of the Florida House of Representatives.
St. Johns (1)	St. Augustine	July 21, 1821	From the Spanish "San Juan" the name of the river.
St. Lucie (46)	Fort Pierce	March 14, 1844	Named for St. Lucie of Syracuse a Christian executed in 304 A.D.

County	County Seat	Date Formed	Origin of Name
Santa Rosa (21)	Milton	February 18, 1842	Named from Santa Rosa Island which was named for the Catholic saint, St. Rose de Viterbo.
Sarasota (60)	Sarasota	May 14, 1921	Not positively known. Said to be Spanish for an Indian "place of dancing," but no modern Spanish equivalent has been found. Another legend gives the origin to a beautiful daughter of Hernando de Soto, Sara Sota.
Seminole (50)	Sanford	April 25, 1913	Named for the Seminole Indians. The word itself possibly comes from the Spanish "cimarrones" or runaways or the Creek "ishti semoli" for "wild men."
Sumter (29)	Bushnell	January 8, 1853	General Thomas Sumter, a South Carolinian who fought in the American Revolution.
Suwannee (35)	Live Oak	December 21, 1858	The origin is disputed. It could be an Indian mispronunciation of the Spanish "San Juan" or from the Cherokee "sawani" meaning "echo river," or the Creek "suwani" for "echo."
Taylor (34)	Perry	December 23, 1856	President Zachary Taylor. He Commanded U.S. Troops in Florida during part of the Second Seminole War.
Union (61)	Lake Butler	May 20, 1921	When Union County separated from Bradford County it was said that the two parts were "united" in the opinion that a new county should be formed. Some say it refers to the "Union of the United States."
Volusia (30)	DeLand	December 29, 1854	The origin is disputed. It may be Indian or French, but no definite evidence has been found.
Wakulla (23)	Crawfordville	March 11, 1843	The word may be Timucuan and its meaning lost or from the the Indian word "kala" meaning "spring of water." Another possibility is that it is the Creek "wahkola" for "loon," a bird which winters in Florida.
Walton (8)	DeFuniak Springs	December 29, 1824	Colonel George Walton, Secretary of the Territory of West Florida.
Washington (12)	Chipley	December 9, 1825	President George Washington

FLORIDA'S TERRITORIAL GOVERNORS

Governor

Term

1. Andrew Jackson   March 10, 1821-December 31, 1821
   (March 15, 1767-June 8, 1845)

   Jackson's place of birth is not definite, but it was probably in South Carolina. He led a colorful military and political life. He helped form the state of Tennessee and served as a representative to both houses of the U.S. Congress from that state. As a military officer he led troops in the Creek War of 1813, at the Battle of New Orleans in 1815, and the capture of Florida in 1818. Jackson served as Commissioner and Governor of Florida during 1821, but left the territory in October to return to Tennessee. He later served again in the U.S. Senate and then as President of the United States.

2. William Pope DuVal   April 17, 1822-April 24, 1834
   (1784-March 18, 1854)

   DuVal was born in Virginia and was associated with several of the founders of the United States, like Patrick Henry. He moved to Kentucky, became a lawyer, and represented Kentucky in the U.S. Congress. He was appointed first Territorial Governor of Florida by President Monroe on the recommendation of John C. Calhoun. He was reappointed by President Adams and Jackson. During his tenure as Governor, Tallahassee was made the capital. He enjoyed friendly relations with the Indians and spread knowledge about Florida through his literary friends like Washington Irving. He signed his name DuVal, though it often appears as Duval, like in Duval County.

Governor	Term
3. John Henry Eaton	April 24, 1834-March 16, 1836

(June 18, 1790-November 17, 1856)

The second territorial Governor of Florida was born in North Carolina and lived in Tennessee where he was elected to the U.S. Senate. His friend Andrew Jackson appointed him Secretary of War, but he resigned in a controversy over his wife, Peggy O'Neale. He was then given his Florida appointment, but spent seven months getting to Tallahassee. During his term as Governor there were many problems, especially with the Indians. He was appointed American Minister to Spain and later wrote a biography of Jackson.

4. Richard K. Call   March 16, 1836-December 2, 1839

(October 1792-September 14, 1862)   March 19, 1841-August 11, 1844

Governor Call served as territorial Governor of Florida two different times. He was born in Virginia and served in the Creek War with Jackson. He served with Jackson in his military and political ventures into Florida. Call decided to live in Florida as a lawyer in Pensacola. He served as a member of the Legislative Council, delegate to Congress, and an officer in the West Florida militia. He commanded troops in the Seminole War. He ran for Governor when Florida became a state but was defeated. His home in Tallahassee, "The Grove," is still in use and is owned by former Governor LeRoy Collins and his wife, Mary Call Darby, a great granddaughter of Governor Call.

5. Robert R. Reid   December 2, 1839-March 19, 1841

(September 8, 1789-July 1, 1841)

He was born in South Carolina, educated in Georgia and practiced law there. Reid served as a congressman and Judge from Georgia. Jackson appointed him Federal Judge to East Florida and President Van Buren appointed him Governor. He believed in strict control of the Indians. Reid presided over the convention which drew up Florida's first constitution.

6. John Branch   August 11, 1844-June 25, 1845

(November 4, 1782-January 3, 1863)

The sixth and last territorial Governor of Florida was a native of North Carolina. He had served in the state legislature, as Governor and U.S. Senator. Jackson appointed him Secretary of the Navy. He resigned this position during the controversy over Peggy O'Neale. President John Tyler appointed him territorial Governor of Florida for the short period preceding Florida's statehood.

From Allen Morris' Florida Handbook

GOVERNORS OF THE STATE OF FLORIDA

Governor	Political Party	Term
1. William D. Mosely	Democrat	June 25, 1845-October 1, 1849

(February 1, 1795-January 4, 1863)

He was born in North Carolina and ran for Governor of that state but lost by three votes. He moved to the Lake Miccosukee area and was elected as the first governor of the state of Florida. After leaving office, he moved to Palatka where he became a fruit grower.

2. Thomas Brown	Whig	October 1, 1849-October 3, 1853

(October 24, 1785-August 24, 1867)

He was born in Virginia where he served in the legislature and invented the post office letter box. Brown moved to Tallahassee where he operated a hotel. His political career included being a member of the first constitutional convention and the legislature. While Governor he was concerned with internal improvements, agriculture and made cost studies on draining the Everglades.

3. James E. Broome	Democrat	October 3, 1853-October 5, 1857

(December 15, 1808-November 23, 1883)

Broome was born in South Carolina and moved to Tallahassee in 1837. He was appointed as a judge and administered the oath of office to the state's first governor. Elected governor in 1853 he was a strong supporter of State's Rights. He vetoed more Acts than either of the first two Governors and was given the title of the "veto-governor." After leaving office, he became a state senator and one of the state's largest landowners.

4. Madison S. Perry	Democrat	October 5, 1857-October 7, 1861

(1814-March, 1865)

He was born in South Carolina and became a leading planter in Alachua County. While Governor he settled a border dispute with Georgia, encouraged the extension of railroads in the state and urged reestablishment of the state militia because of the shadow of the Civil War. Florida seceded from the Union on January 11, 1861, during his administration.

5. John Milton	Democrat	October 7, 1861-April 1, 1865

(April 20, 1807-April 1, 1865)

Milton was born in Georgia and became a lawyer. He served in Florida during the Seminole Wars and moved to the state in 1846. Operating from Jackson County, he became a power in the Democratic party. He was a strong States Righter and encouraged Florida's secession. As governor during the war he advocated Florida's position as a source of salt and food for the Confederacy. When the war ended, Milton committed suicide, prefering "...death to reunion."

Governor	Political Party	Term

6. Abraham K. Allison — Democrat — April 1, 1865-May 9, 1865
(December 10, 1810-July 8, 1893)

The sixth governor of Florida was born in Georgia. He moved to Apalachicola where he was Mayor, County Judge and a member of the legislature. Allison twice acted as Governor. In 1853 he informally acted as Governor as Speaker of the House when the Governor was out of state. As Senate President he took over the office in 1865 after Milton's death. Allison was jailed by Federal Troops at the end of the war and later under Reconstruction for intimidating blacks.

7. William Marvin — Democrat — July 13, 1865-December 20, 1865
(April 14, 1808-July 9, 1902)

Marvin was born in New York and was practicing law when appointed as U.S. District Attorney to Key West by President Jackson. He served as a Federal Judge and on the state's first constitutional convention. He was appointed Provisional Governor by President Andrew Johnson to aid in restoring Florida to the Union. Marvin later was elected to the U.S. Senate from Florida, but the "radical" Republicans refused to seat him.

8. David S. Walker — Conservative — December 20, 1865-July 4, 1868
(May 2, 1815-July 20, 1891)

The eighth Governor was born in Kentucky and moved to Leon County in 1837. His political career included being State Senator, State Superintendent of Public Instruction, Mayor of Tallahassee, Justice of the Supreme Court and Governor. He helped create a system of free public schools in Tallahassee. While Governor he helped restore civil government under military rule. After his term he once again became a judge. The Constitution of 1868 was approved while he was governor. It gave the right to vote to all races.

9. Harrison Reed — Republican — July 4, 1868-January 7, 1873
(August 26, 1813-May 25, 1899)

Reed was born in Massachusetts and traveled through the Midwest, until he moved to Washington D.C. in 1861. He was sent to Fernandina as a tax commissioner by President Lincoln in 1863. President Johnson appointed him Postal Commissioner in 1865. He became Governor in 1868 under the new constitution. There were two attempts to impeach him while he was in office and William Gleason and Samuel Day tried to take over the governor's office. After leaving office he edited a magazine for Southern growth, served in the House of Representatives and as Tallahassee's postmaster.

10. Ossian B. Hart — Republican — January 7, 1873-March 18, 1874
(January 17, 1821-March 18, 1874)

Hart was born in Jacksonville in the last year of Spanish rule. His father had founded the city of Jacksonville. He became a lawyer and was a member of the House of Representatives of Florida. He opposed secession and was active in the reconstruction of the state. He served as an associate Justice of the Supreme Court and then as Governor. After 14 months in office he died of pneumonia.

11. Marcellus L. Stearns — Republican — March 18, 1874-January 2, 1877
April 29, 1839-December 8, 1891)

Stearns was born in Maine and joined the Union Army in 1861. He lost an arm in battle and turned to the study of law in the army. After the war he served in the Freedman's Bureau in Quincy. He served on the constitutional convention and in the Florida House. He was elected Lieutenant-governor in 1872 and succeeded to the governorship when Governor Hart died. He lost the next election in 1877 when the Hayes-Tilden dispute took place. Stearns was appointed to a federal post in Arkansas and left the state.

12. George F. Drew — Democrat — January 2, 1877-January 4, 1881
(August 6, 1827-September 26, 1900)

The state's twelfth Governor was born in New Hampshire and moved to Florida in 1865 to establish the state's largest sawmill. His election ended the reconstruction period in Florida and began a period of industrial expansion in the state. He returned to the sawmill business after leaving office.

13. William Bloxham — Democrat — January 4, 1881-January 6, 1885
(July 9, 1835-March 15, 1911)

Bloxham was the first Florida Governor who had been born in Florida after it became part of the United States. He was born in Leon County and received a law degree but turned to planting. He served in the Florida house and was the first Florida Governor who had served in the Confederate Army. He served as Secretary of State and then Governor of Florida. His first term in office was marked by the sale to Hamilton Disston of large amounts of the Everglades for $1,000,000. This saved the state from financial disaster.

14. Edward A. Perry — Democrat — January 6, 1885-January 8, 1889
(March 15, 1831-October 15, 1889)

He was born in Massachusetts and moved to Florida in 1853. He was a lawyer and served in the Confederate Army. While he was Governor a new constitution was adopted and a State Board of Education created.

15. Francis P. Fleming — Democrat — January 8, 1889-January 3, 1893
(September 28, 1841-December 20, 1908)

He was born at Panama Park in Duval County. Fleming served at the Battle of Natural Bridge. The Yellow Fever epidemic of 1889 caused him to push for a State Board of Health while Governor.

Governor	Political Party	Term

16. Henry L. Mitchell   Democrat   January 3, 1893-January 5, 1897
(September 3, 1831-October 14, 1903)
> Mitchell was born in Alabama and moved to Tampa when he was 15. He studied law, became an attorney, served in the Civil War, the House of Representatives and member of the Supreme Court. During his term frosts in northern Florida drove the industry southward and hurt the state's economy. Mitchell served Hillsborough County offices after his term in office.

17. William D. Bloxham   Democrat   January 5, 1897-January 8, 1901
> Bloxham was elected for the second time as governor in 1880. His second term was marked by natural disasters. Severe freezes and a hurricane in 1896 almost destroyed the citrus industry and the state's tax base.

18. William S. Jennings   Democrat   January 8, 1901-January 3, 1905
March 24, 1863-February 27, 1920)
> The 18th Governor of Florida was born in Illinois and came to Florida in 1885. His political career included county offices in Hernando County, the Speaker of the House, and Governor. During his term in office the primary system replaced the convention system for nominating candidates for office. He pushed for saving public lands for the people and for reclamation of the Everglades.

19. Napoleon B. Broward   Democrat   January 3, 1905-January 5, 1909
(April 19, 1857-October 1, 1910)
> Broward was the first Governor born in Florida after it became a state. He was born in Duval County and led a colorful life. Orphaned at age 12, he worked in a log camp on a farm, on a steamboat, as a cod fisherman, pilot on the St. Johns, operated a lumberyard, and was a phosphate developer. He also aided Cuban revolutionaries by blockade running supplies. Politically, he was Sheriff of Duval County, city councilman and member of the Florida House. During his term as Governor colleges were consolidated under a Board of Control, an automobile registration law, enacted and drainage and reclamation of the Everglades took place. Broward was elected U.S. Senator but died before taking office.

20. Albert W. Gilchrist   Democrat   January 5, 1909-January 7, 1913
(January 15, 1858-May 15, 1926)
> He was born in South Carolina while his mother was visiting there from Florida. He graduated from West Point and engaged in real estate and orange growing in Punta Gorda. He served in the Spanish-American War and in the House of Representatives. As Governor he encouraged legislation concerning the health of Florida's citizens and livestock.

21. Park Trammell   Democrat   January 7, 1913-January 2, 1917
(April 9, 1876-May 8, 1936)
> He was born in Alabama and he moved to Polk County when he was young. He held many public offices during his lifetime including: Mayor of Lakeland, member of the House, President of the State Senate, Attorney General, Governor and United States Senator. As Governor he caused the passage of election reform laws on spending and equalized property taxes.

22. Sidney J. Catts   Democrat   January 2, 1917-January 4, 1921
(July 31, 1863-March 9, 1936)   (elected as candidate of Prohibition Party)
> He was born in Alabama and was an ordained Baptist minister. He served as Governor of Florida during World War I. Many of the Democratic party leaders opposed him because he was elected without their support. Catts was later defeated in attempts to become a U.S. Senator and Governor again.

23. Cary A. Hardee   Democrat   January 4, 1921-January 6, 1925
(November 13, 1876-November 21, 1957)
> He was born in Taylor county and became a school teacher and lawyer. He was State Attorney and Speaker of the House. While Governor several constitutional amendments were passed including: legislative reapportionment, prohibition of state income and inheritance taxes. Leasing of convicts to private businesses was outlawed.

24. John W. Martin   Democrat   January 6, 1925-January 8, 1929
(June 21, 1884-February 22, 1958)
> The 24th Governor was born in Plainfield, Marion County. He was Mayor of Jacksonville for three terms. As Governor, he led Florida through its biggest land boom. Many progressive actions took place including: statewide highway construction, financing of schools by state appropriations, and free textbooks for elementary schools.

25. Doyle E. Carlton   Democrat   January 8, 1929-January 3, 1933
(July 6, 1887-October 25, 1972)
> He was born in Wauchula and began practicing law in Tampa in 1912. He served in the State Senate and then as Governor. His terms as Governor was during one of the most difficult periods of Florida's history. The national depression wrecked the economy and put thousands of Floridiands out of work. The land boom collapsed, a severe hurricane and infestation of the Mediterranean fruit fly all combined to slow down the state's growth.

Governor	Political Party	Term

26. David Sholtz   Democrat   January 3, 1933-January 5, 1937
(October 6, 1891-March 21, 1953)

He was born in New York and later moved to Daytona Beach. He served as a member of the House, State Attorney and City Judge. The worst of the Depression was in effect when he became Governor. He utilized the new federal programs to help the state's citizens and economy to recover.

27. Frederick P. Cone   Democrat   January 5, 1937-January 7, 1941
(September 28, 1871-July 28, 1948)

Cone was born in Benton, Columbia County. He was a lawyer and served as Speaker of the State Senate. During his term as Governor the licensing of drivers began in order to finance a highway patrol.

28. Spessard Holland   Democrat   January 7, 1941-January 2, 1945
(July 10, 1892-November 6, 1971)

Holland was born in Bartow and educated as a lawyer. He held many political positions during his lifetime including: County Prosecuting Attorney, County Judge, State Senator, Governor and U.S. Senator. As Governor he aided in Florida's participation in World War II, strengthened the state tax structure, helped establish Everglades National Park, recommended a gasoline tax for better highways, and established the Game and Fresh Water Fish Commission.

29. Millard F. Caldwell   Democrat   January 2, 1945-January 4, 1949
(February 6, 1897-   )

He was born in Tennessee and came to Florida in 1924. He served Santa Rosa County in both the state and U.S. Houses of Representatives. Under his administration public schools were strengthened and the Capitol Center was begun. He was a Justice of the Florida Supreme Court.

30. Fuller Warren   Democrat   January 4, 1949-January 6, 1953
(October 3, 1905-September 23, 1973)

He was born in Blountstown and was elected to the Florida House of Representatives while a student at the University of Florida. He was a lawyer and a writer. While Governor he actively sponsored and saw enacted: prohibition of cattle on highways, a strong citrus code, a reforestation program and active modern highway construction. This included the Florida Turnpike, Jacksonville Expressway and the Sunshine Skyway at St. Petersburg. He also actively promoted Florida's tourism industry.

31. Daniel T. McCarty   Democrat   January 6-September 28, 1953
(January 18, 1912-September 28, 1953)

He was born in Fort Pierce. He was a citrus grower and cattleman. McCarty served as Speaker of the House and in World War II. He died of a heart attack during his first year in office.

32. Charley E. Johns   Democrat   September 28, 1953-January 4, 1955
(February 27, 1905-   )

Johns was born in Starke and became Governor when Governor McCarty died in office. Johns was President of the Senate and served as Governor until an unexpired term election could be held. He pushed highway construction and prison reform. He returned to the Senate after serving as Governor.

33. Leroy Collins   Democrat   January 4, 1955-January 3, 1961
(March 10, 1909-   )

Collins was born in Tallahassee and served in both House and Senate in Florida. He was the first Florida Governor to succeed himself. He was elected to complete the unexpired term of Governor McCarty and then reelected for another four-year term. Collins pushed for creation of a State Development Commission to help diversify the state's economy basing it on industry, tourism and agriculture. He worked to modernize Florida's school system, sponsored educational television, nuclear research and a community college program. During this period of racial unrest he took a moderate progress under the law approach. The state experienced less unrest than other southern states. He served later as a Director under the 1964 Federal Civil Rights Act.

34. Farris Bryant   Democrat   January 3, 1961-January 5, 1965
(July 26, 1914-   )

He was born in Marion County and became an accountant. Governor Bryant had served in the Florida House for five terms and upon election as Governor stressed education. A constitutional amendment was passed allowing the sale of bonds to construct buildings for colleges and universities. He started the construction of the Cross-Florida Canal. Highway construction was pushed and an amendment was passed allowing the sale of bonds for purchase of land for conservation and recreation purposes. Bryant later served in Federal posts in the administration of Lyndon Johnson.

35. Haydon Burns   Democrat   January 5, 1965-January 3, 1967
(March 17, 1912-   )

Burns was born in Illinois and moved to Jacksonville in 1922. He was in business when elected as Mayor-Commissioner of Jacksonville. When he was elected Governor the cycle of office had been changed to move it from presidential election years and Burns had to run after two years in office. Under Burns there was constitutional reform, industrial development and tax reform.

Governor	Political Party	Term
36. Claude R. Kirk, Jr.	Republican	January 3, 1967-January 5, 1971

36. Claude R. Kirk, Jr.   Republican   January 3, 1967-January 5, 1971

(January 7, 1926-   )

Kirk was born in California and became the first Republican Governor of Florida since reconstruction. He came to Florida after military service and obtaining a law degree. He was a successful businessman and former Democrat. During his term in office a substantial revision of the 1885 Constitution took place. The executive branch was reorganized giving more power to the Governor. He later ran unsuccessfully as a Democrat for Governor.

37. Reuben Askew   Democrat   January 5, 1971-January 2, 1979

(September 11, 1928-   )

He was born in Oklahoma and moved to Pensacola in 1937. Askew was County Solicitor for Escambia County, a member of the Florida House and President pro tempore of the Senate. He was the first Florida Governor elected to consecutive four- year terms. Under Askew a corporate income tax was enacted along with other tax reforms. State revenues were shared with local governments to ease property taxes. He took a "sunshine" amendment to the citizens to require financial disclosure by public officials and candidates. He opposed a casino gambling amendment, named the first black justice to the Supreme Court, appointed the first woman to the cabinet and the first black since reconstruction. He received many awards for his defense of equality and justice.

38. Daniel Robert Graham   Democrat   January 2, 1979-

(November 9, 1936-   )

Governor Graham was born in Coral Gables and obtained a law degree. Graham was elected to the Florida House of Representatives in 1966 and four years later to the State Senate. As a representative and Senator he stressed education and health services. While Governor he continued to stress these two points. He also has had to deal with the illegal immigrant problem and crime problems. Economic growth was emphasized and a Mediterranean fruit fly problem was attacked immediately to protect the citrus industry.

INDEX